# OUT OF POVERTY
### and into something more comfortable

# OUT OF POVERTY

and into something more comfortable

John Stackhouse

Vintage Canada

*A Division of Random House of Canada Limited*

VINTAGE CANADA EDITION 2001

Copyright © 2000 by John Stackhouse

All rights reserved under International and Pan-American Copyright
Conventions. Published in 2001 by Vintage Canada, a division of Random
House of Canada Limited. Originally published in hardcover in 2000 by
Random House Canada. Distributed by Random House of Canada Limited.

Vintage Canada and colophon are trademarks
of Random House of Canada Limited.

**Canadian Cataloguing in Publication Data**

Stackhouse, John
        Out of poverty : and into something more comfortable

ISBN 0-679-31098-3

1. Stackhouse, John, 1962–    –Journeys — Developing Countries. 2. Poor —
Developing countries. 3. Developing countries — Economic conditions. I. Title.

HC59.72.P6S72 2001        362.5'09172'4        C00-932468-2

Cover and interior design: Jenny Armour
Cover photos: Cindy Andrew
Inside photos: Cindy Andrew and John Stackhouse (pages 80, 99, 105, 115, 152,
        229, 275, 313, 347)

www.randomhouse.ca

Printed and bound in the United States of America

10  9  8  7  6  5  4  3  2  1

# CONTENTS

# INTRODUCTION

When I left Canada in the fall of 1991 to become *The Globe and Mail*'s first overseas development writer, I had no idea what I was getting into. Of course, I had been exposed to charities and missionaries and knew what they did in lands far away. After graduating from university, I had wanted to teach in Africa. But I was trained in macroeconomics and *Macbeth*, not chemistry or computers, and was turned down by most of the organizations I approached. I travelled, instead, largely in Asia, writing about development as I went. With my wife, Cindy Andrew, a photographer, I met slum children in Bombay, aboriginal women in the Indian interior and scattered hill tribes in northern Thailand. And, for a brief time, I believed that improving their circumstances was a straightforward matter.

Perhaps it was my middle-class upbringing in Toronto, as the son of children of the Great Depression, but during my early travels I equated development with material progress. I was hardly alone in such thinking. By the 1980s, development organizations believed they had a pretty clear idea of how wealth was generated, as if the centuries-old struggle to end poverty and deprivation was a problem that could finally be solved just as science had unravelled the mysteries of nuclear fission. Establishing a fair and open economy and a reasonable standard of civil liberties were important. Add to that the right public investments—in education, health care, affordable housing and accessible credit—and any human life anywhere could be transformed. If the tribal women we met hauling rocks for fifty cents a day were given half a chance, I was convinced they could change their lives, their villages and their countries for the better.

At the start of the 1990s, this simple formula—democracy plus free markets equals progress—was treated as the new universal truth. The massive, interventionist, government development schemes of the sixties and seventies had been swept away by the tide of Reaganomics and Thatcherism. The Cold War against Communism was over, the Soviet Union and its satellite nations were bankrupt, while the statist beliefs that towered over much of

the developing world since the fifties were discredited. If governments restricted their economic role to regulation and guidance
and invested judiciously in building an attractively educated work-
force, it was believed, poverty could be wiped out in a generation.

In November 1991, as I boarded a flight to Hong Kong and then
Bangkok to begin a new journey as a foreign correspondent, I thought
of the tribal rock haulers and how their lives could be changed if only
their country and their community followed this kind of advice. It was
all laid out in a pile of briefing papers I had received from the World
Bank and the International Monetary Fund—the two Washington-
based organizations that finance most of the world's poorest governments. They were about to hold their joint annual meetings in
Bangkok, and they wanted the world, especially the developing world,
to know that there was a clear path ahead. For proof, delegates had
to look no further than the Thai capital, where my flight landed eighteen hours later in a thick aerial swamp of humidity. Bangkok was
material evidence of the most astonishing creation of wealth since
post-war Japan. Cindy and I had explored the city five years earlier,
wandering along its fetid canals and through its ragged shantytowns;
now it was dressed to the nines in commerce and trade. Glass bank
towers and high-rise hotels had grown from the noodle stalls we had
frequented. A new expressway ran over the old shantytowns, and
many more like it were planned. Thailand, which had the world's
fastest-growing economy through the eighties, had become the
world's second largest market for Mercedes-Benz (after Germany)
and the biggest consumer of Johnnie Walker Scotch whisky. As a measure of progress, opulence was definitely in.

From the airport, I headed into the city centre, along roads free
from traffic, thanks to a national holiday to welcome the World
Bank and the IMF. Bangkok was playing host to every leading development figure, finance minister and international banker in the
world—the Olympics of development, some were calling it. This
was a defining moment for an era. Mikhail Gorbachev's financial
advisers had come from Moscow to try one more time to stave off
the inevitable collapse and financial implosion of the Soviet Union.
The Soviet team, humiliated enough to beg in front of the world,
stood in sharp contrast to their Thai hosts, who had built a sumptu-
ous conference centre, with its own lake and park in the city centre,

just for the meetings. Across the road next to the conference centre, the government erected billboards to block the delegates' view of an unsightly slum, and every evening, the Thais served us champagne and shrimp studded on ice sculptures.

Thailand was displaying its star development status, setting an example of how other impoverished countries could move out of poverty. A crucial ally of the United States, it provided air bases during the Vietnam War and a constant bulwark against Indochina's Communism. For that, it received huge amounts of foreign aid. But Thailand was also smart enough to invest heavily in primary education, land reforms and economic infrastructure, and to buy in to the IMF and World Bank free-market dreams.

None of the delegates seemed to care that the star student was a military regime that had ousted an elected government only ten months earlier. No one seemed to care that the wealth all around us was the creation of a select few Thais. Most of the planet was too busy realigning itself with the West. From Beijing to Bolivia, the triumph of capitalism seemed absolute and complete, the pursuit of wealth never more entrenched as a universal goal. To the believers, an end to the long, noble project of development was in sight, just two hundred years after the great Scottish economist Adam Smith wrote, "Little else is requisite to carry a state to the highest degrees of opulence from the lowest barbarism, but peace, easy taxes and tolerant administration of justice."

The following May, after Cindy and I had settled in New Delhi, where we would live for the next seven years, I started to see the folly in Adam Smith's assumptions and my own. As I travelled from country to country, village to village, it became glaringly clear that human development is not about creating wealth, though income and material assets are important. It is not about outside interventions, whether they are massive government projects or simply the imposition of free-market ideologies. I came to see development as a process, even a struggle, that was internal to a place and deeply democratic in nature. This book is about those struggles, quiet as they are, carried out in hamlets and slums, on riverbanks and mountainsides, by people who until now have been largely excluded from public decision-making. These are villagers arguing with each other about where to put a school rather than merely accepting a World Bank recommendation. These are men running their own forests for profit, and girls sitting down to talk about their fathers and about how to break traditional bonds. In May 1992, these were also thousands of Thais—professionals, office workers, students—blocking off central Bangkok, the very capital of new opulence, to demand a public voice.

I flew into Bangkok this time shortly before a night-long curfew as the military government tried to shut down the city. The previous night, an army unit had opened fire on a group of demonstrators inside the downtown Royal Hotel, killing dozens of unarmed people. Although another crackdown seemed certain, peaceful protests continued around Democracy Monument, a simple column with a painted flame on top built in memory of a student uprising in 1972.

Seven months after the development Olympics, when every major hotel in Bangkok had been sold out, tourists and investors had fled the city, along with most of Bangkok's taxis. From my near-deserted hotel, I hired a motorcycle-taxi, the only one willing to head for the monument, where gunfire had already been heard. We raced down a wide boulevard, past an empty shopping mall and through a shantytown behind it, and then wove a maze of back lanes to avoid the troops moving throughout central Bangkok.

The driver dropped me at the monument and took off. I couldn't see why. All around me, there were men in tailored suits and women in short skirts and silk blouses chatting on mobile phones. I heard one of them wonder aloud if he was illegally parked. This was not a poor and dispossessed mob rioting over bread shortages or fuel prices, but a cellphone revolution, driven by anger at the constant looting of the country. The protestors' bank savings and hopes were disappearing while a small group of Thais grew fabulously rich. The people around me were the people who had created this new model for development so admired in the West, and here they were telling the world that it was wrong. They were saying, loudly and boldly, that if people have little say in the decisions affecting their lives and are not allowed to help shape the civil and economic structures around them, then occasional elections and healthy bank accounts are not enough.

Trying to steer clear of the soldiers, I moved carefully with the protestors, who were calling for the resignation of Prime Minister Suchinda Kraprayoon, the former military commander who had led the January 1991 coup. Tear gas saturated the evening air and military helicopters hovered overhead, while platoons of soldiers moved up and down Ratchadamnoen Klang, the tree-lined, twelve-lane boulevard leading to Democracy Monument. At the next intersection, a mob was setting fire to cars and garbage cans, smashing street lights and telephone booths—reiterating its demand for the prime minister to go. In the middle of the intersection, young men in red bandanas built a bonfire of garbage, which motorcyclists circled, revving their Kawasaki engines. This was not Bangkok the opulent, but a congestion of anger and fear.

I stopped and looked back. A column of troops stood watch, ready to march toward us. The noise grew more maddening as more motorcycles emerged from the back streets. Suddenly, a fat middle-aged man in shorts, T-shirt and flip-flops appeared in the middle of the intersection. Waving a newspaper and shouting for the prime minister's removal, he looked like a corner grocer who had pulled himself off his couch to join the free-for-all.

And that was where my notes stopped.

Gunfire filled the air. From the corner of my eye as I turned to run, I saw troops pouring out of half a dozen little alleyways like ants from a hole. The motorcycles screeched down an unmanned lane to a footbridge and over a canal. I fled on foot with the crowd, down a back alley in full stride, my heart feeling as if it was about to rip through my rib cage. The end of the lane was blocked with barbed wire. Following half a dozen others, I ran up the exterior stairs of a low-rise apartment block. Soldiers shouted and people screamed, the gunfire sounding like a thousand firecrackers going off. On the second or third floor—I was not counting—a teenaged boy grabbed my arm and yanked me into a dark apartment with another boy, his brother.

After they bolted the door we stood frozen for a moment. Someone banged on the wooden door, shouting, but quickly moved on to the next apartment. Trembling, the boys led me into a dark bedroom and showed me where I could huddle behind a door. They sat in a corner, holding hands and staring at each other, listening to the shots outside. Each burst of gunfire felt like a sharp jab to the stomach. Thais firing on Thais. Thais screaming at Thais. It was so thunderous the apartment felt as if it would collapse, and it stopped only when the rains began, the sky releasing a tropical fury of water that seemed to drown the madness.

Across the room, the two boys had turned on a small lamp and were reading their school books. One rose to get me a tin cup of water while the other telephoned an English-speaking Thai friend, who told me to stay put for the night on the bedroom floor. Outside the window, troops were still on the street. I thanked the boys for sheltering me and waited till first light to slip out the back entrance of the apartment block. The soldiers and barbed wire were gone. Overnight, Prime Minister Suchinda had resigned, disgraced that his soldiers had killed several dozen protestors. Up the street, only a few troops lingered around Democracy Monument, preparing for a fresh Bangkok dawn of newspaper trucks, taxis and traffic.

In the years following the Bangkok riots, I travelled to more than forty countries. From Vietnam's central highlands to the far reaches of Eritrea, much of humanity was struggling for control of their lives and gaining it with remarkable speed, less because of the national elections and parliaments the West so often confuses with democracy than because of a new tenor in local democracy.

In Somalia and Tanzania, I found two very different and awful results of dictatorship and foreign intervention, two countries paying the price for not allowing their peoples to set their own course. In Uganda, I came across a generous man struggling to break the ancient bonds of culture in his own family, just as in West Africa I met women who were struggling in the shadow of despots and cumbersome aid programs to take charge of their own interests.

In Bangladesh, I came across villagers gaining control of their land and waters with the most basic tools of economic democracy. And in India, I met forest dwellers, village insurgents and low-caste widows using the political and legal system to achieve what decades and billions of dollars in government money had not. But it was in Indonesia, once one of the greatest "successes" of international development, that I discovered how ignoring and suppressing the democratic needs of a people can ruin a nation and all that was once considered development.

From East Timor to Timbuktu, I saw how some of the world's poorest and most oppressed people are changing our world. But nowhere was my journey through development more influenced than in an unassuming village in northern India where I stayed whenever I had the chance over the last eight years. This village, Biharipur, became a microcosm of all I saw elsewhere, stuck as it was in centuries of tradition, only the names changing. It was the place I came to know best. It provided me with friends and joyful moments and sometimes gave me hope in human progress. But, just as often, it crushed that hope in the nasty friction of social divisions that seemed unresolvable, and have frustrated so many other visions for development. Even in the violence that submerged my village, however, I saw the hope of people breaking the status quo and gaining a voice.

Fortunately, at the beginning of a new millennium, the world's poor probably have a greater say over their lives than at any other time in history. Almost everywhere I went, I found local campaigns to share basic resources like land and water, to build democratic school boards, trading co-operatives and credit movements, and to make government accountable at the highest and lowest levels. These are the small revolutions that are changing the world. It is barely a start, but the people in this book have at least brought us this far and have shown us a way forward.

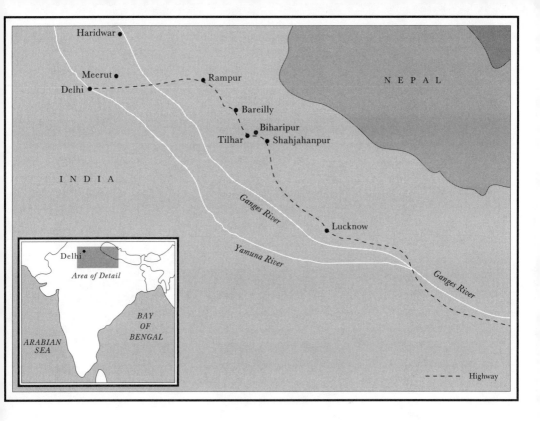

# THE VILLAGE I

"No one along the highway could tell us where Biharipur was, not the paan shop men or the bidi wallahs or the horse-cart drivers. . . . It was as if the village of seven hundred people had vanished from the earth."

# I

# A Man with a Title, a Widow with No Name

No one along the highway could tell us where Biharipur was, not the paan shop men or the bidi wallahs or the horse-cart drivers. We tried the hospital, the police stand, the local pharmacy. "Biharipur?" Each person looked equally confused, as if the village of seven hundred people had vanished from the earth. And maybe it had.

My Indian colleague Rama and I looked at each. Neither of us had a suggestion. We had travelled more than three hundred kilometres southeast from New Delhi to find a little hamlet called Biharipur that had been recommended to us by a social activist, Suman Sahai, as a quintessential north Indian village. Suman had been there once and was struck by the poverty and its permanence.

I had been living in India less than a year and hardly knew my way around New Delhi, let alone the countryside. Rama, who worked as a researcher-reporter for *The Washington Post*, wasn't much help with directions either. An ethnic Tamil, Brahmin and graduate in English literature from Delhi University, she was as out of place here as I was. She was also drugged silly to prevent car sickness. But Rama did have a passion for the poor and an uncanny ear for the dialects of north India, where Hindi is more a framework than a language. She finally thought to rephrase the question, asking a chai wallah, "What about Rajinder Singh Yadav? He is a *lambardar*."

"Ohhhh. He is a lambardar, is he?" the chai wallah replied. The tea-seller's sarcasm suggested he doubted that such an important man could be found in such an obscure place. No one knew Biharipur. The lambardar, the chief, that was something else.

Out on the Gangetic plains, where three hundred million people base their existence on fertile soils, abundant rains and ancient traditions, a lambardar is king of the locality and master of all he surveys. He is a man of prestige and influence. Little happens without his approval. Nothing proceeds unless he benefits. And his name is known at tea shops.

I knew nothing of this tradition, or that it determined the success of all development efforts in northern India, as social customs and political behaviours do just about everywhere. All I knew was that Rajinder Singh Yadav was a farmer whose approval we needed in order to stay in his village.

"You go straight," the chai wallah said. "At the culvert, there is a big tree. You turn left."

We left the chai wallah to his vat of buffalo's milk boiling on a clay stove, over some sticks and straw, a scene so rustic it was hard to believe this was the beginning of the nineties, a decade that would create more wealth than any other in history. Bill Clinton was in the White House, Boris Yeltsin was almost in the Kremlin, North America's tough recession was over and a new decade of liberal reforms, of free markets and free speech, was underway in dozens of developing countries. The World Bank and IMF promises in Bangkok were starting to pay off, it seemed, despite those nasty riots. For most of the world's poor, this was at last a time when the rise of individual rights and opportunities would overcome the ages of dictatorship, monopolies and state control, a season of victories for students, entrepreneurs and subsistence farmers who for generations were the serfs of the developing world. Biharipur, I hoped, would be one of the new liberation zones.

But Suman Sahai was more ambivalent about the village's prospects. "Biharipur is five kilometres from Tilhar town," she had told us before we set off. "Five kilometres is not such a distance. One would think that if the nucleus is strong and developed, the benefits would filter down to the peripheral villages. But that has not happened there. Biharipur is isolated and untouched." She spoke with the remorse of her heritage. Suman's ancestors included the royal princes who once ruled the countryside around Tilhar. They were gone, but a new class of lambardars had taken their place—and so little else had changed.

We found the big tree described by the chai wallah, and turned on to a narrow tarred road, which followed a lazy path of broad curves, unannounced bumps, potholes filled with broken bricks and sudden turns around barren rice paddies that were so whimsical they seemed to be the design of a mad engineer, or a contractor trying to unload a lot of asphalt. We passed a fishing pond, a small hamlet of mud huts and more rice fields, and soon the national highway was well behind us. Still no one had heard of Biharipur, but more and more people knew of Rajinder Singh Yadav. "Over the railway tracks, and straight," a young man on a bicycle told us. "You follow a dirt track to another dirt track and turn left at the next dirt track. He is living there."

Sleepy, the driver who came with our rental car, balked. He had barely said two words since we'd left New Delhi the previous day, covering one of the world's most dangerous highways with little comment and his eyes half-shut. But now Sleepy looked ready to argue. It was not so much the railway tracks that threatened the undercarriage of his low-riding V-8 Contessa Classic, the car favoured by north Indian gangsters, but the road beyond the tracks, which looked as if it had been bombed recently by the Pakistani air force. Sleepy told us to walk.

With our backpacks, water bottles and Suman's letter of introduction, Rama and I set off by foot, down the bumpy dirt road, on to a narrow footpath and across the glorious golden wheat fields of a north Indian winter. It was still early. The mist had not yet risen from the small forests, while a thick dew covered the wheat. As we walked, a gentle winter breeze rustled through the fields, shaking the young wheat stalks as though it was shuffling paper. Hawks soared high above us, looking for snakes and field mice. In the distance, on a small hillock where someone had built a little one-room temple, kingfishers darted from tree to tree. We were in the heart of civilization, and there was not a person in sight or a human sound in the air.

We continued along the narrow embankment, trying to spot Biharipur on the horizon, but I was too concerned with staying on the footpath, away from the snake-infested fields, to keep an eye out for anything. I probably would have missed the boy across the field had he not yelled to us. He called again and ran along the embankment, barefoot, as nimble as a squirrel on a tree branch. The boy wanted to know where we were going, but Rama, the cautious one, wanted to know first who he was.

"Dhanvir," the boy said. "A Dalit. From the next village."

The Dalits are the people once known as "untouchables" in the pernicious Hindu caste hierarchy. Dhanvir said he was in the fields watching water pumps for the higher-caste landlords. Rather than getting an education, he spent his time watching water gush from the ground through a machine of nineteenth-century design. Rama asked Dhanvir if he knew the way to Biharipur, which he did. It was his village. Rajinder probably was his landlord, I thought. The boy pointed across the fields to a clump of mango trees, and beyond it, beneath the mist that was melting in the winter sun, to something resembling a medieval compound, a cluster of mud buildings packed tightly together.

We thanked Dhanvir and continued to walk to the village, which seemed more like an outgrowth of the mango grove than a planned settlement. There were no signposts, electrical wires, telephone poles, sewers, ditches or pavement to interrupt the natural landscape. At first glance, the only evidence of modern development was a cement culvert that connected the rice fields with a buffalo pond.

A few boys, enjoying the graceful recess between planting and harvest, splashed about in the pond with their water buffalo submerged to their snouts. On the other side of the culvert, a small boy squatted to shit in the same place where many others had apparently done the same recently. Above him, on the culvert wall, two men basked in the morning sun and smoked *bidis*, oblivious to all around them, until they noticed Rama and stared curiously at this Indian woman in a baseball cap, jeans and short-sleeved shirt.

"What is your caste?" one of them asked.

It was an odd greeting, but one I learned was the basis for most introductions in northern India. Other castes were to be distrusted. Lower castes were to be shunned. But Rama was a Brahmin. More than that, she was a Brahmin from New Delhi, the capital of all India. The men, who were probably no more than halfway up the caste ladder and had never been to the capital, nodded respectfully.

When they turned to me, I said I had no caste because I came from a country called Canada. They looked perplexed.

"How far is it to Canada?" one man asked.

I said it was on the other side of the world, next to America.

"Is that beyond Bombay?"

Well beyond Bombay, I said. Maybe a month by ship.

They stared at me blankly, and I realized we were no longer in the global village.

"Did the British rule you?" the other man asked.

When I said yes, both men smiled. A common heritage. We were almost brothers. But when we asked for directions to Rajinder's house, saying we were friends of the lambardar's friends, the men looked at us again with suspicion. Not only were we from different castes, we had just declared our loyalties.

One of the men pointed to a mud lane that led into Biharipur. He told us to follow it, and turn at the second left. Though we thanked them, there were no more smiles.

From high in the air, the villages of central Uttar Pradesh are so compact they look like farmhouses in Nebraska: spread out neatly in equidistant fashion, each surrounded by a clump of trees and about one hundred hectares of open fields. Except that here in the district of Shahjahanpur, each habitation is not a farmhouse but a village of seven hundred or eight hundred people. According to the 1991 census, there were 2,124 such villages in the area, scattered randomly around the chaotic, unplanned district centre, Shahjahanpur (named inappropriately for Shah Jahan, the Taj Mahal's creator, a man who loved order and symmetry in his work).

Biharipur was anything but symmetrical, more a maze than a community. The main track gave way to half a dozen smaller laneways that led deeper into the village in no apparent order. Despite the vast open fields and the scattering of mango groves all around us, the mud huts were jammed together as tightly as they would be in a Bombay slum. This was not unusual. The architecture and layout of a typical north Indian village conveys a medieval sense of protection. At night, most families bring their livestock into their courtyards to protect them from rustlers. No window faces outward, and the only way in is through a short door that forces you to bend to pass through.

The main laneway was lined on each side by thick mud walls spotted with hundreds of dung patties, a mix of manure and straw, slapped on to dry in the warm winter sun. Once the dung cakes were dry, the village women stored them in mounds, which they sealed with more mud, giving them the appearance of anthills. They were the family woodpiles. Every few metres along the dung-lined walls, a wooden door opened to a private courtyard surrounded by huts made of mud, straw and bamboo poles. In the centre of these modest homesteads were cows and buffalo tethered to more poles. In a few courtyards there was also a tree or two, mostly a neem, whose thin branches make good toothbrushes. A few families had invested in clay roof tiles, the only manufactured building material in sight. To keep out the rain and harsh sun, everyone else relied on roofs of sticks thatched with straw.

As we ventured deeper into the village, I noticed the first women we had seen since the highway, drawing water at a well. When they saw us coming, they pulled veils over their faces and hastened their work, hauling their buckets up by rope. Other women slipped quickly into their houses, and closed their doors.

"These are the Britishers!" a young man yelped to his friend as they rode past on bicycles, careful to avoid the deep ruts carved by a steady traffic of bullock carts. "These are the ones who ruled us!"

A small pack of children had begun to follow us, giggling in excitement. One of them asked if we really were the British. "No," Rama said. "We are from Delhi only."

Most of the children, boys and girls, were dressed only in shorts. A couple wore tattered shirts. None had shoes. Their bare chests and arms exposed the marks of scabies, a highly contagious disease caused by itch-mites burrowing into the skin. One young girl was covered with red spots that looked like measles. I stopped to take a picture of the children and noticed one boy behind all the others, crawling on his hands and knees like a lame dog, manoeuvring his frail body around patches of mud that the others simply stepped over. He was crooked, probably from polio.

Another young boy, hearing what we wanted, offered to lead us to the lambardar's house. We went down the main path, then left, right and left again. How could we miss it? No other structure in the village was made of brick. No other structure had a second storey, even if it was only a small room built on the roof. No other structure could be seen from every corner of Biharipur.

The boy swung open a gate to a small courtyard, where he suggested we sit on two charpoys, the woven cots used across rural India for sleeping and lounging. The courtyard, with a cement floor and small room at the back filled with fertilizer sacks, appeared to be a kind of open-air receiving room where the lambardar could greet visitors and talk business without violating his wife's privacy.

"Take rest," the boy said. He offered us a couple of hand-held fans attached to twirling handles, and disappeared, shouting on his way out that some strangers had come and they might be British.

No one knows when Biharipur was settled, but the lush green fields in this region were farmed as early as the third century B.C., when the Mauryan empire laid roads, built irrigation canals and water reservoirs across northern India. Only a millennium ago, the fields we had crossed that morning were part of a Hindu heartland that was home to a vibrant and liberal culture and a wealthy economy, which produced a golden age of culture, art and international trade, supported by a neatly hierarchical caste system, with priests at the top and permanently indentured labourers at the bottom.

Then came six centuries of Muslim conquest and rule led by some of the great Afghan and central Asian warriors—Baber and Sultan Mahmud of Ghazna among them—who poured into the subcontinent to seize its abundant rivers, lush forests and bountiful fields, and convert its oppressed labourers to Islam. The conquerors destroyed Hindu temples, burned centres of learning and drove northern India into an inward shell of feudalism and regional fiefdoms, but eventually the conquest gave way to a more enlightened and tolerant Mogul age, during which the lands around present-day Biharipur were controlled by the nawab of Oudh, a wealthy prince who at one time claimed much of the Ganges basin and developed a successor state to the Moguls. As legend has it, the nawab was so rich he used his agriculture rents to build a three-hundred-kilometre-long tunnel between his palace in Lucknow and the Taj Mahal in Agra, in case the emerging British colonial power tried to capture him. The tunnel, if it ever existed, proved useless, for the British took Lucknow, declared the nawab insane and, in 1856, parcelled him off to an asylum in Calcutta.[1]

In the nawab's place, the British patronized the region's junior princes and wealthy landlords, who were known as zamindars, and assigned property titles and revenue-collecting powers to those who were friendly with Her Majesty's loyal representatives. When India became an independent nation in 1947, the new government abolished the zamindari system and announced a program to redistribute land to the peasants. But in fact, most of the titles went to a new generation of landlords who were able to disguise their holdings in the names of women, children and deceased ancestors. In place of Suman Sahai's relatives came a hundred Rajinder Singh Yadavs. The official record of land titles mattered little anyway, because the new lambardars, the village chiefs, were given power over their village's land records. They also controlled village councils, village welfare funds and village development projects, as the ruling elite had done

---

[1] The nawab's Great Imambara in Lucknow, a prize of Asian-Islamic architecture, is overrun by squatters who have pitched tents on the palace grounds and redecorated its grand hall with a tapestry of illegal electrical connections. Inside the grand hall, one of the few treasures preserved is a 1920s photograph of the area, labelled "General Bird's eye view." Its frame is marked with pigeon droppings. As for the remaining royal descendants, many live in tents around the Imambara and collect a royal allowance of 1.53 rupees a month, or about four cents.

through Hindu, Muslim and British rule. Aristocracy had not been abolished. It was merely decentralized, pulled down the caste ladder by the heavy weight of democracy.

Out of political shrewdness as well as a commitment to social justice, India's post-independence governments had assigned land that belonged to the so-called forward castes to the larger group known officially as Other Backward Castes, including Rajinder's Yadavs, who were cowherds by tradition. For the first time in a millennium, the kings of the land lived in the villages. In the sixties they were further aided by the Green Revolution, which brought hybrid seeds, subsidized fertilizer and massive irrigation networks to rural India and turned subsistence landholdings into profitable ventures. With so much economic change going on, political revolution could not be far off.

I was dozing on a charpoy, and would have been fast asleep were it not for the flies landing every few seconds on my face, when the wooden gates to the courtyard swung open and in walked a tall man with broad shoulders and city clothes: polyester pants, a dress shirt he wore tucked in and leather sandals. His thin moustache and neatly combed hair were all urban. His freshly washed hands did not feel rough like those of most villagers, as if to show he did not do fieldwork. Ever. His stomach also protruded, rock hard, not fat, as if to show he was not hungry. Ever.

We jumped to our feet and greeted Rajinder Singh Yadav with folded hands and the Hindi "*Namaskar.*" He reciprocated, but remained guarded. He asked Rama her caste, and me my country, and held us in a suspicious gaze until we handed him Suman's letter—then he smiled. India has thousands of castes and sub-castes but none is quite like royalty.

Once Rajinder knew our association, he called for his Number Two son, Chandra Prakash, to bring tea and biscuits. He offered us water as well, but we stuck to our bottled water, telling him it contained medicines as we were not feeling well. My constant sneezing, from the winter wheat fields, helped the charade but it also prompted some concern from our new host. Rajinder called back Chandra Prakash and told him to bring a special tea made with Ayurvedic herbs that Rajinder had bought recently during his pilgrimage to Haridwar, the holy site where the Ganges leaves the mountains and enters the plains. No visitor to his house would be allowed to feel unwell, he said.

We had not even begun our tea when Rajinder informed us that he was not a lambardar by birth. He was born and raised in Shahjahanpur. At twenty, he entered the Indian army, shortly after its great victory in 1971 over Pakistan in the Bangladesh liberation war. A year later, after he was kicked out for starting too many fights, he completed his undergraduate degree at a local college and, in 1975, passed his teacher's exam. But he hadn't stood a chance of getting a teaching job until 1989, when his caste-mate Mulayam Singh Yadav, a former teacher and village wrestling champion, became chief minister of Uttar Pradesh, India's most populous state, which straddles the Ganges and considers all politics to be caste politics. The new premier launched a Yadav hiring spree that came Rajinder's way in 1991. At last he had a government job, as soon as he paid local officials a share of his first year's salary in return for them signing his employment papers.

Despite his checkered past in the army, Rajinder's parents were able to arrange his marriage to another landed peasant, a Yadav, of course. The attraction for Ram Beti in marrying a city boy was clear, until Rajinder announced that, against custom, he would move his bride to Biharipur rather than bring her to his father's house. He took over the management of her family's ten hectares, which were mostly harvested by lower-caste sharecroppers, and quickly pushed aside her brother, a man who was the elected *pradhan*, or village chief. The brother, Abhivaran, proved no match for a man with a college education and army training. Rajinder was soon the dominant force in Biharipur. He and only he was the lambardar, and he wore the crown well.

These appeared to be very good days for Rajinder. He had a motorcycle and enough money to go on pilgrimages. Thanks to India's economic reforms, which freed most agriculture prices from government control, his fields were more rewarding than ever, earning him the equivalent of four to five thousand dollars a year. His teaching post in the next village gave him another twelve hundred dollars a year and a social status that farming could not. On the side, he had also become the village quack, using the knowledge he gained many years earlier working part-time for an army pharmacist in Shahjahanpur.

As landlord, teacher and medical practitioner, Rajinder was able to rule the village without challenge, not even from his hapless brother-in-law. As a teacher, Rajinder was put in charge of a polling station during every election, though not in his village. He also became the political boss for the Samajwadi Party, the one led by Mulayam Singh, commanding four hundred votes in Biharipur, and thus was given authority over all development works that came this way. When the Samajwadi Party rose to power, he received the village's only licence for a firearm, which he used to buy a shotgun from a Bombay mail-order catalogue. A gun, Rajinder explained, was a useful thing to have, especially in Sonora, the neighbouring village where he taught. Sonora was dominated by upper-caste Thakurs, the last of their kind in the area. They were the big losers in land redistribution and now they had to share their school as well, which many of them could not accept. The Sonora men had beaten up two of Rajinder's predecessors because of their caste, and run them off.

A gun was a sign that Rajinder could defend himself and, that he had the right connections to get a licence. Clearly impressed, the Thakurs were soon inviting him to their weddings, while back in Biharipur, a gun also kept the increasingly restless Dalit youths in line. Rajinder knew that no matter where he stood on the ladder of development, there was always someone above him and below him, trying to knock him down or pull him off. He could not be too protective of all that he had.

Chandra Prakash entered the courtyard with a tray of glasses filled with steamy hot chai, Indian tea boiled with fresh buffalo's milk, sugar and the Ayurvedic herbs. We talked for another hour about the many development agencies that had been to Biharipur, and what they had left behind. Three hand pumps for drinking water were installed in the eighties, as part of the International Decade for Safe Water and Sanitation. A health worker also visited every few months with vaccines for babies, and birth control pills and condoms for young married couples. Under development programs for the lowest castes, the Dalits had received some additional special benefits, but Rajinder wasn't sure what they were. And that was all there was for seven hundred people.

It seemed astonishing that here, in the golden days of reformation for some of the world's poorest farmers, there was so little visible development. Biharipur seemed no better than it had been a century ago, with filthy ponds, unprotected wells, scabies, measles, polio and mud huts that in the West would be declared unfit for animals. Why, I asked, couldn't Rajinder as an educated lambardar help the village do more for itself: build its own school, fix its own road, perhaps expand its cow pond?

He said he had appealed for a school and health clinic. He also desperately wanted to see the badly broken trail beyond the railway tracks paved, or at least bricked. But, he concluded, in Uttar Pradesh, crowded, corrupt, violent and saddled by a millennium of invasion and imperial rule, change was a grand promise.

The state of 140 million was in a perpetual mess. Slightly smaller than California, Uttar Pradesh has five times as many people, with rates of infant mortality, fertility and illiteracy that rival those in the poorest corners of Africa. The fact that seven of India's prime ministers have come from the state, including the once revered Nehru-Gandhi dynasty, seems only to make the situation worse. They showered districts like Shahjahanpur with public sector industries, hefty subsidies and grandiose development schemes, and did little to change the underlying structure of power in villages like Biharipur. Livelihoods and ambitions are still carefully transported from one generation to the next, only now they must be shared by more and more people.

"Everyone wants to change but who will do the change?" Rajinder said. "Politicians don't want to change. Farmers don't know how to change."

"Has nothing changed since you moved here?" I asked.

"Since the British left, no change has come to this village," he answered without hesitation. "You can say sixty percent are poor. They rely on the forty percent who can do something." He paused to finish his tea, handed his glass to Chandra Prakash and emitted a deep burp.

We asked Rajinder if we could look around the village, and talk to other farmers, especially the Dalits. He looked perplexed. A German team sent by Suman Sahai, the only other foreigners to visit Biharipur, had also wanted to talk to the Dalits. He wasn't sure what the Dalits could tell us that he couldn't, but, he insisted, we were free to do as we pleased in his village. Before we left his house, though, he wanted to make a final point. "The main problem is population," he said, though it was clear he was not talking about his own five children. From one troublesome Dalit woman, he said, there were now more than thirty offspring. "If the population continues to grow," he went on, pointing us to the Dalit quarter, on the other side of a small swamp, "it will be disastrous."

And so it was.

We followed a narrow cobbled path beyond one of the big new water pumps, around the hyacinth-covered swamp and past two women bickering about a broken wall between their huts.

"I swear on the Ganges you broke it!" one of the women shouted.

"I swear on the Ganges you broke it!" the other shrieked.

Beyond the squabble stood a walled compound that was home to the thirty people Rajinder had mentioned, most of them children, given the big crowd of barefoot, shirtless boys and girls who followed us. Biharipur's biggest Dalit family lived only thirty metres from Rajinder's house, but a world away in comfort and privilege.

Outside the compound, an old woman sat on a charpoy basking in the winter sun. She nodded as we approached, and before we could introduce ourselves hauled her frail body from the charpoy and planted herself on the dirt next to it. She looked to be in pain, but we as her honoured guests were expected to take the only seat. We tried to persuade her to stay on the charpoy. Perhaps she should lie down, Rama suggested. Her son, himself an oldish man, carried another cot from the house, but the old woman refused to leave the floor. Her place was on the ground, she explained, where she had sat for more than sixty years.

The woman was a widow, the mother, grandmother and great-grandmother of all those around us. She also had no name. Her parents, whom she never knew, had not given her one. No one else had bothered either. Her family called her Amma, "Mother." Others, derogatorily, called her Burhi, "Old Woman." But most villagers were like Rajinder. They simply ignored her.

Amma held her head in her hands, complaining of fever. These horribly cold January nights cut through her bones and sat heavily in her lungs. And now all this noise. A buffalo was loose and all the children gave chase, shouting and throwing stones. There must have been two dozen children running about. The commotion served to stir two mangy dogs, who barked loud enough to wake the dead but not loud enough to drown out the two women a few doors down, always bickering about something.

Amma shook her head. "Yes, the government has given many things," she said bitterly. "Look around. You can see what it means for us. Nothing!"

Before independence in 1947, in another village whose name and location she could not remember, Amma was married off to a young Dalit man from Biharipur. She moved here and gave birth to four sons and a daughter before he died, from what she does not know. Like all Hindu widows were supposed to do, she shaved her head, to mark an end and a new beginning, a symbol that was not lost on her neighbours or all who saw her. She had a new status: she was an untouchable widow, cursed by gender, caste and death. In all of India, there could be no one lower.

Mahatma Gandhi had tried to lift the untouchables by calling them Harijans, "Children of God," but redistributed power would come slower than sympathy. The Dalits, lacking political organization, got little during the land reform movement. At least the new Indian government, led by Jawaharlal Nehru, said it would protect widows, and in 1956 gave them property rights. But the states, which were responsible for land issues, took their time enacting legislation. Uttar Pradesh did not pass the necessary law until 1965, which was far too late for Amma. Her husband's brothers had taken all the land and all her possessions, and told her she was lucky they did not throw her out of the village, too.

"After my husband died, I didn't even get this much space in his house," she said, holding up her index finger. She could not return to her father's village because he was dead. Besides, she was obliged to raise her late husband's children on their own soil.

Amma turned to a moneylender for a bit of cash to build a house, and went to work as a field labourer until her sons, and later their sons, were old enough to work by her side. Her sole good fortune was to have just one daughter, and thus be required to pay only one dowry to see her married.

"I had to work in other people's fields to raise my children," she said, handing a plastic wrapper to one of her great-grandchildren to chew. That was all the Dalits had for a snack. "This work was my life. I had no time with my children. When I went to the fields, I left the children behind to take care of themselves."

Over the decades, much was announced in the name of the widow with no name, for the poor, for widows, for Dalit welfare. First there was the water pump near her home, one of three installed in 1992 as part of a big Unicef-aided project. It was set aside for the Dalits under a quota system and then built closer to Rajinder's house, where he had told the water board engineers to put it. He already had two pumps inside his compound, but this big new India Mark II, with its powerful flow, was especially good for bathing and drawing water for animals. The Dalits could use it when he was finished.

The government also gave the Dalits a dung-fuelled gas generator, the size of a small septic tank. Biogas, as the technology is known, is a naturally produced fuel that requires women (I've never seen a man do this) to mix cow dung, leaves and water in a tank, which in turn produces a gas that can be piped into a hut for cooking. The fuel saves women hours every day searching for scarce firewood, and prevents them from breathing harmful smoke over wood fires. As such, it was embraced by all the big aid agencies as one of the ultimate "intermediate technologies"—neither high tech nor rudimentary—that could help women, forests and the poor. *Deen Bandhu*, the machine was called when its image was put on the ten-rupee stamp. "Friend of the poor."

Amma took her walking stick and slowly rose to an uncomfortable stoop to lead us around back of her hut where we could see the three-hundred-dollar contraption, her "friend." Two square metres in size, and dug partly into the earth, it was broken, and covered with leaves and sticks.

"It did not work when they built it, and it does not work now," she said.

I asked if anyone in the family knew how it worked.

"No one in the village knows how this works!" she snapped in disgust. "Only the government people know."

Even if the contraption had functioned, the Dalits did not have enough livestock to produce sufficient dung for fuel. The biogas plant required fifty kilograms of dung a day and fifty litres of water. Moreover, the biogas flame was not hot enough to cook roti, the staple of every meal in Biharipur. And then there was the acrid smell. No one liked to talk about that.

There were many other well-intentioned programs ("schemes," the Indians call them), but somehow they never made it this far. A reforestation scheme resulted in five hundred fruit trees left to rot in the government seeds warehouse in Tilhar, the local county seat; Rajinder's brother-in-law Abhivaran forgot to pick up his quota. A shipment of smokeless stoves, called *chulas*, was also sent to Tilhar, although no one could say where they ended up. Even when the government announced a pension scheme for widows, in the early nineties, it was for a ridiculous few hundred rupees a year, which Amma never saw. It was supposed to be distributed by Abhivaran, the *pradhan*. But neither he nor Rajinder had seen the money. Or so they told us later.

Amma was not one to wait for help anyway. She retired on her own private pension, known as her sons, who worked as sharecroppers in Rajinder's and other landlords' fields. In return for their labour, they kept half the harvest. Rajinder paid for the seeds, fertilizer and irrigation water, but the arrangement was not always enough for the Dalits to make ends meet. During the lean season, some of the young men also worked at a brick kiln at the end of the road, where the temperatures made the summer heat, at forty-five degrees Celsius, seem cool. If a pair of them could make one thousand bricks in a day, they would each take home $1.25.[2] Or they could try their luck in Shahjahanpur, twenty-five kilometres away, where the roads were cluttered with Dalits pedalling cycle-rickshaws.

The boys always found some way to survive. Amma was more concerned for the future of her oldest great-granddaughter, Archana, who had reached the marriageable age of twelve. The girl had already been hard at work for a few years, tending livestock and rolling dozens of rotis for every meal. Now she would do the same for the family of a fourteen-year-old Dalit boy from Tilhar. For the girl's dowry, Amma had put aside two hundred rupees (about ten dollars) in the hope it would please her new in-laws. They might even treat Archana well

---

[2] all US dollars unless otherwise indicated.

should her husband die, or worse, should she not produce a son. Amma knew enough not to leave the girl's welfare to the state.

As Amma spoke of Archana's uneasy fate, it was hard to imagine how this new generation, no matter how much political power it gained, could ever make great strides. Amma's extended family had half a hectare of land to share among them. And all these children, she was starting to wonder, what would they do? Where would they go? There was no school. In her day, most children died before they needed to talk about school.

"They create so much trouble around here," the old woman said, as the half-naked children continued to chase each other around the compound.

Rajinder taught in a primary school just two kilometres away. Why didn't the children go there? I asked.

"It is a Thakur village," Amma said firmly. "Maybe it is safe for the Yadavs to go to a Thakur village. We would never send our children. They would only get a thrashing, every day."

She had a suggestion. Perhaps we could build a school right here in Biharipur. It would give the children something to do. Besides, a village of seven hundred people had every right to a school it could call its own. It was not Amma's burden, but a matter of global concern, one that had inspired lavish international conferences.

When I suggested she take up the idea with the lambardar, she said that would be difficult. A man with a title, a woman with no name. I volunteered to mention the idea, which I put to Rajinder before we walked back across the fields to find our driver. The lambardar said he already had a plan, one that only a village leader could carry forward, one that was his duty to carry out.

And this, to my knowledge, was how Biharipur's crusade for a school began. It was as innocuous and virtuous a quest as one could find, I thought. The desire for a school was not something that could turn a village against itself. It was not something that could lead to violence, allegations of rape and murder. How could it undermine the process of development when something so noble as a school, I had always believed, truly was development.

RAJINDER AND HIS FEMALE STUDENTS PLAYING MUSICAL CHAIRS AT SONORA SCHOOL

# 2

# "They fear she will start saying 'No'"

A month after our first visit to Biharipur, Rama and I returned to the village to see the Sonora school, the one the Dalits refused to attend. Cindy had come along to start photographing village life. Rajinder, our new friend, was happy to see us and to have us stay with him until classes resumed. The school was closed to celebrate the winter harvest, a holiday that would culminate the next day with a trip to the county fair. We were welcome to come along.

The next morning after the chores were done, Rajinder harnessed his wooden cart to his two white oxen, and invited the village children, regardless of caste, to the travelling fair, which had set up camp for a few days near a mango grove by the highway. Some farmers walked all the way to the fair only to get a knife sharpened, but most came to witness the exotic and taste the bizarre. We wandered past magic shows, games, a Ferris wheel propelled deftly by three young men who stepped on the axle as if it were a treadmill, and an array of luxury goods such as homemade sunglasses, lipstick and a new brand of skin powder called Luxury Talc. Some of the unmarried girls bought earrings and facial creams that promised to make their complexions lighter. A few of the village boys loaded up with plastic toy guns while the older ones, who had come on bicycles, tried their luck shooting balloons with a real pellet gun. The food at the fair was also unending: *chaat masala*, milky sweets, grapes and this year's new exotic offering, Pepsi-Cola. For ten rupees each, about thirty cents, Biharipur's children could eat themselves silly, which most did.

In the far corner of the mango grove, we found a small puppet theatre in which the afternoon show featured two tattered hand puppets, a man and wife, dressed in village clothes. The act opened with the male puppet beating his wife for refusing to do his laundry. "You can't get a woman to understand unless you beat her," he told the audience after hitting her so hard she fell from the stage. The female puppet then reappeared and clobbered her husband with a big hammer, which drew great cheers from the little girls sitting on the dirt in front of the stage. A bit dazed, the male puppet agreed to press his own clothes, until he regained his senses and flattened his wife's head with a steam iron.

And that was the end of the show.

All the children laughed, some of them hysterically, especially little Geeta, the girl we called Hot Pants because short shorts were all she usually wore. Dressed in an old kurta for the fair, Geeta laughed and laughed as she left the open-air theatre to get ice cream, some local variety called Denmark, and meander again through the crowds of strange adults, back to Rajinder's ox cart. The ice cream, the rides, the afternoon of spending their meagre savings had exhausted the children. Rajinder was keen to leave the fair before dark, too, as classes were to resume the next morning at eight-thirty.

Most of the children fell asleep on the way home but I could not take my eyes off the full moon, brilliant and white, which rose from the horizon until it was above the mango trees and seemed bigger than the earth itself. As our ox cart lumbered ahead, the moon's radiant light grew stronger, cutting like a scythe through the spindly stalks of dal in the field beside us. There were more than a dozen of us resting on straw in the cart but once the crickets found their peace, the only sounds I could hear were of the ox team's hooves pounding the dirt and the cart's wheels gnawing the ruts of the country lane. Then, a train passed in the distance, whistling in the still of the cool night, and I knew we were close to Biharipur.

When we reached the village, the moon was high above us. Rajinder said we would have to be up early the next morning if we wanted to follow him to school, as if there was any way to sleep through dawn when dogs barked at the new light and babies cried. Like all the other women in the village, Cindy and Rama had to be up by daybreak anyway, to go to the dal fields and relieve themselves before we men rose and took our turn. The women also had to bathe, light fires and boil water for tea before their husbands awoke. Their daughters had their own sets of chores: sweeping the house, feeding the animals, helping their mothers make rotis for breakfast and getting their younger brothers and sisters ready for a new day. To get to an eight-thirty class in a school two kilometres away was a challenge for everyone, least of all us. We said we would be ready.

When eight-thirty came, we were still at Rajinder's house, finishing our roti and eggplant and waiting for the teacher to get ready. Dressed in his city clothes, Rajinder darted about as he tried to get his older sons prepared for the elementary school they attended in another village and explain what they had to do in the fields after class. Sharecroppers had to be lined up for the next planting season. The tractor needed diesel fuel. He was running through the list when, suddenly, a strange man appeared in the courtyard and took a seat on the broad wooden bench where we had slept after the fair. There was a land dispute, the man told Rajinder. Nothing divides a community in northern India like a land dispute, and only the lambardar's mediation, the man explained, could stop this one from turning violent.

Rajinder nodded and asked us to meet him at the school, across the fields in the Thakur village. A simple dirt road led directly there.

"Arun!" he shouted. "Arun, come here." Arun was the Number Four son, the top student in grade three and a seasoned mischief-maker. He appeared in the courtyard with a jute satchel of books and a toy gun he had bought at the fair, his hair combed with coconut oil.

"Go to school," Rajinder told Arun. "Tell the other children to sweep the classroom until I get there."

After stopping to pick up a few of Arun's friends, we walked along the dirt road to Sonora, the boys' dogs trailing loyally at a distance. Behind the dogs, a few barefoot Dalit boys walked at their own pace. Their hair was not combed with coconut oil. They did not carry bags or books. They were on their way to the pond with a small herd of buffalo.

No sight in rural India is bleaker or more depressing than a government school, and Rajinder's two-room schoolhouse was about as bad as it got. Built only two years earlier, it had a cracked and broken floor. Its roof had holes. During the rains, the teachers and children had to seek refuge in a nearby villager's house. At the best of times there was not enough space for even half of the 141 children who had registered, but that was seldom a concern. On most days, fewer than a third of the children showed up. A latrine, required by standard government school design, was missing. A water pump was installed only recently. The paint on the walls was so thin you could see raw cement. The rest of the unlit interior was so dark and dank it felt like a Himalayan cave.

There was ample money assigned for all these things, but Rajinder said the Thakurs, who dominated the local school construction committee, had stolen much of the building fund. The committee president kept the latrine money, he said. About the only bright spot was a Lipton Tea ad painted on one of the school's outer walls. No one was sure who paid for that.

Arun, pudgy and short, tried to take charge as soon as we reached the school, but it was no use. None of the higher-caste boys would listen to him but went straight to the mango grove to play tag. Only

Arun and a few girls picked up brooms and swept the two dark class-rooms of the dilapidated cement schoolhouse. Their sweeping also made no difference, not when there were piles of unused construction bricks in both rooms, and the shelves were layered with dirt, broken cement and cobwebs. After a few minutes, even Arun dropped his whisk and joined the other boys in the mango grove.

At nine-thirty, an hour late, the rumbling sound of Rajinder's Rajdut motorcycle sent the children scurrying for their books and slates. With sunglasses and the rifle slung around his shoulder, the lambardar looked like a Bombay film villain as he parked his machine beside the school, but the children respected him. When he clapped firmly three times to bring the school to order, all the students pushed to get into line. They were less enthusiastic about the headmaster who had also just arrived, late as he was on most days. The man explained (to us, not the children) that he owned a shop in a nearby town, which he had to open every day before school. The school's third teacher was away on "official leave," the headmaster explained. A fourth teaching post had not been filled because of a fight over caste quotas.

After clapping the children to order, Rajinder announced that there would be no classes in the crumbling schoolhouse today, not when it was sunny and warm outside. He told his pupils to lay out their jute sacks under a mango tree, and sit in neat rows, according to grade. Then he appointed two boys to carry chairs and a couple of desks for him and the headmaster. I counted sixty children from grades one to five, about a 40 percent turnout. Only ten of those present were girls, and just two were from Biharipur, daughters of one of Rajinder's neighbours. It was par for the region. In 1991, according to a UN estimate, the literacy rate for village women in Shahjahanpur, the local district, was 12.3 percent, one of the lowest in the world. At this pace, Biharipur would need another ninety-two years—five full generations—to reach universal female literacy.

Undeterred, Rajinder took charge of his forty pupils, moving nimbly from one row to the next to keep the first three grades occupied. Ranging in age from five to eleven, they had a great gap in learning skills, one so big it was a remarkable feat just to keep them all busy. Rajinder dealt first with his grade threes, asking a small boy to read a passage from "My Dog," the story of a girl who catches a group of thieves with the help of her dog. He told the other children in the class to draw a mango and lotus. When it came time for the grade ones and twos, Rajinder instructed the youngest children, who sat listlessly in the shade, to write on their slates the Hindi words for "stranger," "welcome," "India" and "literate." Only a few were able to complete any of the words, except a little Thakur girl who also volunteered to write out the English alphabet on Rajinder's slate. She said her mother, a grade eight graduate, had taught her that at home.

I looked over to the headmaster, who sat at his desk smoking a bidi while the twenty older children in his charge sat on jute sacks with their slates and notebooks. "If ten chairs cost fifteen hundred rupees, how much will twenty-five chairs cost?" he asked his grade fours. Their next lesson, science, was about carbon dioxide, and the relationship between humans and trees. In history, they were taught about the men who once ruled India, the British, the very people we had been mistaken for. In the next row, most of the grade fives were struggling with a basic arithmetic problem ($[125-50-40]$ x 9), which seemed like a serious issue since the state-wide board exams were only two months away. The headmaster would be reprimanded if all his students did not achieve at least 33 percent on the exam, the official passing grade for primary school, but he was not the least bit worried. The questions, he explained, could be purchased in Tilhar market. In fact, under the new Yadav-run government, cheating in school was no longer illegal. It was one of the few election promises the Yadav chief minister kept.[1]

---

[1] In 1998, a major private study of north Indian schools confirmed that Sonora was the norm. A team made up of several of India's most respected development thinkers conducted spot checks in 236 primary schools, and found that the headmaster was missing in a third of them. Only 25 percent of the teachers present were engaged in a teaching activity. The rest "were found engaged in a variety of pastimes such as sipping tea, reading comics or eating peanuts, when they were not just sitting idle," the group wrote in the Public Report on Basic Education (PROBE) in India. The PROBE study found that out of 220 official teaching days, teachers spent roughly seventy days on non-teaching functions, such as government surveys, distribution of food rations and election duty. More teaching time was lost to bad weather—all schools are closed during heavy rains—and occasions like the one day a month when teachers go to the county centre to collect their pay. This was in addition to twenty statutory holidays. When teachers did show up, the PROBE team discovered they taught for no more than two hours a day. All in all, this meant that a teacher like Rajinder put in a total of three hundred hours of teaching a year, a minute per day for each student. "And this pattern is not confined to a minority of irresponsible teachers," the study concluded. "It has become a way of life in the profession."

Rajinder's and the headmaster's lessons went on for another thirty minutes, until most of the children's minds seemed adrift in the sun-drenched fields. Some got up and played tag. Others sat idly, picking at twigs and leaves on the ground next to their jute sacks. Finally, the headmaster announced a recess so he could go for tea in Sonora. The older children cheered. We welcomed the break, too, because it gave us a chance to talk to the handful of girl students while the boys ran off and played. There were only four girls in grade five, the highest level in primary school, and I wanted to know how they felt about having to leave at the end of the year. It did not matter that they were the four best students in Sonora. Thakur girls almost never went on to further education.

"My mother said as long as I finish my work at home I can go to school until class five," said twelve-year-old Anita. "After that, I must stay home and help her."

"Will you be married when school is finished?" I asked.

The girls burst into laughter, and covered their faces in embarrassment. Except for Nanhi. She did not laugh. The little pocket knife on a string around her neck told everyone that her marriage had already been fixed. Her parents had arranged her engagement the previous week to a boy from a neighbouring Thakur village, and the ceremony was only a few days away. Nanhi was thirteen.

"Do you want to get married?" I asked.

She shook her head, and for a moment looked angry. "My sister was supposed to be married first. She is fifteen. Then they told me my marriage had been fixed. They said I am more beautiful than my sister."

Nanhi's father was the Thakur village chief, the one who kept the latrine money, and he would soon face re-election under India's new system of village democracy. Rajinder explained to us later that Nanhi's father had hurried up the marriage of his prettier younger daughter in order to win twenty-five votes in the groom's extended family, which lived in his jurisdiction.

When the headmaster returned and agreed to Rajinder's suggestion of a games period, there was another loud cheer from the mango grove. Every Friday and Saturday, the children were supposed to have one hour of games, usually *kabaddi*, the rural Indian sport that is something like British bulldog. But Rajinder—a former district champion in shot put, kabaddi, rope climbing and running—believed athletics were so important they should be offered daily. The games period also afforded the headmaster the opportunity to sit under a mango tree, smoke another bidi and mark notebooks. He chuckled when I asked if he was worried about a school supervisor arriving unexpectedly. The local school superintendent came only once a year, on a scheduled day, to quiz students before their exams, the headmaster explained, and to check for hygiene. Moreover, the Village Education Committee, which was supposed to monitor teachers' attendance, met only twice a year: on Independence Day and Republic Day to hold small flag-raising ceremonies and enjoy refreshments bought with money from the latrine fund. No, he said, there was no need to worry about supervision.

While the headmaster retreated for his smoke, Rajinder stood in the middle of the mango grove and merged the five grades into one for stretches and calisthenics. The most athletic boys were called forward to display headstands, back arches and yoga positions, and then start a game of kabaddi. Rajinder suggested the girls play capture the scarf. It would be the last time Nanhi could play the game with her friends before donning the sari of womanhood and moving to her husband's village.

While the boys tackled each other, the girls found their own space and set up a chair in the middle of a ring, and placed a scarf on it. They shrieked and giggled, then elbowed each other as hard as the boys did as they took turns daring to snatch the scarf and dart back to the boundary before an opponent could touch them. When Nanhi's turn came to capture the scarf, she quickly snatched it and ran, only to be tackled in the open field by two friends. They rolled on the ground, laughing, then put the scarf back on the chair and dared another girl to snatch it.

By noon, it was hot, even in the shade of the mango trees. Rajinder declared school over for the day, and rattled off a homework assignment for each grade. Classes were supposed to go until one-thirty, a five-hour day in theory, but neither teachers nor students seemed concerned. Ninety minutes of class time was enough. They all had other work to do. There was just one more thing, Rajinder said. He asked Nanhi to come forward and say the day's prayer. She would not be coming to school again, he informed the others.

"God, give me strength," the thirteen-year-old girl said solemnly, "so I can perform my duties, and serve others better."

That evening, we sat quietly on Rajinder's rooftop terrace, listening to the crickets and a few dogs barking furiously at strange noises in the fields. Rajinder was appalled by the whole system he had lobbied so hard to join. "Teaching is a spiritual pursuit," he said. "I believe in reincarnation. If you do good work in this life, if you help children, your next birth will be good." His pupils, he feared, were learning nothing to help them in their future lives—in Biharipur, Sonora or elsewhere. "I would teach them about sex but the parents and other teachers won't allow it," he continued. "They do not know how much sex to have and that makes them unhealthy. If they understood sex, they would not deteriorate as adults."

Rajinder was curious about our sex life—specifically why Cindy and I, both in our early thirties, did not have children. "I would like to know what you use for birth control," he said, smiling. "It must be very good." While I fumbled for an answer, he beat me to one. "I hope it is not condoms. You know"—and here he paused to reduce his voice to a whisper—"they inhibit your manliness."

I steered him back to the subject of education.

"Will Biharipur's girls ever go to school?" I asked cautiously.

Rajinder sighed and leaned back in the charpoy, as if to look at the stars above. He said he tried to persuade parents to send their daughters to school during his rounds as the village's medicine man. "An educated girl," he would tell them, "can make good food, stay clean and manage the house. Under her, the children will become literate."

The mothers often told him to take their girls to school, but the fathers invariably objected. "They fear she will start saying 'No,'" Rajinder explained. "They fear she will start having her own opinions. There's also the common thinking, 'She's going to get married. Why does she need an education?'"

The best hope for Biharipur, he reminded us, was for the government to build a school right here, so at least the Dalit boys and a few more girls would feel safe coming to class. Their fathers could even keep an eye on them.

It was the only time I would hear him agree with Amma, who also wanted a school for her great-grandchildren. They had common ground in the Indian constitution, too. That eloquent document, completed in 1950 by the first great Dalit leader, B.R. Ambedkar, called for primary schools to be made accessible to all children. Forty years later, government policy called for a school to be built within a kilometre of every sizeable community, a policy that the World Bank and several other big aid agencies were eager to finance. A huge effort was on to build schools for Biharipur and thousands more villages like it.

But after what we had seen in Sonora, I was no longer sure a school would make much difference unless it was accompanied by some serious social change, starting with the notion of human equality. What good was a school for little Hot Pants, I wondered, when she would be sold off like chattel at puberty? What hope would education bring the shoeless Dalits when it came from their own landlord?

Rajinder remained convinced that a school would help break these caste and social barriers. He had written letters to district authorities in Shahjahanpur, and spoken with the Yadav power brokers. He'd gone to the state capital, Lucknow, to meet the finance minister, a fellow Yadav, who agreed that Biharipur should have a school. When a distant relative was elevated to the Indian cabinet, Rajinder went to a public rally and prostrated himself at the minister's feet, hoping that might advance the file. But our lambardar was beginning to learn that official development, like his headmaster, moved at its own pace, especially for those who lived three kilometres from the main road. The people of Biharipur would not get a school when they decided one was needed. They would get one only when an official in Shahjahanpur or Lucknow, someone they had never met, decided to initial a file, and grant them what was theirs by right.

CHANDRIKA PRASAD, LEADER OF THE ALI BABA BAND

# 3

# Dalchand: Father of the Bride

April in Biharipur is glorious. The winter wheat has been harvested, the summer rice is in the ground and the mango trees are just starting to blossom. Gone are the cold winter nights, when the village is shrouded by the smoke of a hundred fires. Still to come is the deliriously hot summer, with rains, mosquitoes and sickness everywhere. April days are hot, sunny and dry; its evenings warm and still. All things considered, it is the perfect month for a wedding, even for a couple of teenagers.

In rural India there is nothing quite like a wedding, nothing that so excites, enriches or, at times, impoverishes people. It is one of the strongest traditions that hold together communities and families and allow them to endure many hardships. Yet it can also sap families of years of savings, money they could have spent educating their daughters, keeping them healthy or buying land. Cindy, Rama and I returned to Biharipur in April for the marriage of one of the village girls, Kanya Vati.

To pay for Kanya's wedding, her father, Dalchand, a landless labourer from the menial Dheemar caste, had to beg and borrow from his friends and relatives. But most of the twelve-thousand-rupee cost (about four hundred dollars) would come from our host, Rajinder, who made financing simple. Before loaning someone a hundred rupees, he would keep ten rupees as a service charge and then demand ten rupees repayment every month over a year. The interest rate worked out to 33 percent, about double what the local banks charged at the time, and cost Dalchand another harvest.

A sweet man in his fifties, Dalchand had an unflappable manner. He kept a pleasant home, wore a white dhoti and T-shirt every day and was always exceptionally kind to us. But when we found him sitting on the culvert outside the village in a tattered burgundy dinner jacket he had purchased for the wedding, he looked more nervous than most fathers of the bride. He had picked the following day for the wedding on the advice of an astrologer in Tilhar, and astrologers were not always right. A year earlier, Dalchand's first attempt to marry off Kanya, also with an astrologer's blessing, failed miserably when the groom's family broke off the engagement. They said her skin was too dark. At least the family was decent enough to return the five hundred rupees and the cutlery he had provided as a dowry. But now Kanya was fourteen years old and approaching the age when she would be considered undesirable. This could be her last chance.

Dalchand described the new groom as "a good farmer," a sixteen-year-old from a village forty kilometres away. The groom's parents, whom Dalchand met through mutual friends, had accepted his dowry offer of a man's bicycle and gold watch, but still he worried. A few years earlier, his eldest daughter, Shardha, was thrown out of her husband's village when her first son died at six months of age, and had been living in humiliation ever since in Dalchand's home. Not only that, but her in-laws kept the dowry. Would Kanya face the same hardships? Dalchand wondered. What would this boy and his family do to her if she could not bear sons? Would the groom's family get drunk at the ceremony and fight? Or would they stop the wedding before the sacred vows and demand more dowry? Dalchand could bear no more expense. "I'm just nervous about all my duties," he said, walking back to his house with us. "I don't want any complaints. My honour is at stake."

Dalchand was neither comfortable like Rajinder nor desperately poor like Amma. Dheemars, one of the many Other Backward Castes, are traditionally fishermen, but in the middle of the Gangetic plains there are few fish to be had. Even when the government stocked the local pond with fish fry, people like Dalchand couldn't touch it because an official had sold the exclusive fishing rights to a man from Tilhar. Dalchand relied instead on a half hectare of land he worked as a share-cropper, and a small dry-goods store that his wife, Kamla, operated out of their house. The land gave them enough to eat, and a little to save for dowries and clothes. The shop, really just a shelf with a few packages of tea, biscuits, soap and matches on it, earned them a few rupees a day to buy luxuries, such as a used dinner jacket for a wedding.

Like most Dheemars in Biharipur, Dalchand lived at the front of the village, near the pond where they were not allowed to fish. He and Kamla had a small patch of dirt in front of their house that served as a yard, and a small mud porch where they kept their shop. Inside, around a central courtyard, were four more rooms for themselves, Kanya, Shardha and Bishram, their grown son, who was married and had just had his first child, a boy. The whole place was in a tizzy when we reached the house, which helped explain why Dalchand had been sitting on the culvert wall, contemplating. In the front yard, a work crew from Tilhar erected a canopy made of tinsel and expired lottery tickets strung between bamboo poles. (It must have been a good lottery: the top prize was one hundred thousand rupees.) There was also a welcome gate made of banana leaves, gold tinsel and an "Auspicious Marriage" sign. On the front porch, Kamla was busy slapping paint on the exterior walls with her bare hands; it was a Brahmin blue for good luck. Inside, a group of her friends sat around a fire, boiling sugary milk to make sweets for the guests, and teasing Kanya in song. "We know about the boy you're marrying," the women sang over and over. "There's no wheat in the house, and the mother is hard of hearing!" They all laughed. Kanya, whose eyes were fixed demurely on her hennaed hands, did not budge.

Poor Dalchand did not have time to sit down. He remembered he had to check in with the two cooks from Shahjahanpur who were busy in the next-door neighbour's hut, unpacking big vats, ladles and scores of plates for the wedding feast to be served that night. He had already purchased the food: one hundred kilograms of flour, fifteen kilograms of ghee, six kilograms of oil, fifty kilograms of sugar and fifty kilograms of potatoes. But one of the cooks, a big burly man who was clearly unimpressed by the state of the rustic kitchen, felt it was not enough. "Where are the green vegetables?" he demanded of Dalchand. "You must have vegetables!"

The troubled look on Dalchand's face deepened as he calculated the unexpected cost. He slipped into his house, pulled out a wad of rupees hidden behind a brick and dispatched a couple of friends to the nearest market for green vegetables.

We left Dalchand to contemplate his debts, and returned to the porch to see Kamla, mother of the bride. She sat down beside us, careful not to let her blue hands drip any paint on the dirt floor. I asked how she felt seeing Kanya go. "I'm sad to lose my daughter," she said. "I'm also very nervous. My stomach is fluttering. We have to make this boy's family happy." She smiled, exposing a mouthful of stained and broken teeth.

Did she like the groom Dalchand had picked?

"Oh, yes!" Kamla said. "He's good-looking, a good farmer and he can take care of himself. That's all anyone wants for their daughter."

Before Dalchand's friends returned with the vegetables, the crack of a gunshot sounded from the road. The wedding party had arrived. Seated on the back perch of a tractor, the young groom looked as terrified as Kanya. He wore a garland of ten-rupee notes to show his wealth, and a thin wisp of a moustache to show his masculinity. Most of his extended family, about fifty men in all, were squeezed onto two tractors and two carts, which would have made for an unbearable journey had they not all been drunk. At least there were no women from the groom's village for them to abuse. Marriage in northern India is a man's business; Kanya would be the only female returning with the groom and all those men.

As soon as the tractors came to a halt, several members of the groom's family headed straight for a set of charpoys outside Dalchand's house, and fell asleep. A few more lay down on open patches of dirt, and they slept too, which did not bother Dalchand, standing in front of the canopy to welcome his guests. His own son's wedding, a couple of years earlier, had been one of the best times of his life. But once the last of the groom's relatives had been greeted, Dalchand excused himself to walk around the village with a sack of rice to be given out by the handful to each of his neighbours, the customary invitation to a wedding feast.

We arrived at the feast with Rajinder at about nine that night, a time when the village is usually dark and asleep. Most of the groom's party had risen, eaten and were into large bottles of country-made liquor. A rented diesel generator whirred, jerked and belched smoke in Dalchand's front yard, drowned out only by Hindi film music blaring on the cassette player he had rented. The generator also powered four fluorescent bulbs that lit the path to his house, the only electricity some of the young village children had ever seen. After dinner, while the cooks packed up, the older Biharipur boys sat under the bright lights and smoked hand-rolled bidis. Most of the groom's family returned to their cots, except for a few who watched a Hindi movie on the TV and VCR Dalchand had rented for 350 rupees, about twelve dollars.

As the party staggered on, few of the guests noticed that the first ritual, the formal engagement ceremony, had already started in the courtyard inside Dalchand's house. Before a smattering of people, mostly from Biharipur, Kanya and the groom exchanged garlands, and said, "I choose you," a little after the fact, I thought, since their fathers had already done that a few weeks earlier. Kanya, her head veiled, did not look up. The boy, who wore a paper crown, stared nervously at the ground. But Dalchand, dressed in a crisp white dhoti and his used dinner jacket, looked proud. He was upholding his honour well. Once the pledge was made, he marked the groom's forehead with a *tilak* as a sign of respect. And then, as if on cue, one of the groom's relatives shouted for more dowry. Dalchand looked timid.

He kept his eyes cast downward and muttered a soft "No." More men shouted for dowry but most seemed too drunk to stand up. Finally, Dalchand and the groom's father stepped aside, and whispered to each other for a couple of minutes. On top of the bicycle and watch, Dalchand agreed to give the boy's family 1,605 rupees, about fifty-three dollars, plus a set of bowls and serving dishes. The drunk men clapped, and accepted Dalchand's invitation to return to the party in the front yard where the music was blaring.

As a special feature, Dalchand had hired his neighbour, Chandrika Prasad, to perform along with his fifteen-member Ali Baba Band. Chandrika had given up farming and sold his land when he reached middle age to go into the music business, and now had a harmonium, four drums and a trunk full of glittering costumes. He hired men from other villages to play music, usually at weddings, and tonight had brought along a transvestite dancer. For the whole gig, he charged one thousand rupees, less than thirty-five dollars. After the engagement ceremony, we listened to the Ali Baba Band play in front of Dalchand's house for a few minutes before realizing that all fifteen members were drunk. The harmonium sputtered like an old tractor. The drumbeats erupted as unpredictably and loudly as the rented diesel generator backfiring. Rajinder, who steadfastly avoided any food, drink or conversation at the party, was relieved when we said we, too, were ready to leave. Several band members had passed out anyway, and Chandrika was fading, although the dancer, resplendent in makeup and a sari, looked as if he could go all night as he swanned up and down the alley outside Dalchand's, flailing his arms in the moon's shadowy light.

We returned shortly after sunrise for the marriage ceremony, but found only a group of women in the courtyard around the wedding pole—four poles actually, taken from ox plows and propped like a tall teepee with silver tinsel strung around. The couple would have to circle the pole seven times in the ancient Hindu ritual, but not before Kanya returned from the fields where she had gone to graze the family's goats. Her older brother Bishram was in no position to help. His baby had been awake most of the night with a fever, aggravated by the Ali Baba Band, which apparently played off and on until four in the morning.

Once the bride was back home, washed and dressed, and the Brahmin priest had arrived, the ceremony could begin. To invite the gods, Dalchand sprinkled the marriage circle with water that had been purified with mango leaves. He then put a piece of dry grass under the groom's toe to ward off evil spirits, and fed the boy a sweet as a further offering to the gods. I looked around the courtyard. There was Kanya's family, and a few neighbours. The only guest from the groom's side was his brother. The others were still asleep.

As the priest prepared for the ceremony, Dalchand turned to the congregation and said he was willing to accept gifts. The groom's family had presented him and his wife with new clothes. "Is there anyone else who would like to present us with new clothes?" Dalchand asked. There was no response. Sadly, he turned to the priest, and offered him sweets to begin.

But before they would go any further, the priest and his young assistant, who were sitting cross-legged on the courtyard next to Kanya and the groom, announced they would need more money. Dalchand, with a look of disgust on his face, asked a friend to spot him twenty rupees, the equivalent of a day's wage for a field labourer. The assistant rejected the twenty-rupee note because it was torn. Another friend dug into his pocket and found two unblemished ten-rupee notes, which the assistant quickly accepted.

Chanting quietly to the gods, the priest lit a fire in front of the couple so that the creator would be witness to their union, and invited the groom to throw ghee on it. Kanya was asked to drop grain on the fire, to call forth her ancestors so they could bless the marriage. But before she could reach for the grain at her side, the priest stopped the ceremony again, and said another five rupees was needed for the fire. Dalchand huffed angrily, and passed a five-rupee note to the assistant. (Brahmin priests should not touch something as temporal as money.) Bishram, sitting at Dalchand's side with a pen and paper, noted the transaction in the running tally he was keeping of the wedding costs.

"Why don't you speak louder?" one of Dalchand's friends suggested to the priest, who had resumed his mantra. "Even the gods can't hear you."

"He's old and weak!" the assistant snapped.

"I'm not old!" the priest said, quickly looking up from the flames. "Who said that?"

The assistant muttered something.

"Shut up!" the priest said. "Don't open your mouth."

After listening to prayers and mantras for nearly an hour, I looked across the courtyard and out the front door. A work crew was already dismantling the canopy and taking down the "Auspicious Marriage" sign.

Then the priest asked the couple to stand and walk around the ox-plow marriage pole, while he threw blessings of grain at them. Each was asked to repeat a set of vows. Kanya promised to look after the boy's family, bear him sons, feed him food "from the six seasons," help him in his salvation, forgive him for wrongdoings and never return to her father's house uninvited. The groom promised to take Kanya on pilgrimages, share his money with her, treat her well, clothe her and accept her praise. "Even if I am wearing torn clothes," he said solemnly, "you will praise me."

The priest sat silently for a minute. "What else have I forgotten?" he asked the congregation. There was no response. "Okay," he told the two families, "you can take them inside."

Kamla rose to escort her daughter and new son-in-law into a room off the courtyard, but before they could get there the priest's bagman was again clamouring for money. Dalchand made a final offer of fifty rupees for both him and the priest.

"I get twenty-five rupees from labourers, and you're much better than a labourer," the assistant said.

"If you don't take it, there will be nothing," Dalchand replied testily. He handed the assistant fifty rupees for the priest, and twenty-five rupees for himself.

"These days twenty-five rupees is nothing," the assistant complained. Dalchand angrily gave him another ten.

While the groom bathed at Dalchand's hand pump, Kanya stayed in her room, where her mother brushed her hair with coconut oil and helped her into a pink sari, the clothing of womanhood, a present from her new in-laws. Outside, the local women cooked roti and tea for the wedding guests, who were just starting to rise, although across the dirt path, under a clump of eucalyptus trees, the Ali Baba Band slept on.

After the wedding guests ate breakfast, they laughed loudly about the previous night while Dalchand stood to one side, looking relaxed. His house was in one piece, and his daughter looked beautiful as she prepared to climb aboard a tractor to leave Biharipur. The groom's family also seemed happy as they piled into the tractor cart, though they could not agree on where to put the new bicycle.

Of course, Dalchand was in debt again, more than he had counted on, but the marriage seemed secure, and that was worth a very good amount.

"Now," he said, "I can sleep."

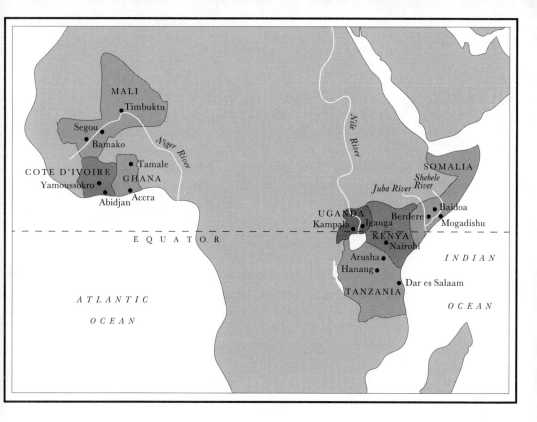

# AFRICA

"Unlike Somalia, which was left by Mr. World to rot, most of Africa was again rising. Its people had seen the inanity of Big Men, the folly of Big Aid and the fickleness of Big Media, and were now mapping their own course."

TECHNICALS IN MOGADISHU

# 4

## Desert Rats

The monsoon pounded New Delhi the day before I was to leave for Africa, where drought and anarchy were devastating Somalia and about to destroy the new hopes of international altruism. From morning to night, rain poured down, flooding the low-lying slums and submerging most of the city's underpasses. The monsoon was so intense that in a matter of hours it flushed out the city's archaic storm drains, driving every living creature to the surface, which in our part of the city meant rats.

With Cindy already in Africa, photographing the lives of AIDS orphans in northern Malawi, I was alone in our ground-floor flat, writing to deadline, nine and a half hours ahead of Toronto, and at first too busy to notice the clanging in the washroom next to my office. When the noise grew louder, I assumed it was the forty-year-old toilet, installed when the house was built. But shortly after midnight, I discovered something much worse than outdated plumbing. When I went to the washroom, I saw that every few minutes a metal drain popped up and a six-inch rat slipped out, bolted through the crack under the washroom's second door and was home free, in *our* home.

I ran out of the washroom and grabbed the first object of self-defence I could find. Even to a smallish rat, the umbrella must have looked ridiculous; they continued to trot about like dinner guests, unfazed by my presence. My first shot with the umbrella missed the rat entirely but dented the metal tip. The next shot clipped the rat's rear but only knocked it off balance. It darted into my office and slipped behind a cardboard box before I could whack it again. I ran straight for the box, kicking it dead centre as hard as I could. The rat emitted such a piercing squeal that surely, I thought, it was dead. But when I pulled back the box to check, it popped out the other side, dashed behind a bookshelf and was gone. I was clearly outwitted. I also had a story to file. I put the heaviest object I could find, a voltage stabilizer, on top of the flimsy bathroom drain, returned to my desk and wrote to the sound of squeaking mischief.

After a while it seemed almost natural to have rats darting about the flat. Then I spun around to retrieve a file from an open drawer, and before me was the biggest, fattest invader of them all, standing somewhere between "India—Population" and "India—Water." I grabbed the *The Globe and Mail Style Book* and launched it at the creature, only to see the book bounce off the file drawer and land between the cabinet and the wall. Unscathed, the rat ducked over the side of the drawer and slipped behind the big metal filing cabinet. This was war, I decided, and quickly sent my story by modem so I could get down to some real work.

I thought first about Cindy. In Malawi, she told me, field mice ran up and down her body every night while she slept in a maize hut. Her solution was to wait for a mouse to reach the top of her foot and then flick her leg, hurling it across the hut she shared with an old woman and eight orphaned grandchildren. The others apparently slept through the swarming.

I opted for a technological solution, using the Indian-made rat traps Cindy had bought at a local hardware store. The traps were nothing more than long rectangular cages with metal doors that snapped shut when something pulled on the small bait levers. There was no catch, nothing to claim the rat other than the bars around it. The cages were a pacifist's dream. At two in the morning, they were also all I had.

I hooked pieces of bread as bait to the levers inside the cages and waited. Twice I heard the cages snap shut but when I looked there was nothing. The rats had nibbled the bread from the outside, and fled when the trap was triggered. Finally a third cage slammed shut and there was a squeal. I ran to the back hallway and found a plump little creature too complacent to be bothered with finishing the rest of the bread in the cage. Fearing I would lose him, I grabbed the handle, walked quickly to the door and was about to step outside when something bounced off my foot. The rat had fallen through the trap door, and was gone.

Fed up with Indian rat traps, I returned to my first weapon, the umbrella, and chased the escapee into my office and then back to the hall, where it tried to squeeze through a small hole in the front door. It was stuck. Here was my perfect chance, a shot so clear and simple it felt like T-ball. But something overcame me. I found myself gently opening the door to let the animal scurry down the dark driveway and into the bushes. The pacifist was me.

Conceding all floor space and open filing cabinet drawers to the rodent army, I went to bed, where, pulling back the single sheet we used in summer, I found two small turds. The rats were obviously not content with the low ground. I retreated to my office to sleep for what remained of the night in my swivel chair, with my feet on the desk. When dawn broke, and the rats sought darker shelter, I moved to the couch and dozed fitfully for a few more hours. I knew they would be back, as sure as the rains. From then on, I would be the guest, and this would be nature's home.

Exhausted from the rat wars, I boarded an Indian Airlines flight that evening for Bombay where I was to catch the next morning's five o'clock flight to Nairobi, and from there, I hoped, on to Somalia.

I was too tired to think about Indian Airlines' main course of dal, spinach and rice, or the partially melted ice cream in a cardboard container, which I ate with regret. Two hours later, in the check-in area of Bombay's international airport, my temperature soared and my face felt flushed. The summer humidity was intense but this was something else. I dashed for the men's washroom and filled three sinks with vomit. Each time I looked up in the yellowing mirror, I noticed a small Tamil man, a cleaner, shaking his head. He left the room before I did. Feeling cooler, but not stronger, I joined the customs and immigration lineup, only to make it to the first counter where I heaved what little remained in my stomach. I mumbled an apology to the immigration officer as I handed him my passport. He nodded knowingly and quickly stamped my pages. I had nothing left to declare.

The bout of food poisoning would have been nothing more than an uncomfortable bump in the road had it not meant that I was one of the last to board the plane, far behind a beefy Nigerian I found well established in my seat. He invited me to take the middle, between him and another two-hundred-pounder, who occupied the window seat. My Kenya Airways boarding card, clearly stamped "15C," made no impression. "This is the way we fly in Africa. It is first come, first served," the man in my aisle seat said, opening his hand again to offer me the middle chair, or at least the part not draped by the Yoruba robes flowing over the armrests. When I protested to a flight attendant, the steward shrugged and continued to the galley, where he spent the rest of the night dozing. I decided to explain to my African co-travellers how we fly in India. I put down my bag in the aisle and announced to the two men, and to those in front and behind us, that I had lost all control of my digestive system. It was only a friendly warning, I assured them, but there was every chance I would throw up my entire Kenya Airways breakfast on someone's beautiful robe should I be trapped in the middle seat and unable to bolt to the toilet if the need arose. The squatter moved, but not without leaving several yards of blue fabric and a large elbow in my air space. And that was the end of it. The three of us snored all the way across the Arabian Sea.

❖

By the time I got to central Nairobi and met up with Cindy, there was no time to worry about my travelling parasites. We needed to get to Mogadishu, which I was told would be more difficult than ousting a Nigerian from 15C. Somalia was in the midst of civil war and a frightful famine. One option was to buy a place on a small private aircraft used for running narcotics and qat, the mind-numbing leaf chewed by almost every Somali man every day. A refugee worker suggested a more reputable carrier, Southern Air Transport, the private company that made its name running guns to Central America in the eighties. Its Hercules aircraft were now running food to Mogadishu for the few relief agencies who dared to stay.

The next morning, just after dawn, we found ourselves on a metal bench in the plane's dim underbelly with a few relief workers and seventeen tonnes of food aid. Oddly, it seemed quite normal to be flying to the rescue with food for the starving and laptops, satellite phones and cameras with which to tell of more horrors. This was the way the world handled crises, I thought. Big problem. Big coverage. Big relief. Big sighs of satisfaction.

Up in the African sky, our big aircraft seemed to float over the Kenyan lowlands that bleed into Somalia's parched interior and then its green coastline and capital. From the cockpit, Mogadishu looked like a sun-baked Mediterranean town, with white villas, rolling hills and a pristine beach that seemed to stretch from the city's edge to the end of the earth. Then some small gunfire ricocheted off the hull, barely causing a dent. The pilots laughed as if it were confetti thrown at a wedding limousine. This happened every time they landed in Mog, they said, in the heart of madness. When the door opened, allowing in a rush of sultry seaside air, I realized I knew little of the land or people outside. Few others on board did either. At the foot of the steps was a pickup truck of gunmen waiting to exact a landing fee from Southern Air and offer us their services for one hundred dollars a day—each. The rate was non-negotiable.

We hitched a ride instead with some relief workers to the Unicef guest house, which was running full with the growing number of reporters, photographers and cameramen arriving each day. At the airport gate, piles of wheat sacks sat under the watch of the same gunmen who had welcomed us. Almost every relief shipment into Somalia was being hijacked by one faction or another, and most of

Mogadishu had been looted, too, even the shark net in the city's harbour. The tragedy we were watching from the relief truck was not just another African disaster; it was a serious test for the West's new order in the wake of the Gulf War, one that called for the perceived forces of right to overcome the perceived forces of wrong. In starving Somalia, this new belief dictated that some form of intervention was inevitable. The great powers would have to provide protection for their food, and some strong advice to straighten the place out. The West would be content only when the rats were driven back underground.

No one was really sure how Somalia got like this, or even what "this" was. Pestilence or nuisance? But we believed we had a better mousetrap, and that Somalia needed it fast. It was as logical a reaction as my traps and umbrella were in New Delhi, and as flawed.

Over the next month, Cindy and I would travel up and down Somalia's famished roads to record suffering that should never be tolerated, and missing the bigger debacle unfolding before us. We had waded inadvertently into an allegory of African aid. The myopia of charity, our ignorance of cultural differences and social stigmas, our impatience and media hype, the passions of Big Men and the egos of big organizations—these sad and destructive forces were all here in this one dreadful quagmire.

Beyond the seized food aid, the first thing I noticed on Mogadishu's main street were the barbershops, and then the tea houses, stands selling gas by the jar and vegetable stalls brimming with big red tomatoes, watermelons and bananas. This was not a disaster zone; this was the capital of relief. To find Somalis who did not have access to fresh fruit, we realized we had to get out of the city as fast as we could, and hired Ali, a young man who was related to one of the Unicef drivers, to take us inland to a place called Baidoa, "City of Death." Ali was not a typical driver. With three friends, a cache of automatic rifles and a pickup truck, the young English student had refashioned himself as a technical—slang for a gunman for hire to relief agencies and journalists who usually expensed the cost as "technical assistance." Cindy and I had no idea that our technicals had the same combat experience as we did, which was none. They were only university students in a country that had no functioning university.

To get to the City of Death, we followed a magnificent American-built desert highway donated to the Somali dictator Mohamed Siad Barre during the Cold War when he was fighting Marxist Ethiopia. The American Highway, as it was known, was said to have been the design of military planners who wanted an emergency airstrip for Somalia's fighter jets, which was perhaps why much of the 185-kilometre-long highway looked like something out of Nevada—smooth and straight as it passed scrubland and ghost towns of abandoned shops, stripped-down hydro poles and broken street lights. At first the road was lined with children and crippled men selling great big bunches of bananas or filling potholes with dirt in the hope drivers would throw a few shillings out their windows. It was probably the world's only voluntary toll road, and a sign of the country's remarkable enterprise. Farther ahead, the road was littered with remnants of construction equipment, stripped of every part that could be removed and shipped to the Middle East, usually in an open container of goats headed for slaughter.

The ghosts of better days did not linger out in the desert, however, not in places like Bur Hakkaba, "Mountain of Rest," a great rock on the American Highway where hundreds of women and children sat, waiting for food. Their husbands and fathers were at war, or dead, and now they were too weak to walk any farther. In an empty tin shed once used to store food, we found sixty women and children asleep at midday on a dirt floor that reeked of urine. The rest of the camp stank of death. Waiting here by the great rock, hoping for some of that food in Mogadishu, the lucky ones got one bowl of gruel a day. The rest had to get by on a soup made from boiled animal skins they had begged from an abattoir.

We continued up the highway to Baidoa, only to be told by an Irish nurse that there was a small town called Berdale, deeper in the desert, and it was "much, much worse" than the City of Death. When we got to Berdale, we found a group of middle-aged men sitting in a pleasant garden drinking tea. They invited us to join them, and told us of their abandoned farms and broken tractors. One man had lost two hundred hectares for want of water. He said a nearby river was full, but ever since the war started in 1991 the local irrigation canals had not been dredged; the private company that used to clear the canal every season had seen its machinery looted and its staff had fled.

Judging by their generous stomachs and hearty laughs, these men had food, but they requested we appeal to the West for more. To make their point, they took us to a crumbling building outside of town where hundreds of skeletal children waited for their daily ration of beans and rice under an expansive abag tree that was the only other sign of life on the hard scrabble land. I did not appreciate the difference between the fat elders and bony children until I realized that these were some-one else's children, the sons and daughters of nomads who had gravi-tated to Berdale when the fighting factions stole their herds. There were scores of them before us, and hundreds more on the horizon, coming toward us from the desert in columns of dust. The children, dressed in rags and covered with grey dust, looked like ghosts as they walked through the scrub brush, many with small empty pots on their heads. Ten-year-olds lacked any hair. The younger ones had feet swollen like balloons from blisters and cuts infected during their trek for survival. On our way out of town, we stopped at several homes that had been burned and gutted by retreating militias. There were bodies still strewn in the rooms, some adults but mostly children, their rigid corpses curled up in their last try at comfort.

We told other journalists on the road about Berdale, and over the next few days, North American newspapers and magazines were deluged with pictures of the emaciated children and only them. The well-fed elders had vanished like ghosts.

When we returned to the City of Death for the night, we found on the edge of town a restaurant named Bikini, which served large plates of surprisingly good spaghetti and meat sauce. While we ate, Ali and his friends waited in the back of the pickup truck, which they feared would be stolen by the many freelance gunmen wandering around. Bikini did a surprisingly brisk business with journalists, aid workers, gunmen and food traders, despite its location on the main path for women and children shuffling to a feeding station. From our table, I could see a Red Crescent truck rolling down the street, collecting the corpses of those who could not complete the journey. There were hundreds falling every day.

After our spaghetti and tea, I stood up to pull ten dollars out of my moneybelt, when suddenly my arms were jerked back and I was ripped away from the table. A gunman stood a short distance away, pointing his AK-47 at my stomach while another held my arms behind my back. For some reason, I shouted, "What the fuck are you doing?" over and over again. It was obvious to everyone else in the restaurant what the thugs, whose only English word seemed to be "dollars," were doing. The gunman staring at me was so dazed on qat he seemed barely able to stand up or train his bloodshot eyes on anything other than my moneybelt. Between his drooping eyes and my idiotic shouting, there was enough confusion for the restaurant owner to grab his own gun and jump over the wooden bar that lined one end of the Bikini. The Somalis started shouting at each other. Some men at the next table grabbed Cindy and hustled her into the back room, apparently for her safety; Ali and our own gunmen rushed in. Unimpressed by our freshmen technicals, the robbers let go of me and went after the camera bag of another journalist just as the gunmen of a local warlord entered. The chief of security apologized, and promised to take care of the assailants. Baidoa, he assured us, was a perfectly safe place for journalists, relief workers and food aid.

After sleeping the night at the Unicef office in town, we were woken at dawn by the moans and grunts of hundreds of people rising from their beds on the street to get to the local feeding centre. It consisted of a firepit and pot in an abandoned yard. When the centre opened at seven, several dozen women and children pushed through the yard's big metal gate and ran toward the pot. An emaciated boy was slammed against the gate by a crush of people behind him. A woman, running barefoot with two tiny children in her arms, tripped over a rock, but managed not to drop the children as she fell to her knees. The best that two guards could do to keep the crowd in order was to hit the smallest and weakest with sticks. The stronger ones had already reached the pot of gruel.

A couple of weeks later, after the world started flooding Somalia with food, I joined the first Canadian airlift from Nairobi to Bardera, the desert headquarters of the most cunning of all the warlords, Gen. Mohamed Farrah Aidid. On a sparkling clear Sunday morning, six Canadian pilots and crew, who had not been to Somalia before, followed a series of parched riverbeds to the upper Juba and then traced the meandering river to the town that once was a tobacco-growing centre and stood like an oasis in the desert. From the air, Bardera hardly looked like the epicentre of a major famine, not when we could see rich maize and tobacco crops running along both banks. Well off the river, the pilots spotted a brown-and-white flag attached to an anthill, and beyond it a long, clear, flat stretch of dirt. They said that it must be the runway, although it looked less than half the distance needed to land a Hercules. It would have to do. The aircraft bounced once off the landing strip, circled around and tried again, skidding to a halt, with a flat tire, right in front of a thicket of scrub brush.

From the airstrip, two lorries, under UN flags, took the sixteen tonnes of food and barrelled down a dirt path into a dry riverbed and up through the bush to Bardera, where three thousand hungry people awaited the airlift. Forty had died that morning. There were hardly any children under two left, although there was no shortage of young men. A group of them, all armed, was waiting for the convoy at a warehouse where the food was to be stored. They said the shipment could go no farther, because of a new "tax" policy. Instead of the usual 10 percent tithe on all relief shipments paid to General Aidid's men for "protection," the warlord required, as of today, 20 percent. A UN representative tried to haggle but the gunmen were unmoved. Twenty percent, or the starving people got nothing, they said, muttering something about orders from the top. More starvation with piles of Canadian food nearby would not play well back home, so 20 percent it was and the young men were gone, in a jeep mounted with an anti-aircraft gun.

I left the warehouse to walk to a three-storey building at the other end of town where Aidid, the new dictator of southern Somalia, was holding court. In a musty waiting room, five teenaged boys, all with guns, sat on carpets drinking tea. I handed one my business card, which he took inside the general's lair. He returned with a fat man in stocking feet, dress shirt and polyester pants that were three inches too short—a colonel who introduced himself with a long embrace, as if I had just come from the front with victory in hand. He then told me to wait. The general was in the middle of a breakfast war meeting with two dozen leaders from his Hiwaye clan who had come from across the desert for their marching orders. It would be a while longer, the colonel apologized, when suddenly the great man emerged and extended his long, thin hand to me. He said he would be happy to receive a Canadian journalist if I did not mind waiting. Another interviewer, former Australian prime minister Bob Hawke, was on his way from the airport with a film crew organized by World Vision.

The moment Hawke arrived, the clan elders were shuffled out of Aidid's room, looking suitably fed and ready for a long nap rather than a bumpy ride across the desert to their various fronts. "Your excellency, the prime minister of Australia," the general announced, greeting Hawke, who had been out of office since 1991. I figured anyone who came to Bardera in a Learjet deserved to be called "prime minister."

I followed the television crew, filming Hawke for a documentary about the famine, and soon realized we were all in Aidid's drawing-room, where he and the elders had been sitting on cushions and piles of carpets. For the "prime minister of Australia," the dictator moved to a poor man's Louis XIV sofa set and offered everyone tea, which he poured himself from a plastic Thermos.

Hawke and Aidid hit it off. The Australian did not correct the mistake about his title, and prefaced one of his first questions with a bold "as one leader to another." Aidid, a former ambassador to India, proceeded to lecture the visiting statesman about his theory of "pastoral democracy," which he had laid out in four unpublished books. The general was in his best diplomatic form, ready to talk through the night, it seemed, but Hawke could not stay more than an hour. He had to film the starving children, and get back to Nairobi by dark.

The suggestion that such an important man should want to wade into the hungry masses took Aidid by surprise, but he quickly insisted that Hawke take his personal bodyguards. The general and I would follow on foot. Walking through his stronghold, Aidid cut a tall and sinister figure, made more imposing by the swagger stick in his hand and the five gunmen around him. The boy guards kept their guns cocked and ready, which seemed odd given that this was Aidid's citadel. It seemed odder that the general scarcely glanced at the rows of hungry people along the street, hundreds of men, women and children barely able to move. But he wanted me to understand the gravity of Somalia's need. He said no fewer than five thousand people were dying every day in his country. "In every region, in every district, you will find hunger and starvation," he said.

If the human crisis was so severe, I asked, why were his men looting food? Only a few days earlier, two food trucks from the International Committee of the Red Cross were stripped clean outside Bardera. A group of his men had also just taken three two-hundred-litre drums of gas from the local CARE International depot to get them to the nearest front, only thirty kilometres away, where a fresh battle was raging. If nothing else, it seemed the agencies weren't getting much for their 20 percent protection money.

"Looting" was definitely the wrong word to use around Aidid. The general stopped in the middle of the dirt road and stared down at me. "They need food because they are working," he said sternly. "They are protecting all this food."

I tried to retreat to happier ground, recalling his days as an ambassador in New Delhi, but the general did not remember much from his six years in India, except his last few months living in the posh Le Meridien Hotel. I suspected it was best not to ask about his embassy's Bank of Tokyo account, which, according to the bank manager, Aidid had tried to clean out before returning to Somalia in 1989 to take up arms against his rival, Siad Barre. Our mutual banker said the general was a "crazed man." But if Aidid had lost most of his mental faculties, as the Americans said he had, his capacity for revenge had not been affected. When I mentioned the United Nations, and the prospect of intervention, Aidid's head cocked back, and his big eyes seemed to expand to the limits of their sockets, stretching their braids of bloodshot veins. He would not forgive the

UN for standing by Siad Barre all those years he, a former defence minister, was in one of the dictator's detention cells, or for evacuating its staff from most of the country in 1992. "If the UN wants to bring in more troops, it will have to do so by force," the general said. "They would be better used in South Africa [which was struggling toward democracy at the time]. It is absolutely illegal and we will not accept it. We are a sovereign state."

In case anyone wanted to doubt his resolve, he rattled off the size of his force: thirty thousand gunmen, two hundred thousand reserves, six thousand "police" already in training. "All they need is equipment," he said, and he meant heavy equipment. "Guns, we can provide."

As we reached the local hospital and walked through its crowded wards, I began to realize why Aidid was so callous about the suffering around us. Most of these people were Bantus and pastoralists from the desert forced into this formerly prosperous tobacco town by drought and war. A simple feeding program would get them on their feet in days, but that was not in Aidid's interest. He, like the fat elders of Berdale, could survive politically and militarily only if the world felt pity for those under his watch. As long as he could parade these living corpses before me, Bob Hawke and the hundreds of others who came calling, the food would come.

Aidid, the diplomat, understood this unstated quid pro quo very well, and I had to at least admire him for that. Out here in the desert, he had built the perfect mousetrap.

"I can't get upset," R.G. Krishnan, the CARE manager in Bardera, said after the fuel-drum robbery. We sat on his front steps that night and listened to the sounds of distant gunfire, presumably triggered by the militia men tooling around the desert on CARE fuel. "This is not my country," Krishnan sighed.

There were only two cultures left in Somalia: the culture of the gun, and the culture of the camel.

Way up the Shabelle River, near the Ethiopian border, we followed a Canadian military team across a barren stretch of desert to find Daud Dir Gulad, a governor and former banker from Siad Barre's Marehan clan. He was a "leader," a man who claimed to own fifty villas in Mogadishu. All the big- and middle-power missions flying into the country wanted to meet the leaders. I never saw them meet women's organizations or traders' associations. But at least Gulad was in an upbeat mood for a man whose wealth had fallen to rubble and rival clans. He would merely have to fight harder to get it back.

"Fighting is the culture of the nomad," the governor of Abduwak said. "We have been fighting for thousands of years. You can bring a million soldiers here and you won't stop it."

Nearby, a fifty-year-old camel herder, Abdulkadiu Ibrahim Hayle, was looking for a wife. He already had several, too many to count, but still he wanted more. He asked how much I would want for mine. I said she was not for sale, but still I was curious about her market value. He said a fine woman like Cindy should fetch fifty camels, then worth about six hundred dollars. Unfortunately, the drought had reduced his herd to twenty camels. He offered them all, but I had to decline. He understood. These days, he said, twenty camels was nothing.

On my next flight into Mogadishu, I discovered that the pickup truck that met us on our first arrival was no longer in service. There was now a black Mercedes parked on the landing strip, with its engine running to keep the air conditioning on. When the cabin door opened, three men got out of the car with guns. On top of the usual aid tithe, they announced, each passenger had to pay a fifty-dollar "arrival fee." They said the money was needed to keep the airport running smoothly.

After losing faith in Ali and the undergraduate gunmen, Cindy and I asked around Mogadishu for a more experienced team of technicals.

Everyone suggested a man named "Two Men." He was six feet tall and about 250 pounds of rock-hard muscle, which in Somalia really was the size of two men. He drove his own two-bench Hilux pickup truck with another two men in the back, each with AK-47s, and a third perched on top of the cab with a gun fixed to the roof. The guns were for show, he boasted, because "no one dared get in the way of Two Men."

We wanted to travel south, along the back roads and flood plains of the Lower Shabelle River, where there was a Somalia I had never seen on television. Huge banana estates lined the roads and, beyond them, there were lush irrigated fields that had been overrun by weeds and grass.

Once we were out of the capital, Two Men insisted we take a detour to an abandoned fruit plantation, where he stopped and bought a sack of fat pineapples; they exploded with juice when he cut them open with a machete he kept under the truck's floor pad. When I said I could not believe the abundance, Two Men took us down another road to a Somitel plantation that had grown 150 hectares of bananas for export to the Persian Gulf before its Italian managers fled in 1991. The estate, complete with a mansion at the end of a dirt road lined with pine trees, was looted bare, but in the fields a group of former employees grew beans, onions, tomatoes and watermelons for their families and the local militia. Somalia had become an international byword for hunger and desperation, but before the war it had everything it needed to feed itself. There was forty-one million head of livestock, two hundred thousand tonnes of fish caught every year and an estimated 8.5 million hectares of highly fertile land, mostly along the Shabelle and Juba rivers, although only seven hundred thousand of those hectares benefited from modern agriculture. That night, we stopped at the Médecins Sans Frontières residence in Marka, a seaside town eighty kilometres south of the capital, just in time for a local feast of jumbo prawns, vegetables and rice, with fresh fruit for dessert, all harvested in famished Somalia. A country that was declared an international orphan and a ward of international benevolence had everything it needed right in its own backyard.

In 1992, most of the people who ran Somalia, and helped run it into the ground, fled to a refugee camp outside the Kenyan port city of Mombasa, just down the road from a string of beach resorts. In exile, the educated elite created their own new order. The Utango refugee camp had eighteen thousand registered residents, fourteen thousand unregistered residents and the most remarkable sense of enterprise I had seen in any refugee camp anywhere. Among the outcasts, mostly from Siad Barre's Marehan clan, were engineers, surgeons, schoolteachers, university professors, poets, filmmakers, journalists, cabinet ministers, retired military officers and the director of Somalia's national museum. There were also murderers, thugs and thieves enjoying the fruits of international relief, but it was hard not to marvel at what they had done here. On my way into the refugee camp from the main road, I counted three video halls (*Rambo III*, *Coming to America* and an Italian romance were playing), a Ping-Pong parlour, several Coke stands and tea houses, a bakery that produced six thousand buns a day, three mosques, an elementary school and a portrait studio. The photo shop was run by a Mogadishu photographer, Mohammad Ahmed Mohammad, who fled with his Nikon F3 and Minolta camera and, in the camps, averaged seventy passport pictures a day, more than he ever did in Somalia. There was also garbage collection, temporary street lights and a community centre where English, French and Arabic were taught by fellow refugees.

While the Somali elite had the potential to be self-reliant, they were also more demanding than any refugees the camp's workers, from the UN High Commissioner for Refugees (UNHCR), had ever encountered. One group filed a complaint when they received only four spoons of sugar with their daily tea ration. Another group successfully lobbied the Italian embassy for special rations of spaghetti and tomato sauce. Finland donated tinned meat. The European Union gave flour.

I continued deeper into the camp, following men who were walking from the bus stop with new mattresses. On a warm Sunday afternoon, a small field in the middle of the camp was filled with more young men and women, reading books of philosophy, politics, poetry and fiction, in English and Italian. I was looking for the house of the museum director, Mahmoud Mohammad Dirios, whom everyone seemed to know. A group of young boys on new BMX bicycles led me to him.

Dirios said my timing was impeccable as he was about to leave for the Intellectuals' Cottage, a hut where a group of men gathered daily to debate politics, test ideas and read poetry aloud. That afternoon, Saeed Salah Ahmed, one of Somalia's best poets and filmmakers, planned to read one of his newest works, a play about civil war and international reaction.

*Mr. World* opens when the title character, who represents international force, arrives in a troubled Somalia with bundles of aid. He gives it to two other characters, the city and the farm, but not to a third, the nomad. Among those unsettled by this arrangement is a small stone that wanted to be used in the wall of a castle but instead winds up in a dam. In anger, the stone pops out, allowing the river to flood the city and farm, while the nomad escapes unscathed. Tragically, a small city girl who cannot swim is swept up in the flood and drowns while people on the shore shout for her to swim. It is too late, they realize, for her to learn. Mr. World is disgusted with the turn of events, and blames the Somalis for not properly building the dam or teaching their children to swim. He suggests they turn to yet another character, the "indigenous brain," and leaves.

After the reading, as we talked over tea with extra UNHCR sugar, it was clear the Somali men would always blame the West, a.k.a. Mr. World, for their nation's problems. For years, Siad Barre was a most favoured ally of American policy against Ethiopia, and his nation was awash in weapons because of it. When he lost his American aid and fled, his one-man state collapsed, and all of Somalia's one-man institutions went with it.

For the men in the Intellectuals' Cottage, it was important to be seen as victims of the Cold War, collateral damage, really. Not that any planned to go back. The Utango refugee camp was fast becoming a transit centre for the rich and educated to move on to Europe and North America. The dam bursts were all behind them, and they seemed content to leave the repairs to someone else.

When I last visited Somalia in 1993, it already seemed like a unique and awful calamity. Most of the world would write it off as a terrible experience that could bring little meaning to anything else, but that was to miss a more lasting tragedy. Like most developing countries,

Somalia was divided between the very rich and the extraordinarily poor. The rich man held up the crying baby, which was not his own, to get into the kitchen of international relief. The rich then controlled the aid that came flowing, sometimes by persuasion, more often at gunpoint. Along the way, no one seriously questioned the country's power structure, or how this painful transition might be used more effectively to build a new system of governance. Somali women, for example, were excluded from the management of almost every aid project I visited. So were the Bantus and nomadic clans.

Clan leaders were not the only ones to misrepresent the troubles. The world's biggest relief organizations, military attachés and the media twisted what was unfolding, each for its own purposes. There was horrific death at our feet, to be sure, the kind I hope never to see again, but there was also a bounty of food crops, rivers, oceans and human talent in Somalia that almost none of us ever reported. The Somalia we created in the world's mind was an invalid. The real country was not.

In all these frightening ways, it reminded me of Biharipur. What Somalia needed more than another Hercules full of food was a new social structure, starting with a bit of grassroots democracy. It was always assumed that such things would come later, that governance was dessert, to be provided after the main course of gruel. Later never came. When things got rough, as General Aidid said they would, we fled. The last international troops left in 1995, not long after Siad Barre, the former president, died in Nigeria. The following year, Aidid himself was wounded in battle and died during surgery. Most obituaries said his death could herald peace, but the fighting continued through the rest of the decade, and when another drought hit in 1999 few people outside Somalia noticed. Mr. World had gone home, confounded by a small, geographically insignificant country of eight million people, with no neighbours of importance and no allies of consequence. Only a handful of relief agencies were still there, and they were frequently looted and their workers occasionally kidnapped.

In this misfortune, at least our misadventures in Somalia brought an end to the arrogant hopes of interventionism—that great Gulf War hoax—that we, the West, have the will, weapons, nerve and right to police the world. In a tragic and often ugly way, the debacle also exposed why decades of Western aid had been so deluded by our need, even out in Bardera and Abduwak, to deal with "leaders," the very people who had created Somalia's troubles.

The misfortune was a metaphor for all that was wrong with development in Africa. Beyond Somalia were dozens of countries that had suffered the same fate, over longer periods and often in less dramatic form. But unlike Somalia, which was left by Mr. World to rot, most of Africa was again rising. Its people had seen the inanity of Big Men, the folly of Big Aid and the fickleness of Big Media, and were now mapping their own course, slowly, patiently and in a direction no outsider could ever chart for them.

GIDAMUHALEDA HABONJU, A BARABAIG ELDER, TANZANIA

# 5

## Big Men and Little Dreams

My romance with Africa began in 1975, in a school auditorium in suburban Scarborough, Ontario, when a volunteer from Canadian University Services Overseas (CUSO) spoke to my grade-eight assembly. The man wore a cream-coloured safari suit and a beard, and seemed terribly serious as he told us of a country in Africa called Tanzania where he had lived for a year and where people— and he had a very long slide show to prove this—lived in grass huts. The man said he wanted us to understand this place known as the

Third World, which was changing by the day, and to understand how very lucky we were to live in Scarborough. What the man didn't seem to understand was that our own school was changing by the day, too. In a matter of months, my predominantly white class had added children from China, Bangladesh, Pakistan and Jamaica, whose families lived in a row of overcrowded government-subsidized apartment blocks near the school.

"What's this Third World you're talkin' about?" one of the Jamaican kids shouted from the middle of the auditorium during question time. "I didn't know there was a Second World."

The CUSO man, who did not see the irony or humour, proceeded for another twenty minutes to talk about Africa's strategic importance, unmindful of the world changing all around us and the great folly of the world trying to change Africa.

Those were the halcyon days of Third Worldism, a time when the North felt that any problem in the South could be solved with money and technical expertise. And there was probably no place where Third Worldism was stronger than in Tanzania. Between 1970 and 1979, official aid disbursements to the country rose from four dollars per capita to thirty-two dollars per capita, making it one of the most aid-dependent nations anywhere. By the eighties, aid was the second biggest part of the Tanzanian economy, after agriculture—and this in a nation of farmers.

I wouldn't perceive the naïveté of the Africanists—those who sought to save a continent—for another two decades, but I was hooked, less by the grass huts and geopolitics than by the incredible relationship this white man in a safari suit had with a place so far away. By the time I finally got to Tanzania, in 1994, most of the aid had been judged a failure, the economy was in ruins and CUSO had all but vanished from the scene. But I still wanted to see one remnant of the age of Third Worldism, a project that stood out from all others. It was a simple scheme to grow wheat, to recreate a piece of Saskatchewan near the Serengeti, on land that was officially vacant. The giant Hanang Wheat Complex was supposed to help Tanzania feed itself in a time of soaring food prices, and that alone seemed worthwhile. But now, more than twenty years after the first Canadian advisers came to Tanzania's outback, there was little more than apology, regret and a monument to a fading zeitgeist.

❖

It was late in the afternoon as I approached the Hanang wheat farms with my guide, Daniel, a development worker from the local trading town of Katesh in northwestern Tanzania. We were alone on a dirt track on the country's northern plains, where tourists rarely venture. Before long, Daniel warned, packs of wild animals would emerge from the bushes, and they would be among the lesser dangers. Robbers ruled the night here, but he also knew I was impatient. I had been travelling most of the day, following a succession of dirt highways, roads and bush tracks. Before we stopped to sleep I wanted to at least catch a glimpse of the wheat farms, sprawling across twenty-eight thousand hectares of land, and some of the bitter harvest that cost Canada seventy million dollars and the Barabaig people their last hope of independence. The farms were operating out here somewhere, almost forgotten by their creators but not by those who endured them still.

"That must be it," Daniel said, bringing the jeep to a halt. "Look at the clouds of dust over there. It's one of your Canadian tractors."

The machine Daniel pointed to looked like a Massey-Ferguson combine, one of dozens given to Tanzania in the early eighties to turn these fields into a wheat mine. Beyond it were scattered acacia trees, their buzz-cut tops the only evidence that this was Africa, and then nothing but vast stretches of golden wheat billowing under a prairie sky so big it could swallow the earth.

We left the jeep and scurried down a small ridge to the wheat fields where Daniel spotted two women hunched over the rich black soil like birds pecking for worms. One appeared to be gathering gleanings scattered on the field while the other bunched the remains and threshed them on the ground. They retrieved the kernels from the dirt and collected them in small coffee cans. Perhaps because of the wind whipping across the plains, obscuring any other noise, the women did not notice us at first, and then jumped when they saw us. They thought we were from the farm office, like those who had come the previous day to seize all they had collected. After losing two cans of wheat to the farm men, who told the women it was illegal to take such scraps, they had spent all of today recouping their loss.

Before we got any closer, the women recognized Daniel. Even

though he was from the big town of Katesh (population: five hundred), he was a known friend of the Barabaig people, and they nodded approvingly for us to come forward. They introduced themselves as Maria. They were both Marias. They were tall, like all Barabaig people. They carried big sticks and had intricate circles tattooed around their eyes. They both had brush cuts and looked very serious. But one of the Marias was much older than the other, judging by the big holes in her earlobes, stretched by a lifetime of heavy stone and wood earrings. Each hole was so big you could slide a Ping-Pong ball through it. The holes in the younger woman's ears would fit only marbles.

"Welcome," Maria the younger said.

"You are most welcome," Maria the elder added. "You are most welcome in our fields."

Here she was referring to "our fields" in front of a Canadian and a Tanzanian, representatives of the peoples who had orchestrated the seizure and total destruction of the Barabaig's land in the name of development. Their ancestors had grazed their cattle here for generations, and now the two Marias had to walk seven kilometres a day to this spot just so they could sneak about like poachers. "Our" fields?

"The land was so beautiful," Maria the elder said, as she began to explain her losses. "There were trees and pastures for all the cows. We had more than one hundred cows, just my family. Now we have four cows."

Her son cared for the animals, walking them every day down a narrow cattle track through the wheat farms to a pond that was half its former size. The track used to be forty metres wide, as mandated by the government, but the wheat fields encroached. Now the track was barely ten metres, and anyone who allowed their livestock to stray off the path faced a severe penalty. In 1987, a British anthropologist named Charles Lane wrote a paper on the Barabaig's demise in which he identified fifty-seven sacred burial sites that had been destroyed to make way for the farms. He quoted one man whose home was surrounded by the wheat fields; every time he tried to cross them he was fined for trespassing. Another man said six farm employees caught him in the wheat fields and attacked him, knocking out his front teeth. Despite international pressure, the assaults continued. In 1991, a man and his wife were jailed for three years for allowing their cattle to wander into the wheat fields. When a nine-year-old boy was caught for a similar offence, he was kept in custody for four months and then released after receiving twelve strokes of a cane. Barabaig huts and corrals were torched on "their" fields, and water sources sealed off.

But after losing all they had built over the centuries, at least this had to be said about the Barabaig: they saw no need for irony. No matter whose combines rolled across the plains, they still had faith in the land and in a greater power. They still believed in the spirits that swirled in the winds around Mount Hanang, which stood on the horizon. Somehow they were still able to see the occupied fields as theirs.

As the Marias spoke, another group of women emerged from the bush with hard leather water jugs strapped to their backs. One wore thick rings of copper the size of small Frisbees around her neck—to show her wealth, and to keep her chin up. The four women said they were walking home from a water hole they had dug on the other side of the farm, complete with a wooden ladder to climb three metres down. The daily trek took about three hours, and only women did it. Their husbands, sons and brothers were busy driving cattle herds to separate water holes even farther away. Sometimes the men had to walk for days with their cattle, with nothing more than the juice of tree bark for nutrition. And the days kept getting longer, sometimes turning to weeks. There was so little water and grass left for the Barabaig cattle, the women said. Cows that used to give five litres of milk per day struggled to produce one. Entire herds were vanishing.

"It is good you did not bring your cows with you today," Maria the elder told me. She stared me in the eye, and looked very earnest. "You should not bring your cows here. If you bring them here, they will die."

"What if you get your land back?" I asked. "Would my cows be safe here?"

"Ahhh, if we get this land back, you are most welcome to bring your cows. They will give you so much milk. You must bring your cows here when we get this land back."

As the sun fell in the distance, showering the equatorial plains with a riot of colour, Daniel and I followed a track back to the main road, beyond the farm gate and past the foot of Mount Hanang, which now stood as the Barabaig's only physical link with the past. Their homes, graves, sacred stones and watering holes were gone, destroyed by men. But here was a mountain, a sacred one, that men could not move.

From a distance, Mount Hanang was unprepossessing—it did not have Mount Meru's beauty or Kilimanjaro's mystical halo of snow. But as we drove past, in the glow of that equatorial dusk, the mountain's presence seemed eternal. Here, on the rim of Africa's mighty Rift Valley where human life began, the sacred hill of the Barabaig people seemed to be watching our every move. In the gullies, in the thorn bushes, but most of all in the cursed Canadian wheat fields, it felt as if the spirit of Mount Hanang was in all places above us and at all times within us.

No one is sure when the Barabaig, who have no written history, first came to the plains of Hanang, but based on their southern Nilotic features and dialect, they are thought to have drifted from Sudan or the western Ethiopian highlands about three thousand years ago. It is known that they lived in the nearby Mbulu highlands, south of Arusha and Mount Kilimanjaro, until early in the twentieth century, when the British colonial administration began a major tsetse-fly-eradication program that allowed their cattle to wander farther afield, and for the Barabaig to follow.

Only thirty years ago, the Barabaig enjoyed almost free rein in the rich and wide-open spaces around Hanang. Maybe seventy-five thousand in number, they wandered between lakes nestled in volcanic craters and fields where the soil was so rich they said it produced "milk grass." Wherever the cows' needs lay, in water or grass, the Barabaig men followed, surviving on cow's meat, milk and urine, and occasionally ashes and tree bark, while the women grew small crops of corn and millet wherever they could find water.

Serene in one sense, the pastoral life was also brutal, a bondage to nature. Their houses were little more than huts made of forked trees, cut and planted in deep holes, with roofs of mud and twigs laid on rafters, and perimeter fences made of thorn bushes with eight-centimetre-long spikes. From afar, a Barabaig hut looks like nothing more than a clump of bushes. Not surprisingly, of every hundred children born, about twenty do not make it to their first birthday— more than double the national rate of infant mortality. A child's chances of attending school are equally poor, since the government curriculum is set in Kiswahili and English, which few Barabaig understand. A survey by a Christian missionary group once found that only 5 percent of Barabaig adults spoke Kiswahili. Most of the pastoralists spoke only Datooga, a language shared by fewer than two hundred thousand people in a country of thirty-two million.

Whatever the Barabaig's hopes and limitations, their prospects were forever changed by two much larger nations bent on their own perceptions of development. One was Tanzania, which wanted—and this was the title of a book by founding president Julius Nyerere—to run while others walked. The other was Canada, which wanted to run by Tanzania's side. They found their mutual vision in a simple strain of wheat, appropriately named "trophy."

The vision reflected common thinking of the sixties and seventies, that development was a race—a race against time, a race against poverty, a race against population growth. People who ran the world back then were full of such cataclysmic thinking, of population bombs and refugee invasions, of disasters near and great if someone did not do something very big and very fast.

The assault on the Barabaig began in the sixties when Nyerere first got scared. The granddaddy of African socialism, he was one of the first African leaders to seriously buy into the population-bomb theory, and act on it. Nyerere feared Tanzania, then home to fifteen million people, would not be able to feed itself in the twenty-first century, when its population was projected to reach seventy-five million. No one seemed to mention that Tanzania, with 120 distinct ethnic groups and two hundred languages, was almost as big as Western Europe with less than half the population of Great Britain. No one seemed to mind that Nyerere was ignoring pleas for both a serious national birth-control program and simple health care for mothers, thousands of whom died in childbirth every year.

Ideology was the Barabaig's greatest foe. Almost from the moment he assumed office in 1961, Nyerere, a devout Christian and former schoolteacher, distrusted private initiative and free enterprise, putting his faith in God and the state. Within six years he announced a stunning new socialist direction for his country—named the Arusha Declaration for the northern city where the manifesto was signed. At the time, most of the world was mesmerized by visions of the Great Society, the welfare state and the powers of big government. The new nations of the Third World also felt they had to do something radical to free themselves from the remaining bonds of colonial cash-crop economies. In Tanzania's case, the nation was dependent on the precarious export of cotton, coffee and sisal. Nyerere wanted something different. Stealing a page from his mentor, India's great Fabian socialist Jawaharlal Nehru, he nationalized most of the country's economic interests—the so-called commanding heights that included banks, urban land, mineral assets, big commercial farms and several industries (the Canadian Bata family's Tanzania Shoe Company, for one).

In the countryside, Nyerere shared a dream called *ujamaa*, or "familyhood," a very African ideal of communal living and equality. He ordered civil servants to lead austere lives, and called on rural Tanzanians to follow a new model of development that would enshrine respect for others, common property and an "obligation to work." The ruling Revolutionary Party also set up "cells" in every region, village and factory to ensure that no one went hungry, and that anyone who called Julius Nyerere a well-meaning idiot would be beaten up or thrown in jail. As a result, the great man won 99 percent of the votes in his first election in 1970, though that declined to 93 percent in both the 1975 and 1980 national votes.

When worldwide inflation hit in the early seventies, Tanzania was forced to ration oil and wheat but Nyerere was not one to give in. In November 1973, he ordered a new program called "villagization" to bring together farmers and peasants like the Barabaig who were scattered across the countryside. At the time, it was estimated that half of rural Tanzanians did not live in villages, and it was assumed they would be better off in clusters, which could be equipped with schools, health clinics and water taps. The village collectives were voluntary at first, and everyone ignored them—a good indicator of a bad idea. Nyerere's bureaucracy resorted to burning huts and crops and forcibly moving people in order to meet his 1976 deadline for the relocation of nine million people into *ujamaa* villages. The CUSO man had not told my school about the village burnings, staged elections or prisons crowded with political opponents, but this was the seventies, the age of Suharto, Pinochet and Amin, and a dictator had to do something really heinous like eat the mortal remains of an opponent to merit condemnation, especially from aid organizations that needed their patronage.

Granted, Nyerere remained a good and God-fearing man, even at the height of his power. Except for sending his children to school in Canada, he maintained a modest lifestyle, seeming to want nothing more than social and economic justice for his people. Ordinary Tanzanians referred to him as *mwalimu*, "teacher." Leaders from Africa, India, China and the former Soviet Union beat a path to his door for advice, which he dispensed with equal sagacity to Pierre Trudeau, Robert McNamara and Chou En-Lai.

With its long coastline and borders with eight other nations, Tanzania, at the time, was seen as a prize catch in the Cold War. Nyerere, *mwalimu* and master planner, was also considered a visionary. Which was all part of Tanzania's curse. As intellectually gifted as Nyerere was—after winning a scholarship to the University of Edinburgh, he translated *Julius Caesar* and *The Merchant of Venice* into Kiswahili—he had little in the way of common sense. Worse, he had no accountability to the people affected by his decisions

Prompted by his population fears, one of Nyerere's greatest concerns was food production—specifically wheat production. In 1968, his government had started an experimental wheat farm outside Arusha to test seeds and planting techniques. Then Nyerere heard about a similar effort in Kenya that was doing rather well. Moreover, it was supported by Canada, the greatest of wheat growers. At the time, no one seemed to question Nyerere's fascination with wheat, perhaps because as a one-party state, he allowed no one to question anything that came from his lips. Looking back from the comfort of a democracy, we can safely say that wheat was a very stupid idea indeed. No more than 10 percent of Tanzania's population ate wheat, and that was in the form of white bread. Moreover, almost all of the white-bread eaters lived in Dar es Salaam, and worked in offices. For the vast majority of poor Tanzanians, who lived on a peasant diet of corn and millet, wheat was as practical as champagne.

Consumer preferences notwithstanding, Tanzania decided to grow wheat on a big scale, with Canada's help. In 1971, the Canadian government provided technical advisers to Tanzania's National

Agriculture and Food Corporation for two large farms, named Basotu and Setchet, operating in Hanang. That the land belonged to the Barabaig seemed irrelevant. This was a national mission, as important to Nyerere's Tanzania as NASA was to Kennedy's America.

The first experiment went as badly as the early Apollo missions. The local soil proved to be so light it could be blown away in a windstorm, or by excessive plowing. Hanang was also parched. A good year's rainfall seldom exceeded fifty centimetres, and it all came between December and April. The Canadians discovered something else they had not seen on the Prairies: qulea-qulea birds, which descended in great hordes to attack the crop. In 1975, the Tanzanians were ready to pack it in when a team from Canada's Department of Agriculture announced surprising results with the new trophy wheat strain and gentler planting techniques that protected the soil and preserved its moisture. The yields at Hanang rose from seven and a half bags per hectare to nearly twenty bags—results the Canadians had not seen since they left home. Bolstered, the Canadian government commissioned a study by Manitoba Pool Elevators (not famous for its African expertise), and announced in 1977 its intention to pump thirty-five million dollars into a giant new wheat complex for Tanzania. In a country where five hectares is considered a big holding, there would be seven farms, each covering four thousand hectares. Naturally, it would all be owned, operated and overseen by the state.

The Hanang wheat complex cannot be seen in isolation, as its emergence coincided with a massive increase in foreign aid to Nyerere's Tanzania. The American-dominated World Bank made the country one of its biggest aid recipients in Africa while China donated a Friendship Textile Mill and a fifteen-hundred-kilometre railway stretching from Dar es Salaam to the copper mines of Zambia. The Dutch, British, Swedes, Norwegians, Germans and Danes were not far behind, nor was Canada to be left out. In 1974, the Trudeau government quintupled official assistance to the Nyerere regime to about thirty million dollars a year, mostly in the form of low-interest loans. Three years later, Ottawa converted most of the assistance to grants.

For Canada, the new commitment was about more than money; it marked a strategic change in foreign aid, away from small poverty-alleviation schemes to bigger and more ambitious projects— works that would make a difference to a country rather than to a selection of villages only. In addition to the wheat farms, there were electricity transmission lines, an eight-million-dollar water filtration plant for Dar es Salaam and ten million dollars a year for Tanzania's railway, in the form of diesel locomotives, wagons and new tracks. And then came the Siha Bakery, an outrageous idea from the start, which drove its privately owned competitors into the ground before it, too, collapsed.[1]

The bakery's downfall preceded the decline of almost every major aid project and nationalized enterprise in Tanzania. The Canadian-built water filtration plant, costing 26.3 million dollars, had to scale back its production by 50 percent when the original Canadian team left with all the imported chlorine and most of the technical expertise. At the nationalized Bata shoe factory, which was built in 1957 with a capacity to make six million shoes a year, production was cut to just over half a million for want of spare parts. The Morogoro Shoe Company, which McNamara's World Bank financed in 1981, cut its production within two years of opening to 4 percent of its capacity, and then to less than 0.6 percent by 1988. The nearby Morogoro tannery, built in 1978 with Bulgarian aid, never ran at full throttle, either. With enough equipment to produce three million metres of leather a year, the plant had a peak output of one million in the early eighties, and then fell to two hundred thousand in 1989, its last year of operation.

---

[1] The Siha, "Goodness" in Kiswahili, represents all that has gone wrong with a trillion dollars of Third World aid over the last half-century. To begin with, there was no obvious need to build a Western-style bakery in Dar es Salaam, already home to ten charcoal-burning bakeries, other than petitions from the head of the state-run National Milling Corporation, which needed a world-class bakery to absorb all his flour. So flawed was the proposal the magnanimous Dutch turned it down, as did Canadian aid officers, until someone pointed out its potential in the form of a million-dollar contract for Canadian Baker Perkins Ltd. The company, a subsidiary of a large British concern, would supply state-of-the-art equipment to Siha, which could produce one hundred thousand loaves of bread a day. The Canadian International Development Agency, Canada's main foreign-aid arm, would pay the whole shot. A UN study later pointed out that similar equipment could have been purchased in Germany or Japan for half the cost, but that was the least of the bakery's problems. Construction costs were three times more than the original forecast, and the machinery, which was installed just before the first OPEC crisis, ran on oil. The bakery's prospects worsened as oil prices rose. In 1981, not long before it was shut down, it lost $4.1 million, about double the original cost. By that time, most of the smaller bakeries had also gone under because they could not compete with the monstrous state-owned, aid-financed Siha.

All around Nyerere the "commanding heights" were falling to the harsh forces of economic reality. The government and many of its aid donors blamed falling commodity prices more than mismanagement, failing to notice how fast the economies of Korea, Thailand and Indonesia were growing on the backs of the footwear industry and commercial cash crops. Nor was there much official notice of the policy forcing Tanzanian grain farmers to sell their crops to the government at one-third the world price, just to keep the bread eaters happy. Nyerere's Soviet-like farce continued, and continued to win aid. By 1990, commitments of foreign assistance to Tanzania—a mere forty-seven million dollars a year in 1970—surpassed one billion dollars.

Nothing created by this aid, not the Morogoro Shoe Company, Siha Bakery or Dar es Salaam Water Filtration Plant, was as breathtaking as the Hanang Wheat Complex. Despite the fact that Nyerere's government was insolvent and Tanzania's economy was entering a depression, Canadian support for the project grew, with money for Canadian combines, big metal silos, advanced seeds, fertilizers and pesticides, and trucks to haul each harvest down the highway to a new rail line also built by Canada. There were late-model Land Cruisers in which farm staff could drive around their realm, and airplanes swooping down from the great East African sky to spray pesticides on each new crop. And at every turn, failure. The trophy strain rarely repeated its initial success, especially when the tractors, combines and trucks began to run out of spare parts and fuel as Canadian support was reduced. A 1986 study commissioned by CIDA also questioned the ability of the Tanzanian staff, after a decade of training, to sustain the project's early success. It seemed the local staff had other priorities, as CIDA discovered in a 1990 report that alleged two hundred hectares of wheat were planted secretly by farm management for their own profit. The truck operators, meanwhile, were using farm vehicles to haul charcoal, as well as wheat, to Arusha, 250 kilometres to the north. This not only reduced the life of each truck, but contributed to the rapid cutting of what little forest remained around Hanang.

Were it not for the destruction of the Barabaig way of life,

Hanang might have been just another wreck on Tanzania's scrap heap of development. But as the farms went on, it became clear that they suffered from more than faulty planning or bad management. They represented nothing less than a perverse notion of human development. In 1991, a British reporter, George Monbiot, stumbled across the farms during his travels to research *No Man's Land: An Investigative Journey through Kenya and Tanzania*, a book about East Africa's endangered pastoralists. He wrote: "I visited the Canadian research director, who said that the project was a complete success. What about the Barabaig? 'The Barabaig,' he informed me, 'are nomadic. They can go to another place.' His Tanzanian assistant, listening to our conversation through the door, stopped me in the corridor and announced: 'I won't shed a tear for anybody if it means development.'"

Daniel and I spent the night in Katesh, a brawling, dusty frontier town that seemed to be enjoying an economic revival following the end of Nyerereism. The beer halls did a brisk business, with a steady flow of mining prospectors, farmers and traders who had to traverse this giant country to make the smallest of sales. It was also harvest time, and big Canadian trucks were loaded up and on their way to the railhead. Katesh was the drivers' first watering hole, and it seemed to mirror the hopes of Hanang district in every way but one: there were no Barabaig in sight.

The next morning, we returned to the Hanang farms to see more of the damage and perhaps find some of the people responsible, the people who so fondly discussed the pastoralists as "nomads." The Barabaig are known as transhumant people, not nomads, meaning they follow their livestock with the seasons, like migratory birds following ancient pathways. They also have a very different idea of development from the one dictated by Dar es Salaam and underwritten by Ottawa. Their guiding principle is land, not money, because land nourishes their cows, and their cows nourish them. At the end of their days, they are buried in this land, alongside their ancestors, in graves that are sacred and under the eye of Mount Hanang.

"Pastoralism is a way of life," Daniel explained as we neared the farms again. "When a pastoralist is moved away and becomes a cultivator, as soon as he has a bit of cash, he buys a cow. When he moves to town, he still buys cows. It is ingrained."

It sounded ridiculous—why buy a cow when you need indoor plumbing?—until we reached the farms and found a Barabaig elder crying in his hut.

The man was Gidamuhaleda Habonju, and there was a time when he towered over these fields and his people. The seventy-eight-year-old was a big man in every sense. He was at least six feet tall, and once had seven hundred cows, seven children, a wristfull of copper bracelets and so much milk from his herd that he had to give it away. But when we found him, he looked defeated in body and spirit. His razor-sharp spear, once used to fend off wild animals, was useless; the only serious danger these days was a jeep like ours running him over. His old bullhorn, sixteen inches long, was no more than a decoration, since his personal herd was down to seventy cows and barely worth summoning. The previous year, twenty of his cattle died for want of grazing land.

"If I wanted to sell the rest of them, they would fetch no money," Habonju said angrily, after he invited us into his hut. "They are so thin that if I wanted to slaughter them, they would give me no meat."

"Do they give much milk?" I asked.

He picked up his spear and tapped a coffee can lying on the mud floor: "Three cows will barely fill this container."

A ring of thorn bushes ran around Habonju's homestead to set his property apart from the wheat farm. Although homesteads and cattle pens are the only land that the Barabaig deem private property, the old man had never marked his holdings before. Now he felt he had to. Several years earlier, after a long trek with his cattle during the dry season, he returned to find his homestead demolished and covered with wheat fields. He moved to another place and again saw his home demolished to make way for the farm.

"The first time, they surrounded our homestead. There was no room for the cows, so we had to move," Habonju explained, taking a seat on a sack of grain. Only a few streams of light broke through the tree branches that formed the walls, and I could barely make out his face.

"The second time, they came and burned our house. They said they would give us two thousand shillings, but the local party officials kept one thousand shillings for the village education fund, to buy food and drinks for whenever someone visits." The party was Nyerere's Revolutionary Party, which was supposed to guide the nation at a local level, and set an example for all in thrift, modesty and respect. By the eighties, it had all the credibility of East Germany's Communists.

Habonju and his family had been forced to move seven times since the wheat farms came. In its defence, the government said it was only upholding land regulations from the British colonial era, stating that a pastoralist forfeited his right to a piece of land unless he made permanent improvements like irrigation, fencing or crop sowing within a five-year period.

The grand old man of the Barabaig stood up, took his long walking stick and led us back outside. Around his half-naked body, he had wrapped a traditional brown-and-orange shawl, to blend in with the landscape. And for a moment, as he stood surveying the fields where he was born, standing as still as the tree beside him, it seemed difficult to differentiate Habonju from his surroundings. Only his curly white hair stood out, although there were moments when it fused with the clouds overhead.

As the old man quietly faced the wind, he looked as if he was ready to rejoin the soil. He had wanted to be buried next to his father and grandfather, but the farms had destroyed their graves. Habonju used to visit the graves regularly, to quench them with milk and honey beer poured from a bull's horn, and occasionally adorn them with the skin of a slaughtered lamb. But all he could find now were his ancestors' spirits in the air, around him but not underneath. Perhaps, he said, almost whispering to the wind, this was the reason for his troubles. "I think the land is angry with me," he said. He paused and spoke again, as if to no one: "I don't know how to please my ancestors."

When I moved closer to Habonju to take a photograph, I noticed tears welling up in his eyes again. He was tired of all this fighting with the wheat farm, and the lawsuits that human rights organizations had suggested he file against the government. Many officials had come to record his statements, including a Tanzanian judicial commission co-funded by CIDA, but little had changed. The government had offered him land elsewhere, and under domestic and international pressure it was pumping more money into Barabaig welfare. Maybe his children and grandchildren would benefit, but for the old man it would not amount to anything. The land and the cattle that defined his life were gone.

"I want to stay and die here, where my father and grandfather are buried," Habonju said before we left. "I was born here. My father was born here. My grandfather was born here. My sons were born here. Where can we move? Anything other than land—what would I do with it? I need land to live. I need land for my cows." He paused. "I need land so I can be buried."

It is fair to say that a person's concerns are not the same at seventy-eight years of age as they are at eighteen, Tanzania's median age. Habonju, for instance, was a man of the soil, a creature of custom. He had spent most of his life under British rule. He was a citizen of a country whose official languages he did not speak. His four grown sons had their own ambitions and pressures. Each had children to care for, and had heard about Katesh's school, health centre and beer halls. The younger Barabaig men were talking about innovations like small dams, cattle troughs and storehouses for the maize they had started to grow. They also knew about veterinarian services that might reduce the death rate of their calves, who stood a 40 percent chance of survival because of tick-borne diseases that went untreated. This life of roaming the plains was not necessarily for them.

Nor was their struggle unique. In new nations across Africa, Asia and Latin America, aboriginal peoples were clashing with the expanding majority, and with the new ambitions of their own youth. They all wanted something similar, to find a less punishing way of life. And yet many also desperately wanted to maintain an identity that stemmed from the ground beneath their feet. Fortunately, there was a way forward, and plenty of lessons to learn from North America's horrible record of dealing with indigenous peoples. People like the Barabaig need not be rounded up and moved to reserves, or *ujamaa* villages, to have schools, health clinics and jobs. Nor do they need cash payments—money that might lead to their destruction as a community—in return for access to traditional lands and waters. What the Barabaig needed, and this they needed most, was the power to make the decisions that affected their land and waters. But in the shadow of Mount Hanang, where Canada had spent seventy million dollars on "development," no one was even talking about this.

After hearing Habonju's story, I wanted to visit the farm office to see if years of controversy had changed anything in favour of Hanang's first tenants. The base looked like a country estate from a distance, but as we got closer I realized that what had seemed to be a tree-lined lane was a row of short, stubby silos, and in place of a manor home there were portable offices, the kind you might see at a mining site. Behind the silos, we found a row of abandoned Canadian vehicles, mostly trucks and off-road types. A Land Cruiser, emblazoned with a Canadian and a Tanzanian flag, was stripped of its wheels, axles, engines and a back door. The older vehicles had to be cannibalized for spare parts, we were told, since the last Canadian advisers had left with the farm's only line of credit for foreign exchange.

The farm manager invited us inside for coffee. He had heard a foreigner was snooping around the property, and was happy to see a Canadian again on his land. He was less happy to hear about the Barabaig.

"If you want to build large farms, you have to move people," the plump little farm man said. The pleasantries were over, and the biscuits had not yet arrived.

"For whose benefit?" I asked.

"For whose benefit?" The manager rocked back in his chair. He seemed genuinely shocked by such a question. "It was done for the benefit of the nation."

This led to a recitation of statistics. The Hanang Wheat Complex provided 40 percent of Tanzania's wheat needs, and paid nearly a million dollars a year in income taxes. It accounted for about three-quarters of the nation's wheat production. If the farms did not exist, the country would have to spend scarce foreign exchange on Canadian or Australian wheat. Or its urban consumers would have to go without bread.

The manager also wanted to draw my attention to local population pressures, and growing food needs. According to a 1984 government survey, Hanang district was home to 130,000 humans, 197,000 cattle, 85,000 goats and 36,000 sheep. There simply was no space any more for a man with 700 cows.

I was about to suggest that a 280-square-kilometre wheat complex was hardly a model of space utilization either, but the manager beat me to the point. His farms fed thousands of economically productive city dwellers, while Habonju's herd supported just one family. The manager was right. Cattle grazing, the world over, is an inefficient use of land. But we were both missing the broader principle: the land in question was Barabaig land. If the Tanzanian government was so concerned about food production, it should have helped the Barabaig become more sophisticated cattle ranchers and dairy farmers, with veterinary services, transportation networks and marketing support. If the Tanzanian government was really desperate to produce wheat, it should have provided economic incentives for the Barabaig to grow wheat.

At last the biscuits arrived.

If the Barabaig could not own any of the seven mega-farms, I asked, how many Barabaig worked on them? "They can't do this kind of work!" the manager exclaimed. "They are cattle herders!"

Not only was I showing a bias for the Barabaig, it seemed I had insulted his technical expertise and years of training. The answer was, "None."

Tired of inefficiency and abuse, Canada slowly withdrew from the Hanang project, leaving more trouble in its wake. After the last Canadian advisers went home in 1993, the complex's production dropped from a peak of forty-nine thousand tonnes a year to thirty thousand tonnes, as it steadily lost market share. The National Milling Corporation, once the Hanang Wheat Complex's sole customer, accounted for less than 10 percent of sales as it began to source subsidized wheat from France, Belgium and Saudi Arabia at almost half the local cost.

Before it withdrew from the farms, CIDA agreed to a seven-year, 4.5-million-dollar project to help the Barabaig and their neighbours, but in no way did the Canadian government want to accept any responsibility for the tragedy it had sponsored in Tanzania. After I wrote about the Barabaig in *The Globe and Mail*, Charles Bassett, CIDA's vice-president of corporate affairs, wrote in a letter to the editor: "The article suggests that the Canadian International Development Agency is responsible for their [the Barabaig's] situation. This is not the case. The wheat-farm project was launched by the Tanzanian government in 1969. Canada was approached by the Tanzanian government for assistance in wheat production and research for the project. Over 25 years, CIDA provided technical assistance and funds to support development of the wheat farms. Canada is not to be held accountable for Tanzania's land-management policy. If this were true, it would amount to a violation of another country's sovereignty."

Once we were beyond the farm gate, Daniel took me on a detour to a small village where CUSO had built a school for 190 children, most of them Barabaig. The money came from CIDA. The two classrooms were jam-packed when we arrived, and many of the children said they walked up to seven kilometres a day to get here, even though one of the two teachers was usually absent, as was the case today. Down the road, CUSO had also installed a corn-milling machine that a local women's group ran for a profit. The machine could mill a sack of corn in twenty minutes; by hand, it used to take a woman two days. The school and machine looked nice, and were greatly appreciated, Daniel explained, but they would not reverse the Barabaig's continuing slide into obscurity. The pastoralists, who accounted for about 40 percent of the district's population, continued to be pushed aside. They held only two seats on Hanang's fourteen-seat district council, the one that agreed to demarcate land in Hanang and allot it as private property. The Barabaig would have none of it. For centuries, they had shared their land. The village well, farm plots and graves belonged to the clan. The rest—grazing lands, trees, lakes, Mount Hanang and the earth itself—belonged to the community, under management of the Barabaig General Assembly. The Barabaig refused to privatize the earth and Mount Hanang, so the district council set up a "friendly relations" committee. It lasted one year.

Tired and disheartened, Daniel and I were silent for the rest of the way back to Katesh. The charitable dreams and promising slide show I had seen back in public school were beginning to feel like a sham. Big wheat farms and white Land Rovers—this is what went on in the name of development, and it was not amounting to much for people living on the fringe. Fortunately, it would not last. The next few years would see remarkable change for Tanzania, and for most of the developing world. It was not the kind of revolutionary change brought on by independence, but the hard struggle of building a democracy in which community rights and individual freedoms would become the guiding lights.

Accepting some responsibility for his failed model of Third Worldism, Nyerere stepped down as president in 1985, but continued as chairman of the Revolutionary Party for another five years, giving him a full three decades in power with no serious opposition. Tanzania did not legalize opposition parties until 1992, and did not hold its first multi-party election until 1995, which the main opposition groups boycotted. Long before the great man died in October 1999, the post-Nyerere government undid all of his policies, and unloaded most of the worthless industries his government had created. The World Bank–funded Morogoro Shoe Company, for example, was sold to a Somali businessman, who spent five million dollars renovating the run-down factory. He increased the payroll from 42 to 260 and tripled sales by developing a niche in army boots.

Just for doing this, Tanzania's first democratic government probably deserves more credit than it has received. From Nyerere, it inherited a debt burden greater than the country's entire economic output. The government now spends four times more every year on its foreign debt than on the nation's entire primary school system. In a country that under the great *mwalimu* championed basic education for all, about half of Tanzanian children no longer go to school.

While debt relief is essential to Tanzania's resurgence, it is not enough. Tanzania's most pressing development challenges are not just economic ones. Human development, and the Barabaig, knew this long ago, is also a political process in which people must gain the power to share equally in decisions about their collective welfare, and to choose among the many paths to these goals.

In this way, the Barabaig's struggle was no different from the struggles underway in Bangkok and Biharipur, or the ones I would find in the Guinean savannah, in the backwaters of Bangladesh and eventually in the heart of an epic forest fire in Borneo. These were not battles to preserve anachronistic or unsustainable ways of life. These were not fights for the past. When the Barabaig spoke to the wind, their words were all about the future.

GEORGE MPANGO IN HIS CASSAVA FIELD, IGANGA DISTRICT, UGANDA

# 6

# Daddy George

Like Tanzania, Uganda had occupied a corner of my mind since the seventies, for two very different reasons. First, the small East African country and I were born on the same day, October 9, 1962, Uganda from the clutches of British colonialism, me from the tenth-generation descendants of English migrants. Second, my father, a theology professor at the University of Toronto, used to invite home for dinner Ugandan students and refugees who had escaped the horror of Idi Amin's dictatorship and were sponsored in Canada by the

Anglican Church. Their stories were more interesting than *The Dogs of War*, which I read after the CUSO volunteer's lament for Africa, and confirmed the atrocities we heard about in the kitchen over CBC Radio. Their stories also gave me the impression that Uganda was a beautiful land, with lush rain forests, mountains, rolling tea plantations, the source of the Nile and a deep reservoir of generous and forgiving people, a place Churchill called the "pearl of Africa," for good reason.

When I finally got to Uganda, in 1993, it looked like anything but a pearl. After twenty years of civil war and border conflicts, it was wartorn and bitter. Along the potholed Kampala Road, which runs from the Entebbe Peninsula in Lake Victoria to the centre of town, most of the buildings lacked windows, and many stood in want of roofs since soldiers had stolen the corrugated iron as prizes of war.

Beyond the dilapidation, however, Kampala was the new darling of Africanists, who cheered its former guerrilla leader, Yoweri Museveni, as a new role model for the continent. Under his leadership, Uganda's economy was growing by nearly 10 percent a year, a rate not seen anywhere else in Africa and higher than that great beacon of economic development, Suharto's Indonesia. The Asian Ugandans expelled by Amin were back in droves, reclaiming and renovating their confiscated properties. Museveni had also set out to lead Ugandans through bold social changes, talking on national radio about condoms and AIDS, while urging priests, imams, gurus and schoolteachers to do the same. His liberal views paid off, winning nearly a billion dollars a year in financial aid and new investment for Uganda, and the first package of multilateral debt relief granted by the G-7 industrial powers to any African state.

Unfortunately, it all sounded a bit too much like Nyerere's Tanzania, except economic growth had replaced *ujamaa* as the driving ambition of a government and its financiers. These bold statements were the facades of national dreams, but beyond them were millions of people trying to forge their own course. Few national governments, good or bad, respected this local initiative, and few development agencies understood it. Fortunately, there was a man in Kampala who knew all about this struggle.

I first heard about George Mpango from an older Canadian couple whom I met in the lobby of Kampala's Fairway Hotel. They knew George from his student days in Canada, where he had completed a PhD in chemistry at the University of Waterloo in southwestern Ontario. Since then, he had given up the good life in North America and a comfortable job in Nigeria to return to his troubled homeland to take on one of the most disruptive, disputatious and dysfunctional institutions in all of Africa: the extended family. The Canadian couple said George's story would teach me more about Africa than perhaps anything else, and if I wanted to hear it I should join them for tea at George's flat, on the campus of Makerere University where he taught chemistry.

Since it was Sunday, and just about everybody in Kampala was on the way to church, I decided to follow the stream of people along the city's sidewalks and footpaths, up the hill from the Fairway, past the Sheraton, where the latest World Bank mission had camped out, and then down through the valley of central Kampala. It was hard not to notice the early signs of Asian investment returning to build or restore office buildings, hotels and shops. On the road, the new cars were imported late models and driven by Asians. The footpaths, by contrast, were all African. People were headed to the only hilltop in Kampala higher than the Sheraton's, the peak of Uganda's domed Anglican cathedral. There I found more than a thousand Africans listening to one visiting white preacher, a dour, admonishing Scot. I was not sure if Kampala, with the World Bank on one summit and God on the other, was cursed, blessed or headed for the final conflict, but I decided to take my chances with God and slipped into a back pew.

The guest preacher delivered his sermon, which, judging by the shuffling in the pews, was much longer than usual, exhorting the congregation to avoid the temptations of greed. Some of the worshippers did not have shoes. Almost all of them had come on foot. I shared a crowded bench with an African woman and her six children, dressed in what looked like second-hand clothing, perhaps from Scotland. Greed? I wondered. How long did the preacher expect this congregation to hold out?

After the service, I walked down to Makerere, once the most respected centre of learning in Africa. It felt like a wooded park, so endowed was its hillside campus with sleepy banyan trees, big clumps of jacaranda and bougainvillea, and wooden bungalows for privileged staff. I could not believe this was a university on the verge of collapse until I reached George's faculty housing, marked by peeling paint, a wobbly cement staircase and a crumbling outdoor passageway so decrepit it would have been condemned back in Waterloo. Upstairs, in the one-bedroom flat he shared with his wife and four children, George welcomed me with such a tight handshake I feared he was mistaking me for an old roommate. This is the way of an East African greeting, however, and he did not let go of my hand until we reached the living room, where the other Canadians sat sipping glasses of Coke.

As I took my seat on a ratty sofa, George launched into his life story, as socially uninhibited as Rajinder had been back in Biharipur. He was a one-man aid agency, the lifeline to his entire community. As a first-born son who was called home to assume the role of clan elder when his father died, the Canadian-trained chemist had become the dole chief for more people than a small village. "There's my beloved mother, of course," George told us. "Three stepmothers, five orphans—no, there are eight—from three of my brothers who passed away. Five orphans left behind by my father. My ten brothers who are still alive, and their children. I don't know how many that is. Plus three sisters who are not married." At least the other eleven sisters and stepsisters were married, and no longer his responsibility. In total, the chief of the Mpango clan figured he supported close to fifty relatives—on three hundred dollars a month. And that did not include his own wife and four children.

In 1987, when he took over from his father, George had fifteen brothers and fourteen sisters. Since then, five of the brothers had died, including three from AIDS. I asked George how many of his twenty-four surviving siblings he considered to be responsible. "Five," he said—one brother and three sisters who are schoolteachers, and one sister who works as a secretary.

Of the nineteen living deadbeats, there was one brother who had fought for President Museveni's bush army, which overthrew Milton Obote's regime in 1986. He did not adjust well to peace, and demanded that George sell all the land and divide the spoils so they could go their separate ways. When George refused, the brother threatened to kill him, but before he got the chance, he was arrested for theft and sentenced to five years in jail. George paid for two other brothers to study in a vocational college, one as a mason, the other as a teacher. Both were now drunks. Two more brothers he offered to set up in business with a maize mill. When they said the work was "dirty," George bought them a pickup truck instead, to start their own transport business. They spent their profits on booze and asked George to repair the truck when it broke down. He refused. They let the business collapse. Both died shortly thereafter from AIDS.

Another brother spent a year's worth of school fees on a drinking binge. George allotted a special plot of his father's land to create a small coffee plantation for yet another brother. Every year, after he sold the harvest, the brother threw a party for all the men in the village, and then asked George for more money. "Anything he gets goes to drinking or to finding another girl," George said. "He can't even build a house for himself." And then there's the aunt, one of his father's four widows, who sold the family's fifteen cows while George was in Kampala.

"She claimed some of them fell ill and the rest died," he said. "I know she gave some to her side of the family. The rest she sold—I know that. I'm aware of that but what can you do? These people are my family."

The poor chemist just wanted to spend a weekend alone in his lab completing work on his latest invention, a high-protein biscuit for pregnant women, which he hoped the health ministry or, better yet, an international aid agency would buy in bulk. Here was a Benjamin Franklin for Africa, and he was having to spend weekends on a bus to his village to bail belligerent brothers out of jail, distribute clothes and food to his nieces and nephews and tend to family land that no one else seemed to care for. The last time he stayed away from the village for too long, a neighbour dug up most of his experimental cassava crop and his precious high-yielding tubers wound up in someone else's stew.

George and his predicament seemed bizarre, ridiculous, even a bit funny, but I was beginning to understand that his was the story of Africa, a continent where the extended family is so extended it flops about like a great big octopus. In some cultures, this creature fosters development: family members lend money to one another, pass on business deals, take care of each other's children. But the clan system can also ensure that no one really gets ahead. Anyone with an education is expected to subsidize those without. Anyone with a job in the city is expected to return to the village with gifts and cash—frequently. And God help anyone who goes abroad. The appeals never stop.

As a boy, George herded cows in his village, and every day ran barefoot to school, five kilometres each way. He was a good student, encouraged by his father to get ahead, and as the eldest son was spoiled by his mother and three stepmothers, who worked together to raise their combined flock of thirty children. Food and love were never in short supply, not when he could choose among four huts to seek comfort or dinner. "All my father's wives were my mothers," George said. "They cooked for me when I was hungry. They cared for me when I was sick." The sorority, however, did not extend beyond child care, and when his biological mother grew weary of the lesser wives and their rivalries, she left the village. George fell out of favour. He retreated to his cows and school work until his father took notice of his discontent and agreed to send him to a free boarding school in the district, and then to Makerere, which in the late sixties offered free tuition and board. During the horrific days of Idi Amin's rule, he completed an undergraduate and then a master's degree in chemistry. "I was so afraid during those days that I spent all my time in the lab. You couldn't go anywhere else," he said. On the side, he worked as a tutorial assistant and plotted his escape from Uganda, saving enough over two years for half the cost of an airline ticket to North America. His father persuaded a local planter to lend him the balance to get to the University of Alabama, the only American college that would enroll him in a doctoral program without his first writing an English-language exam. Only when George reached Tuscaloosa did he discover his thesis adviser was a South Asian who associated all black Africans with Amin. After other graduate students warned him that the South Asian professor was racist to the core, George transferred his thesis project to Ontario, where his wife and their first baby could join him.

After gaining a doctorate in 1980, George found a teaching job in Nigeria and figured he was set for life, with a secure job and plenty of distance from his troublesome brothers. That is, until his father died and the call came from Uganda. "Daddy," his sisters said when he picked up the phone. They were referring to him now. George was thirty-eight, and it was time for him to come home.

The best Makerere University could offer him in the late eighties was an assistant professorship with a salary equal to one hundred dollars a month, plus the free one-bedroom apartment where George topped up our Cokes and alternately regaled and alarmed us with his stories. He doubled his income by teaching part-time at a private Islamic university in northern Uganda once a week, travelling there and back by bus. And there was his father's twenty-hectare farm. Its coffee trees, cassava and maize crops brought in another one hundred dollars or so a month—and a harvest of need from all the dependents George had inherited along with the land.

It wasn't just the family that was bogging him down. Everything about Makerere seemed to be telling him to sit still as well. Opened in 1922 by the British, the university was considered so important to Uganda that it was a line item in the national budget, drawing 2.5 percent of government spending in the seventies as the government increased enrolment sevenfold, to seven thousand places, all with free room and board. By the end of the eighties, when George returned home from Nigeria, Uganda was just about the poorest place on earth, and his beloved Makerere a shantytown among schools. In the university's guest house, the windows had been without glass for more than a decade. In the engineering building, all the men's toilets had been stripped of their handles.

George explained more as we left his crowded flat to walk around the serene campus. His chemistry department was so broke it had to store toxic waste in the basement. Some of the chemicals were thirty years old, and even they had to be rationed. Its academic journals dated from the seventies. The most important chemistry lab in east Africa did not have a simple pH meter. "It's like a high school in Canada," George said. Only worse. Whenever the university's water supply was cut off for nonpayment of bills, which was frequently, students had to bring their own buckets of water to the lab.

Feeling pity, the German government sent a chemical reactor to George's department, without a manual or instructions. It went unused. The European Union provided a fire extinguisher. That seemed like a good idea, but what the faculty really needed was light bulbs. They had none. Some beakers might be nice, too, since they hadn't had a new supply of those in fifteen years. "The donors give us what they have, not what we need," sighed George's boss, Bernard

Kiremire, head of the chemistry department, when we met him outside the lab. Not surprisingly, George had not published any research
since his return to Uganda, and his department had not awarded a
PhD in six years.

As we continued to walk, the campus seemed quiet, even sleepy,
but George warned us not to mistake the calm for Sunday rest.
Classes had been cancelled for a week because the canteen had run
out of food and money, and the administration feared riots. Nothing
angered the students more than food rationing. Every time the canteen was closed, riots erupted.

What amazed me—okay, students hauling buckets of water to
class amazed me—but what really amazed me was that people like
George stuck around this place. With a Canadian doctoral degree,
he had standing offers from universities in Botswana and South
Africa, where he could earn more in a month than he did in a year
at Makerere. Of his faculty's seventeen teaching positions, seven
were vacant for this very reason, and not likely to be filled soon.
George stayed because he was caught in a complex web spun by his
own father and by tradition. His extended family had trapped him.
They had ruined his protein biscuit project. They were destroying
the farm. They were driving him to exhaustion. As George walked
us to the campus gates, I thanked him for a lovely afternoon and
wished him well in his many struggles. But honestly, I thought, how
could such a man break his family's ways before they broke him?

I did not return to Uganda for another six years, a period in which
Africa saw Rwanda's genocide, Zaire's implosion, Sudan's civil war
and Kenya's rapid decay, all on Uganda's borders. Somehow, in this
stormy sea, the pearl stayed safe in its oyster. Uganda's economy had
doubled since my last visit, and it was again a major supplier of fish,
sugar and coffee to Europe. Its policy of welcoming back the Asians
driven out by Amin was also bearing fruit, as the returnees rebuilt
their huge tea and coffee plantations and continued to revamp downtown Kampala with video shops, cell phone dealerships, ice cream
parlours, pizza joints and cyber cafés. And there was music everywhere, as one would want in Africa. The government had awarded

licences for five FM radio stations that not only played lots of African pop, but gave a platform for political humour. It wasn't just a bunch of stodgy newspapers stirring the pot any more. Suddenly people were calling in jokes about President Museveni and his private cattle herd, and everyone was laughing.

Museveni, the former guerrilla leader, was cautious about Western-style democracy, though. He permitted free speech, a parliamentary opposition and political satire but banned political parties, claiming they might divide the country along ethnic lines. In 1996, he allowed a wide-open "partyless" presidential election, which he won with more than 70 percent of the votes, and then pushed ahead with more tough reforms, which he believed would turn Uganda into an economic power in the region.

One of the most important reforms occurred at Makerere, where the university for the first time in more than seventy years was allowed to set its own fees. The government's only condition proved to be a smart move: it said that four thousand students must receive free tuition, the same number as before. Beyond that, the university could do as it pleased.

Makerere increased its enrolment to fourteen thousand, and required ten thousand of those students to pay eight hundred dollars per semester (two thousand dollars if they came from a neighbouring country). The university still had a smaller budget than the salary of a New York Yankees outfielder but at least it could afford light bulbs. In 1993, it also restocked its library, bought new lab equipment and began adding new buildings. Assistant professors saw their salaries triple to three hundred dollars a month. Full professors in competitive fields like medicine got one thousand dollars a month, and students demanded more of them. Instead of riots, there were lineups of young people from Uganda, Rwanda, Kenya and Tanzania to get in. They knew almost every graduate would get a job—not the dead-end civil service positions that were guaranteed to all graduates in the sixties but big-money jobs as accountants, economists, doctors and chemists in food companies.

Unfortunately, the university had yet to figure out a means test for its four thousand free seats, so it awarded them to the top four thousand students on the basis of a nationwide exam. Naturally, most of the toppers came from the best schools in the big towns and cities. Village children, the ones who needed scholarships the most, were largely shut out.

Still, if Makerere students were paying for their own food, I wanted to see it. I also wanted to find George. He had not responded to my letters and cards, and I suspected he had done what I would have done in his situation, which would be to bail out. Thoughts of George's second flight from Uganda, from a different kind of oppression this time, swirled through my imagination as I climbed the crumbling cement stairs to the tenement flat where I had met him six years earlier.

"Mpango is gone," a neighbour shouted to me from her kitchen.

Good for George, I thought.

"They left the day before yesterday," the neighbour said, emerging in the doorway. "You can find them up the hill. Behind Mary Stuart Hall."

Her children led me up the hill, to a new row of staff quarters, compact two-storey townhouses that would not look out of place in Waterloo. George's little boy, who answered the door, was now six feet tall and wearing a Toronto Blue Jays shirt. One of his sisters was at the medical school library, he said. Another sister, a Makerere undergrad, was busy writing application letters to Canadian universities. George's wife came to the door and said he had gone to the village for the weekend.

The very mention of his village brought back a flood of memories of his parasitic relative. I asked how the family was.

"They are there," Mrs. Mpango said.

When George got back the next morning, he called me from the lab (professors are not given home phones) and came straight to my hotel. He had just turned fifty. His hair was streaked with grey and his stomach sagged. Yet he was as exuberant as a thirty-year-old. He could barely sit still as we found some chairs on the lawn, and began to look at photos from his village, not of his drunkard brothers but of cassava, fields of cassava that were taller than George and everything else but the trees. Since my last visit, he had met people from Canada's International Development Research Centre (IRDC) who had helped him start a research project in his home village. He then borrowed some high-yielding cassava seeds from one of the government's agriculture research stations, and grew enough in one year to supply new seeds to hundreds of farmers around him.

In 1996, George had also started a private high school in his district, specializing in the sciences. As a professor, and now head of the chemistry department, he was appalled by how few of his students, especially his best students, came from villages like his. With money he raised from friends, he built the three-room Greenfields High School in Iganga, with a modest lab and small experimental farm, and collected enough fees from hopeful parents to hire a group of part-time teachers for the twenty or thirty children he expected to enrol. On the first day, 120 children showed up, most of them with a full term's tuition in hand. George quickly hired masons and carpenters to add two more small buildings, and more children came. Now, three years later, there were 380 students—most of them village children who boarded with relatives and family friends in Iganga. Two-thirds of them paid their fees in full. The rest brought bricks and timber in lieu of payment.

In Kampala's fading light, we talked for another hour on the hotel lawn about George's many other interests, including the protein biscuit that was now ready for market. "The women in my village, ohhhh, they love it," George said, his baritone laugh filling the air. He was also hard at work on a new orange juice powder, a sort of Tang for rural Africa. The first formula was so good a local businessman agreed to pay George a thousand-dollar down payment for the marketing rights. They shook hands. The man gave George two hundred and disappeared with the formula. A year later, something called Life, which tasted like his drink, appeared on Kampala shelves.

"What can you do with these people?" George sighed. "But you know," and here he leaned forward, "I have a better formula." He leaned back and laughed hard enough to shake the trees behind us.

The highway out of Kampala, as I remembered it, was strewn with ruts and gravel. This time, George and I sailed along at a hundred kilometres an hour toward the Nile, thanks to a resurfaced road financed by the World Bank. Beyond Kampala, a new industrial park was almost completed. And beyond that there were rolling hills of tea bushes, sparkling in the wake of a sun shower, all owned by the Madhvanis, the most successful of Uganda's Asians to return under

Museveni's rule. The Madhvanis were not only the richest people in Uganda, they were richer than some small African countries. They lived well off the highway on an estate said to be the size of a small town, surrounded by vast fields of tea, coffee and sugar cane. With so much concentrated new wealth, I expected more racial resentment. During George's student days, Asians would not sit with him or shake his hand. Some called him "dog." But George felt the Asians had learned to be modest. Besides, he said, Uganda had too many other things to worry about, like AIDS and warfare in three neighbouring countries, to dwell on the past.

When we crossed the Nile at Jinja, just below its source, there was another spectacle. Heavy earthmovers, funded with foreign aid, were remodelling the river's right bank to suit an extension of the Owens Falls hydroelectric dam, the sort of development George loved to see. I think he was spouting praise for the World Bank when suddenly he hit the brakes and jerked his steering wheel to the right and then left. SLAM! We caught a pothole that lifted us out of our seats. Regaining the road, George explained that the crews had not yet made it across the Nile, to his kingdom, the place of the Basoga people, whose influence did not extend to the capital—just as the capital's generosity did not extend to them.

When we reached Iganga, the centre of George's district, we turned off the highway and headed up a rust-coloured dirt track that surged and swelled for the next forty kilometres. When George used to travel to his village, he took a crowded bus to the end of this road, and then drove into the interior by bush taxi, a beat-up old Peugeot that packed up to ten passengers on board before it bashed its way into the bush. The journey often took a full day, but now George had his own vehicle and life was good.

"With peace and freedom there will always be development," he said proudly. "Give me the freedom to choose. Give me a road to drive on. That is all I need."

Ahead of us lay an old cotton station, where turn-of-the-century shops, warehouses and homes were abandoned long ago by the Asians whom the British had brought here to introduce a cash-crop economy. The surviving village had no more than a dozen buildings still in use, as most of the economy had moved outdoors. Along one side of the road, women sat on crates in temporary stalls made of wood and thatch where they sold tomatoes, cabbage and big fat pineapples. A group of men sat on crates behind the shops drinking beer.

As a Coca-Cola truck rumbled past us, rattling from rut to rut, we continued up the road, through Kiyunga village where George went to primary school, and deeper into the bush toward the Mpango homestead, along a bumpy path that was no more than a narrow strip of dirt, overgrown with bushes and trees. George said we had reached his birthplace. The farm that dominated his life, the land that crowded out his biscuit and juice projects and had taken him from his own children every weekend, hardly seemed worth the bother. Although there was a pleasing garden of jacaranda, there was little else other than scrub brush and clumps of acacia trees. Several years ago, a falling tree had crushed George's childhood home, and in its place stood an abandoned two-room brick hut with a rusted corrugated roof. It was the last house George's father had lived in.

"Why do you bother to stay?" I asked.

"The land," George said. "You may not be able to understand this, but our land is more important than anything else. By custom, a man's honour lies in his land. This is something that is passed from generation to generation. It is not something you can claim as your own."

In George's mind and soul, his father's land was less an asset than the home of his ancestors' spirits, as vital as the blood flowing through him. The land under our feet was something he held in trust, from one generation to another, and in this way, George was not beholden to a family of loafers so much as he was committed to their ancestors and children. The present generation, like the scrub brush, merely came with the package. His rationale reminded me of the Barabaig. He could not leave this land, he could not sell, divide or in any way ruin it, without violating all the souls who had spent their mortal years working it. And he hoped it would be the same for his own son, the seventeen-year-old in the Toronto Blue Jays shirt, because in their Masaga tribe there was no greater measure of a man's worth—not cattle, wives or children—than his land.

This tradition was something no economist could quantify, and no government could regulate. To cope with it, however, the Ugandan government had allowed for property to be held by clans under the stewardship of local elders' councils. There was no deed or title. Only the big plantations and urban areas followed modern systems of tenure like freehold and leasehold, with just one other exception— the Bugandan kingdom in central Uganda, where some twenty-three thousand square kilometres of land ceded to the king by the British remained under his stewardship.

Such traditions had become a hot issue among many foreign aid donors who saw them as backward and inefficient in terms of land use, much as they viewed the transhumant Barabaig. Without land certificates, foreign experts argued, farmers like George and his brothers could not use their property as collateral to borrow money from banks to buy fertilizer or build small irrigation systems. The Mpango farm had none of that. In fact, the aid donors argued, all the big reforms going on in Kampala amounted to little out here because small producers could not run their farms like businesses. That was not what George wanted anyway. He would never sign over his ancestral land, title or not, for something so temporal as a bank loan. He was sure the bankers would trick him—him, with a PhD from Canada—into missing payments and defaulting on his loans. Yes, to sign a mortgage would be to tempt the forces of evil, he said. "Those who use land as collateral end up losing it to those who lend the money."

The landed and the moneyed—it's about as old a class struggle as one can find, and George, a rational thinker in every way, feared these foreign-driven reforms would only enlarge the divide.

Not far from his father's abandoned hut, under the magnificent pink splash of a bougainvillea, we found a family member, a woman who was supine and shivering on a dirty cotton sheet. As we approached, she opened her eyes and lifted her head off the ground just slightly, in a motion that seemed to make her pain more acute. She then climbed to her feet slowly and bowed her head respectfully to George. She was the wife of one of his brothers, the delinquent coffee planter.

The woman was suffering from a wicked bout of malaria, and did not know where her husband was. She had not taken any medicines because she could not afford them, not even some Aspirin to relieve the fever and crushing backaches that came and went as the disease slowly devoured her brain.

"I am sure this man has gone with his friends to find a drink," George said, cursing his brother.

Without protest, though, he allowed the woman to shuffle to her brick hut, and return with two chairs for us to sit on. As George took his seat, the sister-in-law got down on both knees to formally welcome him, head of the clan, with a long exchange of greetings he said was customary in rural Uganda.

"How are you?" the woman asked in a hushed tone, her eyes fixed on the ground.

"I am fine," George responded quietly.

"How is your family?"

"They are fine," George said.

"How was your journey?"

"It was long and tiring."

"Mmmmm."

"Mmmmm."

"Mmmmm."

"Mmmmm."

The "mmmmms" rose slowly like a funeral march as the two tried to share some of each other's soul and pay respect to the spirits all around them. The kneeling part was a bit much, but the tonal exchange felt deeply soulful, as if it were a reunification of two persons separated by time—until, that is, George stood up abruptly and bade his sister-in-law a curt and simple farewell: "I will see you when you see me."

As we walked away and the woman returned to her dirty sheet, I asked George if his wife got down on her knees to welcome him home from work.

"Only the village women do it," he laughed. "You can't stop them."

Tradition again. George said he had brought a social-development group from Iganga to coach local women to grow their own crops, away from their husband's land, and keep separate accounts for things like school fees and anti-malaria pills. But change does not come easily in villages.

"If I told them not to kneel down," he said, "they would still do it. But the younger ones don't do this any more. My sisters, they will not kneel when they greet me."

Across the dirt path and beyond a small thicket, a new house had been built, along with a big yard and lovely flower garden. I asked which brother lived there. "It is not a brother," George said a bit testily. "It is someone new here. This man bought the land from my brother."

George had his father's obligations but not his father's powers, and it was becoming apparent that the traditions he so revered might not survive the arrival of his cherished smooth roads, free speech and good schools. Land sales, for one, were becoming a serious problem for the part-time chief, and squatters a bigger one still. As head of the family, he was responsible for all ancestral land, parcelling it out to relatives as he saw fit. He even began to give plots to unmarried sisters and nieces, although once a husband came along, a woman had to move to his land. ("He would try to take our land," George explained, "and our family would never get it back.")

But recently, a couple of his brothers had sold bits and pieces of family property behind his back and outside the boundaries of tradition. George could hardly stop it, at least not without evicting his own brothers or hauling the newcomers before the elders' council. Either way, there would be a violent backlash against him, and he had neither the time nor the fight in him to withstand it. For now, he let it be.

We continued into the bush and past another brother's house, a ramshackle hut of bricks and wood where only a young boy was present, tending a cooking fire. George pointed out that this brother earned upwards of five thousand dollars a year from a plot of maize and coffee, plus enough food for his family, and yet this is all they had. "Look at this hut." He shook his head. "Where does the money go?"

Farther along the path we came to a round mud hut with a straw roof supported by a dozen tree branches staked in the ground. This was home to George's aunt, one of his father's sisters who had agreed to raise the family's eleven orphans, the children of brothers and cousins who had died from AIDS. One of the girls who looked barely ten fetched a plastic cup of water to pour on George's hands so he would feel refreshed. Another girl, the oldest orphan, sat inside tending to a smouldering fire that filled the hut with smoke. Twelve of them slept inside the hut every night, elbow to elbow on the ground. To give the orphans more space, George spent five hundred dollars of his own money, almost two months' salary, to build a two-room brick hut. It was no bigger than a one-car garage, but it was not yet inhabit-able. He needed another hundred dollars to buy more corrugated iron sheets for the roof. With any luck, he said, the children would have elbow room by the rainy season.

We backtracked, cut through a thicket and down a narrow path to more overgrown fields, where George's cassava trial lay. He began the experiment in 1996, when, during a small drought, a mosaic virus destroyed Uganda's cassava crop. With his village facing the threat of starvation, he went to a government research station and got a new higher-yielding variety of cassava that could be spaced much closer than the older varieties. When I suggested that the agriculture exten-sion department should have come to him, he laughed. District offi-cers, he said, were selling the new plants, and he might have got nothing had he not been friends with people at the research station.

With the new varieties in hand, George rented a tractor to clear a field, and hired five men (his brothers refused to do the work, even for cash) to plant bits of the new stem, which is how cassava grows. Why anyone would want to promote the bitter tuber was beyond me, but George explained that across much of Africa, cassava is a poor man's crop. The plant itself looks like an emaciated tree, about two metres in height with spindly branches and a mop of drooping green leaves that taste repulsive. Animals will not touch the leaves, or the tubers that grow underground, because they are laced with cyanide. Moreover, cassava grows pretty much anywhere and can withstand the most threatening weather and pest attacks—an exception being the 1996 mosaic virus, likely from the former Zaire.

Cassava's downside is that excessive consumption has been known to lead to goitre, a morbid swelling of the thyroid gland that often pro-duces a hideous lump in the neck as the cyanide chews up precious body salts. Death due to a cassava overdose is not unheard of, but most African women know enough to crush the tuber to get rid of its high water and cyanide content. They then cook the starchy remains with beans or green vegetables, or bake cassava bread. When drought or pestilence wipes out the maize crop, it may be all a family has.

After a couple of years, George's half-hectare test plot produced thirty-five hundred plants. The previous variety used to give him only forty. He was so thrilled with the results he invited other farm-ers to take some cuttings for their own planting. He did not think his neighbours would take his entire crop. But there before us, beyond the brown grass, thorn bushes and bony trees, was an entire field uprooted. Hundreds of plants were gone. Staring at his looted experiment, George stood still for a moment to contain his emotion. The ailing sister-in-law, his drunken brothers, the helpless orphans and now this. "This is the last blow," he said. "This is very disappointing. A hungry person cannot take this much. Someone who comes and takes a whole plot, that is a thief."

George and I walked quietly back through the bush to the main trail, where the garden's silence was punctured by the driver of another pickup truck honking as if he were in rush hour traffic. It was the maize man, who had come to buy harvested corn at the farm gate. His price today was 130 shillings a kilogram, about ten cents. In Iganga, forty kilometres away, he expected to fetch double that, which led to an obvious question: why couldn't local farmers set up a co-operative, buy a truck, transport their own maize and double their income? The answer, George said in a pained voice, was that no one could be bothered, not when there was cassava to be stolen and coffee trees to be stripped.

"You see," he continued, leading me back to his truck, "we were brought up in a wrong way where business interests were not inculcated in us. People want to be workers and wait for their salary. That's what's happening. People are looking for jobs. They're not trying to create jobs. During our independence days, most of our leaders believed everything should be done by the government. We were brought up to be workers, not thinkers. People see me on the farm and say, 'What are you doing here? You have enough in the city.' I say, 'You can't just stop when you have something.'"

Here was more of George's conflict with tradition. He wanted so much to protect his land, the very representation of his father, and yet he had enough gumption to push for change, to experiment and take risks. He wasn't content sitting on a fixed asset, spending his life protecting it the way so many Africans did. His modern urban self wanted growth. The city and Canada had changed him. His university education had made him more than his father's son. His struggle, I was starting to see, was less with his family than with himself. And the struggle would be greater for his son, the one who wanted to be an engineer, considered English to be his first language and rarely visited the village. It was impossible to see how he, in his Blue Jays shirt, would move ahead with his cousins, the orphan girls in rags.

This was where African tradition was breaking down, leaving great fissures that could swallow entire generations. True, George had his road, and his freedom. More than any of his ancestors, he had the future in his hands. But one man's energy and passion could not transform a village. Until George could find a way to put his delinquent brothers and suffering sisters in charge of their fields and lives, he would remain his clan's Daddy, a one-man aid agency, charitable and forever in demand.

OUR LADY OF PEACE BASILICA, YAMOUSSOUKRO, CÔTE D'IVOIRE

# 7

# A Despot's Delight

If there is a Versailles of Africa, a contemptuous display of wealth that trumpets the need for change, even for revolution, it is Our Lady of Peace, the brownstone basilica that rises from the rain forest of central Côte d'Ivoire as if it was the vestige of some lost civilization. And in many ways it is. The basilica is the tallest Roman Catholic church in the world—it beats out St. Peter's in Rome by a few metres—and was built by one of Africa's most enduring despots, Félix Houphouët-Boigny, in his dying years, when delusion can be at its most dangerous. Every aspect of it, from the air-conditioned pews to the marble driveway to the stone pillars that contain elevator shafts, is an extraordinary waste for a country that should be as wealthy as Malaysia but instead entered the twenty-first century as poor as Zimbabwe. The church itself is a clear argument for democracy. Had it been built in India, the president would have been thrown out of office at the first available opportunity. But it is also an indictment of the many international organizations that claim to be interested in Africa's fate, the ones that have tolerated such abuse, and a useful reminder of the traps that may lie ahead.

In 1995, I had been in West Africa for more than a month to see the region's emergence from the clutches of Big Men like Houphouët-Boigny, and to find many more George Mpangos moving ahead. But I could not resist one backward glance to another age—a pilgrimage to Our Lady of Peace, that age's most outrageous legacy. A few days before Christmas, I set out for the basilica at dawn. There was still a handful of prostitutes outside my hotel in downtown Abidjan, the capital, remnants of the hundreds of Senegalese, Malian and Liberian women who had lined the boulevards the previous night when Abidjan's jazz clubs, Vietnamese restaurants and indoor ice-skating rink were in full swing. The capital seemed all modern, with neatly laid out roads financed by foreign loans that led through suburbs and into the countryside, where we picked up a four-lane motorway that blew straight through the rain forest. For the next two hundred kilometres, from the city's edge all the way to the late president's ancestral village and basilica, it was pure highway, and it felt as if we were out of Africa.

With the sun rising above the dense forest, the only other people on the expressway were a few bicyclists and an occasional clutch of women and girls walking in single file with stacks of wood on their heads. Samuel, the driver of my rental car, belted along at 120 kilometres an hour, leading me to wonder if the road might run right through the Sahara. But after a couple of hours, the glorious motorway became two lanes and assumed the look of a city street, with a median to divide the lanes and lampposts planted every twenty metres. Still in the middle of a forest, Samuel informed me we had reached Yamoussoukro, birthplace of Côte d'Ivoire's founding president, a man who liked to call himself the country's "Number-One Peasant."

The smooth main street continued for another five kilometres, past a semi-pro golf course, the luxurious President Hotel with its revolving rooftop restaurant, the elegantly designed Félix Houphouët-Boigny Foundation for Peace and a hideous monstrosity that turned out to be the presidential palace, although the serving president did not live there. Its ten square kilometres of gardens and forests, protected by a crocodile moat and high security walls, were reserved for Mr. Houphouët-Boigny's widow and their many grown children. When I asked Samuel where the original village was, he laughed. All this, and an international airport, were built on top of it.

Beyond the modern town, over a ridge and across a field where horses ranged, the basilica at first glance looked small and lonely, a church without a community. But as we got closer to the gates and stopped to stare down a driveway paved with marble, it rose like the Emerald City of Oz, towering over all before it. Out here, two hundred kilometres from the nearest big city, in a country that was only one-quarter Christian, the church was built with enough pews to hold seven thousand people comfortably. And it sat empty.

President Houphouët-Boigny claimed until his death in 1993, at the age of 88, that he had financed the basilica, estimated to cost two hundred million dollars, from his plantation earnings. Few people believed him. After the Number One Peasant died, the Vatican had to take over the property because the hugely indebted government could not maintain it. Catholic officials later claimed they had tried to stop the president from building the basilica, but their protests were, at best, feeble, especially since Pope John Paul II had agreed to consecrate the monstrosity in 1990.

Samuel had no interest in seeing the basilica again, and left me at the sovereign gate to the Holy See where I had to show my passport and was greeted by Ohoupo, who introduced himself as a guide—not a tout like one finds at such places but an employee of the church. Ohoupo led me into the basilica through a two-tonne door, designed in France to open as easily as a kitchen cabinet. There were twenty-two such doors around the circular interior, he said proudly, but the engineering feat proved to be among the building's lesser points. What lay inside was the most extraordinary modern creation in Africa.

In a continent shaped by foreign intervention, foreign ideas and foreign aid, almost every aspect of the basilica came from abroad.

Contractors and five construction cranes arrived from France. The pews, made of African kotabe wood, were dried and treated in Italy, and fitted with vents through which cool air could blow on sweaty communicants. The twelve air-conditioned confessionals were assembled in Europe. Three large crystal chandeliers came from Italy. The organ was from the United States. A brass baptismal font was made in France, as were the seventy-four hundred square metres of stained-glass windows, including an immortal scene of President Houphouët-Boigny at the feet of Jesus Christ on Palm Sunday, along with the basilica's French contractor. Above the altar, a fifty-kilogram gold cross hung from a beam. If it were placed on the ground, the cross would stand slightly taller than Michael Jordan, with a broader arm span. At the side of the church stood a one-tonne wood carving of Jesus. In the entire church, the only significant domestic content seemed to be a modest wood statue of Mary, carved in prison by a convicted murderer in search of benediction. The gesture won him a presidential pardon instead.

Ohoupo led me to one of the church's twelve main interior columns—one for each apostle, he said—and pressed a button. It turned out that four of the pillars (as in one for each gospel) contained elevators to whisk visitors up the equivalent of fourteen storeys to a small interior gallery overlooking the pews. The domed ceiling rising above us, Ohoupo explained, was punctured with twenty-nine million tiny holes for acoustic effect. He led me outside along a catwalk that offered a sweeping view of the countryside and, above us, the sixty-metre-high dome plated with gold and topped with a nine-metre-tall gold-plated cross. By design, the magnificent structure is supposed to be lit every night with 2,884 spotlights planted around the church, although a revised budget allowed only for Christmas and Easter.

With the no-cost benefit of daylight, I stopped on the catwalk to enjoy a breathtaking view of the grand boulevard, lined with seven hectares of marble from Italy, Portugal and Spain as it led from the front gate to a duplicate of St. Peter's Square, with its own stone and marble inlay depicting a white dove. Behind the church were two identical mansions—one reserved for the pope, who stayed there once, during the 1990 consecration, the other occupied by a group of Polish priests in charge of the facility. And beyond them, splendid gardens, forty-five of them, boasting no fewer than four hundred thousand flowers, and manicured lawns that rolled like a par-five fairway to the horizon, where they met the edge of the late president's coconut estate.

The basilica took four years and the labour of fifteen hundred workers to complete. But as I surveyed the countryside, I was struck by something odder than the church itself. There were no villages, huts or dirt roads to be seen in any direction, no sign that this stunning creation was even remotely near Africa, or connected to anything of Africa.

We returned inside, and took the elevator down, to find a handful of worshippers scattered in the pews. Ohoupo said the church had been filled only twice: in 1990 for the papal visit and in 1994 for President Houphouët-Boigny's funeral, two months after his death. A whole stratum of kleptocrats was devastated to see him go.

Nearly a decade after the basilica's completion, in 1999, the same Pope John Paul II used his moral weight to pressure Western governments and multilateral agencies to write off all foreign debt owed by the world's poorest nations. This included as much as fifteen billion dollars of debt amassed by Houphouët-Boigny's dictatorial regime, plus all the debts related to Nyerere's bungling and Amin's terror. The big industrial nations agreed to a range of debt reduction measures, assuming that somehow, as if in a stroke of divine intervention, the days of waste were gone. They weren't. Governments continued to borrow in the name of the poor while spending lavishly on themselves. In 1995, Kenya's twenty-year Big Man, Daniel arap Moi, persuaded the World Bank to lend his government money to help rebuild the Nairobi-Mombasa highway while he wrote a twenty-eight-million-dollar line item into the national budget for a new international airport in his hometown of Eldoret. When the World Bank failed to persuade Moi to cancel the airport, it hired a consultant who suggested he shorten the planned runway and reduce the size of the terminal to at least save his government fifteen million dollars. Moi balked, and still got his airport, the improved highway and now a solemn pledge from the West, the pope no less, to cancel Kenya's debts.

It would be futile to blame the lending institutions or foreign aid donors for their clients' follies. Who wouldn't fiddle around with a forty-year, interest-free loan from the World Bank? You'd be dead and buried when it came time for your country to repay. What Africa needed more than debt forgiveness, or tougher foreign aid donors, were public voices that could scream out against abuse, and by the late nineties it had them. Across the continent, a new age was ascendant, possibly a second independence, a time not of liberation wars but of quiet struggles in which millions of people were trying to gain control of their lives and destinies. There have been plenty of setbacks, including a military coup in Côte d'Ivoire in December 1999. But the country's first elected parliament, like many in Africa, had been a sham anyway. A more important struggle lies in the public effort to make governments more accountable and effective, a struggle that is about much more than politics. At the turn of a new century, Africa's future lies in an economic liberation in which its real Number One Peasants are gaining the tools and freedom to build their lives—brick by brick, with no marble inlay.

TAMALE, NORTHERN GHANA

# 8

## The Shea-Nut Gatherers

If any country had buried its inglorious past and laid a foundation for a brighter future, it was supposed to be Ghana. The government had a stable parliamentary system, a shrewd leader and some of the most favourable trade and investment policies in Africa, not to mention a storehouse of gold, cocoa and tropical forests. The economy had grown smartly since 1981, when coups were still cool and a young Ghanaian flight lieutenant named Jerry Rawlings had led one, successfully taking over in the capital, Accra. Although Rawlings was a Big Man in size and ambition, he proved to be cut from a very different cloth than Africa's discredited thugs, tyrants and buffoons. He put an end to the welfare economics of Ghana's founding president, Kwame Nkrumah, who nearly bankrupted the country. He also sold and closed state enterprises, promoted private business, travelled the world to win foreign investment and began to cede power to a new parliamentary democracy. Next door to Houphouët-Boigny's basilica, Ghana was starting to look like a wunderkind. In 1995, the Ghana Stock Exchange was ranked as the world's number one emerging market. For its part, the World Bank said in a comprehensive study there was no serious reason why the country, with roughly the same population, could not match Malaysia's current wealth by the year 2020.

I had often referred to Ghana's promise, in articles about African reforms, but when I finally reached Accra, I noticed little to make me feel that I was entering a new Malaysia. There were no big export processing zones or construction cranes lit up on the horizon as they worked through the night. In the radiance of a West African twilight, the only action in Accra seemed to be the swaying of rich green palms, while the most visible sign of success was a billboard outside the airport—"Congratulations, Dr. and Dr. Rawlings," it read—welcoming home the president and his wife from the United States, where they had received honorary doctorates. Few aid donors protested when Rawlings gave the entire civil service a 60 percent raise, or when he rejected the idea of a value-added tax to help his own government raise revenue, or in the run-up to the 1996 election when there were allegations of funds missing from the treasury—two hundred million dollars, some said. Such hiccups mattered little to an aid community that could not get enough of an African country verging on success.

When I went downtown the next day, to wander the tree-lined boulevards that were supposed to be West Africa's Wall Street, the biggest traders I saw were young men crowding the curbs and medians to sell everything imaginable, and all of it imported: watches, handkerchiefs, coat hangers, chains, ice-cube trays, Christmas lights, Chicago Bulls T-shirts, socks. The only indigenously produced item for sale that I could spot was a plastic bag of water, tied tightly with an elastic band. Despite its new image, Ghana's economic output for a year was still only 6.5 billion dollars, less than Malaysia produced in an average month. By any standard other than Africa's, it remained a very poor country.

Like Malaysia, or Tanzania for that matter, Ghana had been a British colony (called Gold Coast) with a cash crop economy. But since independence in 1957, it had gone a separate way from its colonial cousins in Southeast Asia—along a similar path of state-directed development as that taken by India and increasingly Africa. Like Nehru and Nyerere, President Nkrumah was able to picture himself on the commanding heights with a very altruistic mission. He seemed genuinely to believe that only government could protect the peasants from the profiteers, and that would require a broad portfolio of public ownership. He welcomed foreign and private investment, such as a massive smelter built by America's Kaiser Aluminum, but he always insisted the state be present too. His government built the towering Akosombo dam and hydroelectric plant on Lake Volta, a new port at Tema complete with world-class cocoa silos, and the Kwame Nkrumah divided highway connecting the port with Accra. And it maintained its ownership of the vast Ashanti gold fields and northern cocoa estates. Although Rawlings had liberalized more of his economy than most African leaders—he sold off much of Ashanti, for example—he always found ways for the government to keep its hand in the pot, especially in agriculture, which still dominated millions of lives and affected most political outcomes. As in British times, the government controlled the trade in major cash crops, from world-class produce like cocoa down to the meek shea nut, claiming that the peasants were not yet ready to take on the profiteers, who never seemed to be identified.

I was intrigued by the government's ongoing interest in shea nuts, if only because no more humble a crop could attract state attention. Its economic worth was marginal; its strategic importance was nil. But because it was a mainstay for women in the northern forests, the shea nut remained an essential part of any plan to end poverty in Ghana. Foreign aid donors and non-governmental organizations (NGOs) flocked to the little brown nut, which they saw as a catalyst for generating incomes and earning women a stronger economic voice. This sort of local reform in village enterprise and rural markets was what Africa needed more than its famous cocoa silos and new stock markets, perhaps even more than national elections. Far from the capital, it was this sort of glasnost in the peasant economy that would bridge the greatest divide between Ghana and Malaysia; it would also require the government to accept that the peasants and profiteers were one.

In a handful of villages, this bridge had already been built by one of the most unlikely allies the shea-nut gatherers could find: the Body Shop. The British-based retail chain was one of the world's biggest purchasers of shea butter, which it uses in its Aloe Lotion, Watermelon Sun Block SPF 20+ and Aromatherapy Relaxing Moisture Cream. As part of its global "fair trade" program, the socially conscious retailer wanted to funnel a bigger share of its shelf price to the women who harvested the nuts and processed the butter. In the early nineties, the chain agreed to buy nearly 5,700 kilograms of unrefined shea butter from co-operatives formed by ten villages in northern Ghana, at a price of 1.25 pounds sterling per kilogram. The price was about 50 percent higher than the local rate because the butter had to meet European health and safety requirements as well as the company's own quality standards. As an added incentive, the Body Shop threw in another 0.79 pounds sterling a kilogram for the harvesters to invest in village schools or other development projects of their choice.

"The foundations of fair trade are transparency, mutual respect and empowerment rather than exploitation," the retailer explained in words the women of northern Ghana had never heard from their own government. "The Body Shop views its trading relationships with Trade Not Aid suppliers not as a charitable act but as a viable alternative for trade."

The program was all the rage among development's granola set, and it was pure business. For the shea-nut women, it meant more money because they were selling direct to retail. For the Body Shop, it meant more sales because of heightened public interest, including a picture in *People* magazine of the chain's high-energy founder, Anita Roddick, searching for shea nuts in northern Ghana. The deal seemed like just the sort of thing Ghana needed a lot more of, something that cut out both the middlemen and the Big Men. It came from the countryside, was built on local traditions, bypassed the capital and created more jobs and independence for women, the very opposite of what Nkrumah's cocoa silos and aluminum smelter had achieved or Rawlings' reforms had produced. It seemed like an ideal solution to Ghana's development woes, and for a brief while it was.

❖

For as long as anyone could remember, shea nuts had been under some form of government control. In 1849, Britain's Gold Coast government started a state monopoly to buy and sell processed nuts, which were exported to Europe for the manufacturing of cosmetics. After independence, Nkrumah chose to retain the colonial Produce Buying Company and its power to set prices, license buying agents and make its own purchases in the market, as he feared the trading class, the dreaded profiteers, would exploit the poor, or worse, conspire to overthrow him.

By the 1970s, however, the Produce Buying Company, like most state initiatives of the day, was so rife with embezzlement and waste that it ran out of money, leaving the nut harvesters with a wad of unpaid invoices. It was left to the World Bank and International Monetary Fund to persuade the new Rawlings regime to open up the shea-nut business to competition. At first, the government continued to set prices, control exports and allow only a few new traders into the domestic business, for fear they might exploit the peasants, the same people who were left penniless by the state monopoly. But the government also helped shea-nut villages set up co-operative societies to cut better deals and purchase equipment to process their own butter more efficiently.

All too predictably, though, the Produce Buying Company continued to keep prices well below their international level, pocketing the difference, and it wasn't long before the agency ran out of cash again. Several local co-operative societies folded when they were not paid for their produce. Others started to divert their nuts and butter to black-market traders who offered more than the regulated price. Finally, under more pressure from the IMF, the Rawlings government eliminated price regulations, allowed more private buyers into the market and liberalized exports, all to the benefit of the shea-nut picker. The state-run Produce Buying Company, an agency older then Ghana itself, could not cope with the competition and laid off 80 percent of its staff.

It seemed like a cautionary tale of socialist failure, with only the happy capitalist ending to be played out. But that was not to be, not in an economy that lacked any serious independent regulation. Although the Produce Buying Company had been whittled down to almost nothing in terms of buying power, its remaining executives retained several regulatory powers that could be used to great advantage. One such power was to grant purchase licences, which they did to a company that agreed to buy all the state enterprise's stock in 1994. The bureaucrats were still in business.

The fall, rise and fall of the shea-nut trade seemed to reflect much of what was wrong with Ghana's approach to development, and for that matter Africa's. A newly declared faith in the private sector was not enough. The country needed its people to shape their own economic plans rather than accept the diktats of a national government or the whims of an international market or even the enthusiasm of Dr. and Dr. Rawlings.

To find the shea-nut women, I hired an off-road vehicle and driver in Accra and headed north following the shores of Lake Volta, the sprawling reservoir created by the Akosombo dam. We left behind the lush forests of the south, the big plantations and industrial buzz of machine shops, and were soon in the brown prairie that silently marked the end of the tropics and the beginning of the Sahel, North Africa's great barren steppe. So flat was the new landscape that it seemed to stretch all the way to the Mediterranean, with only wandering cattle, sporadic clumps of trees and a few towns in the way. I had been told about aid pouring into the parched north, where the bulk of Ghana's deepest poverty remained, but if there was any trade or aid here, it had quickly dissipated in the tall grass that billowed all around us in the winter breeze.

We reached Tamale, the capital of Ghana's impoverished Northern Region, on the afternoon of the second day. A town of 150,000 people, its main road was lined with government buildings and parking lots filled with Land Cruisers, Jeeps and Range Rovers, each painted white (the official colour of development's cavalry) and emblazoned with the logo of a benefactor. The only thing bigger than the aid organizations seemed to be an inspirational evening planned for the Police Park, at the end of Tamale's main road, where tents, a stage and a carnival atmosphere heralded the coming attraction, the white American evangelists Eric and Gillian Cowley. According to leaflets distributed on the sidewalk near the park, the Americans would make "the lame walk, the blind see, the deaf hear." One photograph in the leaflet showed Eric, with blow-dried hair, thin beard and a baggy African shirt, leading an ecstatic black man . . . could it be in a dance? In another picture, he shared a joke with an erstwhile blind man. And there was Eric again, whispering in a deaf woman's ear. Poor Gillian, with coiffed hair, pearl white teeth and cheeks the size of plums, was shown only in the couple's official portrait on the leaflet's cover.

The day after we reached Tamale, I met Sheini Abu-Bakr, the manager of a government technology centre who had been involved in the development of new shea-nut processors. Abu-Bakr knew the Body Shop co-operatives well and, to my surprise, said their members were very unhappy. He agreed to take me to a few villages over the next couple of days, to hear the women's stories and judge for myself.

We reached our first destination, the village of Dalung, in the late afternoon, when the sun turns a rich crimson over the savannah. Nestled at the edge of a forest, Dalung showed no sign of having been in the vanguard of a bold market-driven initiative. All the huts were made of mud and brick, and only a few were topped with corrugated roofing. Children stood around listlessly, their stomachs distended. Those lucky enough to have clothes held them together with safety pins.

Zenuba Napuru, head of the Dalung women's committee, welcomed us to her village and led us to a neatly swept dirt courtyard where she presented me with a traditional gift: a bag of shea nuts to be hung on a wall or door for good luck. I thanked her but said I did not want to take any luck away from her or the village. She laughed, not a chuckle but a deep roar. Because of a glut left over from the Body Shop orders, she had sacks and sacks of shea nuts inside—so many, she said, that she would not be able to avoid a torrent of good luck.

We sat down with Zenuba on the ground to listen to all that had gone wrong in an experiment that had meant only good. For generations, the women of Dalung had collected shea nuts for oil and processed them by hand. One sack of nuts could take four hours of heavy labour. A woman had to boil, dry and crack each nut, boil the kernel until it was soft and then pound it with a thick piece of wood. The resulting brown paste, when mixed with water, produced the oily butter. Although the more industrious women sold their surpluses in Tamale, or to traders from the south, the money they earned was never enough to move them out of poverty. Then, a few years ago, someone from the Dutch embassy came down the dirt lane to Dalung with a woman from town, one who worked for the 31st December Women's Movement, an organization affiliated with the government. The outsiders offered the villagers a processing machine for their nut business, complete with an air cooler from southern Ghana that could be financed with a low-interest loan.

At first, Zenuba and her friends were thrilled with the new machines, which they set up in an empty community hut near her home. The processor reduced four hours of grinding to thirty minutes, the only hitch being that the machine had to be kept cool and clean in a region that is hot, dry and dusty.

Not long after the new machines arrived, the village's fortunes improved again when the Body Shop decided to expand its fair trade program to shea nuts and selected the local Dalung co-operative as one of its new partners. The company initially ordered fifteen hundred dollars' worth of shea butter, and as part of the deal required the village to invest some of the profits in their community. Dalung's women decided to buy cement and iron rods to build a new primary school. They also made a neat little sign and hooked it to a post outside the door of their round community hut, announcing that this was the home of shea butter.

Gender-sensitive technology. Trendy products. International markets. The women of Dalung did not know how hip they were about to become. Soon, diplomatic missions, aid agencies and NGOs from Accra were flocking to Tamale to get a piece of the New Age shea nut action. Small lending programs were announced for co-operatives to buy nuts and invest in more machines. New boilers and crushers also arrived, many as unsolicited gifts to villages eager to jump on the shea-nut bandwagon.

All the communities around Dalung jacked up their output, sure that the Body Shop's first order was only the beginning of something big for the region. A shea-nut rush was on, and neither the British chain nor the aid agencies were in a position to absorb the glut. In the first season, the northern villages, which normally produced about two tonnes of shea butter a year, churned out twenty tonnes, nearly four times what the Body Shop wanted. The growing inventory worsened when the Body Shop and other European buyers began to return shea butter that had been delivered too late or judged to be too coarse. Making matters worse, the Body Shop, after discovering it had overestimated the international market for shea-related products, quickly scaled back its orders for the next season. In northern Ghana, it wasn't long before shea-butter prices plunged.

Zenuba stood up and took us inside the round hut, where the machines were kept, including the air cooler that had broken down from all the dust. The cooler needed a new gasket that would cost about six times as much as one for the old water cooler. Next to the machines were sacks of nuts reaching up to the ceiling—five hundred kilograms left over from the Body Shop deal that could not be sold that year. "They've been lying here since January," Zenuba said. It was now December.

The Dalung women had never seen anything quite like it. They had never worked with timetables, deadlines or market orders before, or seen such whimsical behaviour. One year, they were the toast of development circles, visited and photographed by *People* magazine. The next year, they were sitting on broken equipment and sacks of unused shea nuts, unable to complete the school or repay the original loan. On our way out of the idle shea-butter factory, I noticed the signboard the women had erected so enthusiastically, obscured by tall grass.

When I contacted the Body Shop in London about the troubles, its fair trade officers downplayed the episode. They spoke of it as a trial that had not worked perfectly, not a failure, and certainly not one their company should be blamed for. They were right, in a sense. It was not the buyer's fault that so many producers misjudged the market, or that the other agencies got involved and didn't supply the best machinery. But if the company did not cause Dalung's troubles, it cannot disassociate itself from them, either. It gained invaluable publicity from its jaunt, enabling it to sell Watermelon Sun Block to consumers who genuinely believed they were helping poor, hard-working women in some very remote villages.

Later, the Body Shop went back to the village co-ops and helped them regroup to complete projects like the unfinished Dalung school. The next year, in 1996, the company also increased its orders for shea butter, certain in the long run that fair trade would succeed. If it does, the real benefit to the shea-nut gatherers may not be the higher prices, new equipment or school, welcome as those are. It will be this new bargaining process that has allowed the women of northern Ghana to sit at the table with a multinational corporation and, for the first time, demand what is best for them.

In the land of charity, miracle workers and Big Daddy development, this sort of collective and democratic movement was fast becoming the way forward. Such movements were already emerging across Africa, and in the strangest places. I had read all about them. I just didn't know I would find one on the road to Timbuktu.

BABO COULIBALY, PRESIDENT OF A VILLAGE CAISSE, BANANKOURINI, MALI

# 9

# Mama Benz

Anyone who doubts the assertiveness of a West African woman has never flown on Air Ivoire. The best seats, sometimes the only seats, are taken by Mama Benzes who manage to consume every inch of available space with their fulsome girth, garishly coloured head-pieces, and the duffel bags and garbage pails they use as carry-on luggage. The women of West Africa should be declared a hazard to airline safety. The Mama Benzes are praised instead as the great hope for their lands.

West Africa's most intriguing entrepreneurs and traders get their nickname from their imposing physiques and their preference in automobiles, although only a small number of them actually own a Mercedes. For decades, these women have flown from country to country hauling clothing, car parts, electronics, fresh fruit, toys and kitchen utensils that can't cross land borders because of ancient and inflexible trading rules. Airport officials are more easily fooled or bought off than border guards. But the Mamas are more than smugglers; they are a lifeline of commerce in their region, and often the only source of good relations between English and French Africa, between old rivals like Mali and Senegal, or between war zones. Thousands more Mama Benzes produce their own goods and trade locally.

I first encountered the Mama Benzes on an Air Ivoire flight from Abidjan to Mali. More precisely, I was run over by them. My problems started when I learned of Air Ivoire's tendency to oversell flights, but only after the boarding process had become a full sprint across the tarmac to the airplane. The winners got business class. The losers had to wait for the next flight. Feeling young and fit, with only a laptop computer and day pack to carry, I was already tasting champagne in my mind when a group of plump middle-aged women—no, they were huge—pushed past me. They had pails, buckets, sacks and boxes splitting from the weight of their contents. I stepped up the pace to pass the women, only to be knocked off balance by a gunny sack to the chest. At the steps to the aircraft, a few more women nudged me out of line. When I protested, six of them stared me down. They said I should be thankful to get a seat. And, it turned out, they were right. I got the last one, which I politely enjoyed with my legs stuck out in the aisle, displaced by a garbage pail full of shoes.

The Mama Benzes remained the bane of my journey, filling the immigration and customs lines before I could get to them, breaking the luggage carousel with their checked-in bags and then, on the curb outside Bamako's rustic airport, hiring the entire queue of taxis, which they proceeded to saddle like a camel train heading into the desert. Two young men, sitting on the curb for a cigarette break, offered to take me to town for ten dollars. What more could go wrong? If they robbed me, at least my computer would end up in good hands; the Mama Benz convoy was just behind us on the highway.

The women knew a good thing in Mali; it was suddenly the

hottest economy in West Africa. As exuberance waned for Ghana and
the two Dr. Rawlingses, it grew for a more distant, exotic and roman-
tic land that was beginning to look like a serious friend of the West's.
Mali's democratic elections, economic reforms, massive investments
in primary schools and general disdain for France, its former colonial
ruler, could not please Washington more.

The desert outpost's season of hope had been ushered in by Alpha
Oumar Konaré, a former student leader, one-time minister of youth,
sports and culture, and founder of the country's first private newspaper. Konaré was elected president in 1992 after leading mass protests
against his former boss, Moussa Traoré, the military dictator who had
been in power since 1969. Keen to win favour with the U.S., President
Konaré quickly arranged visits to his country from the Clinton administration, the head of the IMF, Michel Camdessus, and the World Bank
president, James Wolfensohn, who was so keen on the new Mali that
he brought dozens of staff with him.

Isolated and insignificant Mali was to become an important
African test case for democratic reform. It was also central to
America's hopes of stopping the spread of Islam in Africa, checking
the loss of good land to the Sahara and halting France's efforts to
regain diplomatic sway in the region. Ideologically, Mali was considered such an important linchpin that by the late nineties foreign aid
commitments to the country with a population smaller than Calcutta
had reached 450 million dollars a year.

For all this hope, Mali's ten million people could tap little natural
wealth, and continued to face hardship. So broke was the government
that it employed only thirty-seven school inspectors for a country
twice the size of France, and could hire only four hundred additional
teachers a year, when it needed eighteen thousand. To see Mali
through the painful transition, many Western aid agencies recommended a Bangladesh model, the nation-state equivalent of outsourc-
ing in which non-governmental organizations took up the bulk of
basic development work such as running primary schools and maternal health clinics while the government tried to get its act together.
Under the new democratic regime, some five hundred NGOs had
already set up shop in Mali, helping to channel aid and start innovative programs like community-managed girls' schools.

When I went for a few days to the northern town of Timbuktu, the desert village's only hotel, the Bouctou, was filled with aid workers bringing new hope to the fabled medieval trading centre, which is sinking irretrievably in sand. The UN Development Programme had planted trees and thorn bushes around the town, only to see the greenbelt eaten by sand. The European Union suggested building a wall. Others felt employment opportunities were the answer, that somehow if the people of Timbuktu had occupations and more money they would at least be happier living in a sand dune. A Belgian group called Islands of Peace—an odd name out in the desert—failed miserably when it tried to teach women to grow lettuce and onions. The Christian aid agency World Vision took a more unusual tack in this historic centre of Islamic teaching, where a thirteenth-century copy of the Koran is housed. It opened a women's training centre for tailoring, handicrafts and Bible teaching. A much bigger international agency funded a hospital, which the government could not afford to staff or maintain. It opened two years late, complete with a European-style dentist's chair and a facility for making false teeth. No dental technician lived in Timbuktu, and there was no money for one, anyway.

The aid rush was often so frantic and misguided that despair seemed to be the easiest response, but in some cases foreign advice was not only useful, it was eagerly sought after. One of Mali's most successful development initiatives, for example, had been launched by Quebec's Mouvement des caisses Desjardins, the core of the province's credit union movement. In towns and villages along the Niger River, where cotton was once king, the Mouvement des caisses was helping women organize new enterprises from which both they and their communities could profit. It was not a cold start. The local Mama Benzes had proven their business skills. All they needed was credit.

To find the Mama Benzes at work, I hired a small car in Bamako and headed north, following the south bank of the Niger, where every small tributary looked bone dry. In the capital, where the waters were only knee-deep and a stone's throw wide, a truck could have driven straight across the riverbed. Moussa, my driver, said that when he was a child the Niger and its tributaries were always full in December.

"Six months of the year we got rain," he said. "It is good now if we get three." More remarkable than its low waters is the fact that the Niger flows another one thousand kilometres northeast from Bamako, past Timbuktu and into the Sahara, before turning around and tumbling back fifteen hundred kilometres, through four countries, to the sea.

The dwindling rains and rapid population growth had left little in the way of forest in southern Mali, which like Timbuktu was being lost to desert. In a vain attempt to arrest the stripping of Mali's remaining woodlands, the government provided cheap gas cooking ranges to rural communities, but someone forgot to do the math. A month's worth of gas for the average family cost about fifteen dollars. A month's worth of firewood was four dollars. And so on both sides of the road, women walked in twos and threes, with stacks of wood on their heads, the harvest of an ever-lengthening daily trek.

An hour up the road, when we stopped at a roadside shack for a small glass of sugary tea, we found a group of farmers in the village café, huddled under woollen blankets to fend off the early morning chill. None would refute Moussa's claim about the abundant rains of his youth, or about the paucity of rain now that made their crops vulnerable and trees scarce. To get by, most had switched to hardier, if less profitable, grains. Their wives, when they weren't searching for firewood, had taken up handicrafts. The younger people, they said, had moved to Bamako.

"You can spend all your energy on the land," Dramane, an old man, said to us, "but the land does not answer to your effort."

Moussa and I finished our tea, and continued on to Banankourini, a roadside village we might have sailed right through had we not been told of something important underway that Saturday morning. Shortly after breakfast, the village's women were gathering in their large cement hut of a meeting hall to hear about this novel *caisse* from Quebec. The session began with a local Bambara woman, who had arrived on a motorcycle, chastising the group for allowing ten of its forty members to be absent. Absenteeism, she explained, was not to be tolerated because this new movement was not about finance so much as women working together. Gathered on small wooden stools in a semicircle, the other women nodded politely. They didn't need the lecture. They already knew how to stick together, and quite a bit about finance and savings, too. They knew not to keep their earnings in a

state-run bank, for example. The bank could collapse or simply hand
over a woman's savings to her husband, since it was his legal right to
claim any of her assets.

Because of these threats, generations of Malian women had developed their own version of the financial system known as a *tontine*, in
which groups of women pooled their savings every week, often only
twenty cents at a time, and then held votes, or in some cases lotter-
ies, to decide who should receive a loan from the fund. The money
helped finance the purchase of goats and cows, and sometimes paid
for weddings and medical care. The debtor had to pay interest, usually at the same rate as the local bank, and seldom defaulted because
her creditors were her sisters and neighbours. A woman's only other
source of credit was her husband, whose loyalties were usually divided. Under Islamic law, he could take up to four wives. He would provide each one with seed at the beginning of a planting season to
grow food for herself and her children. The wives had to repay their
seed loans with harvest grain while the husband kept his own plot to
grow food to sell at market.

For a woman who wanted to hide some money from her husband, the tontine system worked remarkably well—few bad loans,
no overhead, forget about marketing costs—but it absorbed only a
small fraction of village savings. Most women stashed the bulk of
their money in boxes in the ground, or in local investments like livestock, which was what the caisse wanted to change.

In the dim room with no lights, Sylvie Gauvin, a financial adviser
with the Mouvement des caisses, took the dirt floor and began to tell
the women, through a Bambara translator, how they could build their
own caisse and link it with a much larger credit union movement.
Unlike the fail-safe tontine system, Sylvie explained, the caisse was
designed to make the women's money work more effectively, and to
push them to think about changes in their finances, their businesses
and the ways they relate to their husbands.

A few months earlier, these women had formed a new local savings group and started to collect small bits of cash as a sort of dry run
for the caisse. Using development funds from the Canadian government, similar groups were being coached across southern Mali, and in
many other African countries, too.

The movement required villagers—mostly but not always

women—to organize themselves in *groupes de solidarité* of four to seven members who had to meet every week for at least three months and save at least a hundred dollars to prove their interest. Once that was done, four to seven savings groups could come together to form a caisse, which was when the lending would start. A new collective, with anywhere from sixteen to forty-nine members, was eligible for a bulk loan of up to ten thousand dollars from the main organization, which it had to repay, with interest, within eighteen weeks. How the money was distributed and collected was up to each caisse, and its member groups.

Under the caisse system, a typical group borrowed more than two hundred dollars a month, which was about ten times more than they got under the old tontine system. For most women, a starter loan of eighty dollars or so was enough to finance seeds and fertilizer for a decent vegetable crop. Loans of six hundred dollars for seasoned members was enough to see a woman through the rice harvest. But if one member defaulted, the others had to cover the difference or risk expulsion of the whole group. This sort of collective goodwill was essential to any success; the women had no other collateral.

The caisse movement was about more than getting rich, however. Each group met every Saturday morning to collect their weekly savings and talk about their financial, marital and family health problems. Business advisers were also brought in to coach the women on accounting, budgeting and planning. The Bambara women called the process *nyesigiso,* "to plan for a better future," which doubled as a local name for the caisse movement.

Since the first caisse in Mali opened in 1990, the number of branches had grown to nearly four hundred, mostly in the agriculturally rich Niger Valley. All told, about seventy-five hundred women had joined the movement and pooled the equivalent of 1.2 million dollars in savings. By the end of 1995, the new network had extended nearly two hundred thousand dollars worth of loans, mostly for agriculture and trading.

The more Sylvie explained the process to the villagers, the more they were intrigued. The women agreed to continue meeting every week to pool their savings so that they could join. But doubts lingered. Each woman had children to feed, a husband to please, a home to keep and fields to tend. They could not afford to lose even a few hundred francs on some crazy idea from this place called Quebec. Babo Coulibaly, one of the older women who had been elected that morning as the new group's president, suggested they keep the tontine system, at least for a few more months, while they tried out the caisse.

"We need to see whether we can trust each other," Babo said. Her comment drew murmurs of disagreement.

"Of course we trust each other!" she continued, trying to clarify her views. "But no one knows what will happen. Only God knows. If we get a lot of money, anything can happen. What do you think our husbands will do?"

"They will not touch our money at first," one woman suggested. "When that money brings more money, then they will ask for something. They will demand a lot of money, and probably will not be able to repay it."

The women voted unanimously to keep the old tontine system alongside the caisse.

This sort of reaction, Sylvie explained, was common in villages, where women tend to be extremely cautious with money. A more dynamic group awaited us in the next town, where just about every avenue of trade was driven by a Mama Benz.

We headed for Segou, clear across a landscape of charcoal black soil, the colour you see only in cotton country. In the thirties, these were the fields that France turned into a motherlode of cash for its teetering empire. With local forced labour, the Office du Niger carved hundreds of kilometres of irrigation canals in the land, and sowed expansive plantations. After independence, the new Malian government continued to suck all it could from the cotton fields, depleting the soil. But as we drove, it was clear that some life was returning to agriculture. Mali's farm markets had been liberalized and much of its land privatized. France also relented on West Africa's regional currency, the CFA franc, which for decades was fixed to the French franc at a high rate so as to make French imports affordable and African exports uncompetitive. When Paris allowed the CFA franc to fall 50 percent in value in 1994, Mali's cotton exports soared.

By the end of the nineties, West Africa was leading the continent, and much of the developing world, in economic growth, thanks largely to agriculture and the disappearance of despots like Mali's Moussa Traoré. The country's crop production was up 31 percent over the eighties, but it had further to go than most just to catch up with twentieth-century farming. Per hectare of farmland, impoverished India had ten times more tractors than Mali; Israel had a hundred times as many. In the past, Mali's government would have borrowed money or pleaded for aid to buy all those tractors, but that era had passed. The development gurus were slowly learning that the money for such things, or at least a good down payment, was right here in Segou. If only a credible banking system could be created to bring the cash out of huts and mattresses.

As we entered the farm town, it did not seem to offer much more than a few rundown cafés on the main street and an endless line of drab cement-block buildings that looked imported from Bulgaria. One of them, with a ten-foot-tall green metal door, was different from the rest: a women's caisse that was fast absorbing savings and funnelling loans to bright local entrepreneurs like Nené Coulibaly (Mali's most common surname).

Nené had a taste for flamboyant turbans and robes—pinks and blues today—and had been in business since long before the caisse came to town. For thirty years, she had been a Mama Benz, buying cloth and thread in markets around Mali for a group of seven Segou stitchers she had working on old Chinese sewing machines in their homes, making clothes and blankets. Her son sold their output in a local market. The old style of business drew no complaint from Nené, except whenever she needed cash to buy more materials. The tontine system wasn't big enough to finance her business. There were only the textile suppliers, who sometimes offered her credit, and, failing them, the local loan sharks.

The arrival of a credit union was perhaps one of the biggest changes in Nené's adult life. No longer did she have to hide CFA francs in her house, or plead for loans at usurious interest rates. Now she could manage her money with confidence, and some degree of predictability. After joining the caisse, she first borrowed about five hundred dollars, which she paid off in six months instead of twelve; her profits were so good that she wanted to get another loan. In just six months, she had netted three hundred dollars, giving her a 60 percent return.

There were more than four hundred women like Nené in Segou with accounts at the local caisse. Three hundred of them had enrolled in training courses sponsored by the movement. Together, the women had collected about fifty thousand dollars in savings, and received more than thirty thousand dollars of the money back in the form of business loans.

Nené did not have a Mercedes yet, but she had plans to expand her trade. She wanted to make a new line of clothes, and try her luck at importing children's toys. Her ambition seemed to know no limits, other than her growing credit line. "That was just a test," she said proudly at the branch, where she came every week with more profits to deposit. "Now I'll borrow more. I want to make the business bigger."

After five weeks in Africa, I returned to New Delhi with a bewildering feeling of confidence in much of the continent. For most of the twentieth century, Africa had been controlled by colonial powers and managed for its resources, from shea nuts in northern Ghana to cotton along the Niger. That was followed by three or four more decades of malevolence and incompetence at the hands of Africa's own Big Men, from the erudite Julius Nyerere to the preposterous Number-One Peasant, Félix Houphouët-Boigny. While the world watched, and sometimes lent a hand, these men crushed communities, drove scarce talent into exile, mortgaged their nations and left absurd legacies, if they left anything at all.

But now, after a century of pillage and plunder, the people of Africa were stepping forward, not in dramatic revolutions but in millions of small struggles of courage and risk. The George Mpangos, shea-nut gatherers and Mama Benzes of Africa wanted the world to know they did not need aid, though it often helped. For these people, development was no longer a question of them or their nations getting rich—of running while others walk. What they needed was to reorganize their societies and communities so that the only Big Men and Women were themselves, and all the tools of development—banks, laws, roads, schools, local councils and national parliaments—were accountable to them.

Democracy's resurgence had helped Africans embrace this sort of change, but they needed more than a choice of government. The freedom to make and sell shea butter was, in many ways, as essential as the free vote. The ability to start a co-operative to sell that shea butter was no less so.

Would this be enough to secure Africa a better century than the one it had just endured?

It is tempting to look at the decline of Somalia, along with Zaire, Sudan, Liberia and Sierra Leone, and to say no, to say that tribal divisions, colonial boundaries and ancient hatreds are so inexorable that a decline into violence and anarchy is inevitable. It is tempting to look at Ethiopia, Burkina Faso, Niger and Chad and say that much of the continent is so naturally poor and overpopulated that it will never escape from mere subsistence. But it is equally tempting to look at Uganda, Ghana and Mali, and say yes, if these countries, so tortured by history and nature, can regain hope by simply allowing people to direct their own development, then so can all of Africa.

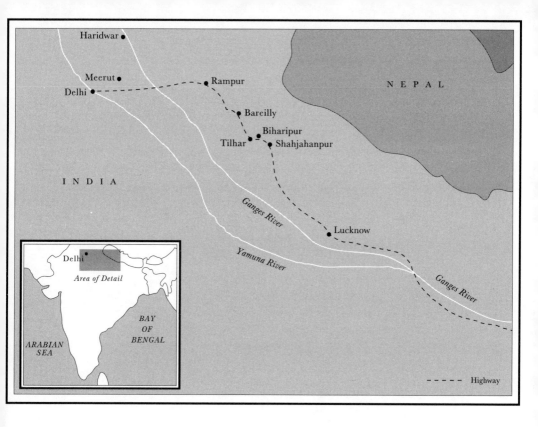

# THE VILLAGE II

"I only know my son's name," the woman said, looking at us strangely for asking. "How can I know my daughter-in-law's name? I only call her daughter-in-law."

# 10

## Where the Spirit Dwells

In the winter, we slept on charpoys in Rajinder's courtyard, bundled under thick moth-eaten quilts. Although the temperature often fell to five degrees Celsius, and one February brought with it hail that destroyed most of the wheat crop, it was the damp chill rolling off the Ramganga River, forty kilometres away, that made sleeping so difficult. The woven cots on their big wooden legs offered little comfort. Even with an extra layer of clothes on, I woke up numb every couple of hours, and often could not get back to sleep for the noise of villagers coughing. The smoke from the night fires made breathing a task, and almost everyone had some form of respiratory infection.

During the searing heat of May and June, our approach to sleeping changed considerably, when we used Rajinder's bamboo-and-rope ladder to hoist our charpoys onto the roof, in the hope of a cool breeze coming our way. But now it was July, the monsoon, hot and wet, day and night. We had to stay in the courtyard, under the awning, where sleep was never easy. If it wasn't a deluge, it was the mosquitoes, and DEET spray only rolled off with a midnight sweat. Cindy and I tried hanging chemical-laced mosquito nets from the awning's underside, only to discover that the loosely strung charpoys were nothing but beds of holes, offering clear flight paths for any hungry insect. We often wrapped ourselves in the nets but that was not foolproof either. I usually threw mine off in the night's heat and accepted the mosquitoes as they came. When the biting got to be too much, I would slip socks over my hands, drape a bandana over my face and lie silently in my sweat until dawn.

On our first night back in Biharipur the mosquitoes were so fierce I could not sleep, even with a net around me. Cindy wisely bedded down on a wooden table with no holes for mosquitoes to pass through, and fell into a deep sleep. I dozed fitfully until sunrise, when Rajinder's boys were upon us, sweeping the courtyard and organizing chairs. It was the lambardar's turn to host his clairvoyant, and before we could gather up our mosquito nets, he too was upon us, combing his hair with coconut oil as he walked. Coming to a halt, Rajinder emitted a loud and deep burp and offered us tea. He had more Ayurvedic herbs from Haridwar on the Ganges—the perfect remedy, he said, for back pain from the night.

No sooner was the tea ready than the guests started to arrive. Two men entered the courtyard on bicycles, and took their seats on my charpoy. They were followed by an old man, who shuffled with a cane and smoked a pipe, and a few more farmers, all in buoyant spirits after a good night's rain for their crops. Then came the clairvoyant. Short and balding, with a slight paunch, he looked more like a low-level clerk than a high-minded mystic, but who was I to judge? The man was welcomed with obsequious greetings. Even Rajinder touched his feet and presented him with a glass of warm milk taken that hour from a buffalo.

Under the guidance of their guru, these men met like this irregularly to discuss matters of faith and mind. Today they wanted to question whether modern science had built an insurmountable wall between their spirits and those of their ancestors. But before they could start, one of the men on bicycles, an electrical engineer from Tilhar, said he had to chant a mantra to the sun god Surya. The other cyclist smiled at us sympathetically. "If you are fond of your pen," he said, "you keep it close to you. If it is close to you, you will never understand it." I would have to give up my pen to understand it, he explained, as we would with all our worldly possessions. I jotted down his comments.

While the clairvoyant sat silently in cross-legged meditation on Cindy's table-bed, the old man with the pipe kicked off the discussion by postulating that all fundamental problems are eternal and inherited, and while they could be delayed by science, they could never be resolved.

"That's not true," said Radhey Shyam, a young farmer who was one of the few men in Biharipur other than Rajinder to go to college. "My grandfather had different problems than mine. I must find my own truth."

The engineer said medicine had solved many problems faced by our ancestors, and allowed us to better understand life.

"People are too caught up in medicines," Rajinder replied. This was an odd comment, since he pushed medicines on just about everyone in the village. "It's like they want to climb a tree and use a ladder," he explained. "Me, I would just start climbing. If I want to know you, can I go through someone else? I must know you directly."

I didn't get a chance to ask Rajinder what he meant by this remarkable renunciation of his amateur doctor routine because the clairvoyant suddenly opened his eyes and said that the outsiders would have to leave. He meant us. We hadn't even sipped our Ayurvedic tea, but the mystic was firm. Some strangers, he said, were blocking his path to the spirit world.

Slightly ashamed, we left the courtyard for a walk around the village as a crimson sun rose over the rain-drenched fields, a spectacular splash of green that looked like a Monet—except for three boys squatting before a cow pond, latecomers to the morning rituals. Latrines, awkward, dirty and expensive devices, were unpopular in much of rural India, and Biharipur was no exception. We continued strolling the village perimeter, past the hut of Ganganath, a great big bearded mystic who lived in isolation; past the compound of a mentally ill man who lay on a charpoy all day alternately giggling and moaning; and past the small hut of Manna, the Muslim woman who had recently given birth to her tenth child.

For Manna, ten children in twenty years had taken their toll. She was in her mid-thirties but looked fifty. "An empty cage" was how Bhagwati, the village midwife, described her. Manna's newest boy, born two months premature, weighed only a few pounds. Too weak to breast-feed, he was surviving on cow's milk. He looked in desperate need of an incubator. He was so frail that he could barely cry, and Manna did not know what to do about his persistent diarrhea and gas. She had not taken the baby to a doctor because she had not taken any of her children to a doctor, not even for basic immunization shots. How she hated to give the little ones needles, Manna said, because that made them cry more. She prayed, but in the end their health and their lives would be God's wish, as it had been for four children who died in infancy and a fifth who was crippled by polio.

We left the Muslim house and followed the path to Jair Devi's, a young mother who was perched in front of a smouldering fire of rice stalks, poking a handful of sweet potatoes she had laid in the embers to cook for breakfast. Her five children sat silently watching. We squatted next to them and listened to their mother explain the horrors of the monsoon now passing. The rains that had made the crops so rich were flooding the village and filling the water table with things Jair Devi could not explain. Disease was now rampant, and it seemed no household would be spared. Those fortunate to have a bit of cash stored in their thatched roofs had spent most of it on medicines. Jair Devi had nothing for new clothes, not even for her eldest daughter, Sri Devi, who had just turned eleven and would soon be eligible for marriage. No one would want a girl like this, dressed in an old sari, as Sri Devi was, but what could her mother do?

Other women, who watched us from their doorways, ventured out to the lane to tell of similar suffering. One of them, Veeta, only eighteen, had lost her four-month-old daughter a few weeks earlier, before she had named the child. "There was no sign of illness," Veeta said, trying to explain something that seemed as incomprehensible to her as the hailstorm that had ruined their crop. "One evening she started to cry. She cried uncontrollably. In the middle of the night, she stopped crying. She was dead in the moonlight."

"Some spirit came to take her away," said Champa, Veeta's mother-in-law, who lived next door to Dalchand and controlled all affairs in the household, including the teenaged girl's life. "What else could it be? It happens all the time."

She referred to it as *buri hawa*, literally "bad air" but meaning a dangerous spirit.

"*Buri hawa lag gaya*," Champa said. "Bad air got to her."

Across the lane, a little boy came out of his house, dropped his shorts and defecated on the path. No one objected. The muddy lane was littered with animal and human waste.

Champa continued to explain what had happened to her grand-daughter. There was no question of taking the baby to a doctor that night. The family had already cut down their only tree, a towering sissoo, to pay off the equivalent of eighty dollars in debts. There was no money for medicines, which the villagers had little faith in any-way. Down the lane, Jagdish Singh's baby daughter had died vomit-ing after they went to a private hospital in Tilhar and spent nearly forty dollars on medicines. The drugs kept the baby stable for just two weeks, and then she was dead.

Since no one kept a record of births in the village, there was no way of knowing how many children had died that summer. We count-ed ten. Someone said thirty buffalo had also fallen to the rains and disease. The dead buffalo were sold to tanners. The children were buried at night in the ditch next to the culvert, opposite the cow pond, by fathers and uncles and brothers. Their mothers stayed home to mourn alone.

After Champa's account of her granddaughter's death, a passage really, I stood silently for a moment, stunned by it all, until Bhagwati, the chubby little midwife, chided me for my emotions. She had joined the other women in the lane, listening to their tales of endurance and suffering. A baby's death was God's wish, she said, and one that we should not question. She gave us an example. Her last delivery, six weeks ago, was a breech birth. In the middle of the night, she took the mother by bullock cart to the nearest hospital, down the dirt road to the national highway and on to Tilhar. "Everything but the head came out," she said. By the time they reached a doctor, the baby was dead. Bhagwati was not aware the woman had lost a child during delivery a year earlier, an indication she might face complications again. But that would not matter, the midwife said, because "God had wanted the baby to be abnormal."

Bhagwati was the closest Biharipur had to a trained midwife, having learned her trade from her mother and her own six successful births—five of them boys, she pointed out. "There is not much difference from one birth to the next," she went on. The average labour lasts about four or five hours, during which she massages the belly with mustard oil. A mother-in-law is almost always present to push on the womb. Once the baby is born, Bhagwati explained, she cuts the umbilical cord with a razor that has been dipped in boiling water and washes the child with well water. The baby is then placed in the mother-in-law's arms and given a spoonful of honey with water, while Bhagwati serves the new mother tea. Her payment for delivering a girl is never more than a bunch of wheat and some rupees, maybe five or ten, equivalent to a quarter. "If it's a boy," Bhagwati said, beaming, "some people give me a new sari."

When we asked Bhagwati to introduce us to the woman she had taken by bullock cart to Tilhar, she led us to the house of a man, Mahinder Singh. She could not remember the young mother's name. The mother-in-law, who sat at the front door, could not remember the girl's name either.

"I only know my son's name," she said, looking at us strangely for asking. "How can I know my daughter-in-law's name? I only call her daughter-in-law."

She paused to think again. "Maybe my son knows."

"Mahinder!" she shouted through the door. "What is your wife's name?"

"I don't know." Mahinder stepped through the doorway and greeted us with quickly folded hands. "I only call her woman."

Woman was not home, and neither Mahinder nor his mother knew where she was. I turned around to ask Bhagwati more about birthing techniques in the village, but she had lost interest. She was more concerned about a rip in Cindy's Gap jeans. The midwife couldn't stop looking at it. "You are a rich man," Bhagwati said to me. "You should dress your wife in finer garments."

We returned to Rajinder's house an hour later to find the clairvoyant gone and the group disbanded. As it was yet another school holiday, the lambardar was now free for the day. He suggested we follow him on his rounds as village doctor.

"I thought you did not believe in medicine!" I reminded him.

"These people are not spiritual," Rajinder said of his neighbours. "They need medicines."

He sent his Number Two Son, Chandra Prakash, into the house to fetch a little black bag of basic drugs and needles he had purchased in Shahjahanpur. At least it made him look professional.

As we headed down the lane, our first stop was at the newly painted home of Rameshawar Dayal, a former railway man who had retired to his family's land in Biharipur. Rameshawar, who looked as if he had spent his career eating deep-fried samosas on railway platforms, was sitting in front of his house, complaining of stomach pains. Rajinder told the chubby pensioner to roll up his left sleeve for a shot of oxytetracycline, a common antibiotic, which he administered in a few seconds. Rajinder put the needle back in his bag. "Drink these herbal medicines with tea," he said, handing the man a small packet. "They are from Haridwar."

Rameshawar wanted to tell us about his other troubles, about how he had to pay a thousand-rupee bribe to get his nineteen hundred-rupee monthly pension, and how his former boss had asked him for twenty thousand rupees to hire his son for a measly two-thousand-rupee-a-month job. But Rajinder pleaded with his pot-bellied patient to rest. He collected twelve rupees—ten for the medicines, two for the house call—and pushed on.

We turned down another alleyway, past a blind man who spent most of his days sitting there, on a log. At the next house, a man complained of worms. Rajinder gave him some anti-worm tablets. Farther down the lane a little girl had a fever. Rajinder told her to roll up her left sleeve for a shot of oxytetracycline, and gave her mother a handful of anti-malarial chloroquine tablets along with some vitamin B capsules and a lemon drink powder with wheat complex for strength—all for seven rupees. Rajinder washed the needle at the family's hand pump and left.

I asked him if he felt qualified to make such diagnoses.

"There are only two things you need to know to stay healthy," Rajinder told us. "Test your nostrils by blowing. If the right one is not clear, you need heat. You should eat food, take a bath and have intercourse. If your left one is not clear, you need to cool down. You need water."

I hated to ask what to do if both nostrils were clogged, and laughed off his remark. (A few years later, *The New York Times* quoted a medical study that found people who had sex once or twice a week tended to develop stronger immune systems than those who abstained.)

We had been making house calls for less than an hour when Rajinder announced he had other business to tend to. He gave his black bag to Chandra Prakash and pointed out three more people who needed shots. It was nothing the thirteen-year-old had not done before—he was so efficient and courteous that we had started to call him the DM, for district magistrate, the most powerful bureaucrat in the countryside. He liked the nickname.

We followed the DM to Lata Ram's house, where he listened to the elderly woman complain about how unwell she'd been ever since she bathed in the holy, and befouled, Ganges River a month earlier. She had been to a doctor in Tilhar and took the medicines he prescribed, but still she was dizzy and in pain with headaches. After she'd spent fifty-two rupees on pills and an injection, only a pink cream that she had bought in the Tilhar bazaar offered any relief. The DM's needle would not help, she said. "It must be a spirit."

When a spirit takes hold of one's body and mind, there is only one place in Biharipur, indeed in all of Tilhar county, to go: Natu Lal, the last surviving witch doctor in the area. He lived on the far side of the village, in a mud house with a courtyard that, unlike most of the village's enclosed compounds, opened on to a pathway.

We found Natu Lal sitting on a charpoy under the graceful neem tree that adorned his yard. Though he appeared unoccupied, the witch doctor told us to go away and come back after sundown. During the day, he explained, he was an ordinary farmer. It was only at night that he tilled the fallow fields of the spirit. I needed a nap anyway. After a long night of sweat, rain and mosquitoes, there was no other way to survive the monsoon.

In the evening, when torpid air hung over the village like a wet sheet, a candle flickered gently in front of Natu Lal sitting cross-legged on his charpoy. We asked him to explain his vanishing craft of *jhad phus*, the act of dealing with spirits by blowing and waving his hands. He learned the trade thirty-five years earlier from a guru, long since dead, in a village far from Biharipur. Natu Lal was not sure how he found the guru, except to say "I found him the same way you found me. When a man is thirsty, he will find the tap." The guru taught the young farmer to conduct his mystical travels only by candlelight, to put his faith in the monkey-god Hanuman, conqueror of evil, and never to chant mantras at noon or midnight, when the gods are resting. Everything else was easy. Hanuman, when offered the right sweets, could chase away almost any evil spirit. Dirt, properly smeared on the forehead, did wonders for dizziness. But there were some people Natu Lal claimed he could not cure—"a lunatic or a non-vegetarian," for example. "If a man eats eggs," he cautioned us, "there is nothing that can help him."

Being the only faith healer on the horizon, Natu Lal saw no end to the steady flow of evil spirits and patients. A year earlier, Kashi Ram, a young farmer, had come to him complaining of frequent dizzy spells. "I went to lots of doctors, but nothing worked," the young man said when Natu Lal sent for him to give us a testimonial. "I figured there must be a spirit inside me." Natu Lal sprinkled water in front of Kashi Ram and chanted mantras in his ear to drive out the spirit. The young man had felt fine ever since.

But slowly, Natu Lal sensed, the other villagers were losing their faith. It did not help when Rajinder took up the medicine bag and started to refer to evil spirits as headaches and feverish ghosts as malaria. India's bicycle boom also enabled villagers to get to the nearest government health centre, a couple of kilometres away, and to ride to Tilhar for medicines. But the biggest blow was to come from his own sons. They refused to learn their father's trade. They refused to share his faith.

"Young people have no faith these days," Natu Lal warned us, sensing that we, too, did not share his conviction.

We had to excuse ourselves. It felt like rain, and we were already late for dinner. We had bought tomatoes on the highway, and Rajinder's wife, whom we rarely saw, had cooked them in a curry with potatoes from their fields, to be served with steaming fresh rotis from her fire.

After dinner, with the prospect of another monsoon night of rain and mosquitoes ahead, we covered our exposed skin with insect repellent and climbed under the nets. I pulled out an extra pair of socks, put them on my hands and fell into a deep sleep. A couple of hours later, just after midnight, a crack of thunder awoke me. The courtyard was dry but the air felt wet. I was dripping in sweat, and chilled to the bone. My hand trembled as I lifted my wrist to look at my watch; I could not control the shaking. Shuffling across the courtyard to the gate, I threw up everything I had eaten for two days. The trembling increased, and I felt colder, and then suddenly a flash of heat. I pulled my charpoy into the open air, and went back to sleep, shaking, only to be woken again by pouring rain. After I dragged the cot back to the shelter, I slept till dawn, with my right hand, stripped of its sock, dangling outside the mosquito net to stay cool. When I woke up, my hand was red with bites, but the fever was gone.

I went to a doctor back in New Delhi, and then another. There was nothing wrong with me, they said. It was as if, for a few wretched hours, I had been possessed by an evil spirit.

MANNA, WITH HER OLDEST AND YOUNGEST CHILDREN

# II

# Third Child, Never

By the mid-nineties, everyone in New Delhi was talking about the
great tiger awakening. The Indian economy, shackled by decades of
bureaucratic controls, had been unleashed by the Congress Party government, which itself had undergone a remarkable transformation in
its ideology from Fabian socialism to muted capitalism. So many foreign companies were coming to New Delhi and Bombay to find investment deals that you couldn't get a good hotel room for under $250
a night. They talked of India being the next China, and more. The

educated classes spoke English. A British system of law and parliamentary democracy were firmly established. Most important of all, the economic gurus said, there was that great middle class. When we moved to India in 1992, the government estimated it at fifty million people. Three years later, some of the world's biggest companies said, no, the Indian middle class, meaning anyone who could afford a television, was closer to three hundred million. The hype was so great that the world's biggest telephone companies collectively bid twenty-five billion dollars for new licences, convinced that one-third of India, including many people in villages like Biharipur, would pay market rates for new phones if they were made available.

As we set off again for a weekend in the village, signs of the business boom were everywhere, with new industrial estates and colonies of apartment blocks surging into the tranquility of rural India. Along National Highway 24, the old farming villages and their art deco mansions were painted with so many Pepsi signs that they seemed to be sponsored by the soft-drink giant. Even the highway, the commercial lifeline of northern India, was overrun with economic growth, and the government could no longer keep pace. So many trucks and buses now plied the single-strip road—and plied it with abandon—that our 330-kilometre journey to Biharipur took eight hours instead of five. On this, my fifth trip to the village with Cindy and Rama, I counted twenty accidents, including three trucks that had careered into the ditch and two buses that collided head-on. Next to the bus accident, at least two dozen bodies were laid on the gravel shoulder, shrouded with blankets provided by local farmers. Other delays and roadblocks were caused by trucks, driven well beyond their prime, that lost axles or wheels and were abandoned in the middle of the road. In a few more places, trucks overloaded with huge bales of goods had toppled over, spewing bricks, sand, cotton and, in one place, women's shoes along the road. In each case, the driver marked his wreckage with tree branches and waited for help, while the rest of us forged a bypass through a gutter or field.

Much of India's trouble lay with its administration, which was wholly incapable of managing the sort of growth brought on by private investment and the endless public disputes it unleashed. Public commissions held hearings and wrote reports about the need for more and bigger highways, and the obvious solution of toll roads, but little action resulted. The same was true of the many towns along our route, former trading posts that had become cities of five hundred thousand or more people, with no planning. A national highway simply became the town's main street and livestock bazaar, and then a highway again. In Bereilly, one of these new urban confusions, the only way to avoid a one-hour crawl through the mad gridlock of livestock and vehicles was to wave our press cards and zip through the local military base, home to the Indian army's animal division. And for five minutes we were out of India, on a lovely tree-lined lane that passed scores of black stallions that lived in spacious stables and got to romp across fields that looked more like Kentucky than Uttar Pradesh.

The resonance of India's economic boom dissipated with each passing kilometre. The capital gave way to smaller towns, and then open rice fields, tea shops and the first signs of mud-walled villages, where the resurgence was merely folklore. For most farmers, the grim reality was that while they were undoubtedly better off than they had been in the eighties, they remained very poor. Theirs was the class that numbered in the hundreds of millions, a class still more beholden to the whims of the state than the frenzy of a market.

The disparity between India's urban industrial growth and its rural stagnation was nowhere more evident than at the Tilhar sugar mill, where a great stretch of ox carts was parked as farmers waited their turn to sell cane. After we got to Biharipur and asked Rajinder about the lineup at the local mill, he told us more about the woes of a sugar cane farmer in the midst of a sugar boom. After every harvest, he had to wait up to three days at the mill to sell his crop, forcing him or a son to sleep in the cart at night to protect both the load and the family's place in queue. A government fiat required farmers like Rajinder to sell 40 percent of their cane to state-owned mills like the one in Tilhar at below-market prices before they could sell any to the new private mills sprouting up across the countryside. And this was only for credit. Like something out of the Soviet Union before its final collapse, the Tilhar mill, which employed seven hundred people, had run out of money. So had most of India's public sector.

After hearing Rajinder's lament, we decided to visit the mill the next day. Just off the highway before Tilhar, we drove by the line of bullock carts and honked at the gate, which swung open immediately.

Maybe a car horn, I thought, was what Rajinder needed for his cart. Once inside, we did what we always did at factories or offices: we told the security guard we had a very important appointment with the very important manager, and handed him our business cards. The guard looked at my card upside-down, nodded appreciatively and led us to the office, past a row of broken windows and a cavern of machinery that verged on the antique.

In the office, we were told that the manager was "on leave" but the chief engineer, J.P. Raungta, would be delighted to receive us— as long as we were not irate farmers. We assured Mr. Raungta we were not. I said I was only curious as to why the government had not raised prices to match the thriving private market.

"Why should we change?" the chief engineer asked. "We are having certain procedures. Those private mills are opportunists."

Our conversation did not go much further, since the engineer had no idea why a factory with a guaranteed supply and guaranteed rate of profit could lose so much money.

The Tilhar mill eventually closed, in 1997, when most of the state-owned mills shut their doors. It owed fifteen million rupees to local farmers, including fifty-five thousand rupees (about eighteen hundred dollars at the time) to Rajinder. Such bankruptcies should have tamed the scorn that India's public servants held for the farming population, but they didn't. Of the twenty million people employed by the Indian government and its many agencies, only a few even knew about Biharipur, let alone cared about its struggles. The sole government worker I ever saw in the village was Sushma Singh, the local barefoot nurse. And that was because we brought her there.

Biharipur was one of five villages that Sushma was supposed to visit every month. With three thousand people in her care, she was responsible for vaccinating children and pregnant women, monitoring the weight of infants, and chatting with every fecund woman in her territory. The trouble was no one in the village knew her name. Some called her the ANM, for auxiliary nurse-midwife, her official title. Most referred to her as "the woman with the needle." Everyone said they had not seen her in four months.

After leaving the sugar mill, we went to find Sushma at the government hospital in Tilhar, where the local administrative block's twenty-four ANMs congregated every day, and tried to persuade her to take us on her next village tour. She agreed, but when we suggested she come that day, she hesitated, and then reluctantly accepted the invitation, admitting she had not been to Biharipur in "some time." She seemed more excited to get a ride with us to the railway tracks. Usually she had to take a horse cart and then walk alone across the fields.

As we drove down the highway and then toward the tracks, Sushma described the ANM system. It was created to reach mothers and children in villages where many women are too intimidated or busy to leave their homes to go to a public health centre, or are forbidden to do so by their husbands. In each of her five villages, Sushma was responsible for early childhood vaccinations, monitoring pregnancies, advising new mothers and coaching traditional midwives like Bhagwati. Every Monday and Tuesday were designated for paperwork, training and "free time." On Wednesday, the ANMs had to attend a weekly prenatal clinic in Tilhar. Thursday, they visited child-feeding centres. Friday, they were supposed to visit one of their five villages, but preferably two. On Saturday, all the ANMs in Tilhar met to discuss their week. In return, Sushma received a decent wage of 1,924 rupees a month (about seventy dollars). "The ANM system is perfect," she said as we parked under a big tree by the railway tracks and started to walk.

Perfect, that is, but for the people. Back in Tilhar, the doctors, all of them men, treated Sushma like a peon whose field intelligence was as valuable to them as an expired medicine. Out here in the countryside, men taunted her as she walked from village to village, while few women listened to her once she got there. In northern India, someone from a lower caste, a lower profession or a lower place, even if they carry a medical kit, is rarely welcome. Sushma made me think of Rajinder's low-caste predecessors at the Sonora school who were beaten up by the Thakur villagers.

After twenty minutes of walking, she stopped at an irrigation channel and put down the white cooler that she carried on her field trips. She had to adjust her sari, a garment not designed for long hikes. She also wanted to warn us not to veer off the path. The remaining uncut cane was now a couple of metres in height, an ideal shelter for snakes, and she had nothing in her cooler for snakebites.

In the cooler, Sushma carried measles and mumps vaccines for infants, tetanus vaccines for pregnant women and rehydration salts for children with severe diarrhea. It was a reasonable and well-planned arsenal with which to combat the most common killers of children. But there was never time to properly examine a child or prescribe a treatment. Over the years, Sushma was also given more responsibilities by a health ministry that had no one else going to the front line. They gave her chloroquine tablets and asked her to look out for malaria. They gave her birth control pills and asked her to give them to young couples. She was even expected to teach villagers about tuberculosis and AIDS, and distribute condoms (to the same people who would not listen to her warnings about measles).

I asked Sushma if she knew what AIDS was.

"It's a disease you get from sex," she said. "It kills people."

She did not know what to do with all the condoms in her bag, though. No one in the village wanted condoms, not when they were seen as unmanly and certainly not when the government-made Nirodh brand had the texture of a radial tire. Even if she had lubricated brands, I had to wonder how her patients would ever dispose of a used condom in a mud hut inhabited by ten others.

Before we reached Biharipur, Sushma stopped at a small hut under a large tamarind tree. A man sat on a rock by the hut, holding a young child and tormenting his pet monkey, chained to the tree, with a stick. When Sushma asked to see the child, the man called inside the hut for his young wife, Champa.

"Where is your card?" Sushma asked the woman when she emerged, referring to the pink vaccination record.

Champa blushed. "I lost it," she said, taking the child, her eighth, from her husband. She hesitated for a moment and stared at the dirt. "It flew away in the wind."

"How did you do such a thing?" Sushma snapped.

"Oh, it was a very stormy night," Champa said.

Sushma sighed and told the woman to get the baby ready for a needle. She would have to start the vaccination process from scratch, with a new record book.

The baby was still screaming from the injection when we left the shaded compound and walked down the path toward Biharipur where Sushma intended to hold an impromptu clinic. At the village entrance, she asked a few idle children to tell their mothers that the government nurse was here and ready to set up camp. We continued walking to a spot near Rajinder's house, where I noticed a new Hindi slogan painted on the wall: "First child, not now. Second child, in a while. Third child, never." Here, Sushma declared. This was where she would hold the travelling clinic.

The first woman to come was Dhan Devi, a young Dalit mother, with her fourth child, a small boy who had not yet been named because the family could not afford to hire a Brahmin priest for the ceremony. When Sushma asked for the pink vaccination card, Dhan looked perplexed. She, too, did not have a card.

"You've lost your card. What can I do?" Sushma scolded the Dalit mother who is married to one of Amma's grandsons.

"I thought you were supposed to keep records," Dhan replied testily.

She had the ANM on that one. Sushma had no record of her previous visits, certainly not records that would show she had missed the last four months or that no child in Biharipur had been vaccinated against measles.

Sushma prepared the tiny baby for an injection, which made him scream wildly until Dhan could sit down on the dirt and comfort him with her breast. Now that Dhan had four children, Sushma wondered if she planned to use birth control pills, or perhaps consider an intrauterine device or even sterilization. Dhan balked at the suggestion. Since puberty, she had given birth every two years, and only one baby had died. It was, if nothing else, a great display of her worth to her husband's family.

"If I have more children, I don't mind," she said indifferently. "My body tells me it's not good but . . ." Her voice trailed off. She wanted to say something to Sushma but others were listening. Dhan picked up her baby and left.

"All your man does is eat and have children," said a woman in the lineup of mothers and little children that had formed down the lane.

"He's good at that," another said, laughing at Dhan.

We followed Dhan as she walked away from the makeshift clinic, holding her unnamed son. She said she would talk to her husband about birth control pills, although she had her own concerns. Her husband's uncle, Shankar Lal, and aunt, Ram Sri, had tried these pills, after nine children, with miserable results. A doctor in Tilhar had prescribed them a year's supply of birth control pills—twenty-one white ones to be followed by seven red ones every month. Every day both husband and wife took the pills, until the year's supply ran out after six months.

When I later asked Shankar Lal about the mix-up, he still looked confused. "The doctor said they were for both of us," he muttered. "I started to take them every night with warm milk."

We returned to Sushma, who had concluded her clinic in less than an hour. She had made no house calls or moved beyond her perch to find more women and children, but now she was eager to get home to feed lunch to her two daughters and her son.

"The biggest problem in this village is these women," she said as we started to walk back with her to the railway tracks. "They have too many children."

We returned to Tilhar hospital at the end of the town's only road, past a confusion of shops, trading centres and paan stalls, where it hid behind a clump of ancient banyan trees that looked as old as the Mogul empire that once ruled here. The maternal-and-child health clinic inside the hospital was the nerve centre of women's health care for the county, and it was empty. We looked at the posters of umbilical cords being cut and smiling children being vaccinated, and beyond the posters at charts showing Tilhar's public health data. The numbers were written as they would be on a baseball scoreboard, and the home team was not doing well. Tilhar's infant mortality rate was 116 for every 1,000 live births, which meant more than one in ten babies died before the age of one, more than in the Central African Republic. The crude birth rate was not much healthier at 404 children born for every 10,000 people living, a rate on par with Nigeria's. With no school or health clinic, Biharipur could expect twenty-eight new children every year. Amazingly, given all we had seen that morning, the administrative block's measles vaccination rate was 98.5 percent. The missing 1.5 percent must all be in Biharipur, I thought.

A ward boy finally appeared in the empty hall to inform us the clinic was open only for a couple of hours every morning. He suggested we find S.K. Jain, Tilhar's public health officer, at his private clinic back on the town's chaotic main street.

With the ANMs as his field intelligence, Dr. Jain was in charge of keeping ten thousand mothers and their children alive and healthy. His walk-in clinic, which he euphemistically called a medical centre, was a different proposition, seeing as it was little bigger than a walk-in closet. When we tried to enter, a few mothers had to step outside to make room for us in the reception area. A medical assistant told the other women, all carrying emaciated babies, to clear a bigger path, and then whisked us straight into the doctor's office.

The country physician was so thrilled to have visitors from New Delhi, where he had studied, that he told the assistant to hold all calls and inform the crowd of women and babies outside that they would have to wait.

"Tea or coffee?" Dr. Jain asked us enthusiastically.

"No, really, thank you," I said. "I've had six cups today."

"So what?" he replied, pressing a buzzer under his desk to bring the assistant back so he could order a tray of tea.

I asked Dr. Jain why so many women came to his private clinic when there was a free public clinic every morning at his hospital, the one with the big airy waiting room. "This is more convenient for them," he said.

I was also curious about a sign in the hospital indicating the office of a "smallpox supervisor." Wasn't smallpox eradicated in the seventies? "Yes, you're right," he said, laughing. "We're waiting for instructions to change the name. But the officer does have other duties. Many other duties. Measles, for example."

Ah, measles. Was it really true that 98.5 percent of Tilhar's children were vaccinated against the disease?

"No, of course not," Dr. Jain said as bluntly as he had insisted we have tea. "We just give that number to the state government. We have our targets to meet. They have their targets. It keeps them happy."

The tea arrived with a plate of salted biscuits. I asked if this were true of most public health issues in rural Uttar Pradesh: that what the government and international aid donors reported was far different from what was happening on the ground.

"Yes. Absolutely," Dr. Jain replied, and for the next half hour he proceeded to tell us about the sick state of Tilhar and its public health service.

The hospital had not received vitamin A capsules in two years, despite a Canadian-funded program to flood the region with vitamin A supplements to prevent childhood blindness. There had been no iodine supplements for pregnant women, either. Only a shipment of iron and folic acid tablets had arrived. Without sufficient outside supplies, Dr. Jain had to buy what he could with the hospital's annual discretionary budget of about one thousand dollars, which worked out to two cents per person in the county.

It wasn't just the sugar mills that were in ruin. The entire district of Shahjahanpur, with two million people, had only one government doctor for every nineteen thousand people and one nurse for every sixty thousand, and their wages came irregularly. The public hospitals were short-staffed by fifty-nine doctors, about one-third of their sanctioned number. More nurses were supposed to be hired but there was a fight over how many jobs should be allocated to each of the major castes. The Uttar Pradesh government was broke anyway, and couldn't afford more salaries. Its medical budget for Shahjahanpur, a district with the same population as Toronto, was just fifty thousand dollars a year.

With no spare cash, the Tilhar officials had turned to local volunteers and community leaders for assistance. Biharipur's one elected official, Abhivaran Singh Yadav (Rajinder's brother-in-law), was provided with oral rehydration salts to give to mothers, and chlorine tablets to put in the village wells. Prem Pal Singh, a college student from the village, was also recruited as a "health motivator" and paid fifty rupees a month to tell people about basic ideas of hygiene and disease control. Dr. Jain doubted the materials or information ever got distributed to those in need. I had never seen chlorine used in Biharipur's wells, and Manna, the "empty cage" who had lost so many children, obviously had no access to rehydration salts for her emaciated boy.

This mattered little outside the village because India's health system did not focus on access or results. The emphasis was on targets—for vaccinations, tubectomies and condom distributions. Dr. Jain, for example, was required by the state to sterilize twelve men and women a year, and he was paid a ten-rupee incentive bonus for each one. Across much of the developing world, this new approach to health care was known as "targetitis," a campaign, largely started by Unicef in the eighties, to turn development into an exercise in management by objectives. Development became a race to get X children vaccinated, Y women sterilized and Z villages fitted with water pumps. The process of changing a community and a society, and of building accountable and stable institutions to serve people, was neglected. In Tilhar, it was completely ignored.

"I admit there is a problem," Dr. Jain said. "We are both at fault. The women don't come out because they are afraid or they are illiterate. Our staff is not always punctual, too."

Tilhar's health information officer, R.K. Saxena, dropped by, necessitating another round of tea. He had his own troubles to share, and for the next twenty minutes the two men went on, unprompted and uninterrupted, seemingly oblivious of each other. They spoke of the villagers—"poor," "sick," "illiterate"—as one might hear men at a Canadian curling club speak of the homeless.

"I go to villages with all the materials and say, 'Here it is, on your doorstep, free.' And they still don't understand," Mr. Saxena said breathlessly. "They agree with us, and the next day forget about it."

"I don't know what kind of country this is," Dr. Jain said. "I've been doing this for twenty-five years and have no idea what's wrong with them."

"We're not changing the attitude of the public," Mr. Saxena added. "We're just buying them. We give ten rupees to a leprosy patient to take MDT [multi-drug therapy], and they throw away the medicines."

"When I go to villages, they have no respect for me," Dr. Jain continued. "When they come here, they line up for hours like animals just to come into my office. They come here and listen to me. They don't respect these 'on-the-foot' doctors."

Here was rural India: health workers who had no incentive to work in villages; villagers who had blind faith in city doctors; city doctors who did not respect patients; patients who were beyond the reach of the public health service. The public health system wasn't sick. It was dead. And in its place rose Rajinder's black bag and Dr. Jain's private "medical centre."

We thanked the doctor for the tea, and left through his reception area, crowded with village women waiting patiently to weigh and vaccinate their babies at full price. We wanted to get back to Biharipur before dark. I also wanted to find Manna, the frail mother, and her frailer newborn son. We had not seen them that day at the ANM's clinic.

Manna was standing in front of her house, under a small clump of eucalyptus trees that had sucked the soil dry but provided some shade and a good place to tie up the family's goats. She was negotiating with a vegetable wallah who carried sacks of eggplant, jamfruit, brinjal and tomatoes on the back of his bicycle, though she did not have enough money to buy food for dinner. She gave the trader a handful of wheat instead of cash for a dozen small tomatoes and returned to her hut. She asked us to follow.

The three of us—Cindy, Rama and I—sat on one charpoy next to the family's water pump, while Manna and her eldest daughter, Shakila, sat opposite us on another. A few weeks earlier, the mother said solemnly, her baby had suffered an especially bad bout of diarrhea. He died in the middle of the night, with barely a cry. A week later, her youngest daughter, Meskina, also fell ill with diarrhea and fever. Both Rajinder and Prem Pal gave the girl injections. When they failed to help, Manna's husband took the girl to Tilhar and paid a private physician fifty rupees for another injection and some pills. They did not have enough money for more treatment, and they never found out what ailed little Meskina. She died a few days later, at age four.

From ten births, Manna was down to five living children, but her main concern now was Shakila, who was to be wedded in a week's time, just before she turned sixteen. Manna felt she had taught Shakila well. The girl could make rotis, sew clothes and haul water on her head. She could sweep the house and make mounds of cow dung patties for fuel. All that was left to test was Shakila's fertility, and over that a mother had no control.

Once we had said our condolences to Manna, Shakila followed us out the door. She stopped by the eucalyptus trees and stood quietly for a moment. We had always marvelled at the young girl's lively spirit, the way she bossed around other children and spoke boldly to us each time we walked past her hut. But now she seemed timid and sad. She was upset at not being able to finish school. She also worried about her new husband and his family, whom she had not seen before. She would like to have a small family. She certainly did not want to bear children anytime soon. But those decisions would not be hers. A new family would decide when she could stop having children, when she could rest and when she could eat. That was the way of womanhood.

"Whatever my husband's family wants," Shakila said, before saying goodbye to us for the last time, "I will do."

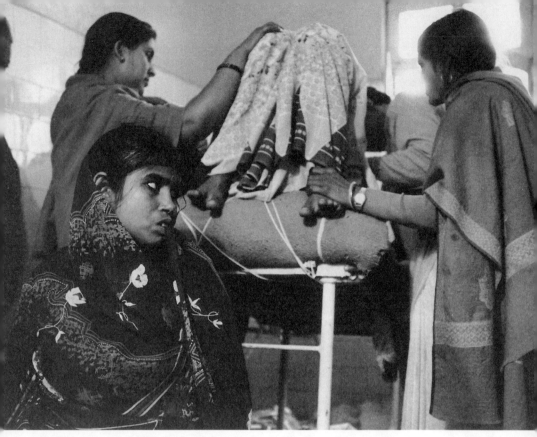

A FEMALE STERILIZATION CAMP IN JAUNPUR DISTRICT

# 12

## "Slight pain is inevitable"

On paper, a young woman like Shakila faced no shortage of family planning options. The Indian government produced those coarse Nirodh condoms and cheap birth control pills, and allowed foreign aid agencies to flood the countryside with intrauterine devices. In the nineties, the government also developed the world's first birth control vaccine, although women's rights groups, fearing the drug would be used forcibly, blocked its introduction to the mass market.

Sadly for a young woman like Shakila, this was the same

government that ran its sugar mills into the ground. One district in Biharipur's state needed fifty thousand IUDs a year, but received only fifteen thousand from the health ministry. When officials in the same district of Jaunpur requested 3.6 million condoms, they got only 2.2 million Nirodhs. As for birth control pills, the whole district of 3.2 million people had recently gone several months without a fresh supply; then only seven thousand packets of the unfortunately named Mala-D brand arrived.

Short of refusing sex with her husband—a capital offence in some villages—a confident young woman like Shakila had little hope of controlling her family's size. Uneducated and repressed since birth, few young women had the confidence to shape their own lives, entrusting their fates instead to in-laws and the divine. "You can choose your wife," Bhagwati, the midwife, once told me. "How many children you have is up to God."

And so India's population juggernaut rolled on. Another fifty-five thousand children every day—thirty thousand of them right here on the Gangetic plains. Another twenty million people every year. Between independence in 1947 and the end of the century, India had tripled in size, from 350 million people to more than one billion, making it bigger in numbers than the entire Western world.

Since the seventies, the rate of population growth has slowed considerably, but probably not enough to prevent India from hitting 1.5 billion in the next few decades and surpassing China as the world's most populous nation. To reduce fertility rates more quickly, some family planning activists believed the central and state governments needed to focus all their efforts on getting good contraceptives to the millions of Shakilas. Others, and this included many senior people in government, believed something more drastic, something more permanent was needed. They got their way every winter. When the autumn harvest was over and the fresh cane crop safely planted, the government went to work, cutting the weeds of a nation's prolific growth with the most extraordinary tool available. It was known as the sterilization camp.

Every Saturday through the winter, the camps were held at district and county health centres across northern India, offering village women tubectomies as a "permanent solution" to their growing families. In some ways, the camps were a fair and decent option. They were said to be voluntary, and each woman was given a small cash compensation for her time and suffering after the brief operation. Because the camps were centralized and staffed with at least one surgeon, an anesthesiologist and a few nurses, the women were also in the hands of health care professionals, often for the first time.

But as with so many good ideas formulated in New Delhi, the sterilization camps were something else in practice. Besides the medical staff, each camp was assigned a battery of "motivators"—government people who spread the word and were paid ten rupees for every woman they recruited. In heavily populated districts, careers depended on a good performance in family planning, and sterilization camps were the most measurable sign of success. A promotion or transfer out of a backwater often rested on nothing other than a successful camp.

In few places were such pressures greater than in Jaunpur, a crowded farming community in eastern Uttar Pradesh, six hundred kilometres southeast of New Delhi. It was already one of the most densely populated rural areas in India, and it was growing by one hundred thousand people every year. Fittingly, it was also the birthplace of Nafiz Sadiq, head of the UN population program.

When I heard a new season of sterilization camps was planned for Jaunpur, I had to see it. Rama and I took the overnight train to Benares, the great centre of Hinduism on the Ganges, though we didn't need to leave New Delhi to see that India had reached its limits. No matter how much we offered the ticket collector, he could not find us a seat. The train was so crowded that many passengers slept on newspapers spread across cabin floors and down passageways. For a "gift" of three hundred rupees, the best the collector could offer was a couple of luggage racks, which we slept on.

The next morning, with bruised backs and aching legs, we hired a car from Benares to Jaunpur, a serene journey through a corridor of trees that seemed dream-like until, two hours later, we entered the most crowded town I had seen in India. People and bicycle carts pushed their way through the main street like the coolies back at the train platform, forcing our rented Ambassador to inch its way through the bazaar, past children's faces and livestock that brushed against the windows and disappeared. Then I realized it was them crawling past us. All traffic, such as it was, had come to a halt because up ahead a rickshaw was so overloaded with boxes that the wallah could not push its back wheel out of a pothole.

This sort of crush had made Jaunpur a frontline in the population struggle, and the all-powerful bureaucracy was told to do something about it. This year, the district collector, who serves as chief administrator, had been strongly urged to ensure that his service completed 12,265 tubectomies and vasectomies. It was only a suggestion, he assured us when we stopped at his office to get a list of camps planned for the next day. India would not assign targets to something so fundamental as a man's or woman's reproductive rights. But it was a strong suggestion nonetheless, and on these few Saturdays between harvests every available public sector employee, every doctor, veterinarian, revenue collector, teacher and irrigation engineer, would become a "motivator" with instructions to find "volunteers," who are almost always women. Official or not, the sterilization hunt was on.

The collector handed us a list of camps with directions—a sign he said of his sheer happiness to show his performance to the international media, consisting of me and Rama. Why, he would even telephone the government Circuit House, home of travelling public servants, and tell the attendant personally to vacate two rooms for us. "We have nothing to hide," said the collector, whose next promotion rested on a good camp.

The Circuit House, a quaint, shaded bungalow, was built during British times and was once a comfortable spot, perhaps many decades ago. Although buffalo carts, box wallahs and other evidence of Jaunpur's population explosion were not permitted in the leafy government quarter, the rest house could not escape time. It was crumbling, literally, as north India's tumultuous seasons quietly and gradually stripped the paint and cement from its walls, ceilings and floors. But we didn't complain. The nearest hotel was in Benares, nearly a hundred kilometres behind us.

When we reached the Circuit House, most of it was in darkness thanks to more power rationing. Mercifully, though, candles were placed along the steps, at the doorway and in the dining room, where we found a group of engineers eating reheated vegetable curry and stale roti. The men were "on tour" from the state capital, Lucknow, in search of sites for new irrigation channels. They would not have to join the next day's tubectomy hunt, but agreed it was a worthy campaign.

"These illiterate village people are having too many children," one of the engineers said, suggesting we join them for a whisky to wash down our meal. "There is not enough food for these people. They are so illiterate. They are so dirty. Look at them. India will always be a poor nation if they continue like this."

The others nodded. Another man chirped up: "Every problem in India is being a population problem."

Rama wisely retired to her room, as I sat down with the men on the guest-house terrace to drink Indian whisky in the dark. At about nine, the power came on. It was off again in twenty minutes.

"There is no hope for this country," one of the engineers said.

This was a harsh reaction to a power shortage, I thought. Here was a five-thousand-year-old civilization that had endured invasions and colonial rule and had remained largely intact. Only Egypt and China could lay similar claims. India, moreover, was progressing with big domestic industries, producing everything from advanced computer software to ships, enough agricultural production to feed the country and export some, and a hopeful young space program. Surely a few glitches in the power company operations were not enough to write off the whole nation.

The engineer explained more. "You will not find anything in the world that we Indians cannot make, but the same is true in China. Look at China!" he said. The others nodded. "Our problem is that we Indians do not work together."

I was not sure the camaraderie was any stronger in China, but the engineers had a point. Even in my few years in India, I had seen an explosion of self-interest. As the population grew and resources dwindled, people were out for themselves. When I suggested this to the engineers, one offered his own example. Once his group had selected an area for an irrigation project, they would inform relatives and friends to buy the land from farmers and flip it to the government at a higher price. I was astonished less by their cunning than by their willingness to describe it to a journalist. Maybe it was the whisky, but the men said there was nothing to hide, since everyone in the state capital knew how land purchases were handled. If this group didn't scoop up land, another explained, someone else would, probably a Member of Parliament. And as I must be knowing, he added cautiously, all MPs from Uttar Pradesh are crooks.

After breakfast, Rama and I set off for the small town of Rampur, where a camp was scheduled. Along a series of secondary highways, the roads were so straight, narrow and elegantly shaded by poplar trees that they could fit into the French countryside—except that every few minutes a maniacal truck or demonic bus hurtled through the mist, scaring us on to the gravel as it roared down the middle of a road barely wide enough for an ox cart. The sterilization camp was no harder to miss as the morning sun burned off a cool winter mist. At the side of the road before Rampur were big banners, posters. The festive mood seemed more suited to election day than a family planning exercise. After depositing fresh loads of women at the centre, dozens of enthusiastic men shook hands and patted each other on the back. Some five thousand government workers were out in force in Jaunpur, along with the big political parties and community organizations, using every official vehicle available to round up "volunteers."

Away from the cheer, we found a group of women sitting under a tree in a decidedly less gleeful mood. The women had been promised 155 rupees and a free blanket to come here today for an operation that would change their lives. What they were doing for their country was less clear. Each of the women was in her thirties and had at least five children. A few had seven or eight. The family planners had already lost on this front, but they had their "suggested" targets to meet and incentives to collect. These women would have to do.

We sat on the ground under the tree with a short, stocky woman named Gulabdai, and a group of her friends from a village twenty kilometres from here. Earlier that morning, a local revenue officer had brought the women by public bus to the Rampur centre. Their husbands and lambardars had urged most of the women to come, but one woman said she had lied to her husband, who wanted more children. She said she was off to the bazaar. Although he would be furious to learn that she was about to deny him the privilege of an even larger family, she knew how little food there was for their six children. He didn't. He always ate first.

Gulabdai, who had seven children, admitted she could not afford any more either. The older ones were already working in a small carpet factory, and there was no money to send the younger ones to school. She knew the operation would hurt, and that she would remain uncomfortable for weeks, perhaps months. It might well affect her strength in the fields and her ability to cook, clean and raise the family. But more children would only add to her burden, so here she was, overriding her husband's last-minute suggestion that he come instead.

"He needs his strength. He does so much physical work," she explained.

"Don't you do most of the field work?" I asked.

She nodded. "Yes."

There was no point in pursuing the question. A vasectomy would leave a permanent cloud of shame over her husband. There appeared to be no male volunteers, anyway—only male motivators, a whole bunch of them, on the other side of the parking lot, where they appeared to be helping themselves to a refreshment table of tea and biscuits before returning to the field for more recruits.

A junior official came over to our tree to tell Gulabdai to visit the registration table, the one decorated with reassuring posters about the joys of a two-child family, not the seven, eight or nine that she and her friends had borne. They were required to give their names, their husbands' names, their age, number of children and caste. A medical officer tested their blood pressure, and sugar levels in their urine. Then the women were asked to sign forms with their fingerprints. It was the Indian equivalent of a waiver. The document declared, in Hindi, that the woman "willingly and independently came to this clinic. I also know there are other ways to control family size. I also know this is the most stable and permanent way of controlling the family size, and I will have no children after this. I know these operations are not always successful. I know for this failure, the doctor or hospital will not be held responsible. People have taught us about the benefits of this operation and I understand them."

Gulabdai said she could not read the form, nor could any of her friends. They fingerprinted it just the same.

As we continued to talk in the lineup, a camp official wandered over to listen. He remained silent for a few minutes, although the shuffling of his feet and shaking of his head suggested he wanted to voice his own opinion more than he wanted to listen to those of a few village women. "You should ask me," he finally said, interrupting the second question. "These women are all illiterate. I will tell you what they think." Rama suggested he leave. He was distracted anyway by a Congress Party jeep that had rolled into the camp with a fresh batch of recruits, sparking cheers and more handshakes among the motivators, and a photo for the local newspaper.

When the time came for Gulabdai and her friends to move inside the clinic, they walked solemnly, their heads bowed, as if entering a temple. The lobby was already crowded with the bodies of women recuperating, laid out side by side under frayed red blankets. Some women were shivering. A few moaned. Most slept. It looked like a chilling scene from another century, perhaps the Crimean War. The whole place reeked of ammonia and, for the first time, Gulabdai and her friends admitted they were frightened. "The smell is making me dizzy, and listening to all these women crying scares me," her neighbour Nari said. "What can I do? My husband said I should come here. We can't afford any more children."

Beyond the lobby of affliction, outside an operating theatre, the women were made to squat in the hallway like children waiting to enter class. Then, one at a time, they were asked for their registration cards by a medical assistant and told to go through the door. We followed Gulabdai, who was instructed to lie on a cold metal operating table while nearby a doctor finished work on another woman. There was no need for Gulabdai to wash or undress. Flat on her back, she simply lifted the upper portion of her sari to expose her abdomen, where one of the assistants rubbed a swab doused in antiseptic. After the anesthesiologist gave a quick injection, she was ready.

Before we could find a spot to stand in the operating room—we were not asked to wash, either—the chief medical officer, Dr. A.S. Kushwala, had finished at the other table and was already at work on Gulabdai. He cut a slight hole in her midriff to pump her abdomen full of air and inserted a metal contraption that was needle, thread and ocular lens in one, which was all he needed to tie a Fallopian tube. As Dr. Kushwala worked, Gulabdai's bare toes curled tightly and she moaned. "Slight pain is inevitable," he said—to us, not her. She moaned again and clutched the metal table, and then it was over. An assistant took Dr. Kushwala's instrument, dipped it in a pot of hot water and returned it to him as he went to work at the next table, slicing open another woman's midsection.

Dr. Kushwala figured he could do 125 sterilizations a day. Both he and the anesthesiologist were paid four rupees for each operation. Both assistants got two rupees. The sweeper, who cleaned up the mess, got one. On a good day, each of the doctors would earn a bonus equivalent to about fifteen dollars, double the regular pay they also received. Dr. Kushwala wanted to do more. The previous year, another surgeon he knew had received a new car, an official white Ambassador, for exceeding his "suggested" target.

We followed Gulabdai as she staggered down the hall to find a resting place on the lobby floor. She took her gift, a ragged red blanket, and lay down with fifteen other women. She was too weak to talk. She had only one hour to recuperate, and then it was back on the bus home. There was no mention of the three follow-up tests she was supposed to receive in the next week. There was no nurse or assistant around to discuss anything.

As we left the Rampur centre, I noticed another Congress Party team posing for more photographs after dropping off a fresh batch of "volunteers." I started to take a picture of the ridiculous sight, but was interrupted by an imposing figure, a handsome older man whom I had not seen earlier. He was uncommonly tall for these impoverished parts and stood with his feet together and chest puffed out.

"Please," the man said. "You must have tea."

Subhash Chandra Pandey was a retired army officer who had returned to his village in Jaunpur district and taken up social work. He had heard some of our impertinent questions repeated by other motivators—"What would happen if only vasectomies were offered?" was one—and thought we had reacted wrongly to the whole exercise. When he was discharged from the military, he was shocked to see the population growth in his own backyard.

Before we could get to the car, he steered us across the grassy parking lot to the refreshments table, where he wanted to introduce us to the others who had helped him bring a dozen women here today, enough to earn them 120 rupees. No one in his village wanted more children, he said. "People come of their own will."

I asked how difficult it was for an educated army man like himself to broach a subject as sensitive as birth control with the illiterate women of his village.

"I just have to approach the husband," Pandey explained. "They basically all trust me so much that they say, 'Okay, you can take her.'"

Slightly barbaric, the sterilization camp was also legal and sanctioned by the highest levels of government. And it was doing little to curtail India's population growth. Elsewhere, a huge variety of poor countries had shown that, in the long run, family planning can never be forced and is best achieved through educating girls (to delay the age of marriage), improving health care for women and children (to increase their odds of survival) and providing better access to a broad range of affordable, safe and reliable contraceptives.

Jaunpur's doctors, administrators and motivators did not have to look far for evidence to support these suggestions. These practices had worked for years in southern India, in the states of Kerala and Tamil Nadu. More recently, down the Ganges, the otherwise troubled nation of Bangladesh was making big strides in family planning, improving the lives of women while rapidly reducing their fertility rates. Thanks to the work of a pioneering doctor and his army of village paramedics, the world's most crowded nation was showing that population control is not about the quantity of life. It's all about the quality.

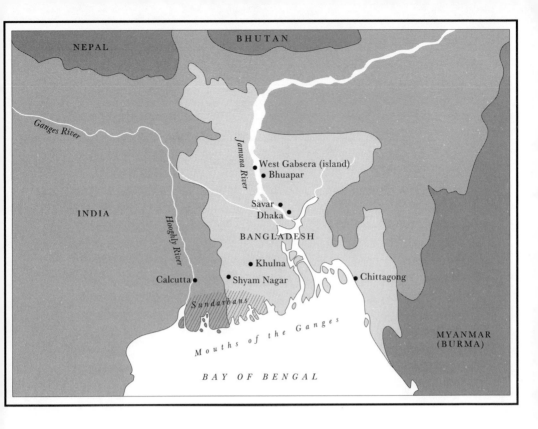

# BANGLADESH

"Strips of roadway rose from the inland waters and then disappeared, only to resurface somewhere else on the seascape like a mythical serpent slithering across a loch. Two-thirds of the country was like this, submerged but survivng, a poor man's version of Atlantis."

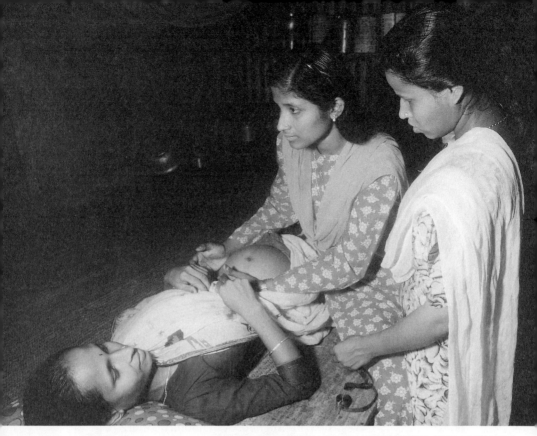

FEROZA YASMIN SHAHIDA, VILLAGE HEALTH WORKER. SAVAR, BANGLADESH

# 13

# Dr. Zaf

Joytun started to hemorrhage at night, in her hut, well off the main road in central Bangladesh. She had just given birth to her first child, a boy, but her placenta had failed to come out. When the village midwife tried to remove it, the bleeding only grew more profuse. The night was hot, and mosquitoes buzzed everywhere, but Joytun was told there was nothing to do but wait, to remain quiet and on her back while she slowly bled, perhaps to death. It would be light soon, her neighbour Azufah explained in a gentle whisper. One of the children could run to the road to fetch a rickshaw. They both knew not to disturb Joytun's husband who was asleep in the next hut. He had to work in the fields the next morning.

At daybreak, when the rickshaw finally came, there was no time to haggle over the price. Azufah paid fifty taka, about one dollar, which was more than anyone in the village earned in a day, and bundled Joytun in, leaving the new baby with his paternal grandmother. Azufah thought the four-kilometre journey to the Savar district hospital would kill the child. She wasn't sure if it would kill his mother, too.

As they cycled out of the village that June morning, the humidity was so thick that it seemed to drip from every palm tree along the broken dirt road. Blood seeped through Joytun's sari and over the plastic seat. For the next harrowing hour, over dirt roads that rose and fell like a tumultuous sea, the young mother was transported in excruciating pain to the Savar hospital, the only one in the district. The terror of a botched childbirth, of the curse and suffering from hemorrhaging, eclampsia or a fistula, swirled through Joytun's mind as she struggled to remain conscious. In her country alone, thirty-five thousand women a year died in pregnancy or childbirth, more than all the men killed in the Bosnian war. Women died anemic, splattered with blood, children wedged in their wombs. Often, the last words they heard were from a neighbour telling them to keep quiet so as not to wake the village or from a midwife advising them to swallow the pain.

Joytun knew, too, about the women who survived childbirth with damaged wombs, hundreds of thousands of them who struggled through life with permanent injuries that made them outcasts from their own homes. If Joytun's labour had torn the tissues of her birth canal, causing a fistula, she might never be allowed in her husband's home again. So disgusting was the resulting leakage from an afflicted woman's bladder and rectum that she might not be allowed to live in her village, either. She had heard about women who could not afford an operation to stop the incontinence that stained their ragged saris and soiled their beds, and how they'd been discarded by their husbands in favour of new unscathed wives. Such women were doomed to spend the rest of their days wandering from house to hut to field, never escaping the shame. Many women suffering from a fistula committed suicide, but no one kept track of how many. In rural Bangladesh, a woman's death is not recorded.

By the time the rickshaw reached the hospital, Joytun was so weak that the doctors said she would not have lived another thirty minutes. They removed the placenta, gave her 450 cubic centimetres of fresh blood and allowed her to rest on a cot. Her birth canal was intact, but the doctors were not sure yet whether she would be able to bear more children. At least she had borne a son, Azufah sighed with relief.

Joytun's survival, in its way, was a quiet miracle. In many parts of the developing world, and in many parts of Bangladesh, the chances of a woman's overcoming an obstetrical emergency such as this were as thin as they had been for their grandmothers. During the twentieth century, thirty million women, most of them too poor to get to a doctor, had died from such nineteenth-century scourges. Joytun survived because of geography and development—she lived within a cycle-rickshaw's haul of Bangladesh's most famous private hospital, an institution that grew from the ashes of a liberation war.

The Savar hospital that saved Joytun was created by a rebel doctor who believed that the health and independence of women were worth as much as the health and independence of a nation. Dr. Zafrullah Chowdhury started his first clinic here in 1971 after he returned from London to build and operate a field hospital for the liberation forces. During an intense rebel offensive against the Pakistani army, Dr. Chowdhury looked at the field nurses around him and wondered what they would do after the liberation forces captured Dhaka. He wanted political freedom for a Muslim Bengal; he also saw how this could be the first battle in a new war against poverty.

When peace came, Dr. Zaf (as he quickly became known around Savar) started the Gonoshasthaya Kendra, People's Health Centre, with a small army of female paramedics who had served during the war. The GK recruits lived in the villages they served and knew their patients as friends. Most of them had no more than an elementary education, but they were trained to treat common ailments in their villages, provide basic prenatal and postnatal care for mothers, promote birth control to their friends and report trouble immediately to the hospital that Dr. Zaf also built. They were the only link most women had with trained doctors and nurses.

❖

I met Bangladesh's most exceptional doctor during a Dhaka curfew in June 1996. The capital was shut down to control an outbreak of election violence. When I telephoned him at about nine p.m., hoping to set up an interview for the next day, he asked why I wanted to wait. He could see me right away if I came by the new hospital he was building. Police barricades were nothing I could not duck. Leaving Cindy at the guest house where we'd rented a room, I hired a rickshaw wallah who weaved his way through Dhanmondi, the leafy heart of Dhaka, and then darted across a broad boulevard to the hospital. Dr. Zaf was right. A Dhaka curfew was only a suggestion.

In the only room with lights on, I found a group of hospital staff drinking tea and arguing about the latest bit of election news. Without missing a word of the exchange, a slight man with a mop of unruly grey hair handed me a business card that read, "Dr. Zafrullah Chowdhury, Projects Co-ordinator." By this time I was used to NGO leaders who called themselves chief executive officers or chairmen and worked in the upper reaches of office buildings when they were not at international conferences. Few of them drank tea. They were served tea. Dr. Zaf poured me some and gave me the quick version of GK's history.

When he started out, the new Bangladesh was so desperately poor that a public hospital was a luxury almost unimaginable outside Dhaka. The retreating Pakistani forces had burned health clinics and factories, and had killed many of the educated people who had hoped to lead the new government. After the war, an American aid embargo followed by a drought pushed the crowded little country deeper into crisis. Finally a state of emergency was declared by the leftist leader, Sheikh Mujibur Rahman, on December 28, 1974. Eight months later, military gunmen burst into the president's home in Dhanmondi and killed him, his wife and most of their children, beginning a disastrous cycle of military coups and authoritarian rule. The young country's only hope seemed to be a Bengali tradition of social work that ran deeper than the Ganges itself, from Raja Ram Mohan Roy, the great nineteenth-century advocate of women's emancipation, to the Nobel laureate Rabindranath Tagore and a more recent Nobel Prize winner, the Cambridge economist Amartya Sen, whose life's work presents a passionate argument for public investment in people.

Cut from this tradition, Dr. Zaf brought the poor around Savar low-cost health services unprecedented in rural South Asia, and soon came to the attention of the generals. In 1977, the young doctor was granted an audience with the new military dictator Zia-ur Rahman. The president wanted to know why birth rates were falling in the area around Savar hospital without a major program for contraceptives in place. Dr. Zaf explained that in his experience women who led healthier lives and delivered their babies safely generally had fewer children. If those children stood a better chance of survival, their mothers, confident that none would die, had fewer children still.

It was a startling revelation (one that finally became gospel seventeen years later at a major UN population conference in Cairo). But this was 1977. Next door in India, the government had embarked on a brutal forced vasectomy campaign and its first sterilization camps. China was opting for an authoritarian one-child policy. In Indonesia, the government was running amok with what it called "family planning safaris," rounding up women and fitting them with IUDs. But here, in supposedly backward Bangladesh, the country Henry Kissinger labelled a "basket case," something very different was going on in the name of family planning. Maternal and child health care had become the country's most successful contraceptive. And General Zia, who had spent much of the liberation war in a Pakistani prison, was all ears. He granted Dr. Zaf permission to build hospitals in ten districts and expand his army of village health workers across central Bangladesh.

In the eighties, the GK hospitals still relied on outside support, but Dr. Zaf also experimented with new ways to raise money from the poor, creating user fees and a health insurance program for villages. No service was free. A destitute woman or widow had to pay five taka, about ten cents, to join the program and another fifteen taka as a deductible for each visit to the hospital. Better-off people paid more, a few dollars for a standard delivery or a hundred dollars for a Caesarean. Dr. Zaf had made another important discovery: when the service is good, poor people, even poor women, are willing to pay a share of their health care costs.

By the mid-nineties, about half of GK's ten-million-dollar operating budget came from the national government, much of it generated by the Savar hospital's second specialty, treating the victims of highway accidents. Only 10 percent of the operating budget now came from foreign aid, mainly the Danish government and Christian Aid. The remaining four million dollars was paid by health care consumers, the very people who would complain loudest if they did not receive good service. Demand-based development was catching on.

"Here, if a woman dies, the worker has to face the village," Dr. Zaf explained. "Accountability is there."

Since the liberation war, GK had produced stunning results in reduced maternal mortality, lower infant death rates and, unexpectedly, lower birth rates—all by building a bridge from the island of medical science to the vast continent of poor, illiterate, unwell and overburdened mothers. For his work, Dr. Zaf won the 1985 Ramon Magsaysay Award for community development, which is Asia's equivalent of the Nobel Prize. In 1992, GK was granted the Right Livelihood Award by Sweden's Nobel committee.

Twenty years after Dr. Zaf's meeting with General Zia, the organization continued to work in ten districts, employing a village health worker for every four thousand people, and did foot-soldier work during the country's many natural disasters and calamities. But perhaps most important was this: Dr. Zaf and his health army (along with hundreds of similar organizations) were showing the world how Bangladesh—desperately poor, crowded and perpetually inclement—could become a leader in some aspects of human development.

"We are still fighting," the revolutionary doctor said. "It's just a different war now."

It was approaching midnight, and there was lots more to discuss. Dr. Zaf suggested I meet him in Savar, at his original hospital.

"When?" I asked.

"If you leave by seven, you'll miss the worst traffic," he said. "I'll see you there by nine."

He meant the next morning.

Cindy and I took Dr. Zaf's advice and left shortly after dawn, just in time to run into a surge of humanity on the only road northwest from Dhaka. This could not be described as traffic. This was a flow of a thousand different human currents and eddies, each swirling, swelling or surging at different paces and in different directions. Everywhere there were people, on foot and bicycle, in rickshaws, trucks and cars, on buses that keeled to one side under the weight of thirty or forty passengers on the roofs, all headed in or out of the most wildly unmanageable city on earth on two narrow lanes of road that doubled as the city's northern flood embankment.

The early morning rush grew worse the closer we got to a narrow crumbling bridge, the only one over the Turag River; drivers were so eager to get ahead of the pack that two lanes turned to eight. We spent the next hour sorting our way through trucks, buses, cars and mule carts just to get to the other side of the bridge, where the eddy of vehicles once again turned into a torrential stream. Trucks and buses raced recklessly past each other on the narrow highway. I hung on to my undigested breakfast, barely, by watching the side of the road—an unending strip of factories, each decorated with palm and coconut trees. They were so uniformly bland I did not notice that we had sailed straight through Savar and had to double back to find the long, three-storey hospital, which looked like a shoe factory set behind a row of coconut trees, the same as scores of buildings we had passed on the way from Dhaka.

Dr. Zaf was already at the hospital, in surgical garb, quizzing his staff about the newest truck driver in intensive care. All around him was an astonishing sight: a South Asian health facility that was clean, organized, efficient, even caring. Next to the hospital was a pharmaceutical factory where GK produced generic drugs for as little as 15 percent of the international cost. Dr. Zaf showed us the production line and then led us to a tiny office where he continued with the previous night's account of Savar's real success, its outreach program.

Across the local district, the hospital was linked to six village health posts, each staffed with six to eight paramedics who kept a watch on their communities and all expectant or lactating women, checking them as many as ten times during a pregnancy. The village health workers provided anemic women with iron and folic acid tablets, and persuaded their patients to come to special tetanus vaccination days at one of the district's four local health centres. If a field worker spotted complications, she was to refer the patient to the hospital and a doctor who assumed responsibility for the case and could prepare for a possible obstetrical emergency. They also coached local midwives on birthing techniques, supplying them with plastic gloves, string, cotton gauze and fresh razor blades for cutting umbilical cords.

A faster way to reduce maternal mortality would be to build more health centres to handle deliveries, but Bangladesh could not afford it. The culture and economy do not allow for women to be away from home and field for more than a few hours anyway. The most viable option was to train and equip village birth attendants, as had been done across much of Asia and Africa. The challenge remained to get women to professional care when unexpected complications such as Joytun's arose, as happened in about one case in ten. The simplest link, an ambulance, did not exist in Savar, and if it did, it couldn't make it to most villages off the main road. Two-way radios might have worked, but GK was denied a licence for "national security" reasons, Dr. Zaf said. For this generation, at least, maternal survival would have to rest on the village paramedic and her ability to spot warning signs and monitor each case through a healthy delivery and infancy.

Dr. Zaf wanted us to meet one of his best paramedics, a nineteen-year-old woman named Feroza Yasmin Shahida, who was sitting on a small bench outside the hospital with a dozen other young women preparing their medical kits for a new day in the field. The daughter of peasant farmers outside Savar town, Feroza had been able to complete grade twelve thanks to a scholarship program for teenaged girls designed by the U.S. Agency for International Development and sponsored by the World Bank. Feroza joined GK immediately after secondary school, learned the basics of modern maternal health care and was given responsibility for all pregnant women and new mothers in her family's village and two neighbouring villages. She had 515 fecund couples in her care, and one GK-issued bicycle to reach them all. A teenager, born well after her country's independence, Feroza was the only health worker in her area.

"Can you ride a bicycle?" Dr. Zaf asked us, suggesting we join Feroza on her rounds.

I enthusiastically said yes, though nothing in Canada had prepared me for riding an Indian-made bicycle on a Bangladeshi highway.

Trucks and buses roared past us on the narrow undivided road, and whenever I sought sanctuary on the gravel shoulder there was sure to be a crowd of pedestrians, cows or goats in the way. The best I could do was frantically work the crooked handlebars and stick close to Cindy, who with a camera bag over her shoulder seemed to be better balanced. Far ahead, Feroza, medical bag in one hand, cycled merrily along as if she were alone on an English country lane. Veering off the highway, she led us down a steep bank and through a crowded trading post to another embankment that served as a village access road. Nourished by a good monsoon, the jute crop was six feet high, and every house seemed to have a duck pond quacking with life. Many farmers had also replaced their mud walls with brick and added sheet-metal roofing. Slowly, very slowly, rural Bangladesh was slipping out of poverty and into something more comfortable.

For another kilometre we peddled easily along the dirt embankment, grateful that it was too small for trucks, until we reached the first village, Gopinapur. Feroza did not bother to don her head scarf when we entered the village. None of the young women in Savar did. The rapid spread of girls' education in the countryside, combined with the creation of hundreds of thousands of jobs for young women in the new garment-manufacturing industry, had led to a quiet and remarkable change in their self-confidence.

Feroza's first patient was Lata Rani, a nineteen-year-old who had dropped out of school early (parental pressure, she said) to get married and was now expecting her second child in three years. The pregnancy, in its third trimester, had gone relatively well, except that Lata was now losing weight. Feroza gave her folic acid tablets and showed her a chart illustrating the green leafy vegetables she should eat. When a loud thunderclap shook the thatched hut, I imagined riding back to Savar in the mud, but Feroza continued with her examination, undeterred by the weather as she checked Lata's blood pressure and then handed her a test tube to urinate in.

Lata slipped behind a sheet of corrugated metal that served as the only wall of the household's latrine, leaving Feroza to explain the toughest part of her job—the dispelling of old wives' tales. "Some women eat almost nothing in their final weeks," she said. "They fear if they eat well, the baby will be too big to come out." Others won't eat tart foods, a lemon for example, which they believe will affect the baby's temperament. "The Hindus!" Feroza exclaimed, appalled at their purification rites after birth. "Some of the women are required to live in isolation with their baby for fifteen days, in a hut or tent outside the village."

Lata returned with the test tube, which Feroza applied to a small fire she had lit while we were talking. Aluminum dropped in the test tube would turn cloudy if Lata was at risk of eclampsia, the sudden seizure in pregnancy that was the leading cause of maternal deaths in this area. The urine remained clear, a reassuring fact Feroza noted in her little pink book. She proceeded to review other foods the expectant mother should eat: eggs, bananas, rice. They went over a breast-feeding chart and a formula for a homemade diarrhea remedy. Lata seemed well prepared. But as we left, Feroza wanted to speak to one more person, the local *dhai*, or midwife. Almost every village has a dhai, most of them little more than helpful grandmothers. They rarely know what to do when complications arise, and Feroza had some concerns about Lata. She went over the symptoms again with the dhai, making her swear she would send for help if problems arose. Feroza lived only one village away—close enough to come in an emergency, and close enough to be held responsible by the whole community if something went wrong.

We cycled to another village, grateful the rains had held off, and checked on a few more patients. Feroza had to finish her rounds by noon so that she could help her mother at home and around the family's duck pond. Her GK salary of twenty-five dollars a month was not enough to live on, but if Feroza did well, she would be promoted to supervisor, earning one hundred dollars a month and zipping around the back roads on a scooter instead of a bicycle. She beamed at the thought.

It had been five years since a woman died during pregnancy or childbirth in Gopinapur. Across the district, the maternal mortality rate was down to two hundred for every one hundred thousand births—less than one-quarter the national average. The birth rate had also dropped to eighteen births per year for every one thousand people in the area, compared with a national average of twenty-eight. Largely through the work of GK, Savar's birth rate was lower than Indonesia's, where Suharto had won a special UN award for population control. The Bangladeshi government was so impressed by GK's paramedic force that it hired ten thousand village health workers in the late eighties and watched the country's fertility rate, already half what it was at independence, continue to drop to levels not seen in any other poor country.

As a small drizzle started, we left Feroza in her village and manoeuvred our way back down the highway to Savar, where we found Dr. Zaf in the hospital canteen, eating a typical Bangladeshi doctor's lunch of dal, rice and Coca-Cola. We joined him. The GK system, he conceded, was far from ideal. The young paramedics could never give their full attention to each of the five hundred couples under their care, nor could they hope to understand the complexities of pregnancy and childbirth, especially since many were still in their teens and unmarried. But by relying on local paraprofessionals instead of barefoot doctors, and by actively recruiting women, GK was at least able to link isolated villages and a local hospital.

Two decades after its first military coup, Bangladesh was teeming with non-governmental organizations like GK, each fighting its own little revolution, lobbying for fishermen, organizing villages to build irrigation canals or running rural banking networks. In 1991, a new democracy had replaced military rule and, by 1998, the country had 1,045 local and 140 foreign NGOs to fill the horrible void left by civil war, corrupt governments and natural disasters. They claimed to reach thirty million of the country's fifty million poor and were helping to break down ancient social barriers and overcome extraordinary environmental pressures with new opportunities. In many ways, they had saved young Bangladesh from becoming a Somalia.

NGO leaders like Dr. Zaf, or Muhammad Yunus, of the microcredit institution Grameen Bank, got most of the credit, but Bangladesh's second war of independence was being won by thousands of local women and men, on their bicycles and scooters, working in villages where a woman's life was once not worth the rickshaw fare to a hospital. This was the liberated Bangladesh of Feroza Yasmin Shahida. But as we left Savar for Dhaka, I had to wonder why—if there were so many Dr. Zafs and Ferozas—Bangladesh remained so poor.

HAJERA ON HER CHAR; BADANA ON THE MAINLAND

# 14

## Two Sisters, One River

At the end of the twentieth century, Bangladesh remained a place of political violence and natural disasters. It also had become one of the world's most ambitious developing countries, and not only because of its famous non-governmental organizations. The government was writing new laws, restructuring its massive bureaucracy and transferring power to elected local councils that were charged with building roads, allocating schools and running local credit schemes. Slowly, the rising sun of democracy was casting its rays across the drenched Bengali landscape. Slowly, Bangladesh, the helpless, impoverished basket case of the seventies, was becoming an archetype of change for the twenty-first century.

But for those who placed some confidence in the country's future, there were nagging doubts about nature, a volatile force in any human life. For all the Dr. Zafs and young Ferozas, Bangladesh remained a nation of 125 million people crammed on to a river delta the size of Michigan. It was three times as crowded as Japan and so starved for natural resources that it even imported rocks from India to help protect itself from a perennial whipping by some of the world's most unforgiving floods, cyclones and droughts.

If there is a perfect representation of this precarious existence, of everything that gives the populace hope and all that consumes its dreams, it has to be the wash-away islands called chars in the hundreds of rivers that pour through the country to the Bay of Bengal. Some three million Bangladeshis live on these chars, where their lives depend on a river's meandering whims and torrential moods.

The Jamuna, the greatest of these rivers, cuts the country in two and every summer carries awesome flood waters and billions of tonnes of silt from the Himalayas. It has given rise to no fewer than three hundred chars, alluvial islands so rich in silt that every winter they produce a bounty of mustard, jute, rice and wheat. But the same flood waters that create the chars eventually submerge them, destroying livelihoods just as they had created them. A char disappears. Another one emerges. And the charlanders move on, hopping from island home to island home, as they have for centuries.

Cindy and I were staying in the small town of Bhuapur, near the Jamuna's east bank, when we met our first charlander, a woman named Hajera. Slight and timid, Hajera had come to the mainland to borrow grain from her sister, Badana, whom I was interviewing in a village hut for a story about moneylenders. I asked Hajera more about the chars; she described them as a collapsing house that had beggared her life. That much was obvious just from looking at the two sisters. Hajera, the charlander, was gaunt. Badana, the mainlander, was plump. At fifty, Hajera had a life of troubles on the river. At forty-five, Badana was on the move. Hajera's life was a daily struggle for survival on the char, a place she insisted we had to see in order to understand how the earth could impoverish her so. All we needed to do was find a sinking char called West Gabsera, where any ox cart would take us to her house.

The next day, we left for the chars with Shiraz, a university student we had hired in Dhaka as a translator. In a rickety outrigger rented at the nearest river crossing, we skimmed along the placid and misty Jamuna as if we were alone in paradise rather than in the middle of the world's most crowded country. There was not a sound on the open river, other than our boat's small diesel motor, and no sign of life beyond the grassy banks that faded as the river broadened and then branched into an intricate brocade of streams flowing together and drifting apart. Because of unusually dry weather, the Jamuna had created a maze of tiny rivers in its sprawling, ten-kilometre-wide bed, with only a few channels big enough for a boat like ours and only our boatman's feel for the river to guide us, as he nipped from stream to stream like a tracker picking his way along a jungle path.

On the horizon, there was a long string of islands that looked like silhouettes dancing on the still water, and beyond them more chars a few kilometres in length, with forests, cropland and hundreds of people living in established villages. Our boatman warned us not to be fooled. All these islands were silt deposits, he said, and only that. Every islander knew the river gave them life and the river took it away.

The driver sat at the back of the boat, under a lean-to made of bamboo and straw, steering with a long pole connected to the propeller, which he lifted and dipped in the water like an egg beater to fix our direction. With an empty oil can, he also bailed the water trickling into the boat from a small leak that was apparently growing between floor boards that had been slapped hastily together. Thankfully, the boatman said, we were within sight of Hajera's island. It was one of the biggest chars of all, a silt deposit that covered ten square kilometres of riverbed and housed eight thousand people. It had schools, a hospital, a police station and thriving markets. It would also not survive another flood.

The bank on Hajera's side of the char rose ten metres above the Jamuna, and was crumbling fast. Ever since a new levee was built upriver to protect the fifty thousand people in the town of Sirajgunj—also being consumed by the river's westward shift—the charlanders believed the currents had intensified, causing their land to disappear ever more rapidly. It was a moot point. No one expected the char to see out the decade. We paid the boat driver, and asked him to come back for us the next morning, provided he could fix the leak, and then scrambled up the fragile bank to find emerald green rice paddies, banana groves and forests of palm and bamboo growing on some of the richest alluvial soil in South Asia. And all of it doomed to slide into the river.

When we reached Hajera's by ox-cart, following a trail that hugged the riverbank, her family had finished breakfast and was sitting in the warmth of a December sun, listening to migratory birds from Siberia flutter from tree to tree. The family compound, next to the ox-cart path and protected only by a little gate made of jute stalks, was built around a small courtyard, where everyone sat, talked, cooked, bathed, milked their cows and stored their harvest. There were four small huts, each made of bamboo and jute. One was for Hajera, her husband and two youngest children; one for their married son, his wife and new baby; one for the cows; and one for a small flour mill.

A dugout canoe, a sort of village lifeboat waiting for the next flood, rested on solid ground, tied to a palm tree. It was not the only reminder that disaster was never far away. The family's small beds sat on a raised platform, as did the earthen stove. During the last major flood, Hajera's husband had to put a cow in the wobbly little boat and pull it across the inundated fields to dry ground. From there, Hajera hired a larger boat to transport her children and the cow to her sister's village, where they stayed until the dry season. Her husband slept on the thatched roof of their flooded hut, to maintain their land claim, should the land return.

Such was nature's passion in summer, but these were the winter months, a time of plenty. A large mound of dal filled the centre of Hajera's courtyard, and a pile of rice stalks was in a corner. There were ducks waddling to and fro. A hen poked a dozen chicks toward some cooked food spilled from breakfast. Out on the river, a rusting ferry chugged by, billowing black smoke into the clear sky as it lurched under the weight of hundreds of passengers. And then it was gone. Hajera's unadorned farmstead, shaded by banana and palm trees, was left to bask in its own serenity and a cooling winter breeze.

All seemed calm, except for Hajera, who greeted us but continued with her morning chores: sweeping the courtyard, scrubbing pots with dry leaves, tethering cows to new grazing positions and then cutting grass with a knife to feed them at night. Her husband, his brothers and their sons could sit around smoking hand-rolled cigarettes, but Hajera told us she had no time to relax. She feared this winter would be her last one here. During the previous summer, the Jamuna had devoured a neighbouring village and was now only fifty metres from her compound, ready to consume her land during the next rainy season. After harvesting what they could, Hajera and her family planned to move to another plot they had claimed a couple of hundred metres into the char's interior. Sandy and seldom inundated and replenished with silt, it was less fertile but would tide them over until better land emerged somewhere else.

When Hajera was finished sweeping the yard, she sat down for a few minutes on the golden mound of dal in the middle of her courtyard and began to describe a little of her life. Forty years ago, she'd moved to the chars as a child bride, to a new existence of shock and adjustment. She and her husband seldom stayed on one island for more than six or seven years; every major flood pushed them on. They had lived on West Gabsera in the seventies, around the time of Bangladesh's independence, and then had to leave it. They came back to the island when it re-emerged in the eighties and stayed until the great flood of 1988, when it disappeared again. During the disaster, their extended family had to pack up their animals, cooking utensils and bedding, and paddle to one of six smaller chars where they had land. They would suffer for a year or two, but always move back to West Gabsera, as they did in the early nineties when the new soil gave them their best harvest ever.

"There will always be a char, maybe not here, but there will always be one," Hajera declared.

She invited us to sit down beside her on the mound of dal, less out of courtesy than the hope that our ample North American weight would help crack open the dry, brittle pods. As we took a seat, she returned to her chores. Although Hajera looked faint, she stopped working only to spit out a wad of betel-nut juice that had stained her teeth a dark red. Her cheekbones protruded more because of her leanness than her bone structure. Though her hair flowed youthfully in a braid down to her waist, it was greying. The more we spoke, the clearer it became that Hajera had no time for rest. Unlike her sister who was building a new life, Hajera devoted most of her day to protecting an old one. There were house repairs to be finished from the previous monsoon, and the cows needed to be moved again and tethered in another field; the char had no room for free-ranging cows.

Because the chars had no irrigation or fertilizer either, Hajera's land yielded only half the harvest of her sister's fields and produced only one crop a year. One tube-well on Hajera's corner of the island served twenty families. The government was not willing to invest any more in a place that disappeared and reappeared according to the dictates of a river, and so Hajera's family survived on dirty water and struggled in their fields to earn a couple hundred dollars from each hectare of rice, jute, wheat, dal and radish—750 dollars a year in all to support twenty-five people in her husband's extended family.

Hajera eventually put down her small broom and settled into the long task of pounding rice stalks. Ever since she'd enrolled her youngest daughter and son in school to take advantage of a free food program for poor children—they each got fifteen kilograms a month of wheat—there was no one to help her at home. Her husband, Shahor, the eldest male in his family and thus the patriarch, suffered from what a visiting doctor once said was Parkinson's disease. As we watched Hajera work, he sat quietly in a corner of the courtyard, trembling. All the neighbours believed Shahor was possessed by a spirit— one of his younger brothers had died when a similar condition set in—and Hajera could not afford the medicines prescribed by the visiting doctor to prove them wrong. The drugs alone cost one hundred taka every ten days, or about two dollars, and were supposed to be supplemented with a high-protein diet and lots of Vitamin B foods like milk, spinach, eggs and liver—items Hajera could not afford. She could not even afford to buy basic medicines for one of her sisters-in-law, who was down with malaria. The family's health had seldom been worse, now that several of the children were showing signs of measles, for which none had been vaccinated.

The tranquility of char-life aside, this is what it meant to live in extreme poverty, to live at the mercy of nature and disease, and be without a little money to buy the most basic of treatments. When her husband fell ill, Hajera sold a hut on another char to pay his medical bills. She had also sold two plots of char land to cope with the growing cost of living. The family still held four hectares, an enormous amount by Bangladeshi standards, but two-thirds of it was under water. And all of it had to be shared by the ever-expanding clan: Hajera and her husband, their five children, his elderly mother and two brothers, their wives and thirteen children. Understandably, Hajera's older boys had moved to the mainland. Her youngest son and daughter would likely join them as environmental refugees, probably stuck in a Dhaka slum seeking factory work. Only one son, the eldest, would stay to help with the land, and that was out of duty to his parents, whose lives, I began to realize, were eroding as quickly as the land around them.

Other people began to arrive in the compound, mostly neighbours dropping by on their way to the local market. Hajera politely offered them well-water and suggested the heavier men sit on her unbroken pods of dal. Tea was a luxury she could not afford, but still they were her guests, and they each accepted a glass.

The older men and women remembered only one white person who visited their island before, shortly after the 1988 flood. "He was white and had white hair," Hajera said, laughing for the first time since our arrival. "We were so scared. We thought he was a spirit."

She was at last taking a break, if only to watch in bemusement as Cindy moved around the dal pile, photographing her. Cindy gave Hajera the camera to take a picture. "Did you make this yourself?" Hajera asked, hefting the Nikon like a handful of potatoes at the market. When Cindy said no, Hajera seemed let down. She had made her own house, rice pounder and boat. Why couldn't this foreign woman make a camera?

The men who were now lying back on the dal, a very effective Bengali beanbag, started to lecture me about food. I was only surprised that it took them this long. Food, especially food from the water, dominates the Bengali mind. A national maxim holds that a Bengali who does not eat fish and rice at least once a day is an unhappy Bengali.

"There used to be so many fish. They used to be this big," said Ali Akbar, one of Hajera's brothers-in-law. He stretched his arms as wide as he could, almost tearing his mauve kurta. "Now we only get tiny fish. They're like shrimps."

He shook his head in disgust at the thought of such fish, careful not to dislodge the white prayer cap he wore. A pious man in middle age, he had taken to growing his beard, with long strands of white and grey now overtaking the black undergrowth. "We can only get fish in the market now," he continued. "Fifteen, twenty years back, we never had to buy fish."

"If we could have bread and potatoes, maybe we would be better off," said Mohammad Shamshar Ali, a neighbour. "Rice by itself is not good. It makes us sleepy and weak." He seemed to be rehearsing a lecture on nutrition, and could not be stopped. "I met a man once who was so strong. He said he ate bread for breakfast and dinner, and only a bit of rice for lunch. He hit me so hard it still hurts."

The others nodded sympathetically, until a new voice turned their heads. It was Shahor, quivering in the corner as he fidgeted with his only possession, a silver locket containing a miniature Koranic verse.

"Is your country crowded like this?" Hajera's husband asked.

I started to explain that Canada had thirty million people in an area seventy times larger than Bangladesh but Jomarion, Shahor's mother, decided it was her turn to speak. She was tiny, frail and who knows how old, though age had not dampened her spirit. This generation of charlanders, she said, had nothing to complain about compared with those who had seen the great flood of 1938. "We made high platforms and stayed with the land. We always stayed on the char!" she said, holding the growing audience in Hajera's courtyard in rapt attention. "Right after that, there was a very big famine, and most people died. It felt like everyone was going to die. The government did nothing for us. No one came to help us, not like today. At least some people come now when there are big problems, but the government always tries to save the people on the mainland first. They say they don't care about us. We are the poorest people in all of Bangladesh. No one is poorer than the char people."

Jomarion's lament cast a pall over the dirt courtyard. What else could be said about the charlanders? They limped from disaster to disaster, and she was right, no one cared about them. All the shiploads of aid seldom made it to these disposable islands. It was assumed their inhabitants, nomads of the river, were too transient to receive anything other than relief. And the government—Jomarion had sized it up pretty well, too.

As a young man, her son Ali Akbar had only one dream, to become a primary schoolteacher and escape from the chars. But he couldn't afford the eight-thousand-taka bribe to get a job. He was destined to be a transient char farmer, whose dream of reading Bengali folk tales to large classes of children was now confined to his own small hut where his five sons and daughters gathered every night around a kerosene lantern to hear his stories. Maybe one day, his children would get off the char, and he could follow them in retirement. "I have only one dream remaining," he said, "and that is that one day I will be able to live on the mainland. That is what I pray for."

The crowd was starting to disperse, and we could see Hajera had plenty still to do. We suggested we would find our own way to the local school, to see where her children studied. The school had 156 students in grades one to five, and 131 more children in a preschool play group. For this collection of nearly three hundred pupils, there were just four teaching posts, and only two were filled.

Ali Akbar led us out the jute-pole gate and down the rutted lane, pointing across a field to a clump of trees where we would find the school. Shahor had set off limping in another direction, shaking badly as he traversed a field to move one of the cows to another tether, while Hajera headed to the river to fetch a couple of pails of water and to see how much of her land had disappeared overnight.

By the time we reached the school, the morning students were on their way home. We found the headmaster, another Akbar, inside the cement building. He was also the *matbar*, or local chief, a distinguished man with a proud grey beard and thick glasses in black square frames. He had started this school several years earlier with funds from local parents, after district officials told him the government was not willing to build anything permanent. The education ministry at least agreed to pay salaries for four teachers, but then hired only him and another man and delivered only half the food it was supposed to give under a national food-for-education program.

"They said the remainder is needed for the administration," Akbar told us, as we sat on the porch of his two-room school. "I went to the union [county] office to complain, and one woman said we were lucky to get anything. She said the union chairman usually sells everything."

Even if half the grain was skimmed on the mainland, what was left made a difference. For many parents, three or four dollars a month in food meant a child was of more value sitting in a classroom than working in a field. Unfortunately, that did not translate directly into an educated child, not in classes of a hundred or more.

Akbar had to eat lunch and prepare for his afternoon shift, but he suggested we come to his house in the evening and stay overnight in his children's room. The five of them would pile into the only other bedroom with him and his wife. He said Hajera's huts were too crowded for company, and he was right. She could not afford so much as a charpoy for a guest to sleep on.

We spent the afternoon exploring the char and talking more with Hajera, who was at work in her fields, before returning to Akbar's in the early evening, guided by a full moon that sparkled in the Jamuna as we walked along the bank. Akbar had a three-room cement house, a sign that he had prospered in his decades on and off this char. "Yes, many years ago the people of Gabsera were the richest in the area," he said. His wife, unlike Hajera, did not say a word as she served bowls of rice and curry-fried vegetables. "But in the last seven or eight years," the headmaster continued, "we have all become poor."

When we finished dinner, we moved to a set of wooden chairs around a kerosene lantern and talked more about the levee. Akbar felt it was accelerating his island's demise. Although the government had sent a few missions to study the char's fate, nothing had been done. "The government people came and asked our opinion," the headmaster said. "Then they said, 'You don't understand the solutions. Only educated people understand. Only government people understand.'"

I could not make out Akbar's face in the dim, flickering light, but he sounded distressed. As sure as the next flood, he would be forced to the mainland, leaving behind all he had built here. I could not imagine what would become of him in the great human sea of Bangladesh so we sat silently, almost in meditation, until it was time to say good-night to West Gabsera's first and probably last headmaster.

The next morning, Christmas Day, we returned to Hajera's to wish her well before we tried to track down our boatman. She was already hard at work, boiling a pot of water to make a rice, dal and vegetable *khichuri*, a kind of stew, for breakfast—the same meal they would have for lunch and dinner. While she sliced a green pepper, she asked little Phulbanu to climb to the roof of their main hut and fetch an extra *lau*, a long white vegetable that grows on vines. Hajera added some dal and a couple of onions to the stew and continued to stir the big pot with a stick.

It was all she could do to get her ailing husband dressed in a lungi and old T-shirt and the children off to school, and yet there were always other people dropping in and expecting to be fed. Her only daughter-in-law, Nurjahan, was usually some help, cleaning pots and cutting vegetables, but this morning she was in bed with her newborn baby, Hajera's first grandchild. Another mouth to feed. Only when Shahjahan and Phulbanu had left for school could Hajera sit down with us on the pile of dal. She said she was ready to collapse, and it was not yet nine o'clock.

"It's extremely hard to keep moving," she went on. "I feel like I am going to become crazy. We worked so hard for this house. We built it. We planted the trees."

She shook her head. All that was around us would be gone, and so soon. But Hajera had more than the char to worry about. Exhausted and anemic, she could no longer keep pace. There was never enough food or medicine, and now the children's free education was getting expensive, what with the cost of books and clothes.

"People who knew me before, they know I could carry a *maund* of rice [about twenty-two kilograms] from here to there," she said, pointing across the field. "I had five children and was never sick during childbirth." She paused as if to catch her breath. "The last few months, I have felt so weak. I get fever. I get dysentery. Lately I have not been able to sleep. I lie down on a pile of hay in the hut, but I cannot sleep, not in the day, not at night."

Hajera had few places to turn and fewer people to share her troubles. Her only sister lived a morning's journey away by boat and rickshaw. The other women in the compound were either ill or preoccupied with children; her husband could no longer help. His balding head, white beard and wasted frame made him look too old to be the father of young children. He sat in the courtyard, shaking more than the day before. What seemed to weigh most heavily on Hajera's mind, though, was her own fate, a concern that women were not supposed to have. Hajera could not stop thinking about her mother. She invited us into her hut, where it was dim and cool, to talk more about her mother. She didn't want her husband to hear. "When she was my age, she died," Hajera said. "One of the last things she told me was I would die at this age, too." She looked at us and asked rather pointedly, "Do you think this will happen?"

I was struggling to think of a polite way to say the obvious, that Hajera did not look well, when a strange man walked through the jute gate and called for her. Hajera excused herself and slipped out of the hut and into the courtyard. She returned a few minutes later and stood on her wooden bed to reach for a hole in the thatched roof, where she kept a stash of money. This did not look like a good sign, handing money to a strange man, so I asked, perhaps impertinently, what she was doing. As she stepped down from her bed and counted the taka, she began to explain more of what had gone wrong. Ever since the big flood of 1988, her family's income had lost ground, literally to soil erosion and figuratively to inflation. She and Shahor had sold off huts, livestock and bits of land to make ends meet, but his debilitating disease had put their survival in doubt.

No matter how early she rose to fetch water or how late she worked to cut grass for her cows in the moonlight, she could not keep her husband and children clothed and fed. Four months earlier, when she needed to buy food and winter clothing, she borrowed twelve hundred taka, about twenty-five dollars at the time, from a man in a neighbouring village. Now it was time to repay the loan, along with three hundred taka of interest. But she was short one thousand taka, not counting the other loans she had taken just to get through the dry season. So deep was she in debt that she planned to sell a piece of land for five thousand taka. It did not take much imagination to see that Hajera was staring at destitution.

I asked her to stay in the hut for a moment, and reached into my knapsack for five thousand taka, the equivalent of one hundred dollars. She refused. She said she could not afford to go any deeper into debt. I said it was a gift, that people where I came from were really quite rich.

Hajera paused for a moment and then said she would accept the money, on the same terms as the local moneylender, which meant in one year's time she would repay the five thousand taka, plus another five thousand taka interest. With this one deal, made in desperation, she would owe me her entire year's income. I made a counteroffer: I would buy the land from her if she would manage it for me on a share-cropping basis. She and Shahor could keep half the harvest and invest my share in her children's education. I would collect the money later, maybe when the children were older and working. Hajera smiled, took the cash and ducked out the door to dismiss the moneylender.

Before we left to meet our boat, proud to be landowners in Bangladesh, Hajera insisted we listen to her once more. "You have nothing to worry about," she said earnestly. "The money will not be wasted. We will not drink it away like other people do."

Back down the river, I was astonished to see from the water how far the Jamuna receded during the dry season. About two hundred metres from its banks, the boat beached on a mud flat, leaving us to follow a series of wooden planks on foot to higher ground where cycle rickshaws congregated to ferry people to Bhuapur. That was all the traffic there was, a stream of rickshaws gently clanging their bells as they passed one another in the shade of the stately pepil trees that lined the road.

Beyond the trees, everyone in Tangail district seemed to be at work. In the depths of the dry season, farmers had planted rice in ditches and parched irrigation canals, and filled their fields with golden mustard and wheat. In the few unplanted fields, women and children were busy digging blocks of earth by hand and with shovels, and carrying them in baskets on their heads to the brick kilns that popped up every kilometre or so along the road. Where there was a pond or stream, the banks were crowded with old men and young boys trying to catch a few fish before the water disappeared. It was only when we approached Bhuapur market that traffic, of a sort, emerged in the form of an ox cart lumbering toward us with a load of tree stumps and logs, followed by a dozen men labouring with bamboo poles to carry an entire dry-goods shop to a more profitable intersection.

We returned to a small room we had rented for a week above the Grameen Bank's Bhuapur branch, a two-storey red brick building set in a rice paddy. We had already spent several days there before travelling to Hajera's char, trying to figure out the complex world of money-lenders, commercial banks and charities claiming to be suppliers of credit to the poor. Grameen Bank, Bangladesh's most famous development organization, was the biggest player in this game, especially in the farm districts of central Bangladesh. A pioneer of the capitalistic idea known as microcredit, the bank had loaned hundreds of millions of dollars to the poor at market rates of interest. Like the caisses in Mali, Grameen's method was to lend to groups of five people rather than to individuals. If one person defaulted, the other four would be thrown out of the program, costing them future capital and causing them much disgrace. "Social collateral," the bank called it.

In many ways, the bank's belief in group capitalism for the poor was the antithesis of traditional Keynesian aid, which often amounted to international welfare, and in this way had helped change the very nature of development in the nineties. Microcredit had been copied in dozens of places, as diverse as Kenya, Malaysia and Chicago. But whether Grameen Bank had seriously reduced poverty was in some doubt. Its loans appeared to mostly help people who had something to start with. Whether this sort of financing could create anything meaningful for someone like Hajera was another matter. We figured her younger sister, Badana, a long-time Grameen client, might give us a good indication, and we planned to return to her hut the next day, after a Christmas dinner of stringy chicken and rice. In a largely Muslim country, we figured that should be the extent of our celebration.

Shortly after dawn on Boxing Day the mist was already rising from the dew-soaked mustard fields when we set out for Badana's village,

Lokerpara, literally "meeting place." Like her desperate sister, Badana was in top gear before breakfast as she fetched water and got the children ready for school, but unlike her sister she gave no hint of collapse.

"Before Grameen Bank, I was zero," Badana told us as she sat down to finger through her ten-year-old daughter's hair for lice, another morning chore. Her teenaged son, dressed in a lungi and a blue-and-white rugby shirt, swept the courtyard beside them. "We were sharecroppers. We could not find enough food to feed our children or clothes to dress them in. Now we can buy food and lease land and send our son to school. I have repaid thirty thousand taka to Grameen, and I have money left over."

Badana slipped out to the banana grove to move two cows, much fatter ones than Hajera's, to a tether in the open field, and then returned to join her husband, children, brother-in-law and a couple of nieces in the new home enterprise. Wrapped in blankets in the early morning sunlight, the entire family was weaving baskets. Only Badana's sister-in-law did not join in. She sat on a pile of hay, holding her head as she waited for someone to fetch some medicine for her fever.

A series of small loans had helped Badana and her husband, Javed Ali, purchase bamboo to cut and weave. The profits of this small business were not going to make them rich, but they were the difference between comfort and despair, judging by the extra saris hanging from a pole inside Badana's hut next to a display of new cooking vessels and aluminum plates.

While the others wove, Badana returned to her outdoor earthen stove in a corner of the yard and stoked it with straw to boil a pot of water for rice. She would eat later, after her weekly Grameen Bank meeting, but she wanted to get breakfast started. She also had to collect her small pink bank book inside the hut, along with a wad of taka from her husband to repay their latest loan.

Once everything was organized, Badana told her daughter Shakuri to watch that the rice didn't burn, and then she was off, leading us across a narrow embankment to the heart of Lokerpara. For their weekly meetings, the village women's group had built a small clubhouse from jute and thatch and added a corrugated sheet-metal roof. Badana kicked off her size-four rubber sandals at the door, stepped inside the cramped three-by-six-metre hut and took her place on a burlap mat with nineteen other women. The borrowers sat in front of a Grameen lending officer in rows of five to designate their groups. He was there to collect their money, disburse new loans and mark the tallies in each woman's pink booklet.

Before the meeting could begin, the women had to rise to their feet and do ten squats, followed by the Grameen salute—hands crossed in front of their chests—and three quick chants of their slogan, "Unity and work is our motto." Then they punched the air with their right fists and took their seats. The routine seemed odd for a group trying to foster independence, especially since it was led by a man. It was not as if these women, who would spend the rest of their day in the fields, needed the exercise. But Grameen believed firmly that its fight was a collective one, and that this struggle was about more than money. The members stood together against domestic violence, local corruption, illiteracy and dowry, a very Indian custom that also penetrated Bangladesh.

Once the exercises were finished, the women returned to their mats and waited patiently for Haider Ali, the lending officer, to call their names and collect their cash. Each time, he had to mark the entry in his book and the woman's book, and recount the taka, which he did as fast as a casino dealer. One woman who had not brought enough cash wedged her hand through the jute wall to collect more from her husband, who was standing outside ready to give her instructions. Another woman who had forgotten her pink book sent her daughter running home to get it. But Badana sat quietly with her weekly payment of 230 taka to cover the three loans she was juggling. When it was time, she handed the cash to her group chairwoman, who put it with the other women's money and passed it on to Haider Ali. He did not care who supplied the money, as long as the group repaid its debts.

Within an hour, Haider Ali had collected 8,720 taka for the week and could put away his books and cycle back to the Bhuapur branch. There was plenty of work to do there, with the year-end approaching and ledgers piled on desks and filing cabinets up to the ceiling. By the end of the week, the local lending officers had to calculate compound interest on the six thousand accounts in the area and enter it in their books by hand.

This system was created in the seventies by an American-educated economics professor, Muhammad Yunus, as an experiment in poverty alleviation at the University of Chittagong, on the southern coast. Yunus was intrigued by a group of women who made bamboo stools for a living but who were perpetually in debt to their suppliers. They could not scrape together twenty-five cents on their own to buy more bamboo, so he decided to lend them money from his own pocket. When the women repaid him in full and on time, he arranged a larger bank loan for them in his name.

Eventually, in 1983, Yunus secured his own banking licence and launched Grameen, which means "rural," as a profit-oriented, commercial bank for the poor. Bangladesh's central bank provided most of the initial capital, while foreign aid donors covered the bulk of the overhead—subsidies, in effect, that allowed the poor persons' bank to grow at an astonishing rate. By the late nineties, it operated in forty thousand villages and reached 2.3 million borrowers, about 94 percent of them women, who were a much better credit risk than men. Grameen claimed that 98 percent of its loans were repaid on or before their due dates. One reason women did so well was that they took their family's honour much more seriously than did their men, who often drank away new capital. Unlike their husbands, they also liked the smaller loans that were easy to manage and could finance micro-enterprises they could run in their spare time.

Badana and her friends formed their group when they saw other women in Lokerpara borrowing from Grameen and making money, mostly from cows and leased land. "They were earning money. They were saving money. We wanted to be like that," she said. Badana started with a two-thousand-taka loan, which she used to buy a raw harvest of rice from another farmer who did not have time to thresh it. There were seven more loans, each one bigger than the last, which Badana invested in cows (she had two, plus a calf), chickens (there were ten now), ducks (three) and banana trees (twelve). The animals meant more milk and thirty eggs a week, some of which her family consumed, the rest of which she sold. Another loan helped her and her husband buy the bamboo that they sliced into thin strips and wove into large grain storage baskets to sell at Bhuapur's weekend market. Saving as much as they could, she and Javed Ali accumulated forty thousand taka, which they used to buy land to grow rice, jute and mustard. No longer did they need to work as sharecroppers.

Despite the fact that the loans carried commercial rates of interest as high as 20 percent a year, Badana's group had not missed a payment in seven years. Before Grameen, the villagers had to pay 100 percent or more a year to local Hindu moneylenders, the *mahajans*.

Still, I had to wonder why Javed Ali, a shrewd farmer, could not turn to a commercial bank, even if his wife was intimidated by them. There were three commercial banks with branches in Bhuapur, each with government-set quotas for loans to small farmers like him. He just didn't trust them.

"My father always said, 'Don't rely on the banks. You're illiterate. They'll take advantage of you,'" Javed Ali told us when we got back to the family hut after the meeting. "That was why we were reluctant to borrow from Grameen, but they didn't have paperwork or anything like that. You just went in every week, and that was it."

To its credit, Grameen dealt a body blow to the mahajan monopoly. It also caused a major transfer of wealth from urban to rural Bangladesh, much more efficiently than food aid, make-work projects and other government schemes. Its little hundred-dollar loans had amounted to more than two billion dollars in capital. But as Grameen sailed ahead, there was disturbing evidence that it didn't make that much difference to poverty. An extensive World Bank study, published in 1995, found that 62 percent of the Grameen borrowers it surveyed still lived below the poverty line, while 72 percent of non-borrowers in the same villages were poor. Given the enormous scale of the bank's operations, the 10 percent difference was hardly striking.

Grameen also seemed to know no limits to its own growth. In the early nineties, it built a big new office building for itself in Dhaka. Its staff grew to twelve thousand, and then grew more demanding. In 1991, Grameen raised salaries by 25 percent to match a government wage increase, but rather than offsetting the cost with efficient new technologies or productivity gains, the so-called poor persons' bank passed on the costs to its borrowers, raising interest rates from 16 percent to 20. And yet branches like the one in Bhuapur still struggled to break even.

More troubles were exposed by a University of Manitoba doctoral student, Amin Rahman, a Bangladeshi by birth, who lived for a year in a Grameen-serviced village in Tangail, not far from Lokerpara. To Rahman's astonishment, many of the 154 borrowers he studied in 1994–95 actually lived as migrant workers in Dhaka, Malaysia or the Persian Gulf while their names were used by others to get new loans. Moreover, many of the women borrowers were fronts for their husbands or fathers. Out of the 120 women Rahman interviewed, 108 said that "male guardians in the household either sent or influenced them to become members of the Grameen Bank loan group." As well, 78 percent said the money was used for a different purpose from the one in the loan agreement. Badana herself told us she had used a three-thousand-taka tube-well loan to pay for her eldest daughter's dowry, the very practice she disavowed during every Grameen meeting. "No one will take your daughter without dowry," she explained.

A much more disturbing finding was a belief among women that their small loans led to an increase in domestic violence. Sixty-nine said they encountered verbal aggression more often than they had before joining Grameen. Another sixteen members cited an increase in both verbal aggression and physical assault. Six of those women said they were beaten when they refused to hand over the Grameen money to a male family member. Only twenty-one reported a decrease in domestic violence after joining the bank. It was not just the male family members who abused the women. Grameen lending officers, most of them men, regularly threatened the borrowers if they did not repay their loans on time. Across Bangladesh, development workers told stories of Grameen officers storming into huts to snatch pots, pans and utensils from defaulters, even though they had not been required to put up any collateral in the first place. In most cases, the threat to a woman of *durnam*, a bad reputation, was enough to drive her to repay.

The longer we stayed in Bhuapur, the more we also realized all was not right with Grameen. It had been refreshing to see a development organization get tough with its members. Most microcredit schemes wrote off loans as if they were rotten potatoes to be plowed under. But the male lending officers, coming and going on their Grameen-issued bicycles, seemed more concerned with balancing their accounts than seeing poverty and injustice disappear from the countryside. Despite Grameen's own promotion as a poor women's bank, it remained an institution run by men in an economy run by men.

"In the field it is hard to work with male members," Rahman quoted a Grameen officer as saying. "They do not come to meetings, they are arrogant, they argue with bank workers and sometimes they even threaten and scare the bank workers. It is good that our superior officers have decided not to recruit new male members, although we do not have any written instruction about it."

On the morning we left, we returned to Lokerpara to say goodbye to Badana. From across the field, her compound looked radiant in a frame of muted green banana palms and bamboo thickets. Four years earlier, when her hut was leaking badly in the monsoon, she had signed her biggest loan yet, a special ten-year Grameen home loan for twenty thousand taka, to pay for some badly needed repairs. She and Javed Ali hired a carpenter and mason to raise their mud foundation, replace bamboo crossbars with fresh poles and add corrugated sheet-metal roofing, as well as a new latrine. She also installed a new clay oven and small mud wall to keep smoke from wafting into the cooking areas used by her two sisters-in-law, who shared the compound.

Javed Ali did not approve of the house loan. Renovations did not increase the family income, he argued. He wanted to use the money to buy farm equipment and more livestock, or perhaps lease some new land. "I think it would be better if I was the (Grameen) member," he said. "I make all the decisions anyway." But he lost that argument. It was Badana's name on the loan, and she would repay the eighty taka a week from her weaving business. For all of Grameen's faults, which really were no more than the faults of its society, its loans had at least given Badana an economic voice.

After their son left for school, Javed Ali harnessed the two cows to a plow and headed for the fields, affording Badana a few moments to relax. She decided to pop some rice puffs with garlic on the smouldering breakfast fire as a snack for young Shakuri and her friends, who were hanging around the compound. And then it was back to work, weaving another basket. Badana liked to complete at least one every day, she said.

"Does your husband treat you differently since you started this business?" I asked.

"He treats me better," Badana said. "Before, when we didn't have money, he would always be irritated. His mood was different. Now that we have money we can concentrate on what we're doing."

As she worked, she continued to talk about all the changes in her life. The food was much better. Badana and her family used to live on rice and flour. Now they ate vegetables, drank milk and at least once a week bought small *gura* fish at the local market. There was less diarrhea and disease, too, and Badana could afford two thousand taka a year to send her son to a local private school, although she saw no reason to educate her three daughters, two of whom were married off with handsome dowries and now living in other villages.

I asked if the Grameen loans were the main difference between her life and Hajera's.

"It's two different pictures," Badana said, her eyes lighting up. "Here in our village we were poor, and because of Grameen we have money. In my sister's village, even the rich have been made poor. They have lost everything."

Thanks mostly to these tiny loans, there were now thirty irrigation pumps in Lokerpara instead of the three that were there in the eighties, and twenty metal roofs instead of two. There was electricity, private schooling, health care and three crops a year—luxuries that could not be imagined on the chars. Grameen Bank could not take full credit for these changes. Rural Bangladesh had undergone a remarkable transition, with an intensive government-led investment in irrigation, subsidized fertilizer and distribution of hybrid seeds.

As international aid dwindled, however, the government in Dhaka began to understand that Bangladesh could not escape a lifetime of poverty on the backs of basket weavers. As hard as the country tried, it was so poor that even if it magically achieved Japan's post-war rate of economic growth every year for the next forty-five years, its per capita income would hardly reach one thousand dollars. The government believed the economy needed to take a few giant leaps forward instead of a thousand tiny steps. It had done just that with a low-end garment industry that had created one hundred thousand jobs for young women in Dhaka. But to reach Badana, Hajera and their children, Bangladesh would have to grow through agriculture, by turning its abundant waters and soil into more profitable resources. Most Bangladeshis knew how hard that would be in a crowded river delta continuously knocked down by nature; that is, until someone suggested shrimp.

For centuries, the islands, chars and estuaries where millions of Bangladeshis eked out the barest of existences had been home to shrimp harvesters, and now shrimp was the hot commodity of international cuisine. In Thailand, Taiwan, Malaysia and China, big commercial shrimp farms were earning small fortunes, and the insatiable Japanese and American markets only wanted more. Shrimp produced jobs, hard currency, new farming skills and a step into the bright new world of aqua-industries. Shrimp also fitted the new free-market zeitgeist of development. All Bangladesh needed was a bit of capital, some training and lots of land. It got the first from the World Bank, with a low-interest, thirty-six-million-dollar loan to build embankments, canals and roads for a new landscape of shrimp farms. The UN Development Programme came up with another project for technical advice. As for the land, the government said it would find some— 140,000 hectares, to be precise.

That many of East Asia's big shrimp farms were already falling apart, destroying the soil and ousting thousands of peasant farmers from their land seemed to deter no one, at least not in Bangladesh. The World Bank went so far as to predict the new industry "would not have any detrimental effect on the environment." Shrimp was not just good business, Bangladesh was told. Shrimp would be good for the land and good for the poor.

THE PENGUIN ICE AND FISH PROCESSING FACTORY, SHYAM NAGAR, BANGLADESH

# 15

# The Shrimp Wars

Bangladesh's pink gold rush was in full swing in July 1996 when Cindy and I flew south from Dhaka to the shrimp zone to find out how a country could continue to be so bent on this new harvest when elsewhere the affair had ended in disaster. In southern Thailand, for instance, where one hundred thousand hectares of mangrove forests were felled to make way for shrimp farms, the soil was so badly damaged by salt water inundations that nothing else could grow there, leaving little but wasteland. The ecological destruction continued in

Taiwan, Vietnam, Malaysia and later China, as large food producers moved from country to country, eager to keep Western freezers stocked. It was only the thousands of small farmers who suffered, stuck as they were with enormous debts, lost incomes and land laced with salt, lime, urea phosphate and other chemicals.

Aware of the problems in East Asia, India's Supreme Court issued an order restricting the growth of private farms and directed state governments to experiment with special shrimp zones, like industrial parks, with plots allotted to local farmers. But Bangladesh had stuck to its poverty mantra, claiming it could neither afford such precautions nor risk losing an unprecedented wave of foreign investment. To monitor, advise and regulate ten thousand shrimp farms, the fisheries ministry employed only twenty-five people. They had no policy to follow anyway. An official plan for the shrimp industry, written in 1985, had yet to be approved. True to the original promise, aqua-culture had heralded a new age of capitalism, only it was more unfettered than anyone had imagined.

We followed the shrimp craze to the town of Khulna and then to the edge of the great Sundarban mangrove forest that straddles the Bangladeshi-Indian border. Literally "beautiful forest," the Sundarbans are like Florida's Everglades, exotic and pristine. Covering 3,600 square kilometres, the forest forms a natural break between the Bay of Bengal and the labyrinth of Ganges distributaries whose channels unwind like a frayed rope into the sea. Its countless islands, shifting creeks and the perpetual shade provided by twenty-five-metre-tall *sundari* trees once offered a glorious sanctuary for crocodiles, python, spotted deer, boar and Royal Bengal tigers. But like the Everglades, the Sundarbans have been besieged by human development—two hundred million humans, to be precise, developing all around it.

In recent years, the edge of the Sundarbans had gained new fame for the tiger prawns that flourish in the forested fringe, on land that barely rose above sea level. Every autumn the delta is flooded with tidal seawater. Then, in spring, it is flushed clean by the great flow of the Ganges. The ecology of southwestern Bangladesh is almost perfect for raising shrimp. It allows farmers to trap the brackish waters that prawns thrive in, and then, after a good harvest, clean their fields so they can start anew.

With nature's blessing and the government's support, hundreds of big farms had emerged around the Sundarbans, but one operation stood out like a towering sundari tree. Manik Saha, a newspaper reporter we met in Khulna, told us about this one enterprise that, in a nation of half-hectare farms, was a hundred hectares in size, and under the control of one businessman, Wazed Ali Biswas. To see it, Manik said, all we needed to do was travel down a branch of the Shibsa River, toward the forest, in a rickety diesel-powered boat that looked something like the *African Queen*.

As we chugged out of a small river port south of Khulna, our boatman had to work his way through an early morning flotilla of rowboats carrying illegally felled sundari logs to the docks, where they were strapped to rickshaws and hauled to a mill. Farther downstream, the first shrimp farms emerged on what used to be swampland but was now banked, drained and shaped like Dutch polders. I lay on the boat's roof, watching the farms pass and waving at children on the huge embankments until the engine, vibrating every plank on the boat, lulled me to sleep. We were an hour down river when Cindy woke me to see an extraordinary sight. Up ahead, the right bank was marked with guard towers, and all along the shore small figures bobbed in the water. They appeared to be women, up to their necks, pushing something as they walked. It was the Biswas farm.

"What are they pushing?" I asked Manik.

"Nets," he said. "They're collecting shrimp fry. It's what people here do to survive."

"And the towers, what are they for?" I asked. Two storeys high, with thatched roofs propped up by long bamboo poles, they looked like something out of a Vietnam War movie.

"Those are to make sure the fishermen stay outside, and to keep the shrimp inside," Manik said.

Before we landed, he explained how industrialists put together impressive estates like this one. Because of Bangladesh's old socialist land reforms, landlords had to collect small parcels of property, mostly on a leased basis, which they only later could merge into a bigger farm. If a neighbour refused to lease his land to the new estate, he might find it inundated with brackish water anyway, forcing him to cultivate shrimp and sell it to the estate owner, who often doubled as a trader. As for the displaced tenants, sharecroppers and field workers, they had to find a new subsistence searching for wild shrimp fry in the river.

But sometimes there was resistance, the kind a landlord could not ignore. When commercial farmers in this area tried to expand their enterprises to the other side of the river, they ran into a wall of human will. Most farmers on the left bank were small producers who grew rice on their land during the monsoon and grazed cattle on the dry pastureland in winter. Fearing they would be reduced to serfdom, the farmers declared their lands to be a "shrimp-free zone" and refused to allow any developer in. Armed thugs stormed their village on November 9, 1990. A young woman, Karunamoi, was shot dead by the gang, and forty other villagers were injured in the brief battle, but the villagers held their ground and the thugs retreated. Whether it was because of the attention the assault gained in the national press or the local police investigation, the intimidation stopped and the people of the left bank went back to their small farms.

As our boat approached the right bank, our driver cut the engine and turned the starboard side to the tall mud embankment. Our arrival was no longer a surprise. On top of the levee stood an armed guard and what looked like a farm manager. Manik reminded us that no matter the situation in South Asia, hospitality is paramount, so we waved courteously from the boat and were welcomed ashore. The guard came down the bank to help us off the bow and up the slope. The manager was even more gracious, especially when we said we had come all this way to learn more about the shrimp business. Why else would a few journalists hire a boat and travel down river to his polder?

"Good," the manager said when I explained our intentions in the broadest way possible. "We must talk over tea."

As we walked along the embankment toward the estate office, the manager explained two very different worlds: one outside the levee, the other inside.

On the outside, women and children, most of them not in school, skimmed the river for shrimp fry. These hardy local shrimp breed on shallow banks in the open sea, where tides and currents pick up their larvae and carry them inland to estuaries, ponds and lagoons. After growing quickly in the brackish water, they return to sea to repeat the cycle. It was like raw material delivered to a commercial farm's door.

The estate paid five hundred taka, or about ten dollars, for every thousand fry, which on a good day might mean fifty cents for the average local woman. "We used to pay a thousand taka," the manager explained, "but there's such a big supply now that the price has come down."

Once the fry were purchased from the people outside the embankment, they were transferred to the big saline ponds constructed inside the levee, built by the government and financed by the World Bank. But that was only the beginning. Running a tiger prawn farm, the manager explained, was high maintenance. A staff of twenty workers had to continuously add or remove water, using motorized pumps and sluice gates, to keep the saline level just right, and apply antibiotics to fend off disease. They also had to feed the carnivorous tiger prawns sacks of fish-meal pellets every day, along with urea phosphate to help them grow to a size worthy of their name. To maintain the right acidity level, lime was added regularly, along with oxygen pumped in by an aerator. Only then, once the biggest prawns had reached thirty centimetres in length, were the local women and children brought in to collect them by hand.

Properly managed, Biswas stood to harvest sixteen tonnes of prawns and gross 1.5 million dollars for the season — about ten times what he would gain from a winter rice crop. But if any aspect were botched, the fickle tiger prawns would die en masse, and he would lose his investment.

After tea with the estate manager, we walked back to the boat, where a group of river women had gathered. They were keen to tell Manik of their troubles. Fatima Shahad was the first to step forward. Her brown patterned sari was drenched by the muddy waters; in her hands she held a small basket containing a few dozen shrimp fry, worth a few pennies at best. Her account of her experience on the shrimp farm sounded Orwellian, so small and vulnerable was her life compared with the big and domineering forces of government, development and commerce.

For years, she and her husband had worked as sharecroppers on this land, before the government built the big embankment around it and renamed it Polder 23. In those days, they worked on a local farm in return for half the rice crop. They had never earned much, perhaps enough rice in the summer to feed their ten children, and a little more dry-land rice, vegetables and animal fodder in the winter. In a small pond next to their hut, they raised ducks and they had some hens, while their sons kept a small herd of goats in the open pastures. At least the livestock provided the children with a steady supply of eggs and milk.

But when Fatima's landlord announced he had leased his land to the new Biswas shrimp farm, her modest tenancy changed forever. Her husband had to move to Khulna to find work on a road-building crew, and unless he sent money home, which he rarely did, she and the children had to fend for themselves. In the summer, when the fields were inundated, they trawled the river for fish. A good summer month earned the family ten dollars. In winter, when the ponds were drained, they returned to the land but found most crops yielded only half what they had before the shrimp, so damaged was the soil. And that was all they had.

The estate allowed Fatima and her children to stay in their hut, perched on one of the embankments, but said they had to get rid of their ducks and chickens, which were declared a hazard to the shrimp. Since there was no grazing land, the goats also had to go. "We had ten animals," Fatima said, her eyes widening in awe at thoughts of the past. "Now we have nothing." Even the clump of trees around her hut had started to wither on the saline fields, forcing her to cross the river every few days by canoe to search for firewood on the other side.

Hers was a staggering contrast to Biswas's venture, the one that could gross 1.5 million dollars in a single season.

Rather than getting into the boat, we decided to walk to another side of the estate to see if the farmers who leased land to Biswas were faring any better than their tenants. Fatima warned us to be careful while walking along the narrow footpaths between the shrimp ponds. A few days earlier, she had slipped into a pond and a guard had chased her home, swatting her across the head. Did she not know she had muddied the waters? the guard asked. Did she not know tenants like her were supposed to keep to their huts and small yards when they weren't trawling for fry or harvesting prawns?

We managed to cross half a dozen shrimp ponds without slipping, and came to a banana grove, where Fatima's landlord, Tamir Gazi, lived in a small thatched hut. A father of eight with a thick beard and few teeth, Tamir sat inside, slouching cross-legged on a bed, looking stripped of his pride. He barely lifted his sullen eyes when we entered, or as he detailed his plight since the shrimp farm's arrival. The old man said that before he signed over his two hectares of cropland to the estate, he was a wealthy man, at least for a villager in these parts. He owned six cows, four buffalo and a herd of goats, and harvested half a tonne of rice a year. Now, the estate pays him a thousand taka, or about forty dollars, a year in rent, on top of the two hundred dollars he got for his livestock, which he is no longer allowed to keep.

Only a few years had gone by, and the money Tamir had earned for his livestock was gone, spent mostly on food. Some of his trees and most of his vegetables had also wilted in the increasingly salinated soil, and his older sons had moved to Khulna for work as day labourers and rickshaw wallahs. The old man knew they would not come back.

When I suggested Tamir not renew his lease to the estate, he shook his head angrily. The big farm, he said, would still flood his land, and then what would he do? Go to the police? He laughed. "The police are on the landlord's side," he said.

As we continued to talk in the hut, Manik appeared increasingly edgy. Heavy clouds were rolling overhead from the Sundarbans, and he said we would have to leave right away if we hoped to reach Khulna, upriver against a monsoon current, by dark. Mindful of the guard towers ahead, we walked carefully along the banks and scurried down the big embankment in a teeming rain to our boat. Fatima and her children were already back in the water, trawling for shrimp fry.

After a night in Khulna, we left with Manik for Shyam Nagar, the last town on the last road in southwestern Bangladesh. It was the informal capital of the shrimp belt, and a place where we hoped to see the better side of the sunrise industry.

The road to the Indian border was dotted with gangs of women and children breaking Indian rocks for the road-paving crews who would come along shortly. Other than a few men hauling logs by cycle-rickshaw, there was no other industry to see, until we were almost at Shyam Nagar and began to notice a patchwork of small farms, half a hectare at most, on the horizon.

We stopped and walked across a field, parched like a dustbowl, to find a farmer struggling with a hoe to save what was left from the pink gold rush. Abdul Aziz said he had once worked as a labourer in the surrounding fields, earning up to two dollars a day. This little patch of land once grew rice for his family of four, but that was before he planned to get rich quick. After hearing about the great promise of shrimp, Abdul flooded his land and borrowed money from a local bank to buy enough fry for his first crop. He enjoyed a few good years, enough to repay his loan. Then a black spot virus from China wiped out his entire farm as it cut a devastating swath across the shrimp belt. There was nothing left, just his sixth of a hectare of land, bone white with salt. All Abdul could do now was turn over the dry, gray dirt beneath the salt and wait for new life to come to the surface, maybe after a few more rainy seasons.

Abdul put down his hoe and led us to the end of his small field where he lived in a tiny hut of bamboo thatch. With his fields in ruin, he said he had taken a job cutting mud bricks at a local kiln, just to earn enough money to buy cow dung for his wife to use as cooking fuel. Their trees, the only other source of firewood, were gone, killed by the saline soil. He was not even sure how he would repay his brothers the fifty dollars he had borrowed to get through this monsoon.

"I lost forty-five hundred taka in one year," he said. "Pardon me. No, it was more."

The local fields looked like a picture out of an Ethiopian famine, so desolate and cracked was the ground. At a nearby tea stand, some of Abdul's neighbours had told us that morning they owed a thousand dollars or more to local banks, money they were not sure they could repay. Only three months earlier, a local farmer, Moheen Ali Sardar, had killed himself by drinking chemical pesticide after his shrimp business collapsed, saddling him with the equivalent of five thousand dollars in debts. With credit lines from the World Bank, Bangladesh's rural banks had loaned aggressively to smaller farmers to get the shrimp rush going. A big industrialist like Biswas, with his hundred-hectare estate, could default on this kind of loan. With one-sixth of a hectare, Abdul would have a harder time of it.

"Before the prawn farms this was a beautiful paddy field," Abdul said. "People destroyed it for profit."

❖

On the road closer to Shyam Nagar, we saw the first sign that the shrimp industry was creating anything other than misery. The Penguin Ice and Fish Processing Factory was built on the main road outside town, and seemed worth a closer look, notwithstanding all the guards at the thick metal front gate. Cindy and I strode straight past them to the main processing room, with Manik in pursuit, trying to explain our audacity to the security men who followed him.

Inside and up a flight of stairs, we found a room the size of a school cafeteria, stinking of fresh shrimp spread across the floor being cleaned in quick order by a legion of women and children. I asked Manik to ask one of the women why they had brought their little boys and girls.

"There is no work for us in the fields," said a woman whose two daughters, dressed in shorts and rag smocks, were helping her cut through a pile of raw shrimp. The woman figured she would earn about seventy cents a day on her own in the factory. With help from her two daughters, Meena and Maya, she could take home the equivalent of $1.20 a day.

Manik tried to drop the subject of child labour as one of the guards motioned frantically for us to leave.

"The guard says the owner is in Dhaka, and we need his permission to stay here," Manik explained to us.

"We'll wait for him," I suggested, careful to stand between the guard and Cindy, who was busy photographing the children.

The guards were clearly uncomfortable with this unrestrained woman and were pleading with Cindy to put away her camera when suddenly the owner appeared.

"You should come to my office," the man said with a warm handshake, introducing himself as Mahbubul Rahman. "Please. Have a cold drink, at least. You must."

We moved to an air-conditioned office, and waited politely for a tray of glasses filled with Coca-Cola, which was fast replacing tea as the official drink of South Asian hospitality. I noticed Rahman's gold Rolex.

"Why do so many children work here?" I asked.

"We absolutely ban children from working here," he replied,

expressing shock at my suggestion. I quickly flipped through my notes. "One girl said she is twelve. Another said she is nine. They both said they've worked here for a year. Some of the others look no older than five."

"My country is poor. That is the only reason," Rahman said, changing his opinion with the same alacrity as he had done with his whereabouts. "It is not legal but the local situation, the poor, it matters. It will continue for a long time because of our population density."

I was more curious to know whether shrimp, for him, a successful industrialist, had turned out to be the sunrise industry that so many had promised. Under the World Bank project, Penguin Ice had been able to borrow twenty million taka (equivalent to about four hundred thousand dollars) to build the factory and finance its initial inventory. The government, the one that can't pay for its own schools, then gave it a nine-year tax holiday. Rahman also assembled a few shrimp farms of his own, two hundred hectares in total. "Sales are not a problem," he said happily. Penguin had produced thirty million dollars' worth of shrimp the previous year, exporting most of it to the U.S.

After we finished the Cokes and a plate of chocolate-cream cookies, Rahman walked us to the factory gate. He offered us a ride back to Khulna in his new Japanese-made Pajero. It looked infinitely more comfortable than the twenty-year-old Toyota Corolla we had rented, but we declined. On our way downstairs, I noticed that Meena, Maya and the other child workers had disappeared from the shop floor. They were outside the gates on the roadside, barefoot, waving to us as we drove past. I turned around just in time to see the little girls scurry back inside the factory, and the gates close behind them.

As we headed north out of Shyam Nagar, the late afternoon light made the rice paddies look like a vast, rich green carpet. Towering cloud sculptures rose into patches of blue sky streaked with crimson. The monsoon was truly upon us.

When the Bangladeshi government and its supporters in the World Bank and the Asian Development Bank launched the pink gold rush, they did not anticipate the consequences that had shattered so many lives on Polder 23 or in Shyam Nagar. In 1985, a World Bank staff appraisal report said embankments would be built only with "the consent of all farmers in one shrimp block." It added, "Farmers not wanting to participate in shrimp-culture activities would be offered equitable lease arrangements." By embracing aqua-technology and its promise of quick profits, the World Bank and other foreign aid donors had failed to appreciate Bangladesh's skewed level of land control and the inability of the poor to negotiate on their own behalf in this feudal business culture. With the prospect of immediate profits, generous tax holidays and free infrastructure, any commercial enterprise like this would naturally fall into the hands of a few powerful landlords, who in turn would push the land beyond its natural limits. There was no legal reason for them not to.

"Big people eat big fish," the Bengali saying went. "Small people eat small fish."

Despite what we had seen (and it was confirmed by several leading environmental groups that surveyed the same area), the World Bank kept its faith in shrimp farming. Its project-completion report for the first loan described the effort as "marginally satisfactory," gave it a B rating for environmental impact and suggested another big loan to the Bangladeshi government to expand cultivation.

Early the next morning, we checked out of Khulna's musty Royal Hotel and hired a cycle-rickshaw to take us to the local office of the national airline, Biman Bangladesh, where we had to catch a bus to the nearest airport, sixty kilometres to the north. Winds and rain had been pounding down all night and grew fiercer as we travelled, at one point filling the rickshaw covering like a parachute. The rickshaw wallah, whose clothes were already soaked and torn, struggled to regain lost ground, clenching his bony feet to the wet pedals. But finally, he had to step down into the water that filled Khulna's streets, and push us the rest of the way. As I gave him a couple of hundred taka, he apologized for the weather, and said he was new to the trade. He used to be a farmer. "Every poor man in Khulna used to be a farmer," he said.

Our plane bounced around in the thunderclouds long enough for a Biman Bangladesh attendant to distribute a Coca-Cola can to every passenger, as if that were a remedy for turbulence, before we inched our way down over Dhaka. From the air, the city already looked like the capital of an aquatic country, surrounded as it was by a stunning patchwork of water that submerged entire counties, except for a village here or a lone hut there built on high ground. Strips of roadway rose from the inland waters and then disappeared, only to resurface somewhere else on the seascape like a mythical serpent slithering across a loch. Two-thirds of the country was like this, submerged but surviving, a poor man's version of Atlantis.

No sooner had the plane hit the wet runway, bouncing twice before finding a hold, than all but two of its passengers were on their feet, unloading boxes of fruit, kitchen utensils, winter and summer clothing. That everyone and the baggage tumbled left and then right and then left again as we taxied to the terminal seemed to be just part of the landing routine, like the pilot's stern instructions to sit down that everyone else ignored. Even before the Biman plane came to a halt, there was a line-up at the exit door, and then a push to the waiting bus.

The sight of a second bus did not deter two young men from climbing on to the rear bumper of the first, so desperate were they, it seems, to beat their luggage to the carousel. They need not have worried. Outside the domestic terminal, trains of luggage carts sat covered with plastic, destined for regional centres like Khulna and Chittagong. An airline official said they would go on the next available military transport plane, as Biman no longer carried big pieces of luggage, not since it had removed all its cargo holds to add more seats.

We had only hand luggage, and breezed through the terminal, past a frenzy of lost baggage claimants and straight into a mayhem of welcoming relatives and taxi drivers. We pushed against the human current, warding off taxi wallahs as they tried to pull us toward their dilapidated cars. I had hoped the fares would drop with every few steps we took away from the airport, but defeat was inevitable. After ten minutes of shouting and cursing, we agreed to pay twenty dollars to get to the city centre, double the normal fare for Bangladeshis, and piled into the back of a tired Toyota.

The airport anarchy was a fitting reintroduction to Dhaka, a megacity of 9.3 million people. By the nineties, the capital had become the world's fastest-growing major city and the centre for Bangladeshi politics, commerce, military affairs and culture, but it lacked a master plan or anything close to it. Just about the only examples of planning in the city were the magnificent national parliament, which American architect Louis Kahn fittingly designed with a moat around it, and a fifteen-million-dollar athletics complex, including a ten-lane swimming pool with underwater video monitors, built for the 1993 South Asian Federation Games. Water was an obvious theme for the capital.

As we drove through half-submerged streets, I tried to imagine an earlier Dhaka, built on a spur of land selected by the Moguls in 1608 for its elevation of eight metres above sea level. It was a more glorious age. In the 1660s, when the French traveller François Bernier came this way, he marvelled that Bengal "produces rice in such abundance that it supplies not only the neighbouring but remote states" and noted "fish of every species, whether fresh or salt, is of the same profusion. In a word, Bengal abounds with every necessity of life." Dhaka's location worked well for centuries, but with Bangladeshi independence the small spur could not hold all that was sent its way. The choicest and driest land went to the bureaucracy, parliament and a military cantonment, all connected by broad boulevards through the city to ensure easy tank access. The medians also had to be wide enough to contain the shells of fighter jets on plinths, which had become the most popular idea for a national monument since no one could agree on a hero—democrat or dictator—to immortalize.

The onslaught of foreign aid—30 billion dollars over twenty-five years—clogged streets with off-road vehicles and filled suburbs with spacious homes and air-conditioned restaurants. By 1995, Dhaka's Institute for Development Studies estimated that two-thirds of Bangladesh's top income earners were intermediaries for the aid business, and almost all of them lived in the capital. This was easy enough to see after any natural disaster when new condominiums and shopping plazas were always among the first signs of revival. Gulshan, "the garden suburb," distinguished itself as the most enduring by-product of the 1974 famine, with bungalows, tennis courts, international banks, grocery stores stocked with Swiss chocolate and Gouda cheese and restaurants with names like Lemon Grass, El Toro, Don Giovanni's Sizzler and Spaghetti Jazz. After the 1988 floods, an even posher colony, Banani, was built on rice paddies beyond Gulshan and laced with houses renting for fifty thousand dollars a year and up.

Bangladesh increasingly struck me as a nation built on good intentions and little foresight. It was a land flourishing with bright ideas, energetic organizations and people as resilient as Hajera and Badana. Yet the void of planning extended to almost every sector of the country's development. Lured by the promise of shrimp and the foreign aid that came with the new industry, the government threw open some of the most vulnerable land and the lives of its poorest people to investors, local and foreign, who had scant interest in human development. There was little regulation or supervision, no one to stop the big people in search of big fish from polluting public waters, destroying scarce land and employing small children. After fifteen years of military rule, there wasn't even a serious public discussion of how to put a stop to this exploitation.

If Bangladesh was to move ahead in a meaningful way, it would have to start making some important collective decisions, and enforcing them; in short, it had to define and protect the public interest, something that NGOs such as the Grameen Bank and Dr. Zaf's public health centres could not do. Although this seemed anathema at the time, especially after the big World Bank and IMF meeting in Bangkok, Bangladesh needed more regulation, supervision and the kind of transparency of decision-making that only a democratic system can provide. It all came back to reasserting the modern idea of government, which had become so maligned in a postmodern world.

On our last night in Bangladesh, I could not sleep for the incessant buzzing of mosquitoes as they hit the lightly toxic mesh of my mosquito net, pulled back and struck again in their blind search for an opening. I lifted the net and quickly reached for a bedside candle that gave me just enough light to read a few pages of a book by Amartya Sen, the great Bengali economist whose insights into social reform were doing much to change development thinking in the nineties.

Sen was born into comfort, the son of a bureaucrat, and grew up in the village of Shantiniketan, before moving to Dhaka, Calcutta and on to a brilliant academic career at Harvard and Cambridge. Early on, Sen demonstrated that famines occurred only in countries with authoritarian regimes, such as British-ruled India in the forties,

Communist China in the fifties and Marxist Ethiopia in the eighties. "A government," he wrote, "that has to face criticism from opposition parties and free newspapers, and that has to seek re-election, cannot afford to neglect famines, since famines are conspicuous miseries which can easily be brought into the arena of public discussion by newspapers, opposition parties, and active Parliamentarians."

In 1998, Sen was awarded the Nobel Prize for his work on welfare economics, but the committee was really lauding him for championing the cause of social investments during the eighties and early nineties when the World Bank and IMF spoke almost exclusively of private investment and market reform. Sen argued passionately, as perhaps only a Bengali economist can, that economic reforms take root only when a developing country promotes more fundamental rights like free speech, which are so necessary to public debate and better governance.

I had brought with me Sen's remarkable 1995 work, *India: Economic Development and Social Opportunity*, which he co-authored with a Belgian economist, Jean Dreze. I opened it to the section on public action and social inequality, hoping to gain some insight into the shrimp debacle. The economists, having studied several similar circumstances in India, said that despite such free enterprise and more open markets there was little change at the village level because local decisions remained in the hands of the local elite. I thought immediately of the shrimp estate owners, the manager of the Penguin Ice Factory and even my friend in Biharipur, Rajinder Singh Yadav.

"The focus of government policy at this time seems to be overwhelmingly concerned with the need to remove counterproductive regulations while continuing the traditional neglect of positive activities," Sen and Dreze wrote.

These "positive activities" could include communities' taking control of local resources—not just natural resources but social resources like schools and health clinics. Parent education committees could curtail South Asia's epidemic of teacher absenteeism. Broad-based farmers' groups could manage irrigation networks. Fishing co-ops could form their own savings and loan societies. Sen and Dreze called it "public action," the common missing element in all we had seen along the rivers, estuaries, polders and chars.

When the candle burned out, I felt eager again to get back to India, which was in the midst of its own social revolution as almost every group imaginable was taking up arms in the form of public action. The struggle was underway from the Himalayas to the Supreme Court to the remote tribal forests of Orissa, and in so many hamlets in between that I realized V.S. Naipaul was wrong only in his head count: there were a billion mutinies now.

If only I could figure out what exactly they were fighting for.

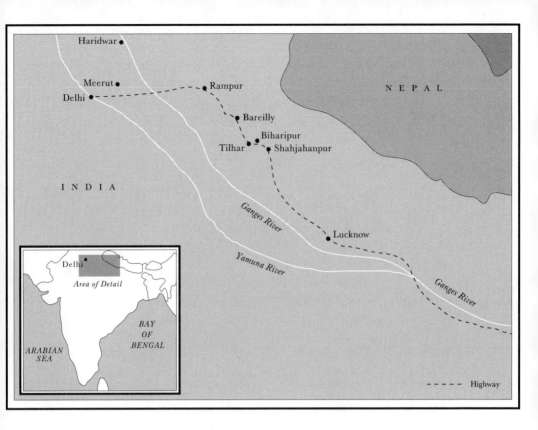

# THE VILLAGE III

"Pollution hung all around us and there was noise everywhere: babies crying, people shouting in the lanes below, cars honking. The smell of open sewers was never far away, either. For Ram, this was paradise"

# 16

## The Sikhs

Whenever a child fell ill in Biharipur, whenever a farmer complained of a bad harvest, whenever a mother spoke of her abusive
husband, I thought of the Sikhs. There they were, living on the
other side of the mango grove, drinking from the same water table,
tilling the same soil and living immeasurably better lives than any
other family in the village except Rajinder's. Kartar Singh, his wife
Jeet Kaur, and their three grown sons worked from dawn to dusk
with barely a complaint. They never gambled or drank the way

most village men did after a good harvest. They saved most of what they earned and invested much of what they saved in farm machinery, higher-yielding seeds, fertilizer and education for all their grandchildren. When one of them fell ill, someone went to Tilhar to fetch medicines from a reputable pharmacist. When a child was born, they did not wait for Sushma Singh, the auxiliary nurse-midwife. They took the baby straight to Dr. Jain for vaccinations. Even at election time they were thinking ahead; Kartar bicycled to chai shops along the highway to read newspapers and weigh opinions about the latest batch of candidates. When it came to their own well-being and the well-being of their children, the Sikhs stopped at nothing.

I tried to visit them every time I was in the village. Jeet always served fresh chai, the best in Biharipur, and often brought out a jar of her mango pickle, better than any I had tasted outside Punjab. Their compound, set well out in the fields, was far enough from the smoke of Biharipur's cooking fires that we could lounge comfortably on charpoys in the warm winter sun and chat, or seek shade under the neem trees they had wisely planted years ago. Everything about their home set them apart from the rest of the village, and there was always something new, like a stronger roof or a smokeless stove. They had barn cats, school books, clothes for their young children, vegetables for dinner, more water pumps. Even their dogs looked healthier than other dogs in the village.

The most intriguing aspect of the Sikhs' situation, however, was the fact that they had moved to Biharipur only a year before our first visit, buying a small plot of land, which over seven years they turned into the village's second-biggest holding. Rajinder could be accused of gaining his land and influence through marriage, caste, city relatives and a gun. The Sikhs seemed to profit only from hard work, motivated by their religion's core values, which condemned poverty, promoted social justice and implored all followers to constantly improve their lives. I often wondered how much of their success was a function of religious tradition, but there are plenty of poor, selfish and lazy Sikhs around India. Kartar Singh and his family had something more, stemming from a migratory life that had taken them from Pakistan Punjab to Indian Punjab, Rajasthan and finally Uttar Pradesh. Through all this, they had learned to take nothing for granted. It was not a better tradition that helped the Sikh family get ahead. It was the courage to break it.

This time I had come to Biharipur only for the day, an exceedingly hot summer day, with my friend Prashant, a marketing manager from the state capital, Lucknow, who was keen to see this low-caste village I kept talking about. I was keen to show the villagers baby pictures of our new son, especially to the midwife Bhagwati, who constantly warned Cindy and me of youth's fleeting gifts. To celebrate the birth of a child, I brought Bhagwati and the others sweets, though to them it would be celebrated as the birth of a son.

On our long walk from the railway tracks, Prashant and I saw the lambardar's tractor in the fields, with a muscular young man behind the wheel. It was the DM. He rattled over to the dirt road but didn't climb down from the machine. Rajinder had already left for town, the DM explained, but he suggested we stop by their house anyway. His older brother, Satya Prakash, was there. He had just been married, and although his wife had not yet moved to Biharipur, the DM laughed, he might take special interest in baby photos. I wasn't sure. Satya Prakash had become one of the most obnoxious youths in Biharipur, wielding his father's gun and political power like a billy club. He did not have the DM's build or even his younger brother's ability to make conversation. Instead, he seemed content to spend most of his day either grooming his wisp of a moustache or torment-ing the Dalits with his Other Backward Caste friends.

Satya Prakash often ribbed us for talking so much with the lower castes, while lower-caste boys taunted me for staying with the lambar-dar. This time as we walked through the village, a few teenagers said loudly enough for me and Prashant to hear that we had come to the village to take their photos, their stories and their land. I was getting my first taste of north India's new caste conflict, which clearly was seeping into Biharipur.

Leaving some sweets for Rajinder's wife, we decided to head for the Sikhs and their small sanctuary in the fields. We walked past Natu Lal the witch doctor's house, along a narrow footpath between rice fields, through a small grove where labourers usually slept during the midday heat and then down a path leading out of the village. The pleasant home was another twenty metres off the path, at the end of a smaller trail that the family's dogs guarded with ferocious barks. Prashant was fearful of dogs and insisted we wait until one of the Sikh children chased the mongrels into the fields with a flurry of small stones.

I could never understand why no one else lived out here. The air was clean, and the breeze always refreshing. There was plenty of room for children and dogs to run. There was no rubbish or sewage from a neighbouring hut to worry about. One could actually taste privacy. Instead, every other family chose to live as if they were in a refugee camp. Rajinder always explained it in terms of the medieval need for protection against marauders, caste rivals, even wolves, which were believed in these parts to steal babies and young livestock at night. The Sikhs laughed at these common fears and enjoyed their peace while they had it.

When we reached the open courtyard, Jeet welcomed us as she always did, by ordering two of her grandchildren to fetch charpoys for us to sit on, and another to run to fetch their grandfather from the fields. Several more children were busy washing the buffalo and milking them. Jeet's daughters-in-law waved hello but stayed by their outdoor kitchens, rolling flour for rotis. No one stopped working when we sat down, not even when I presented Jeet and Kartar with a box of sweets.

When I saw all the children at work, I thought of the interminably sick and scabby Dalit children, of Dhan Devi breast-feeding in the dirt, of the ten children who died a few summers ago and of the measles and polio cases that popped up from time to time. Why, I asked, were Jeet's children and grandchildren so seldom sick? Even the newest granddaughter, number eleven, was plump and cooing, as the Sikh matriarch bounced the little girl on her lap.

"Those people don't know how to take care of their children," Jeet replied.

"That village is dirty," Kartar added. "The children wear no clothes. Look what they sit in!"

"We clothe our children," Jeet said. "It's so hot I bathe the baby four times a day."

"You mean a week?" we asked.

"No. A day!" She looked offended.

"Our houses are not dirty," Kartar said proudly. "Our children are not dirty."

For Kartar and Jeet, it would be heresy to allow their grandchildren to live shoeless or in squalor like the Dalit children on the other side of Biharipur. Sikhism, a faith that grew out of Hinduism and Islam, knows no real poverty because it does not tolerate it. So important was it for them to eschew all signs of the Hindu hierarchy that the Sikhs were the only family not to touch Rajinder's feet when they entered his home.

Kartar wanted to say more but Jeet cut him off, as she often did. No other woman in Biharipur stood so firmly as an equal to her husband. "Once you get into the village, there are all sorts of equations," she said. "Some are lower on the ladder than others. We stay away from all that. Besides, we have so much work in the fields. We don't have time to worry about other people."

One of the daughters-in-law brought us tea and quickly retreated to her chores. Just then, their eldest son, Joginder, who seemed twice as big as any other man in Biharipur, arrived on his bicycle from Tilhar, where he had gone to buy some spices for his wife. After washing his hands, Joginder greeted us and then headed straight to the fields to continue digging an irrigation channel, the task Kartar had set aside when we arrived.

Joginder rarely spent time in the compound. A few years earlier, a feud over how to divide the harvest had separated him from his brothers Prithvi and Sheetal. They had not spoken to each another since, and although Kartar and Jeet did everything they could to bring the sons together, they feared the split was irreparable, so obstinate was the Sikh pride that seemed to flow in their blood. In this compound out in the fields, Joginder had built a metre-high mud wall between his yard and his brothers', and seldom crossed it, though his wife often chatted over the wall with the other women and went to their yards to borrow sugar and fetch water. Only once, when Cindy wanted to take a family portrait, did the entire Sikh clan sit together—silently.

After Joginder left for the fields, I asked Kartar why the other village farmers were not as industrious as he and his sons in improving their land. Most of them had at least half a hectare, which in Thailand or Punjab would be enough to get them out of destitution.

"They are very lazy," Kartar said bluntly.

If he were a white man speaking at the UN, he would be chased out for racism. But I was starting to understand that Kartar Singh, master of the soil, knew more than most.

"These people are not alert," he continued, speaking of the other farmers. "We will plant our crop in ten days. It will take them twenty to twenty-five days. They're not alert to time, the importance of time. They also do not understand money. We see money in our land. We are willing to take loans to develop our land. These people waste a lot of time doing other people's work, doing daily labour jobs. They're more interested in getting a day's wage."

Kartar had been the first local farmer to rent a combine to harvest his winter wheat crop. He was also the one to encourage Rajinder to use more urea and potash on his rice crops. And he was the only one to store a two-hundred-litre diesel drum of fuel in his yard to keep his irrigation pumps going. Other farmers cycled to Tilhar with twenty-litre cans every time they needed fuel.

During each harvest, Kartar employed twenty youths in his fields, and I couldn't help noticing two of them splashing about like children in water spewing from an irrigation pump. "Our race [the Sikhs] sees working as a daily labourer to be beneath us," Kartar went on, shaking his head at the frivolity. "We work morning to night on our land. We don't hang around other people's houses. We only work and take care of our home. That is our life. That is all we do."

As monsoon clouds rolled overhead, I wanted to hear more about this Sikh work ethic. Graciously, Kartar began to tell his story, to explain how a people, a man and a family were able to gain what they had. Born in 1932, Kartar grew up between the Ravi and Chenab rivers in the former princely state of Punjab. Most of his village was Sikh, but the area around Shekhurpura, the nearest city, was predominantly Muslim. When the British withdrew from India in 1947 and decided to grant Muslims a homeland in the form of Pakistan, there was no hope for Kartar's village or his people. Officially, Pakistan was to be a secular state with a Muslim majority. But almost everyone knew it would become a religious state—only the second in the twentieth century after Israel—and minorities would not be welcome.

As the British withdrew, and panic descended on greater Punjab, Hindus, Muslims and Sikhs sought refuge in different directions, in an unprecedented human flight. Ten million people moved from Pakistan to India and from India to Pakistan. One million more were killed trying to cross the line. At the height of the communal slaughter, Kartar's grandfather said the family had to abandon its farm, homes and livestock. In the heat of August, the patriarch led his clan by foot and ox cart on a forty-kilometre trek to Lahore, where they were to board a refugee train to Amritsar, the Sikh holy city in the new India. Before they were crowded into cattle cars, Kartar remembered being stripped of his ceremonial dagger, the *kirpan*, by Pakistani railway guards. He also remembered waiting days for the train to begin its excruciatingly slow journey to the border, only thirty kilometres away. The Sikhs could have walked faster but they knew mobs were slaughtering refugees along the roads, often in retaliation for other slaughters.

When the train finally pulled out of Lahore station, inching slowly toward Amritsar, it did not get much beyond the city limits before a frenzied mob brought it to a halt. Angry crowds shook the cattle cars and tried to wrench open sealed doors, calling for death for all those inside. The bedlam continued through the day and night. Passengers needing to relieve themselves had to do so in a corner of the car, although with only small cans of water and bread to consume there was little need for that. The next day, the mob eased and young Kartar caught some sleep, waking only to discover another tragedy. His grandfather, seated next to him on the floor, had died. There was no time for a dignified interment. The other Sikh men swung open a boxcar door and tossed the body into a Pakistani rail ditch, the last his family would see of its patriarch.

Kartar's eyes welled with the tears of anger and remorse. Five of his own grandchildren had gathered to listen, in the heat of the present summer, crowded on a charpoy under the family neem tree. The youngest played with Kartar's flowing white beard, as he carried on with the story.

On the refugee train, Kartar heard that some of the back cars had been decoupled and burned by zealous mobs. Death seemed certain for all on board, he thought, until he heard an aircraft roar overhead. It was from the new Indian Air Force, dispatched to locate stranded refugees. A few hours later, an Indian locomotive, guarded by soldiers, crossed the new border and hauled the train to safety. As soon as the Sikhs reached Amritsar, they told their horrifying story to waiting crowds, which turned to a packed train destined for Lahore and set it on fire.

Kartar's family joined relatives outside the Punjabi town of Jalandhar and later bought their own land, which gave them fleeting security. In the seventies, Kartar learned of a giant new irrigation canal reaching into the desert state of Rajasthan and moved his wife, five sons and one daughter there. When the land proved infertile, they moved again to Uttar Pradesh, near the Himalayan foothills, where the government was clearing forest to make way for more agriculture. The soil in this new place was good for about fifteen years, but gradually lost its fertility, too, under the pressures of intensive rice farming. Kartar began to ask friends and relatives about new frontiers and heard of a small place called Biharipur, where a family was selling land to move to the city.

Kartar left one son in the old village and another to run a small shop by their old home, and brought three—Prithvi, Sheetal and Joginder—to work on their new land. At first, they could grow only enough to feed their families, so they also worked some of Rajinder's land in return for half the harvest. They saved and borrowed as much as they could to buy small bits of land, mostly from families moving to the city or those falling deeper in debt to Rajinder.

India's economic reforms, which began in earnest in 1991, increased Kartar's reward. An end to government controls allowed prices for several crops to double and triple in the early part of the decade. New private mills meant there were more buyers, although Kartar, like Rajinder, lost more than a thousand dollars when the state-owned sugar mill in Tilhar closed. New capital also emerged from India's rural banks, which were eager to borrow and lend at more competitive rates since traditional government funds started to dry up. When Kartar went to the co-operative bank in Tilhar and deposited five hundred rupees (about twenty-five dollars in 1992), he was immediately eligible for a fifteen-hundred-rupee loan to buy heavily subsidized fertilizer and seeds. There were other government programs to help him buy motorized irrigation pumps. The diesel to run the pumps was subsidized, too, and like all Indian farmers he had no income tax to pay.

The Sikhs were not without their problems, though. On the

advice of state farm extension workers, both Kartar and Rajinder had planted potatoes, only to be told at harvest time that the state purchasing agency would not be buying any in the area because national production was too high. Kartar had to feed some of his potatoes to his livestock and plow the rest into the ground as fertilizer. But all in all, a thrifty farmer like Kartar Singh could not avoid success, as long as the rains were good. And they were.

As Rajinder started to withdraw from agriculture to focus on politics, teaching and attempting to build a school for Biharipur, Kartar picked up more land. He rented plots from the lambardar at the rate of twenty-five hundred rupees for each hectare and spent another four thousand rupees per hectare on fertilizers, seeds and the labour of young Biharipur men. Following the harvest, after subtracting his expenses, he was left with about sixty-two hundred rupees a hectare in profit, or about a hundred and fifty dollars, for each of the ten hectares he and his sons farmed. Over the past five years, Kartar figured, his family's farm income had risen from a modest ten thousand rupees to a very impressive seventy thousand rupees, or close to two thousand dollars, not to mention all the food they grew for themselves. Even when Kartar divided this among his four sons, they had far more money in their hands than anyone in Biharipur—except, of course, Rajinder.

As Kartar spoke, a small boy from Biharipur appeared, announcing that we, the foreigners, had come to exploit them. We would take their photograph and offer nothing in return, the boy said. "Go away!" Jeet snapped at the child. The boy shrugged his shoulders and left.

I often thought the villagers were right to expect something more than sweets but also feared that if I brought lavish gifts it would change the nature of my visits. When I asked Kartar if there was something I should give the village, he looked stunned. He then laughed a bit nervously and said I should give nothing. "Your money would be wasted here."

As much as he liked to ignore caste politics, Kartar was increasingly concerned about his Dalit fieldworkers who had grown more nettlesome since a Dalit woman named Mayawati had become the state's chief minister. Many refused to work for the dollar a day Kartar offered. They didn't care much for his instructions, either, but what could he do? Anyone who so much as raised his voice to a Dalit could be charged under a new harassment law.

Kartar skirted the caste troubles, telling us instead about a freak hailstorm the previous winter that had destroyed much of their crop. I had heard about the storm from other villagers. Some attributed it to unhappy gods. Others saw it as fate. They were so sure of fate they believed fertilizer to be unnecessary, perhaps even displeasing to the greater forces around them.

I had to wonder if Kartar, given all he had suffered, also believed in fate.

"For anything that happens in the field, the farmer is responsible," he said after a long pause to consider the question. "If something bad happened, I would blame myself for not acting earlier, for not seeing the pests and doing something about it."

"Can't the government help you?" I asked.

"The government can do very little in these matters. The most they can do is warn farmers if something bad is coming."

"Is there no such thing as destiny?" I asked, knowing how many Sikhs were intrigued by Hindu mysticism.

"I would never blame destiny," the old man said. "The fields are my responsibility."

"How would the other farmers in the village react to crop failure?"

"Most of them would blame it on destiny," he said.

With that answer, the water pump next to Kartar's homestead stopped. He excused himself to fix it. Ankle-deep in irrigation water, the sixty-five-year-old, who years ago lost his left index finger to another irrigation pump, took hold of the engine as if he were a college wrestler, and in a few minutes it was whirring again.

"Overseeing all this is God," Jeet said while her husband was gone. "If there is no rain, that is His wish."

We thanked Jeet and Kartar for the tea and headed back to the village to the sound of Kartar's irrigation pump clamouring in the stale summer air as it struggled to spew water into the ditches that he and his sons had dug by hand. In the mango grove, a half-dozen men were sleeping on the ground. Beyond them, in the village, there was barely a sign of life, not in heat that seemed torturous for everyone but Kartar Singh and his family.

We reached Rajinder's house to find the landlord back from town where he had again been lobbying for a school. The prospects did not look good, he said, as we all sat down in the courtyard. Mayawati, the new chief minister, had announced she would approve new schools only in villages with a majority Dalit population. Mayawati was determined to right centuries of wrongs suffered by the Dalits and to do it quickly. Besides schools, her administration offered free ten-year land leases to all Dalits, although none of Biharipur's Dalits had found a way to get any land. Some had been told they would have to pay five thousand rupees a hectare in bribe money to get the right papers signed.

Rajinder said he was determined to plod along with his school project, nonetheless. He gave me two sets of letters he had written to district officials—one for the school, another for a paved road—and asked if I would write a cover letter and mail them from New Delhi. Wisely, he knew district officials opened all their mail from New Delhi, especially if their names were written in English. Local Hindi letters went into another file.

Prashant and I left the village in mid-afternoon so we could cover most of the bandit-infested highway back to Lucknow in daylight. Our troubles were not so far afield, however. As we walked toward the railway track, young men quietly jeered at us again. They said we were the lambardar's friends, and here to cheat them, just as the British had done.

Although much of northern India had grown unpleasant under the angry new politics of extraction, in which ethnic, caste and religious groups try to wrench all they can from a weak state, I somehow thought this village, so backward and isolated, was faced with so many pressing concerns that people would finally come together. I was wrong. The Dalits, from the chief minister down to the people of Biharipur, had started to campaign for a bigger share of the wealth. Rajinder, meanwhile, was trying to amass all he could while he was still at the top. Only the Sikhs, I feared, were improving their lives with their own hands.

For anyone else, at least for anyone with even some education, the village's long struggles were hardly worth the while. It was far easier to walk across the fields and over the railway tracks to National Highway 24, where every few minutes a bus passed on its way to the big city, and there was always room on the roof for one more.

# 17

# City Lights

The more I went to Biharipur, the more I realized how hard it is for customs to die in a village. Why walk to Dr. Jain's in Tilhar when a witch doctor lives around the corner? Why build a school yourself when public works had always been carried out by the government or feudal prince or, before him, the emperor? Why try new rice and wheat seeds when the old varieties had kept the village fed for eons? Whenever we suggested something novel, the village elders gave these kinds of responses—with the exception of Rajinder, who came from the city, and, of course, the Sikhs.

The younger people were more curious about change and innovation, regardless of their caste. In the quiet dark of evening, Rajinder's eldest son, Satya Prakash, sometimes shed his virile mask to ask us humbly about birth control. He did not want to have six children as his father and mother now had. Similarly, in the laneways, new mothers pulled us aside to ask about vaccinations and medicine for their children's diarrhea. Teenaged boys were always eager to learn about the big city where we lived. Even the ones who taunted us for being friends with the lambardar turned respectful when it came to Delhi, the ancient city of fourteen million people that included the pampered capital, New Delhi, and its many suburbs that sprawled into two neighbouring states.

The mega-city was the promised land, a vibrant centre where tens of millions of north Indians saw hope for a better future. Hideous pollution, crime, rampant corruption and miserable slums meant little to the village youths. They had heard about the city's verve and seen pictures of city lights. How they shone, brighter than the ones at Kanya's wedding! No matter how little education these villagers had, they knew intuitively that the city was one of humanity's greatest creations, a place where ideas and ambitions flourished, where opportunities abounded, failure was accepted and traditions were broken. The city, and every farm boy knew this, was all about change.

From Biharipur, I knew of three young men, all of them brothers, who were now living in Delhi. Two of them came in 1992 to work in a soft-drink bottling plant. The third followed a year later. They were middle-caste boys, the youngest of five sons who lived a few doors down from Rajinder, opposite the water pump on the way to Amma's. Their father, Mathura, owned less than a hectare of land, a cow and a calf, just enough to keep his two oldest boys in the village. He did not even bother to send his two elder sons to primary school, so clear was their fate. As for the three younger boys, they would have to fend for themselves. Mathura encouraged them to finish grade ten in the great Indian hope of it leading to a government job, in Shahjahanpur or Lucknow. "Government jobs are permanent," Mathura explained to us once. "A private job, they can fire you."

Despite his best wishes, the three boys all failed their grade-ten exams. They were born into the wrong caste for government jobs anyway and would have to continue to fend for themselves in the new urban caste of free enterprise. Luckily, the boys were not alone. The extended family—the agent of so much division and ruin—was there to see the brothers through, as families and clans do in so many other places. Mathura had a cousin in Delhi who said he could find the boys jobs at an ailing Campa-Cola factory. It was a private venture that was taking a beating from the arrival of Coke and Pepsi. Mathura had never heard of Coke or Pepsi, or for that matter Campa-Cola, which got its start in the seventies when Indira Gandhi, in a nationalistic fit, expelled the real thing. But they were good jobs, loading bottles into crates, and crates onto trucks, the kind that clogged National Highway 24. Every month, the boys could take home eleven hundred rupees, about double what their father earned from his land.

When I told Mathura that I wanted to visit his youngest sons, Ram, Ashok and Rajinder, the father went inside his hut to get a recent letter from them, with a return address. My face dropped. The boys lived in an upstairs flat in a place called Mongol Puri. Mathura had not been to Mongol Puri, literally "Mongol Town," nor did he know its reputation. The sprawling tenement on Delhi's northern fringe was in the papers almost every day—on the crime page. Arson. Rape. Bride burnings. Gang wars. Mongol Puri was the South Bronx of Delhi, and poor Mathura could not have been prouder.

Evening had fallen over Delhi when I set off for Mongol Puri in a black-and-yellow Ambassador from our local Punjab Taxi Stand, a relic of a car with one of its doors held tightly in place by a coat hanger that worked for exactly one sharp turn. When the door fell off its hinge, the driver was unfazed. Harbinder, a young farmer who divided his year between driving taxis and tractors, stopped in the middle of the road, retrieved a wrench from the trunk and hammered the door back in place. He suggested I not touch it again.

As we drove north through the city, I wondered why anyone would give up Biharipur's bucolic fields and tranquil mango groves for this. The modern capital was designed for one million people at the beginning of the twentieth century. When Cindy and I arrived in

1992, there were eight million people in the greater city. Seven years later, when we left, the population was approaching fourteen million. For all this growth, there was little in the way of formal planning, no new high-rise buildings, no mass transit system and just one new bridge over the Yamuna River that bisected the city (and that was built only after an older bridge collapsed under the weight of traffic).

In rush hour, Delhi was impenetrable, a gridlock that pumped noxious fumes down every road and lane. I covered my mouth with my arm and hoped my eyes wouldn't sting much longer. A Toronto doctor had warned me that the Delhi air—third worst in the world after Mexico City and Beijing—had already scarred my lung tissue, and the steroid inhaler he prescribed would repair it only temporarily. Many nights I could not sleep for the coughing fits that made me feel like a veteran smoker. And we did not live on the streets like the two million other Delhi wallahs who had to breathe bus and truck fumes through the night. According to a study by India's Centre for Science and Environment, respiratory problems caused by the capital's air pollution kill forty thousand people a year, with no sign of a reprieve.

Nearly an hour after we left the Punjab Taxi Stand, Harbinder stopped at the Mongol Puri police station, near the industrial zones of northern Delhi. He felt safer parking there and suggested I proceed on foot. Fortunately, Mongol Puri was laid out in a grid, the epitome of urban logic, according to Roman numerals and English letters. Unfortunately, the township was built for perhaps fifty thousand and had to house five times that number, with only the narrowest of lanes between buildings piled together like Lego blocks—four and five storeys of brick and mortar with no vertical beams or support bars. A minor earthquake would bring the whole community crashing down. I feared a strong wind might do the same.

Private developers had built the housing blocks to make money, even from tenants who could not afford to pay more than fifteen dollars a month for a one-room flat. A building code would help, but in a city where buses had no pollution controls and cars breezed through red lights, sending unarmed traffic police scurrying, no one talked seriously about building codes.

Deep in the Lego slum, I found the brothers' third-floor flat with remarkable ease, climbing a steep, narrow staircase in the dark, past a landing and then up another one. On the roof, laundry was strung across a small open terrace. And at the end of the laundry line there was a single room slapped on the roof like a brick hut, its interior illuminated by a single light bulb.

Ram was the first person I spotted, a lanky twenty-two-year-old who jumped to his feet, came outside and shook my hand eagerly. We had not met before but he remembered my face from Biharipur; he had seen me the previous year during a visit home for the marriage of an older brother. Twenty-year-old Ashok was right behind him, standing taller than his brother. Nineteen-year-old Rajinder, they explained, was at work on the night shift. The two older brothers had been watching television on a fourteen-inch black-and-white set that Ram quickly turned off so that he could introduce his wife, Guddi, and their one-year-old daughter, Rakhi. I was already in shock. No man in the village, except the Sikhs, had introduced me to his wife. Most wouldn't even know her name.

Brimming with enthusiasm about this new life, Ram wanted to show me everything he could in the room that he shared with his wife, daughter and two younger brothers. I had already noticed two cords threaded through the window that made Mongol Puri profoundly different from Biharipur. One was for electricity. The other was for cable television. While erratic, the electricity powered a "desert cooler," the Indian-made humidifier that serves as a poor man's air conditioner, lodged in the window to blow cool moisture inside. The brothers paid seventy dollars for the machine. Below the bulky contraption was a queen-sized wood-plank bed, with no mattress, and beside it the TV they had bought for seventy-five dollars. In the middle of the room, the forty-watt bulb added four good hours to their days, by Ram's estimation. When darkness fell outside, the brothers could still read, play cards, eat a supper they could see and watch foreign television and rock videos on pirated cable TV. "We don't understand a word of it," Ram said, laughing, "but we like it."

We moved to the small terrace where Guddi had strung the day's washing, and sat in two plastic garden chairs, the brothers' only other furniture. Pollution hung all around us and there was noise everywhere: babies crying, people shouting in the lanes below, cars honking. The smell of open sewers was never far away, either. For Ram, this was paradise. He reclined in one of the plastic chairs as an American steelworker might sink into a La-Z-Boy at the end of a long shift, and looked every bit the citizen. He wore blue polyester slacks and a white dress shirt, the kind of outfit one would never see in the village except on the lambardar. He also fancied his hair cut tightly above the ears and thick on top, with a full moustache to accent his protruding cheekbones in the fashion of a Bombay movie star.

Ashok, who had slipped downstairs during the house tour, emerged with a handful of warm Cokes and straws. I asked why they weren't loyal to their employer, Campa-Cola, though I was quietly delighted they hadn't brought out the mucky drink that tasted like carbonated molasses.

"Didn't you hear?" Ram said, a bit astonished by my ignorance. "The factory closed. We lost our jobs."

The brothers were hardly upset. When the Campa-Cola factory met a predictable death in 1994, crushed by the Coke and Pepsi revolutions, they received severance packages and quickly found work at a nearby plastics-recycling factory that paid them 250 rupees a month more than they earned at the bottling plant.

"Jobs are easy to find here," Ram said. "Anyone can find a job here." There certainly was no chance of them returning to Biharipur. "In the village," he continued, "too much rain or too little rain can change the whole year. There's a steady income in the city. There are many companies. In the village, it is hard to fill your stomach."

"After so much education, why sit around the village and work in the fields?" Ashok chimed in. "It would be a waste of time."

To get their new jobs, the three of them lied again on their application forms, claiming to have completed grade ten. They could read and write Hindi, and do basic math, which was all that mattered to the foreman. The new jobs moved the brothers into a new world of savings. After they paid their rent, food, electricity and cable bills, each of them figured he put away about thirty dollars a month, which they planned to use to buy land back in the village for their retirement. In the village, their older brothers had no savings.

We finished our Cokes and talked longer about the wretched city they liked so much. Guddi had access to tap water in a neighbour's flat downstairs. She wasn't sure of their caste but at least she did not have to wrestle with those big hand pumps down the alleyway or tote buckets on her head. There were also community latrines, maintained by a private organization that charged a small fee for each turn. No more defecating in the open fields. And all around them, in the lanes below, were vegetable carts, sweetmeat shops, restaurants, juice stalls, jewellers and paan wallahs, and at the end of the lane a cinema hall, which sure beat the five-kilometre bicycle trip to Tilhar's only movie house.

Guddi, who was standing behind Ram's chair, offered her own opinion, which in itself was an urban phenomenon. In the village, she would not have been allowed to voice her thoughts or mingle with strange men like me. In the village, she said, she would have to give birth in the family hut, with her mother-in-law and the untrained midwife, Bhagwati, in attendance. In the city, she gave birth to Rakhi at a private hospital. She then teased Ashok about his own teenaged wife, whom he had left in Biharipur with his parents. Guddi was tired of caring for three men and a baby by herself. "It's up to her husband to decide where she will go," Guddi said. "But really, it would be nice to have another woman here. She would like Delhi."

After I said goodbye to the others, Ram walked me back to the taxi and smiled as he stared at the throngs around us: bicycle carts, street vendors, men and women rushing here and there. On his days off, he often took a city bus to Connaught Circus, the capital's central arcade, just to see all the people and neon-lit stores. The anonymous frenzy of city life is what he loved most. But Ram confided there were parts of village life he was starting to miss. The clean air, at least out in the fields, old friends and family ties: these were things he could not replace in the city. If he could save enough from the factory job, he thought one day he might return and farm alongside his brothers.

The steady march of Delhi's population suggests he was hoping against the odds. But the freedom to dream and save, and work toward a goal that was his alone to achieve, these were the new freedoms of Ram's world. Back in Biharipur, his older brothers were wedded to the land and their family's traditions. Out here, in the wide-open mind-space of Mongol Puri, Ram and his younger brothers were tied only to their ambition.

THE DM TRANSPORTING VOTERS ON ELECTION DAY

# 18

# A Village Votes, a Nation Bends

Long before the British brought cities and Parliament to South Asia,
India was experimenting with local councils to represent villagers
and their interests. During the tenth century, the landowners created *panchayats*, "five-member councils," to govern local development.
The earliest panchayats appropriated land for irrigation schemes
and roads, and built the schools that helped India emerge at the
start of the second millennium as one of the world's great civiliza-
tions. Trouble was, the rigid Hindu caste system was so entrenched

that no system of governance could be equitable. Only the forward castes could make decisions affecting their society and thus serve on the councils. Certainly the untouchables would not be allowed to vote. The issue was not even open for debate.

The early panchayats did not preclude rapid economic development, or the gaining of fabulous wealth by those in power. But a model of governance that did not allow or promote full, equal and vigorous public participation was destined to destroy itself, along with much of the economic development it supposedly fostered. India's deeply stratified society, for example, could not grow outward or protect itself from invasion by marauders from Persia and Central Asia who rolled over stunningly meek resistance, not because Indians were cowards but because the masses saw little need to protect one heinous ruler from another.

When northern India was conquered by Afghan armies, giving rise to the great Mogul Empire and new efforts to absorb Hindu civilization into a growing Islamic world, the untouchables and lower castes were among the easiest converts. Many others chose Buddhism or, centuries later, after the arrival of the British, Christianity. Whoever was the ruler in Delhi, divide and rule remained the practice in the hinterland.

As British authority withered in the early decades of the twentieth century, and Indians planned for their first-ever democratically elected government, Mohandas K. Gandhi foresaw the need for a new panchayat system based on universal suffrage. Local governance, he told his followers, was not only fundamental to human progress and development; it was the only way for the world's most diverse nation to rule itself. Without the power of local government—and in India, this means village government—Indians would only doom themselves to more outside rule at the hands of an authoritarian bureaucracy, a self-serving urban elite or perhaps one day a dictatorial military.

Gandhi's model of *gram swaraj*, village self-rule, did not survive his assassination in 1948. The new panchayat system, while written into the constitution, was hijacked by political groups and stripped of its powers. The local councils had no purpose other than cutting ribbons and welcoming state officials, who retained the right to dismiss panchayats at their pleasure. But Gandhi's wisdom prevailed, as rural development in India grew increasingly corrupt and unproductive, and the rural electorate became more disenchanted with those in power.

Finally, in 1993, Parliament passed the Seventy-third Amendment to India's constitution, to resume local council elections and return some of their original powers over local development. The new governing structure had three tiers: a village-level council, a block or county council and a district council, with mandatory elections every five years. To prevent influence peddling, no government employee— not a teacher, policeman or auxiliary nurse-midwife—could seek election. One-third of the seats were also reserved for women, as well as a smaller share for the lower castes. Once they were elected, the councils were to receive as much of their state's development budget as possible, for roads, irrigation ditches, water pumps and schools.

To many political thinkers in New Delhi, the reforms were the most significant step in development in nearly fifty years, something more significant to human progress than all the aid from the Indian government and abroad. To the reformers, the new councils represented nothing less than a second independence, which they called Panchayat Raj. To the cynics, the new panchayats represented something more banal, a gift to the local princes who would now enjoy decentralized corruption and unchecked political abuse. Not since the British granted taxation powers to the zamindars, the skeptics said, had the local bosses had it so good.

Every time I heard a debate in New Delhi about the merits of Panchayat Raj, I thought of Rajinder Singh Yadav. As a schoolteacher, he was not eligible for a council seat representing Biharipur and its neighbouring villages, and his teenaged sons were too young to seek elected office. When Uttar Pradesh held its first council elections in 1994, he fielded his wife, Ram Beti, the woman who rarely left the house and only a few times a year left the village. A couple of women from other villages challenged her for the seat, but none had husbands as influential as Rajinder. He ensured that everyone in Biharipur voted for Ram Beti. That went without saying. His teaching connections, his place in the emergent peasants' Samajwadi Party, his good relations with the higher castes: he had everything to ensure his wife a landslide victory in the surrounding area, and she won.

The vote proved to be a formality anyway. After the council's inaugural meeting and the swearing-in of members, Rajinder attended all meetings on his wife's behalf, voting for her by proxy.

"You know he understands all these things. He is so intelligent,"

Ram Beti later told Rama, who with Cindy was one of the few visitors allowed in her kitchen.

"She gets bored," Rajinder told me in the courtyard where only men were allowed, Rama and Cindy being the exceptions. "She doesn't know anything. She doesn't understand."

Besides, he said, there was only one other woman on the council, the chairwoman, and she did not attend either. Her grown son, a friend of Rajinder's, sat in her place.

Nearly two years had passed since the local election, and although I had been back to Biharipur several times, I figured we would start to see some progress for the village. Instead, we found the road as deeply rutted as ever. The small bridge over the irrigation ditch had also collapsed, forcing us to drive through a rice field to continue. And there was no school. There was not even talk of a school any more. Only when I reached Rajinder's house did I notice something new. Ram Beti's name was painted on the door, with the title "Member, Block Development Council." The whole house was different, for that matter. The family had painted all the bricks a pale pink, added potted plants to the entrance of their courtyard and decorated the yard's walls with Hindu aphorisms such as "Devotion is the last surrender," "All problems are man-made" and "Duty to God is humanity."

The DM, Rajinder's orderly Number Two son, entered the courtyard to greet us and ask why we were so late. We usually arrived in the early afternoon but now it was almost dark. I explained that traffic was horrible. It was bad enough that the road was jammed with trucks and buses trying to beat an election-day highway curfew as this part of northern India prepared to vote, but the same road was also lined with giant cut-out posters of Nehru, Gandhi and the remaining pantheon of dead Brahmin leaders from the Congress Party. The single unlined strip of asphalt was barely wide enough for two trucks side by side, and now we had to worry about Jawaharlal Nehru tumbling into the passing lane. The DM understood. He was nearly crushed by a bus while trying to steer his bicycle around a sizeable image of Indira Gandhi.

Rajinder, the DM explained, had already left for another town where he was to serve as an election officer. Like every teacher and thousands of other government employees in the area, he would spend the next day checking voter lists, fingerprinting people, handing out ballots that were the size of broadsheet newspapers and sealing the big metal ballot boxes. The election would cost him not only a day of teaching; he and every other teacher had been given the entire week off to allow for two days of training, one day of polling and two days of travel.

All opinion polls suggested that voting the next day would help bury the Congress legacy and end nearly fifty years of single-party rule in India. Gandhi—Mohandas, that is—had been right when he predicted absolute power in New Delhi would destroy itself. Rather than in the flames of revolution, however, the political system was burning slowly in a million fires of communal and economic anger. The oppressed, whose interests were claimed by the Congress before independence, no longer trusted the dominant party. New political movements based on caste, religion and ethnicity had emerged in the eighties and were about to peacefully overthrow not only a government but a style of representation.

Rajinder's Yadavs and the Other Backward Castes had been among the first to storm the Congress citadel, thanks to land distribution in the fifties and sixties that soon led to political representation. Forming an alliance with the disenfranchised Muslims of northern India, the so-called backwards gained power in the late eighties in the country's two most populous states, Uttar Pradesh and Bihar. More recently the self-styled "landed peasantry" had joined a larger national coalition that posed the most serious challenge yet to Congress rule, crumbling as it was on all fronts. Meanwhile, the Brahmins and other forward castes had drifted to the Hindu chauvinists in the Bharatiya Janata Party (BJP), which wanted to take away special rights and protections granted to Muslims and other minorities. The Dalits had gone their own way, too, by forming the Bahujan Samaj Party to seek a radical redress of centuries of oppression. In every small town along the highway from New Delhi, I was amazed to see trees and lampposts festooned with the Dalit party's blue-and-white flags, each bearing their emblem, an elephant, quiet and tolerant, yet strong and vengeful. "We are patient," the Dalit slogan said, "and we can crush you."

❖

The DM told us dinner was almost ready, and suggested we eat on the roof, under the stars, where a cool breeze would protect us from mosquitoes. While we waited for Ram Beti, block councillor, to roll and cook rotis, the DM filled us in on what had happened since our last visit. At the school, one of Rajinder's co-teachers had been fired for embezzling grain from a new school lunch program that the Congress government had launched as a last-ditch effort to win back peasant votes. Now the school at Sonora had only two teachers for nearly 150 children. But there was good news. Rajinder's emphasis on sports and daily calisthenics had helped the school win forty-two prizes at the district athletics meet, including a ribbon for the top female sprinter; it went to one of the Thakur girls. Unfortunately, the DM went on, as part of a new public health drive, a government doctor had also visited the school, examined every child and taken sixteen of them away to Tilhar hospital. Most had skin infections. A few had active tuberculosis.

When the DM leaned forward to light a candle on the small wooden table we were sitting around, I noticed a TLC pin on his shirt.

"Total Literacy Campaign," he explained. Another attempt to win peasant votes.

The national government, fed up with India's abysmal literacy figures, had launched a blitz in dozens of troubled districts like Shahjahanpur to bring the national literacy rate up to "cent percent." Under the program, in every village in the district, a literate person, meaning someone with a grade-ten education, was assigned to make ten other people literate. The slogan (no Indian government program can proceed without one) was "Each one, teach ten," a play on one of Gandhi's creed of "Each one, teach one."

In Biharipur, the mission fell to Rajinder, Satya Prakash and the DM, who at the time was only in grade eight. Each of them was given ten names, plus a few dozen more among them since no other instructors could be found, and for the next six months they taught their neighbours how to read and write. The sixteen-year-old DM met his group every night after dark for a half-hour lesson from one of six books provided by the national drive. None of his pupils had been to school before. Most were Dalit field labourers, including

Amma, who otherwise were never allowed in Rajinder's courtyard where the classes were held.

According to the official brochure, the government wanted to do nothing less than "liquidate illiteracy." After six months, it said, Biharipur's Dalits would be able to read aloud at a speed of thirty words a minute "with normal accent" (which was not defined), write a short letter, copy at the rate of seven words a minute and conduct simple arithmetic. It also promised villagers "several wholesome social spinoffs," including confidence building among women and "instances of superstition and social evils getting corrected." Poor Natu Lal, the witch doctor, was doomed.

At the end of the six months, every person in Biharipur was asked to write his name on a card, which Rajinder delivered to the district office, where for the first time in recorded history his village was declared literate. As thanks for their effort, Rajinder and his boys were given lapel pins and a few hundred rupees.

"Do you consider the people here literate?" I asked.

"No, no," the DM said, laughing. "It was just a formality."

He excused himself and returned with a stainless steel dish filled with curried vegetables, a bowl of dal and a big plate of rotis, and he watched while we ate. South Asian etiquette demanded that except for the head of the household, no one could eat until the guests were finished. The boys were next, followed by the girls and finally the mother, who got whatever food remained.

As we ate quickly and sparingly, the DM explained what was planned for voting day. Satya Prakash, had already gone to the village by the railway tracks, where the polling station would be located in a school. He would serve as a scrutineer for the Samajwadi Party and make sure everyone from Biharipur knew whom to vote for. He would also be expected to persuade the polling officials to allow a few extra ballots to be cast. The DM would stay here in the village with his father's tractor and cart—another acquisition since the council election—and transport voters to the poll. I asked if Rajinder had voted in an advance. No, the DM said with a smile. He would vote for his father at tomorrow's poll. He would vote for his mother, too.

I was just beginning to learn how flexible India's postmodern democracy had become.

❖

The next morning, there was no need to rush. The polls were supposed to be open at nine, but like most schools and government
offices they usually started late. After breakfast, we decided to follow the DM through the village as he tried to round up voters. In
elections past, his father simply told people it was time to vote as
they piled into his ox cart. But the air of a new democracy seemed
fresh this morning. The young DM would not have such an easy time
of it, even with Satya Prakash fixing votes at the poll.

He parked his father's red tractor near the main village entrance
and began cajoling people to get in the wagon, starting with elderly
women since they were the most pliant and wanted to avoid the midday heat.

"Whoever gives me a sari, I will vote for him," his first client,
Ram Guddi Yadav, told the teenager. I asked if anyone had given her
a new sari during this election. "No," she sighed. She wore a frayed
old cotton sari with a brown floral pattern on it, the finest apparel she
said she could find for this, a rare journey outside the village. "I guess
I will vote for Mulayam Singh," she said with an air of resignation as
she climbed into the tractor cart and squatted at the front. "He is
from our caste."

Ram Guddi sat alone in the wagon as others gathered around
and debated whom to vote for. Every major party had sent a representative to the village, but they had visited only Rajinder's house,
usually with gifts of liquor to distribute on polling day. The four
hundred or so other voters were left to his persuasion, or in his
absence, their own perceptions.

"We will vote for whoever asks us to," said Lakhan, a Dalit man.
"If they bring us in a vehicle, we will vote for them."

"Mulayam Singh Yadav was good," said Lala Ram, a middle-
aged farmer, referring to the Samajwadi Party leader. "He built
many roads and he increased the price of grain."

I asked why Mulayam Singh, when he was chief minister of
Uttar Pradesh, did not pave the road to Biharipur. "Ohhh, this village is so backward," Lala Ram said. "It does not matter who is in
power. No one does anything for us."

A couple of teenaged boys rode through the village on bicycles, waving red-and-green Samajwadi Party flags that bore its symbol, a bicycle. The youths shouted, "The teacher, the farmer, the consumer—they are all ours," and rode on.

Since the DM planned to wait until the tractor cart was full of voters, we decided to walk the two kilometres to the polling station before the morning sun hit the rice fields from too harsh an angle. The path to the poll cut through the mango grove, past the Sikhs' homestead and into the open fields, where we could follow a zigzag of narrow boundaries between paddies, stopping only at Kartar Singh's to seek his political opinion and a cup of tea. Kartar could usually predict the winner, but this time he said he had never seen so opportunistic a campaign. "It's not like Punjab where candidates come to your house and talk with you and have tea," he lamented. "Here the candidates come to the lambardar's house and then leave. They don't seem very interested in the rest of us."

Just the same, he and his family's seven other adults planned to vote for Rajinder's Samajwadi Party. He doubted they would win, not with the Dalits rising as they were, but that was secondary to their main interest, which was in expanding their land holdings. Eight votes swung the lambardar's way might just help them gain more.

When we reached the polling station shortly after eleven o'clock, voting had scarcely started. At the front steps of the two-room school-house was a corral of bamboo poles, strung together with rope to guide voters into the polling station. Guarding the entrance were two policemen—one fat and disturbed at the appalling lack of food in the village, the other so old he sat most of the day in a chair on the school porch. Their only weapons to chase away criminals, fraudulent voters and meddlesome children were two sticks of sugar cane, which the fat constable gnawed on constantly. Inside, in a corner of the main polling room, a booth was made out of a children's desk, shielded by a sheet of corrugated iron and a piece of sackcloth hanging from the ceiling. Opposite the makeshift booth, four government employees from Shahjahanpur manned a table where ballots were distributed, fingerprints were taken for voter identification and indelible black ink was dabbed on the left index finger of every voter to ensure none voted twice. Two of the polling officers were teachers. One was a bookkeeper. The fourth was an electrical engineer. None of them wanted to be here. They certainly were in no mood to contradict Satya Prakash, the son of a local village chief, an armed Yadav no less, who stood watch behind the table with a few of his teenaged friends.

We exited the school and walked around back to an adjoining yard, where each of the major parties had a table and a local worker to help people find their names on the official voters' list and a voting number they needed to receive a ballot. Most of the villagers also needed a bit of coaching to understand the ballot, which was no easy task. For the constituency of Shahjahanpur, there were thirty-three candidates on today's big pink sheet, each with a unique icon to assist those who had not graduated from the TLC. The big party symbols were all there: the Congress's reassuring hand, the Samajwadi's egalitarian bicycle, the Bahujan Samaj's tolerant yet vengeful elephant and the BJP's ancient lotus. There was also a fan, jeep, ice cream in a cup, hand pump, umbrella, chair, shovel, light bulb, airplane, television, grandfather clock, ox cart and two children, doubtless the party advocating more sterilization camps, I thought.

When we returned to the front of the school, a small line had formed in the corral, led by Dalchand and his neighbour, Chandrika Prasad, leader of the Ali Baba Band. They were followed by Abhivaran Singh Yadav, Rajinder's brother-in-law, and eight more voters I did not recognize. I asked who they were. Abhivaran only smiled, flashing his big paan-stained mouth of gums and crooked teeth. He was drunk.

The pack of Yadav men were challenged by the engineer as soon as they entered the school.

"Your serial number is not valid," he told one of Abhivaran's friends.

"He's okay," Satya Prakash assured the polling official.

"Okay, go ahead," the engineer said.

After the Yadavs, Kartar Singh and his entire family, the feuding sons included, voted quickly, with the same efficiency they applied to their wheat fields. And then they were gone, walking home in single file across the land.

When a lull followed the burst of Yadav and Sikh voters, we saw our chance to talk with the disconsolate electoral officers. The way the bookkeeper described it, polling duty was a severe punishment.

He and the three other officers, plus the two police, were picked up in Shahjahanpur the previous evening and dropped on the highway nearby, with instructions to hire an ox cart or walk to the school. Each had to carry ballot boxes, ballots, rulers, a thick elections rule book, food boxes and bedding.

"We were forced to come," said the bookkeeper, who was employed by the local irrigation department. He lifted a metal ruler to stuff a corner of Jeet's oversized ballot deep into the army-green metal ballot box.

They slept on the school floor, and ate breakfast at the local lambardar's house. The six men then had to open the polls for 1,259 registered voters, hoping no one more dangerous than Satya Prakash would come to harass them. They would be on their own until shortly after five o'clock, when a military truck was supposed to pick them up at the highway.

"Can you imagine anything like this?" the bookkeeper exclaimed. "They expect us to live here like animals and then administer the election."

The late morning heat had left everyone in the schoolhouse sweating. We offered the polling officers some of our bottled water, but they declined. They had come to accept the illnesses that would befall them from the school water pump and force them to take long medical leaves from their jobs. Only later in the afternoon did they succumb to temptation and plead with the local village chief to bring them tea, which he did.

The engineer was about to give his version of hardship, stuck in a village for twenty-four hours, when I heard Rajinder's Eicher tractor rumble up to the school. The DM had at least twenty people, all but one of them women, packed in his cart. This was good, Satya Prakash muttered to his friends. Women always voted the way they were told to. But one woman was different from the rest: Amma. What was she doing here? She didn't have a name. How could she vote? Clearly I knew nothing about rural elections. The Dalit widow calmly announced her dead husband's name, as she had done for more than thirty years, and the polling officer obligingly crossed it off the list, handing her a ballot.

Dressed in their best saris, no matter how ragged they were, the other women could not hide their terror as their hands trembled with each drop of indelible ink applied to them. In many cases, they were too nervous to even say their names, which was when Satya Prakash stepped forward. For each woman, he declared a name. For some, he made one up. For others, he pointed randomly to the voters list. If that person came later, well, they would have to find another name. The polling officers crossed the names off the sheet and handed each woman a ballot and ink-stamp to mark her choice. Then, Satya Prakash or one of his friends led them, one by one, to the polling booth and pointed to the Samajwadi Party's bicycle. At that point, the woman was free to exercise her democratic right. Only Bhagwati, the midwife, messed up Satya Prakash's system. She stamped every symbol on the sheet. "I like all of them," she said eagerly.

When the tractor-load of women had finished voting, the DM came into the polling station to vote for his mother and his under-aged self. Satya Prakash had already voted twice, under his own name and his absent father's. "Everyone does it," he boasted. "The other party agents voted several times. I didn't object."

His friend Shyam Bihari, a twenty-eight-year-old farmer, had voted four times, each time spitting on his left index finger and rubbing out the not-so-indelible ink. "The officials only recognize your finger, not your face," Shyam said. He suggested I approach the voters' registry. "Go there and vote," he insisted. "No one will object." I had to decline. More than thirty names on a ballot, I explained, and I get confused.

The four polling officials seemed to have little problem with any of this. They assumed Biharipur belonged to Satya Prakash's father, and, with it, all four hundred votes. Surely an educated young man like this, one of the teachers suggested, knew what was best for his people. Really, if I wanted to vote, he said, one more ballot would not change India's fate.

Luckily, before the scrutineers started to fight over my vote— would it go to the airplane or ice cream in a cup?—a scuffle erupted outside the polling station. I rushed outside to see the fat policeman trying to hurry along Ganganath, the wandering ascetic who stayed from time to time in a thatched hut off in the fields. The mendicant would have none of it. "I did not choose to come here," Ganganath shouted. His eyes looked glazed, as they usually were, from a morning with his religious pipe. "A boy forced me to come," he told the police. I think he meant the DM, who had ferried the holy man in his father's tractor with all the women. The generosity did not pay off, however, as Ganganath announced he would vote only for the Hindu nationalist BJP, and then raised his conch shell to blow a screeching note in the constable's plump face.

After Ganganath voted and left for home on foot, the chubby constable returned to his battle with a group of children playing in the bamboo corral, threatening them with the sugar cane stalk he had chewed down to an innocuous stub. They were clearly unimpressed, and continued to climb on the fencing, dashing only when the policeman summoned the energy to take a run at them.

Behind the school, the older policeman was preoccupied with a disturbance that grew so loud I thought it might be the arrival of a booth-capturing gang. We rushed around back to see the clamour, only to find that its source was Subash Chandra Jaswal, a local veterinarian. Dr. Jaswal had been deputed as elections supervisor for eight polls, including this one, and given the powers of a sector magistrate, which he took most seriously. Standing before a crowd of party workers and curious children, he declared all banners and posters stapled to trees around the school to be in violation of the Indian Elections Act and ordered their removal. He was also keen to find the DM, or more precisely, a young boy who, according to his sources, was transporting voters to the poll by tractor cart. "Only by bullock cart," the country vet told the crowd. "I want to see people moving only by bullock cart." Satya Prakash and his friends nodded dutifully. The DM was still inside voting.

Rajinder's sons had no reason to resist Dr. Jaswal's injunctions. They figured they had the poll wrapped up, even though barely 500 of the 1,259 registered voters had turned out. It was already noon and too hot for more than a few dozen stragglers to come in the remaining hours. Even when the afternoon cooled, there was too much work in the fields for anyone else to come to the polling station. Both Satya Prakash and the DM seemed ready to pack it in, when I noticed a large group of Dalits heading back to Biharipur by foot. We followed them, curious about why they were not going by tractor. They said they weren't sure the DM would give them a ride after what they had done. "We voted for the elephant," one of them said firmly. "All of us."

None of the Dalits believed their ballots were secret. Years earlier,

a Congress worker had told them the government possessed spy satellites that could see how they voted behind the corrugated iron sheets.
Had they never seen TV? the man asked. How else would they be able
to see inside Parliament all the way from Biharipur? It was the same
principle, he said. And they still believed him.

Of course, no one would ever know how Biharipur or this polling
station voted, since all ballots were trucked to a warehouse, under
army guard, mixed with ballots from around Shahjahanpur and
counted en masse. If the results were any more precise, the Elections
Commission feared they might inspire revenge attacks. But the sentiments were clear enough to tell Rajinder and his sons that something quite remarkable had occurred on this day. Even Amma, who
for nearly five decades had voted for Congress candidates, had tried
a new party today in her dead husband's name. In the quiet, persistent and very forceful way of democracy, the Dalits were asserting
themselves, and no amount of tractoring or multiple voting could
stop them from expressing this most basic right.

At five o'clock, right on schedule, our polling station closed. The
election workers tied each ballot box shut with string, which they
knotted and sealed with red putty. The chief polling officer and each
party agent then initialed the seals, put the boxes in white gunny
sacks and sealed those with more string and putty. When a bullock
cart arrived, the boxes were loaded on it and carried out to the highway, where the election team would wait for a military convoy to
return them to Shahjahanpur's comforts.

At the end of this extraordinary day, we watched the bullocks
saunter into the twilight, their cart full of ballot boxes and all the
tired election officers except one. In the dust of the wheels, the fat
police constable gave chase, struggling desperately to catch up to
the cart and jump on the back. The others reached out, heaving all
of his excess on board. The constable finally seemed at peace, sitting with his legs dangling. He smiled and waved goodbye to us, a
fresh stalk of sugar cane in his hand.

When the final count was announced, Shahjahanpur was deeply
divided. The local town, where most of the Brahmins and upper

castes lived, went to the Hindu nationalist BJP. The village polls like the one near Biharipur were split between the Yadavs' bicycle and the Dalits' elephant. Quite remarkably, the Congress candidate slipped through the middle, with one of the party's few victories in northern India.

Over the next two years, Biharipur would be duly punished for not supporting the successful Congress candidate. The local road remained battered, and its broken bridge unrepaired. The school Rajinder lobbied for did not appear, although this had also been the case when his own party was in power. On the level of basic needs, Biharipur was not doing well by democracy. But on another level, the level of basic rights, Biharipur was doing better than ever. A new more competitive political system was forcing old grievances and divisions into the open where they could be debated peacefully. It would take many more elections, especially many more at the local council level, to make this system more accountable, responsive and effective in Biharipur, but at least democracy was giving every adult Indian, even the widow with no name, a chance to express herself.

Returning to New Delhi, I felt as if I had witnessed a turning point in the life of a village, a small moment when the seeds of change were sown. A change of government was one thing, but today marked a much more important victory for the new Dalit resistance that was taking hold in Biharipur—a change as great as the historic migration of Kartar Singh or Mathura's three youngest sons. And for a brief time, it all seemed good, perhaps because none of us could have imagined in the playful atmosphere of election day what kind of trouble lay ahead. The movement that unsettled this cozy little polling station was about to transform Amma's village and its absent lambardar in ways neither had ever imagined, or perhaps wanted.

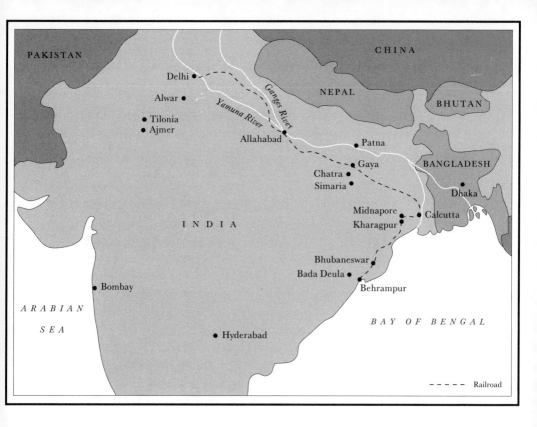

# INDIA

"If an MP felt his or her school needed more chalk, he had to make an argument before cabinet and was usually up against half a dozen other MPs demanding more chalk for their constituents, too. A chalk crisis could bring down the government."

SINDAIGA SABAR, OUTSIDE BADA DEULA, ORISSA

# 19

## The Forest Dwellers

The first time Cindy and I travelled to India's impoverished east coast, we toured the capital of Orissa state with a young couple from Bombay. He was the heir to a local mining fortune, she was a model, and they found Bhubaneswar (literal translation: "Lord of the Universe") horribly boring. Our night on the town consisted of a quick run through a silk shop followed by a few Kalinga ruins seen from the back of their chauffeur-driven Contessa Classic, which the couple had remodelled as a stretch limousine. The only excitement came outside the silk shop, when a lame beggar gamely thrust his torso through the back door as our model friend tried to slam it shut. It seemed like no contest. He had no legs; hers were so long they seemed to extend across half the limousine. But fear is irrational. "Please!" the model shrieked in panic at her liveried driver, who tried to coax the beggar away from the car without soiling his crisply pressed white pants. "Get rid of him!" The driver offered ten rupees to the beggar, who wisely did not budge. The driver upped it to twenty and we were on our way, sipping drinks in air-conditioned comfort as we sped off to dinner.

Living in New Delhi, I had become accustomed to India's extraordinary wealth, some of it centuries old. Now, as India opened its economy to private investment and competition, the rich were getting richer at a ferocious pace. I realized this when one of our neighbours, a man in the building trade, came home with a Ferrari. A few months later, another neighbouring family in the import-export business knocked down its little house and replaced it with a two-hundred-and-eighty-square-metre home with wrought-iron mouldings, teak trim and an atrium looking out on a garden through a two-storey window. When the family decided the mansion was a bit of an awkward shape, they knocked it down and started over. Down the road, the former chief minister of Haryana, a farming state outside New Delhi, bought a new Lexus and paved his driveway with marble and stone to keep its wheels comfortable at night. Eventually, our whole neighbourhood was gated and patrolled nightly by bicycling watchmen dressed in black commando fatigues. We were rich. Anyone making more than ten thousand dollars a year in India was rich. But we weren't among the super-rich. New Delhi's glitterati had moved to farmhouses south of the city, where they could enjoy swimming pools and bathhouses without paying water bills or property taxes because most of the state was designated as farmland and free from government tariff.

As emerging market mania took hold of India and more investment money rolled in, the bounty seemed unending. When I went to a jewellery store to buy a Christmas present, two women beside me—an exceedingly plump Punjabi and her flashy daughter Dimple (whom I had seen at parties around town)—could not decide between an eight-thousand-dollar diamond-and-ruby bracelet and four-thousand-dollar diamond teardrop earrings. Mommy told Dimple to decide over the weekend. She and Papa were off to Bangkok.

If you spent enough time in New Delhi or Bombay or Bhubaneswar, you would get that soothing gin-and-tonic feeling that all was well in the subcontinent. India had gone a bit astray economically after independence, but now everything was on track. Centuries of ingenuity and enterprise were being unleashed. In the few years since we moved to New Delhi, the staid city, which once shut down every night at eight, had given way to pizza home delivery, water parks, go-cart tracks, discos and multiplex cinemas, all built and run by Indians. I wanted to believe in the boom, especially after a relaxing walk with my rich friends and their groomed Alsatians in Lodhi Gardens, the Central Park of south Delhi. But there was always something in the morning paper to flatten the fizz. Like starvation deaths outside Bhubaneswar. According to reports in the fall of 1996, hundreds of people were dying or on the verge of death in Orissa, the kind of catastrophe I expected in Somalia but not in this new land of eight-thousand-dollar bracelets and stretch limousines in a city called Lord of the Universe.

To learn more about Orissa's bleaker side, a friend at an Indian magazine suggested I call Ramani, a doctor working for a charity in the state's impoverished southern hills. On the phone, Ramani described a horrible situation. There were starving and severely malnourished children, entire hillsides of them living on seeds and leaves. I was less shocked by the naked misery than by the abundance of resources she also described. These were people who inhabited a magnificent state of forested hills, alluvial plains, black soil and deep mineral deposits.

Aside from the Bay of Bengal's finest surfing beaches, Orissa offers India's best dance, pottery, stone carvings and colourful appliqué. It also claims one of Hinduism's most important temple towns, Puri, where mighty images of Lord Jagannath are mounted every summer on chariots (thus the word "juggernaut') and pulled through the streets by thousands of men. It has India's biggest lake, Chilka, where every winter exotic Siberian birds nest. And its hinterland is rich with bauxite and manganese.

Yet, for all those gifts, Orissa remains one of India's poorest states, with a rural per capita income of about one hundred dollars in 1994—less than half that in Haryana, where our Lexus-driving neighbour once ruled. Only 6.4 percent of families owned television sets; in Haryana, it was 40.3 percent. Not surprisingly, the Oriya people migrated in droves to other states, where they worked in coal mines, carpet factories and ship-wrecking yards, often indentured to their employers, while most of Orissa's natural wealth was controlled by the national government or industrialists from Calcutta and Bombay.

In this land of disparities, no one suffered more than the state's five million *adavasis*, the indigenous peoples who had inhabited the lush forests and hillsides for countless generations. They were now struggling through what Ramani called "the hunger season," when food stocks were below the subsistence level. But food aid, she insisted, was the last thing these people needed. She said if we could meet her in Bhubaneswar in a few days time, she would show us what she meant. "If the adavasis owned their forests," she explained, "things would be different."

This was not a revolutionary idea, at least not in India. Other state governments had returned control of their forests to the local communities, usually with good results. Not only did the local population profit from the harvest of trees, berries and leaves, but the forest cover under local stewardship was returning with abundance. Community forest management was all the rage in India's development circles, except among those who claimed responsibility for the adavasis. They argued that the indigenous peoples did not need control of their forests because they were considered "special people"— "scheduled tribes" was their official designation.

After hearing Ramani's account, Cindy and I made plans to return to Orissa, right after the official opening of the first McDonald's in New Delhi. The sight of the world's first Maharaja Mac was something not to be missed, not when people on the other side of India were struggling through the hunger season.

The night we arrived in Bhubaneswar, we met Ramani at a hospital. She had driven in that day with a small adavasi girl whom she brought 250 kilometres from her home in a jeep for a foot operation that would allow the child to run for the first time. Since the girl was asleep in the children's ward, Ramani suggested we sit outside on the hospital lawn, under a stunning blanket of stars, where she could describe more of the adavasi struggle. In Rayagada, the administrative block where she worked, close to half the population was listed as moderately or severely malnourished. The official infant mortality rate was 164 deaths for every 1,000 live births—worse than in Mozambique or Mali. So endemic was the poverty that one tribe, the Bhima Saoras, did not even have a word for it. They simply called it *dolai*. Hunger.

As much as the adavasis struggled against nature, they faced a bigger and growing conflict with their own government. Before Ramani had brought the young girl to Bhubaneswar, she had taken a tribal woman with a ruptured uterus to a government hospital in Behrampur, down on the coast. They arrived at noon and were told by a government doctor to come back at four o'clock with the appropriate medicines, to be purchased in the market. A four-hour wait with a ruptured uterus is not something most doctors would wish on any woman but this one was an adavasi, lower than the Dalits, lower even than a Dalit widow with no name. "I'm pretty pessimistic," Ramani said. The three of us were now on our backs staring up at the night sky. "The government's spending on health care is going down," she went on. "The only thing that goes up every year is wages, and government officials treat tribals as lesser beings. It's corrupt, through and through."

Ramani arranged for one of her colleagues, Narayan Gopalakrishnan, to take us back to the Rayagada forests where he lived. He was also in the capital with a group of adavasi girls for a high school athletics meet. The journey would be spectacular, Ramani promised, past the rugged shores of Lake Chilka, by Orissa's pristine beaches and then inland, through some of India's last thickly forested hills. We only had to watch out, she said, for the fabled Naxalites, the Maoist rebels who had taken over pockets of rural India, mostly in the adavasi belts. Named for their original base of Naxalbari in neighbouring West Bengal state, the Naxalites tended to kidnap or kill any traveller with money.

We left in an afternoon downpour, in Narayan's ancient jeep, which an old adavasi man drove for him. Of the four of us, Narayan seemed the most out of his element. A south Indian by birth, he was tall, soft-spoken, polite and exceptionally well read, as is almost everyone in his home state of Kerala. He was also an MBA who had enjoyed a fast-track career at Modi Xerox, one of India's most prominent international joint ventures, and the good life in New Delhi. But three years ago, he'd quit his management job to work among the adavasis. Like us, he had read about them in newspapers and magazines, and increasingly felt if tens of millions of his fellow Indians lived with such suffering he could no longer take pride in his citizenship. His story reminded me that for all of our rich neighbours and friends, there were just as many Indians sacrificing their comfort for a better society.

Narayan left New Delhi to join Gram Vikas, a secular Indian organization that worked with adavasis, and moved with Lady, his German shepherd, to southern Orissa and a small house in the tribal forests. He learned the state language, Oriya, and the local tribal dialects, and became the main intermediary between villages and Gram Vikas's residential school for adavasi children where he coached sports on the side. He was also trying to connect the remote villages and hamlets with the social services—hospitals, travelling clinics, state marketing boards—that had been created in their name but never introduced to them.

Gram Vikas had already built sixty-five schools in the tribal hills and trained fifty local men and women to work as teachers, along with other teachers it recruited from the plains. The organization also built village wells, dispatched doctors and nurses to vaccinate young children, handed out chloriquine to fight the malarial fever that just about everyone seemed to have and trained traditional midwives to use sterilized razors, not rusted scythes, to cut umbilical cords. The only other schools and clinics in the hills were run by Christian missionaries, who had tried to convert most of the local population, although the largely animistic adavasis remained ambiguous in their faith. In 1991, the entire hillside where Narayan lived abandoned Christianity and reconverted to Hinduism after nineteen local children died from meningitis. It was divine retribution, a local Hindu priest had told them.

As we followed the coast south, for 150 kilometres and thousands of years, Narayan explained all that was wrong with adavasi welfare, as he saw it. Shortly after independence, in the name of tribal uplift, the adavasis were made wards of the Indian president while their ancestral land and trees were made property of the state. The government would manage these resources on the tribals' behalf, and distribute benefits among the fifty million people registered in the scheduled tribes. It did not take long for Narayan's analytical mind to discover that the tribals did not need welfare—most of the benefits were stolen by district officials, anyway. What they needed was the most basic right of any aboriginal people, the right of access to their lands.

This had not always been the case, Narayan explained as we reached Behrampur, the last city before rebel country, and turned inland toward the hills, forests and setting sun. In Orissa alone, there are sixty major tribes—each colourful and quaint to the outside world and among the favourites of anthropologists. Most of them had once inhabited the lush plains along the coast but were pushed inland and uphill by a series of invaders and settlers. The tribal hills we were now entering, with towering outcrops of rock, steep hillsides and narrow river valleys, are estimated to be three million years old, among the world's oldest land formations. The natural food supply was spotty. Wildlife was scarce. Malaria was oppressive.

Still, the tribals managed to live off the forests, which they considered sacred, under the authority of regional princes. Their land was seen as common property, to be used and conserved by the inhabitants in return for taxes to the local satrap. The British colonial government changed the system irrevocably with the 1927 Forest Act, which prohibited Indians from cutting anything without a permit. The tribals could not cut their sacred trees or collect bidi leaves, tamarind pods or mangoes without the consent of His Majesty's Government. Two decades later, the newborn Indian government embraced this system of centralized resource control and kept it in place until the seventies, when Indira Gandhi approved some concessions for the adavasis, whose votes her Congress Party traditionally relied on. The new measures included the right to harvest non-timber forest products such as leaves and pods for domestic use. The sale of forest products, however, was restricted to a new state-run tribal co-operative, which kept offices in Bhubaneswar, Behrampur and other big towns but seldom came to the hills where Narayan lived. When the co-operative did make an appearance, the tribals were expected to accept credit vouchers for their harvest. The money, they were always told, would be sent later.

For timber, another state agency was empowered to pick trees in the hills for cutting, and only it could remove them. Forest guards were posted nearby and given police powers to fine anyone caught with cut wood. Most of the tribals Narayan knew had spent time in jail, often for six weeks at a time, because they could not pay up. Some had to sell cows to meet their fines. Others donated chickens and goats to keep the forest guards quiet. But they continued to cut. They knew the forest guards preferred to stay away from the malaria-ridden hills, especially since the Naxalites, a few months earlier, had blown up the local forest rest house.

Except for the forest guards, Gram Vikas and the Christian missions seemed like the only development agencies resembling government that we might find in the hills. No teachers wanted to be posted here, and not that many adavasi children would go to a government school that taught only in Oriya, which few in the hills spoke. Public health workers were also in short supply, so much so that only 15 percent of the tribal children had been vaccinated against measles. Government development officers seldom left their offices in a neighbouring valley, but it was for other reasons that small dam and irrigation projects never got built. Most of the local officials had been transferred here as punishment, and the best they could do with their two-year hardship stints was pocket as much as possible.

After an hour on a road winding uphill from the coast, Narayan's driver came to a sudden halt. Ahead, two trucks had crashed on a narrow strip of road, and a flatbed truck, apparently in an effort to get around them, had sunk in the mud of the shoulder, blocking the only possible bypass. The flatbed would be stuck there for at least a day, if not more, our driver said, turning around quickly. A few hours detour over the hills was nothing, he told us as he sped back down the hill. We would be lucky if we did not have to sleep overnight in the jeep.

He was right. A few hours later, we were within ten kilometres of our destination, Koipur, when we came to another sudden halt. A small river gushing through the forest and onto the road had washed out the only route ahead. The driver took a forest track that cut above the road, only to sink in a patch of mud. Cindy, Narayan and I took off our shoes, rolled up our pant legs and tried to push, but we only sank into the mire, along with the jeep. I feared we would be there for the rest of the rainy season, when I heard a group of adavasi boys laughing. In shorts and bare feet, they gathered some wood and laid a track for our jeep's tires to gain some traction. We were back on dry land in no time, on another narrow track that cut across the stream and rambled back down to the road, which to our weary backs felt flatter and smoother than any stretch of pavement in India, even better than our neighbour's marble driveway.

The driver pointed across a valley to the Gram Vikas school and Narayan's little house. If we did not hit another washout, he said, we would be there by midnight.

The next morning, after a breakfast of mangoes and rice at the school, we went with Narayan on his village rounds to find a man named Arjun Sabar who was thought to be too ill to move. It was the hunger season, Narayan reminded us, the lean autumn months after the rains had stopped. Most of the spring rice was gone, the winter leaves and berries were not ready, and the mosquitoes seemed more virulent than ever. For the next three months, there would be little for the local adavasis to eat other than crushed mango seeds, mango paste and a daily bowl of gruel. At least with the rains gone, the forest people would not have to worry about leaky roofs, or their village washing away.

We drove up the hill behind the school to a small clearing in the forest, where we parked and set off on foot along a narrow rocky path, plowed through thorn bushes and crossed a small creek before heading into the woods. As we stuck to the overgrown path, Narayan explained the Bhima Saora way of life. For as long as anyone could remember on this hillside, all the families had come together every winter, after the hunger season, to select patches of forest to clear for rice planting. Before the Bhima Saoras cleared any land, however, they sought the blessing of a shaman because they believed each tree was inhabited by an ancestral spirit. The tribals cut and sold what they could haul to the road, and carefully burned the remaining undergrowth so as not to damage the stumps or roots needed for the forest to regenerate itself.

Planted in cleared woodlands, the hillside rice fields represented the oldest and most sacred form of cultivation these people knew,
but even this ancient system was under threat as the fast-growing
population down on the plains started to cut the tribals' forests for
their own firewood, new cropland and, increasingly, new villages.
Two generations ago, the Bhima Saoras could let a forest grow for
twenty years before cutting it. Now the rotation was down to six
years. As a result, the trees were smaller and the soil less fertile.

Some families tried growing fruits and vegetables to make ends
meet, with little success. Those who tried banana palms had to carry
their produce ten kilometres by foot to the nearest market. Those
who cultivated tamarind pods said each crop gave six parts—one
part each for the breeze, the monkeys, the boars, the birds and the
rodents, and only one for the farmer.

At last we emerged on a small crest, several hundred metres
above a crazy quilt of green rice paddies that were shimmering in
the wetness of a fresh rain. They were the plains we had crossed the
previous night, running from the foot of the hill to the edge of a
broad, white beach and finally the Bay of Bengal. So mesmerized
were we by the glorious view that we at first did not notice Bada
Deula, a hamlet perched on a narrow terrace above us, or the crowd
of naked children standing at its gate. When we approached, they
told us we could find Arjun Sabar in the last hut up ahead, as if they
had been waiting all season for us to come.

The hamlet was nothing more than a single path with half a
dozen mud-walled, thatched-roofed huts lined up on either side. A
babbling creek ran through the forest beyond the hamlet, and only
nature lay beyond that. There was no electricity, water pumps,
school or anything that might be interpreted as development for the
Bhima Saora tribe.

When we reached Arjun's hut, he was inside, half-naked and trembling with fever on his cot. His coughs were filled with pain. His mus-
cles, supple from years of running down the hill with loads of wood on
his shoulders, visibly sagged from his bones. Arjun had passed his
forty-fifth birthday, which was better than most. If he could survive to
fifty-five, it would be unprecedented in Bada Deula.

I looked back at the narrow doorway, where Arjun's naked children blocked the room's only light as they watched our every move.

In these villages, Narayan explained, children faced such a slim chance of survival that they were not named until the age of two. When they were a bit older, they would be given clothes, purchased from the relatives of dead people.

It was hard to imagine a poorer village in a poorer part in India, and here was its poorest man, his existence more precarious than the bamboo stalks that held up his straw roof. Arjun rolled over in his cot and moaned as Narayan presented him with some medicine to ease his pain. It was a struggle for the adavasi man to speak, but he insisted we hear some of his story. He wanted us and Narayan to tell the outside world what was happening on this hilltop. The emaciated man had been born here and had watched his first wife die of fever during the hunger season many years ago. Their three young children died soon after, followed by his elder brother. Arjun married his brother's wife, adopted their four children and for several years felt that life was getting better. There was more work in other people's fields, picking rice for eight rupees a day (about twenty cents) or hauling wood. He could also count on the three tamarind trees he had inherited from his father to produce pods that he could sell. For a while, it seemed to Arjun that even the most voracious killer, malaria, was on the wane.

But this year, he continued, the curse of the Bhima Saora had returned, afflicting almost every family with dolai. A few weeks ago, one of his four adopted children succumbed to malaria. There was nothing left from the tamarind harvest either, since the monkeys had taken all six parts. A storm then washed away the rice seeds he had hoped to plant on a patch of cleared land, and his only chicken died from a bout of diarrhea. His best hope lay with three goats he had purchased with a loan from the state-run tribal agency, but they died as well. Arjun called them "plains goats," unfit for the hills. He had to repay the loan just the same. Now all he could do was wait for winter when he hoped to plant pumpkins in the forest and gather mahua flowers used by local distillers to make moonshine. His wife would also collect big leaves to sell as disposable plates or for rolling tobacco. In a good month, they might earn the equivalent of ten dollars.

When Arjun's voice failed, a neighbour who had joined us in the dark hut took up his account, which turned out to be the story of their village. Sarat Sabar, a strapping young man dressed only in tattered white underpants, sat next to me on a bamboo mat on the mud floor. He said his biggest regret was not taking his family to the plains when he found a temporary job there a few years earlier. Three of his four children were now dead: one boy from an ulcer, a two-year-old girl from an unexplained illness and a baby girl, only a few weeks earlier, who could not get enough breast milk from her mother. "It is not like this on the plains," Sarat said with hate and remorse. Tears welled up in his eyes, and then he excused himself. He had to continue cutting branches and clearing deadwood to raise enough money for his mother's funeral. She had died of fever the previous week, and by custom he would have to sacrifice a goat and feed the entire village to keep her spirit safe.

Moving to the plains seemed like the most obvious thing to do, but Arjun and Sarat knew of only one person from Bada Deula who had done that. The young man worked as a night watchman in Behrampur. Most of the other men on the hillside were frightened of the plains. Arjun himself had not left these hills in more than forty years. He said he had never seen a train. He had no idea what it was that left a streak of smoke across the sky.

Having regained some strength, Arjun wanted to explain why he would never move to the city. He spoke only the Bhima Saora language, one of 204 languages in the state, which was known to just twenty-five thousand people. His inability to speak Oriya made it difficult for him to find work anywhere but here. Although Oriya was taught at the local school, over the hilltop and a few kilometres down the road, he did not attend the school, nor did any of his children. In fact, he said, every time a child from Bada Deula tried to enrol, usually to take advantage of a government handout, they had no idea what the teachers were saying, so they came home.

To move to the city would also be to encounter crime, Arjun added. A naive tribal would be easy prey. Living on the streets or in a wretched slum, he would not have his deities and ancestral spirits around, for they remained in the forest.

"This is our traditional land," he explained, certain it was better to die hungry on his own land than live dangerously on someone else's. "This is our soil. We cannot leave it."

❖

Narayan wanted to track down another farmer, a middle-aged man named Sindaiga Sabar (the tribe's common surname), who lived half an hour's walk from Bada Deula. We followed the creek partway down the hill and then climbed another steep path that led up to a rocky outcrop, and beyond it to a small hut where farmers took turns warding off wild animals from their crops at night. These outlying fields were illegal, everyone knew, but there was also no government official who would venture this far to enforce the law.

We found Sindaiga in the fields, clearing some small trees with a machete. He shook Narayan's hand, thanking him for some recent medicines, and welcomed us to his outpost down the hill, where he kept a stash of illegal firewood. He had chopped all this wood himself and layered it in twenty-kilogram bundles, which he wanted to show to Narayan, as if to prove his strength.

Although Sindaiga seemed remarkably fit, the opposite of Arjun, he assured us it was not always so. All Bhima Saoras knew their health, like their crops, could change with the winds. Only a year ago, during the last hunger season, Sindaiga almost died and had to spend three hundred rupees on medicine, not to mention the four chickens he sacrificed to renew favour with the local spirits. He had long feared that he was not pleasing his ancestors. Each of his four sons had died soon after birth, and now he had to care for a niece, since both his brother and sister-in-law had died of fever. Just to make ends meet, to buy enough food and medicine to stay alive, he needed to carry these bundles of wood on his lean shoulders to the nearest town, an eight-hour return journey in the searing heat that would earn him the equivalent of seventy-five cents.

Narayan led us back through the forest to the clearing where we had left his jeep. It was difficult not to feel angered by all we had seen, and a little confused. After we got back to his small house and bathed at the water pump, we sat on his porch to take in the sweet smell of hyacinth and watch the brilliant night sky unfold over the hills. On evenings like this, Narayan liked to sit with Lady at his feet and listen to Chopin, played softly enough so as not to muffle the sound of the creek that ran by his house. For a while, we forgot Arjun's pain, until the valley echoed with the noise of a postman staggering down the dirt road behind the school in the dark. He was drunk. "I will kill everybody," he cried. "You will see." He had been paid that day, Narayan said, and whenever money was around, drunkenness prevailed in the hills.

Alcohol abuse was one reason that government planners did not allow the tribals direct control over their resources. Isolation was another. Some of India's brightest development thinkers argued that what the tribals really needed was more exposure to formal education, Oriya classes and health care, followed by roads, irrigation and electricity. "The modern world," they called it.

Instead, the pathetically slow pace of change, the arrogance of the Oriya instructors, and the rot of corruption had given rise to the Naxalites and their violent passion for a Maoist solution. But after three years in these forests, Narayan remained a fervent capitalist, and he believed the solution still lay in ownership and market access. If the tribals were given title to the forests, he believed, they would not have to sell their illegal harvest of timber, fruit and medicinal plants to black-market traders, or in Sindaiga's case, walk excruciatingly long distances to a city market. Just like any farmer with a title in hand, they could plan their harvests, rotate their crops and sell their produce to the highest bidder. There would be no need for charity or for the likes of Narayan.

Such ideas had been proposed many times, but Indian officials remained skeptical. Wouldn't the adavasis just clear the hillsides, they asked, and move on? Wouldn't they just take the windfall and spend it on moonshine, like the village postman did? Weren't they better off as wards of the president?

Narayan said the answer to each question was no, and there was evidence popping up all over India to support him. Community forest management was showing itself to be the most effective way to save the country's dwindling forests, but more important, it was providing communities with the kind of economic resources and political clout they had never had. We did not need to look far to see this. In neighbouring West Bengal state, hundreds of thousands of peasant farmers were working together to manage 450,000 hectares of forest in a program that had become a conservation model for much of the developing world. It was rooted in sound technical management, economic incentives, social cohesion, community responsibility and, most critically, a sense of trust between government and people—something that the adavasis had not enjoyed for centuries.

After a few nights in the hills, and more days spent hiking through the forests and villages, we left Narayan and his dog one midnight to catch the 4 a.m. mail train back to Bhubaneswar. Our third-class compartment was almost empty, perhaps because it had just passed through Naxalite territory or perhaps because few people in southeastern Orissa had money to travel during the hunger season. We spread out on a couple of hard wooden benches and tried to sleep, something one could rarely find room to do on an Indian train. But before I dozed off, I remembered Narayan's smiling face as we left. He had just received news from the capital, from one of his adavasi students, the people the government felt were a bit slow off the mark. The girl had won the Orissa state championship in sprints. She came from a village not unlike Bada Deula, Narayan said, and there she was, the fastest girl in the land.

From Bhubaneswar, the northern train crosses the Mahanadi River, ancient lifeline of Oriya culture and now a sandpit because of a large dam upstream, and then heads towards Calcutta across the Ganges' expansive delta, a stripped-down checkerboard of rice paddies and wasteland. When the British built this line in the nineteenth century, the Orissa and Bengal coast was a very different sight. The plains were thick with forests and deciduous sal trees, three and four metres in diameter. Tigers and elephants roamed freely, and communities managed the forests as they desired. The great Bengal forests started to dwindle when the British East India Company ventured south from Calcutta, in search of timber for shipbuilding and, later, railway ties, as it opened up the hinterland in the 1850s. The growth of Calcutta industry consumed more trees, and in the twentieth century, India's extraordinary rural population growth cleared even more forest. When state governments finally gained control of their forests in 1955, they saw more opportunity for cash and proceeded to cut with abandon.

By the time we crossed into the southern reaches of West

Bengal, forest covered less than 15 percent of the land. The Bengal tiger had all but disappeared from the state's once-fabled jungles, as had most other wildlife. Amazingly, though, in the middle of this environmental ruin, there were pockets where forests flourished, and as our train cut deeper into West Bengal we started to see them.

At first, the forests looked like nothing more than bushy clumps and groves, but then woodlands appeared that were so thick their leafy crowns stretched to the horizon. In the middle of this new growth, we alighted at Kharagpur, the great junction between India's eastern and southern rail lines, where long trains of coal, timber, bauxite and manganese come together from the Orissa and Bihar hinterlands for their final run to Calcutta, 220 kilometres to the northeast. All around the hideous rail yard, there were the rain-drenched forests that had made East Midnapore district a celebrated name in conservation circles. In just six years, the district had doubled its forest cover, adding two hundred square kilometres of woodlands. It was a model for forestry work in ten other states, but the project's greatest success was in social, not environmental, terms. After twenty years of community resource management, the balance of power in West Bengal had shifted from Calcutta to its villages. This was the kind of change, a voice rising more than a tree growing, that was the ultimate hope for Arjun and the Bhima Saoras, and all those who lived in and around India's forests.

In 1972, a Midnapore forestry officer, A.K. Bannerjee, first proposed West Bengal's radical solution to the dwindling forests. A government moratorium on tree felling had proved disastrous, depriving the poor of firewood and inadvertently causing a rash of illegal logging. Bannerjee, who did not have the men or weapons to stop the felling, suggested to his superiors that the state put villagers in charge of the forests and give them a monetary incentive. As long as they guarded the woods against loggers, he suggested, they could collect as much deadwood, twigs, fallen leaves and berries as they wanted. Then, when the forests were mature and ready for harvesting, the village would get one-quarter of the revenue.

The new system of joint forest management allowed forest officials like Bannerjee to assume a new development role, instead of spending their time policing woodlands. They could sit down with village committees, many for the first time, and help draw up forest plans: how much wood was needed, when it would be needed, and which areas were best for planting trees. Poverty rather than protection, he argued, would be the forest department's calling.

The proposal found an enthusiastic sponsor in West Bengal's new Marxist government, the world's first democratically elected Communist authority, which liked the idea of empowering peasants. More pragmatically, it realized forest management committees would be useful vehicles to mobilize mass support for its other programs and during election campaigns. The social forestry drive, as it became known, won more support from the World Bank, which was keen to finance conservation projects that were not run by India's increasingly corrupt state governments. The bank loaned West Bengal twenty-nine million dollars in the 1980s and another thirty-four million dollars in the nineties to invest in local tree nurseries, as well as to train villagers and expand the state's forestry service.

In its early years, the project did not work well. Many of the forests that were supposed to regenerate on their own dwindled because the forest committees planted only one or two species, which matured at the same time and were quickly cut. The committees hadn't planted species that could provide a village with the environmental equivalent of an annuity. The survival rate was also less than expected because villagers did not know how to thin their forests and watch for disease. An enthusiasm for eucalyptus, moreover, caused greater harm than good. Eucalyptus is a man's tree—tall, spindly and excellent for construction poles that provide a quick cash income for the men who cut them. As fast and straight as the eucalyptus grows, it has its disadvantages; it lacks low branches for culling and sucks the soil dry of nitrogen, killing the forest's underbelly, which women rely on for animal feed, kindling and firewood.

Eventually, the West Bengal project set a 30 percent limit on eucalyptus trees in any forest and adopted a much wider inventory in its nurseries—acacia, sal and fruit varieties—that helped replenish the soil and fostered the kind of undergrowth that made for good animal fodder. But there was another concern. The state wanted villages to wait ten years before cutting their first trees, and most farmers considered that to be too long. In ten years, they might be dead.

To tide over the villages while the big trees grew, the state allowed them to harvest as much other forest produce as they liked:

bamboo, cashews, wild mushrooms and wild potatoes, medicinal berries and leaves that could be sold to make bidis, mats and disposable plates. On average, the temporary income worked out to about 135 dollars a year for each member of a forest protection committee—an increase of about 20 percent on the average family income. In some seasons, the mushrooms alone could earn a fast picker two to three dollars a day, about double what they would make in the fields. Then, once the trees were tall enough for cutting, the village was allowed to cull up to 10 percent of the forest every year, in perpetuity. That worked out to another 125 dollars for each family.

By the mid-nineties, some 450,000 hectares of forest in West Bengal was under the protection of village squads—more than twice the area originally projected. Apart from the new greenery, the higher incomes were enough to keep many young men from migrating to Calcutta and other centres for seasonal work. According to a study commissioned by the Ford Foundation, more than half the men in East Midnapore who normally migrated for work had decided to stay in their villages year-round because of the forests. In one of the villages surveyed, where 70 percent of the men used to migrate for seasonal jobs, the rate dropped to 20 percent. In another village, it fell from 30 percent to nil.

A less tangible, but no less important, outcome was the project's contribution to democracy and public debate in rural India, where for centuries princes, colonial officers and, later, bureaucrats have held sway. The forest movement gave rise to 3,300 village committees and involved nearly 350,000 families. A smaller initiative for landless peasants to plant trees on state-owned wastelands had reached more than one million families who for the first time got to sit with district officers, share their problems and find solutions.

We tracked down one of those district officers, Arun Kumar, at the local forestry office. I had called him from New Delhi to ask more about the project and to see if we could visit some villages that had regenerated their forests. He told us of a place called Chandana, a group of four hamlets bordering a forest that had grown to fifteen square kilometres with trees that were big and ripe for cutting. Everyone wanted a share, even people from another state, Arun said. But if we intended to visit Chandana, he felt he should come with us. Given all its new wealth, the forest protection committee was feeling besieged, and the members might mistake us for poachers. He did not want to tell us what they did to poachers.

Our rental car trundled through a forest so lush that I marvelled at the towering trees and thick bush that crept right up to the side of the dirt road. Apparently others had been marvelling, too. The previous week raiders from across the state line in Bihar had come at night with axes, chains and ox carts to take as many of Chandana's thick sal trees as they could. When the forest protection committee got wind of the raid, a team rushed to the woods with bows and arrows. The standoff was ugly but Chandana's defence squad finally persuaded the Biharis to leave with only a small helping of dead-wood. Then, a few days later, a man from the nearby Lodha tribe was caught in the forest, cutting more branches. In some ways, these solo incursions were a greater threat to the forest than the larger raids, especially by the aggressive Lodhas who had no community forest of their own and were thieves by tradition (listed in the old British gazetteers as a "criminal tribe"). If anyone felt they could just wander into the Chandana Forest and cut at will, it would be doomed.

When we reached a clearing, we parked the car under a banyan tree and proceeded on foot to the village, through a small thicket and down a path that led to the house of Anil Shah, a member of the forest protection committee. A dozen committee members had already gathered on Anil's front porch for their monthly meeting, and they were furious.

"I say we cut off his hand or break his leg!" Anil said, before we had a chance to sit down. He was talking about the Lodha poacher, who was the first item of business for the protection committee. "That way we can be sure he will never try to cut our trees again."

The elderly farmer waved a small stick as he spoke and was ready to form a lynch mob, then and there. Most agreed something less aggressive was needed. Perhaps the local forest patrol was right to fine the man 150 rupees and let him go. Legally, the villagers had no power to levy a punishment. They should have sent for a government forest guard to settle the dispute, but village justice tends to be swift and not always rational.

One man said he had a better solution, a verse he had written for their enemies in the hope of inspiring co-operation. He stood up and sang, his voice soft and quavering:

The jungle is my mother,
She's eager to take me in her lap.
But she is very sad.
In this undulating terrain, in this sweet wind and sunlight,
She is not happy.
People are destroying her.
We must respect her and protect her.

The other men clapped politely and then went back to their argument about the Lodhas and whether to lynch them. "So many people try to cut our trees!" Anil said loudly to Arun, the forestry officer, who had tried to position himself inconspicuously behind a wooden post. "How else do you expect us to stop them?"

Arun tried to explain to us that this kind of heated debate was the most common and visible sign of a project's success. For the past eight years, Chandana's twenty-eight families had fended off the Lodhas, Biharis and other tree cutters just for this moment. Their sal trees, nourished by nearly a decade of good monsoons, were four metres high. Under an agreement with the state government, a forest officer like Arun could now mark trees for the villagers to cut. The villagers, in turn, would get one-quarter of the profits from the trees, plus a wage for cutting them. This simple formula was revolutionary. Suddenly, anything stolen by a poacher was no longer just wood from their forest; it was cash from their pockets.

Using money from earlier harvests of leaves, fruit and the faster-growing eucalyptus trees, the villagers of Chandana had already built a new, wider path through the centre of their community. Anil also added a second storey to his brick house, along with a new red-tiled roof that was more effective than the old thatch at keeping out the rains.

The committee members sat back, drank more tea and, having vented their anger, began to marvel at their achievement, something the men apparently liked to do at every meeting. Their new forest reminded the older members of the woods of their youth, when the roar of Bengal tigers could be heard at night. One man made a big ring with his arms to show the girth of trees in those days.

Anil said we had to see their forest to believe them, and proceeded to lead us up the path, past the old banyan tree where our car was parked, and into the woods. A decade ago, this was all wasteland, wide open and barren. Now it was thick with trees, towering, bone-thin eucalyptus, teak, bamboo, acacia, jackfruit and sal, with an undercover of berry bushes, grass and wildflowers. The low growth was so thick that Anil carried a scythe to slash a path for us.

As he forged his way ahead, a few cattle emerged, munching on undergrowth. The farmer looked a bit embarrassed. He did not need Arun to remind him that livestock were not allowed to forage in the woods, as they would slow its growth. The government, majority shareholder in the forest, insisted on it.

"Where else do we send them?" Anil asked. "We have no pasture land." Arun shrugged. He agreed that whoever wrote that rule did not live in a village.

Anil invited us back to his porch for tea so that he could discuss another concern. He had read in a local newspaper that the western state of Maharashtra, in replicating the West Bengal system, gave its villages half the profits, rather than the one-quarter share his village would get when it cut down the big trees. The southern state of Andhra Pradesh went further, allowing villages to keep 100 percent of the forest profits, provided they invested at least half the funds in the community in the form of schools, irrigation projects or expanding their forests. Arun understood the concern. He heard it everywhere he went, but could only tell the men it was up to the government in Calcutta to change the profit-sharing agreement.

Money was not a deciding factor, anyway. The people of Chandana had already seen their forest grow big and bountiful, and had every reason to keep it growing. Their incomes were, on average, 50 percent higher because of the trees. They had also learned how to lobby officials like Arun and negotiate with other communities. In all these ways, the village had changed markedly in one decade, which was why ten other Indian states were eager to copy its success.

As we sat on Anil's porch, though, I could not help noticing there was something missing, something so obvious it was hard to believe no one had yet mentioned it. The village women, who relied on the forest more than the men did, were nowhere to be seen. There were no women on the forest protection committee. Only a handful of the committees across West Bengal had more than one or two women members. The state forest department was an even greater male bastion. Of its 10,800 officers, just two were women. Before 1992, women were even not allowed to join the forestry service.

Ironically, West Bengal saw itself as a leader in India in terms of involving women in public life; it was the first state to establish quotas for female representatives in local government. But when it came down to the daily running of a village and a forest, men still called the shots. Men like Anil sat on a porch and decided which trees to plant, which trees to cut and how to spend the proceeds, while their wives and daughters left quietly at dawn to fetch the firewood needed to make the tea. Until women joined the vanguard of West Bengal's forest movement, it would remain half-hearted and half-complete. This was a well-known truth of development.

If West Bengal's Marxists planned to give women more control of grassroots development, they did not have time on their side. Across India, the poorest and most disenfranchised women were rising up to demand what was theirs by logic and by right. Even next door, in the anarchic state of Bihar where the Naxalite revolt was in full swing, thousands of women were leading their own rebellion. Although it was smaller and quieter than anything the Naxalites or Marxists had done, in the long run it was more profound. The women of central Bihar wanted nothing less than to send their daughters to school.

AN INFORMAL VILLAGE SCHOOL, NORTHERN INDIA

# 20

## "God, why did you make us girls?"

Bihar is the poorest, most divided, mindlessly violent, venally corrupt and generally unwelcoming corner of India, and a nuisance to get to. From New Delhi, I wanted to fly to Calcutta and travel west by train, which seemed straightforward enough since trains had been running that way for more than a century. But all 1.6 million employees of Indian Railways seemed to be conspiring to keep my journey off-track. My first booking, made two weeks in advance, vanished after a computer glitch wiped out the entire reservation list. My travel agent called me at home and said there was no hope of getting a replacement ticket. As soon as the computer system was fixed, all seats on the Rajdhani Express from Calcutta to Bihar were sold within minutes. Even the waiting list was closed. He asked if I would object to driving four hundred kilometres across some of India's most bandit-infested countryside in the relentless heat of July. A friend in Bihar had a better idea: go right to the top, to the railways minister. "Ring up Ram Vilas Paswan," Abdul said when I telephoned him for advice. "He is friendly to journalists."

According to a poster on the gate of his official residence, Mr. Paswan was nothing less than "King of the Dalits." He was also the most senior Bihar minister in cabinet, and the very model of the new rustic politician. No longer was Parliament filled with Oxford-educated lawyers. This was the age of Ram Vilas Paswan, and to prove it he was allotted a ministerial bungalow next door to Sonia Gandhi's. All of New Delhi was talking about how the King of the Dalits had his bungalow's prize-winning rose garden torn up and replaced with vegetables.

Since I was due to fly to Calcutta the next morning, to catch a train for which I had no ticket, I took Abdul's advice and called Mr. Paswan's personal secretary, King of Peons, who, to my surprise, was keen to hear about my troubles. He invited me to his office, in a small cement-block building beside the railway minister's official residence, where I found four men sitting under a ceiling fan in one room and five more huddled around a single, noisy air conditioner in the next. Everyone appeared to be doing nothing other than trying to stay cool; everyone, that is, except the King of Peons, the PS, as all personal secretaries are known, who was busy working three telephones. Holding two phone receivers to his chest, and a third wedged between his ear and shoulder, the PS assured me I would have no problem getting a ticket on the Rajdhani Express. It would require only a telephone call to Calcutta, which he was already in the process of making. A few quick sentences later, followed by the slow spelling of my name, the matter was settled. All I had to do, the PS explained, was go to the office of the General Manager ("Ge-NAY-Rawl"), Eastern Railway ("Not Western, EEEESTERN"), Strand Road (S-T-R-A-N-D), Calcutta. ("You are knowing Calcutta. I can see that.") A ticket would be waiting for me, he said confidently. No friend of Ram Vilas Paswan, King of the Dalits, would be turned away from Bihar for want of a railway ticket. "If you are not in the pressmen's quota, then you will be in the foreigners' quota," he reminded me before I left. "Failing that, there is the manager's quota, or they can always use the minister's quota."

Exceedingly poor, horribly polluted, insufferably congested, Calcutta is my favourite city in the subcontinent. It is home to everything great about India, starting with its maidan, the most wonderful place in South Asia on a warm Sunday when thousands of families come for picnics and cricket. Calcutta has produced four Nobel laureates; India's only Academy Award–winning filmmaker, Satyajit Ray; the world's number-two chess player, Viswanathan Anand; thirty-five national research institutions; and countless coffee houses where people gather in the evenings to argue about everything. What other city would name connecting streets after Shakespeare, Nehru and Ho Chi Minh?[1]

The Eastern Railway headquarters sits at the confluence of these many personalities—Calcutta's regal past and cacophonous present, its charm and chaos, its intellectual verve and pure filth. Outside the Strand Road building, the streets are all India, rutted, dirty and crowded, a migraine of congestion as people, rickshaws and buses vie for space that does not exist. Inside, the building is divided into quadrants, connected by spacious verandahs, long open-air passageways and caged lifts. There are endless corridors and low-angle stairways that seem to rise forever. And in the middle sits the general manager's office, accessible only by a little wooden bridge lined with a red carpet.

The GM was not in when I arrived at 10:30 a.m., nor was his personal staff of eight. For that matter, the entire building seemed deserted, as if today were a national holiday. I finally came across a lone man carrying an armful of files, and asked if I had missed something. "I am

---

[1] Among Calcutta's many attributes was an unwritten municipal code of chivalry. When a leg of the Calcutta subway opened in 1992, I marvelled at a man who took it upon himself to help unescorted women on an escalator, the city's first. After each one, he ran down the stairs to help the next, who stood patiently in line, not wanting to catch her sari in this odd contraption.

afraid that is not the case," said the man, who introduced himself as a personnel officer and could not have been very senior since he carried his own files. "People here tend to start a little late. That is our problem in India."

The personnel man listened sympathetically to my story about not having a ticket, a ticket I was sure sat on the GM's desk at that very moment if only I could walk across the little red-carpeted bridge and look for myself. But then I realized that probably no one but the GM and Ram Vilas Paswan was allowed across the little bridge. The personnel man said my time would be better spent going straight to the ticket office at the building's main entrance, which is where he led me, down a sloping stairwell, along a laneway, through another door, up a narrow staircase, past a sign that read "NO SPITING [sic]"—the one covered with red betel-nut juice—and into, of all things, a ticket office, where in a few minutes a clerk produced a blank ticket for the Rajdhani Express, stopping in Gaya, Bihar. There was no need for a reservation, the clerk explained. The train was half-empty.

Ticket in hand, I crossed Strand Road to the Hooghly docks where I boarded a small ferry to cross the river to Howrah Station. A couple of men volunteered to help women onto the wobbly boat, and then we were off to the great terminus of eastern India.

The entrance, through a decaying Victorian facade and past ornately carved teakwood ticket counters, is merely a curtain to a grand stage that is always crowded with an epic cast. I picked my way across the station, past soldiers, students, salesmen, young families, deformed beggars, vagabond children, at least one herd of goats and five thousand other people headed to every corner of India or just lying on the floor. At the central platform I found the Rajdhani Express sitting idle as a dozen men filled each car's water tanks through the roofs. The ticket clerk was right. The sold-out, waiting-list-closed, please-rent-a-car-instead train was half-empty. As the train began to leave the station, I found my second-class bunk, a padded cot that pulled down from the side of the cabin, and took in a new vista through the steel-grated window as the platform opera slid from view. We headed west through congested suburban slums that soon became a scattering of shacks before giving way to a deep green sea of rice paddies that rolled forward to the horizon, and into a warm Bengal sunset.

And then it was black. Four hours out of Calcutta, past the rejuvenated forests of East Midnapore and west into Bihar, the mining towns around Dhanbad were as dark as the coal fields below them, and so was the rest of the state, which was so rich with minerals it supplied one-third of India's coal, more than half its mica and one-third of its copper ore. It grew enough rice to feed a quarter of the country. Bihar was India's sixth-wealthiest state at independence; now, with more people than France, it was dead last, the poorest of twenty-six states. Its economic output, seventeen dollars per person per month, was less than a third of Punjab's and half that of neighbouring Madhya Pradesh.

Bihar's decay was so advanced that most of the state was in the grip of private armies or Maoist insurgents, and darkness is what they waited for. Shortly after we crossed the state line, railway police with World War II–vintage shotguns boarded the train, bolted the doors shut and took up their defensive positions on stools by the toilet. There had been fourteen train robberies in Bihar in the last two months, and several had occurred on this line. It was unclear if the holdups had anything to do with Mr. Paswan's rise to the railway portfolio, but as if on cue, after the police were in place, the train lights went out, along with the whirring ceiling fans. "This is how it starts, isn't it?" whispered a woman on the bunk opposite me to her husband on the bunk above her. She drew the tattered, musty curtain that separated our four-bunk cabin from the rest of the car, and lay silently. So did everyone else as the train continued through the dark. Slowly, most of us, including the guards, fell asleep, although several times a jolt or jerk slammed me into the cabin's partition. Just before 2 a.m., the train came to a rolling halt at Gaya, the centre of Bihar, four hours behind schedule.

It was so dark outside on the platform I could barely make out the figure of a strapping man in a white kurta, the loose tunic favoured by landlords because it conceals both pot-bellies and guns. The man in the white kurta appeared to be slapping a much smaller man, as a gunman stood watch. Otherwise, the station seemed deserted. I gamely grabbed my knapsack and jumped down to the platform, to the sound of a grunt, short and sharp. I had stepped on an old woman's arm. She fidgeted and resumed sleeping next to another body that lay next to another body. There were bodies, I realized, from one end of the platform to the other, through the station hall and out on to the street. Every step was occupied, even the wet gravel outside. The crunching of steel as the Rajdhani Express left, the clamour of people to get on board and the long, lonely whistle as it left the station: none of it seemed to disturb the sleeping mass as hundreds and hundreds of people just lay there, waiting for their trains to come in.

As I stepped over the last of the sleeping bodies and into the shadows of Gaya, I could hardly believe this was an important site for Buddhists from all over the world, who come here as pilgrims in search of the spot where the great Buddha, Siddhartha Gautama, meditated some twenty-five hundred years ago. Enlightenment was not an obvious local product, especially not during a power outage. Adding to Gaya's anguish, a fierce monsoon storm had cut off half its phone lines, submerged most of the downtown roads and flooded many of its playfully designed art deco mansions, including one with a roof fashioned in the shape of an old propeller airplane. There was so much damage that the storm seemed to have just passed, but the railway hotel clerk, working by candlelight, assured me it had come and gone a week earlier. Any repairs, he guessed, would take another month or two.

This was the epicentre, the heart of Bihar, where all of India's tectonic plates were grinding against each other, leaving no life unrattled as they opened great cracks across society's landscape. A Dalit militia had massacred scores of landowning Bhumihars in recent years, and the private army financed by the Bhumihars had killed hundreds of Dalit peasants in return. The Maoist Naxalites, the ones who had blown up the forest rest house in Orissa, were also on the move, trying to "liberate" villages, blocks and entire districts from the state. Every village had little choice but to arm itself and wait, usually in darkness.

When academics tried to make sense of Bihar's little civil war, they most often pointed to its abysmal record of land reform after independence. The state's average landholding was 0.87 hectares, barely half the 1.68 hectare average for all of India. Yet one study found eighty-four men with holdings of more than two hundred hectares, often listed in the names of wives, children, dead relatives and livestock. It was hard to dispute the baleful nature of such land-holdings, but even if all the big estates and excess government land were put together and given to the poor, there would not be enough to go around. One needed only to look at rural West Bengal or rural Bangladesh, where such reforms were carried out, to see that land was not a panacea.

A growing number of economists, led by Amartya Sen, thought the government, such as it was, should focus on social goods like education rather than land reform. Bihar's literacy rate was below 40 percent, the lowest in India, and thirty years had passed since any government in the state had paid serious attention to public schooling. Few other issues divided people so deeply along caste lines, and for obvious reasons. The upper-caste landlords feared greater education would rob them of their cheapest field labour. The upwardly mobile Yadavs feared educated Dalits would oust them from political power. The Dalit children feared they would be beaten by upper-caste teachers. And they were all right. Schools more than land would trigger the great social quake that Bihar needed so urgently.

Nowhere was India's education system in greater disrepair than in the plains around Gaya, cradle of Buddhist enlightenment. In the early nineties, nearly half of all boys and two-thirds of all girls aged six to fourteen years were not in school. Poverty was one reason many children stayed home and worked in fields, carpet factories and brick kilns, but the major cause was the state's grotesque neglect of the school system itself, especially for girls. Male teachers outnumbered female teachers fifteen to one, a common reason for girls not enrolling or for dropping out young. The lack of female graduates made the pool of potential teachers even smaller, but the real problem was the state's inability to break ancient shackles of caste. Between 1988 and 1995, a dispute over caste quotas prevented Bihar from hiring twenty-five thousand new teachers, which was only one-quarter the number it needed. Once the caste dispute was settled, the government was deluged with so many applications—three million for twenty-five thousand teaching jobs—that the process had to be halted to figure out a way to get through them all. Then, no sooner did the selections begin than court challenges were filed by some of those not hired, and the process was suspended again.

Where schools were constructed, and Bihar needed two thousand more, they were seen as government property and stripped of chairs, desks and window frames for firewood. Some 70 percent of Bihar's primary schools had no latrines, which further discouraged female teachers from coming to class. In the poorest villages, meaning Dalit villages, almost every incentive promised to a child—books, paper, posters, a free lunch program—failed to materialize. Not surprisingly, in an independent state-wide test in 1995, the average grade-five language score was 37 percent. The average math score was 30 percent.

Fed up with the decrepit school systems of Bihar and the other big northern states, the Indian government and most of its major aid donors finally decided to launch what was one of the biggest and most ambitious education drives the world had ever seen. In the late eighties, more than one billion dollars was put forward for the District Primary Education Programme, which aimed to do nothing less than reinvent Indian schooling. Large chunks of money came from the World Bank, the U.S. government and Unicef, but most of the funds came from the Indian government, which for the first time since independence reduced spending on universities in order to improve primary schools. The new approach was not about blitzes to build schools or hire teachers, which invariably led to crumbling and empty schoolhouses; the stress now was on a revolutionary new body that in North America would be called a PTA. For the first time, parents, teachers and local communities were in charge of their local schools, and most seemed determined not to let go.

In Bihar, a new parallel education body was created to bypass the corrupt, inept and generally negligent people who had made a mess of the schools in the first place. The autonomous schooling society handled all the new money and new ideas, and was run by a member of the elite Indian Administrative Service (IAS), which filled most senior positions in the country's bureaucracy. It oversaw the redesign of school books, with radical new features like sketches of local animals and pages of word and number games. All girls and all lower-caste boys received the books free. The society also channelled ten million dollars a year to thousands of district organizers and village education committees, and ranked their performance. If local results on independent exams did not increase by an average of twenty-five percentage points over five years, an entire district would risk losing new education money.

The project initially covered the state's ten worst-performing districts, building a new school or adding classrooms to an old one (along with new toilets and water pumps if they were missing) in every community that put forward a functioning education committee. Unlike the old-style brick-block schools, the new models (painted pink to show solidarity) featured terraces for outdoor classes, hexagonal rooms to promote children's sitting in clusters rather than rows and ceilings made of local clay teacups to absorb noise. Every committee, made up of elected parents and the local headteacher, got to choose their new school design, set school hours and spend a special budget of two thousand rupees a year on games, sports equipment, books or whatever else they felt was missing. In places where there weren't enough teachers, the committees were permitted to recruit local high school graduates to work as temporary teaching assistants until permanent staff could be hired. Parents were also made responsible for an annual education drive that carried a ten-thousand-rupee cash prize, to be spent on local education, for the school in each district with the biggest gain in enrolment.

Although teachers remained employees of the state and continued to receive their salaries as before, the autonomous project provided them with more resources and respect than they had ever seen. For every forty teachers, spread across twenty villages, the project built a small resource centre where they could find pedagogical materials, meet with other teachers to talk about their problems and attend training courses designed to upgrade their skills.

Every teacher was also handed five hundred rupees to spruce up classrooms with whitewash, paint and chalkboards. If they wished, they could draw animals on their walls or sketch illustrated folk tales—initiatives that previously would have been declared acts of vandalism. The audacious spirit was part of a new teaching method known as "joyful learning," which encouraged teachers to put down their canes and sing, dance and use puppets to bring life to their classrooms. To explain colours, some teachers started to send their pupils to the fields to pick flowers. For arithmetic, they counted hardened goat droppings, which every child could find at home. Stones and feathers were used for art. In science class, examination of local seed varieties replaced abstract descriptions of India's space program.

The project led to an immediate and, in many ways, predictable increase in enrolment. Much more surprising was the fact that the best results came from the poorest, most remote and violent parts of Bihar. South of Gaya, in Chatra district where the Naxalites held sway, primary school enrolment grew from 55,000 children in 1994 to 93,225 in 1999, and it was largely because of this basic power shift.

I set off for Chatra shortly after dawn, on a road that was wide, smooth and pleasant for all of ten kilometres, just long enough to pass a military garrison, an unused airport and a "Welcome, Land of Lord Buddha" sign. After crossing the Grand Trunk Road, the secondary highway descended into an unending run of craters and ruts—and, occasionally, the charred frame of a bus, set alight by an angry mob in the wake of an accident. But beyond the remnants of such retribution, in the withering heat of summer, the fields south of Gaya were mostly empty as I headed into a different Bihar, one where government writ ended and Maoist control began. For the next two hours, the only other vehicle I would see was a motorcycle, with the standard two riders: one to steer, the other to carry a shotgun.

The lonely, broken road curved its way up a hill, through abandoned scrub brush, past a few missionary schools and on to Chatra district, stronghold of the Maoist Communist Centre, as the Naxalites were known in Bihar. Locals simply called them the Party. The Maoists had peasant sympathy and ruled with terror. Government officials who ventured outside Chatra town, for example, faced risk of kidnapping or assassination. Police were often shot dead on their motorcycles, or if they were lucky stripped of their weapons and vehicles and told to walk home. As we rolled into the leafy outskirts of Chatra, which seemed more like a tranquil forest retreat than a hotbed of insurgency, I realized my rented white Ambassador, the official car of the Indian government, was almost begging for a grenade. Other than a few score cycle-rickshaws and a single Tata truck trying to ease its way through the mess, there were no other vehicles on Chatra's main road.

At the end of the street, in an upstairs flat, I found Baikunth Pandey, a philosophy lecturer who had quit a university teaching post to join the Bihar education struggle. He was waiting for me with a late breakfast. In 1993, when he began to feel there was no hope for his native Bihar, Pandey left Banaras Hindu University in eastern Uttar Pradesh, a bastion of elitist Brahminical learning, and moved three hundred kilometres east, to a district where a primary school was considered elitist. Instead of campus housing, he and his wife and teenaged son had to settle for this one-room flat. We sat down in the bedroom, which doubled as a living room and office, and his son served us mounds of rice, dal and pau, a local vegetable fried with chilies. The elder Pandey struggled to keep his eyes open. The power, he explained after his head nearly bobbed into his bowl, had been out the entire night, leaving the town to lie awake for hours in the debilitating summer heat.

The corruption of Bihar had made Pandey sympathetic to the Naxalites' goals, though he opposed their violent means. He, too, believed Bihar needed a revolution, one that would transfer power from a landed elite to the landless peasantry through the most basic public institution, a school. "When we construct a building, the process is more important than the building," he explained as we finished breakfast and prepared to head deeper into Naxalite country. "Ownership should come to the community. When government builds a school, ownership goes to the contractor."

The road into the Maoist heartland, under a protective canopy of bo trees, seemed like any other in rural Bihar except for the commerce that bubbled along its shoulders. In rickety wooden shacks, five hours from the nearest big city, there was Johnson's Baby Shampoo and Baby Powder, Coca-Cola stored in unpowered refrigerators and entire shelves of Indian hair dyes. Pandey explained that Chatra's biggest industry was supplying grunt labour, rickshaw pullers, carpet weavers and coolies, to urban India; the small consumer boom had merely followed their remittances home. He pointed ahead to a sight more striking than the unlit Coke fridges. Next to the road, in a small grove of eucalyptus trees, was a two-room pink schoolhouse that belonged to Dandua village, a community, Pandey said, that had left its worst battles behind.

Twenty kilometres south of Chatra, Dandua was a maze of interlocking mud huts and rutted dirt lanes. There was one modern water pump for fifteen hundred residents and one ancient well consisting of a large wooden lever that drew buckets from below. But there were as many signs of change as there were of deprivation, not least of all the TV antennas that sprung from half a dozen huts, car batteries that provided the village with electricity and most of all the little pink schoolhouse.

Dandua was one of the first villages to get a new school under Bihar's primary-education drive, and what the school lacked in size (two cinder-block rooms for 180 children) it made up for with parental management. A village education committee—nine men, five women and one teacher—had taken over most of the school's affairs. Among the committee's victories, it had secured the transfer of a negligent teacher, and regularly canvassed the village to make sure every child between the age of six and eleven was enrolled and attending class. But nothing compared with the public service strike of 1999. When teachers shut down the state school system for three months as part of a larger government employees' protest for higher wages, a group of Dandua parents who had completed grade six took up teaching, working in two-hour shifts to read lessons, hand out assignments, organize games and do their best to keep their children challenged.

Like most of Pandey's schools, Dandua's was in dire need of another teacher or two. The pupil-teacher ratio in Chatra was eighty-six to one, and in many villages was more than a hundred to one. The program's early successes only compounded the load, with schools doubling in size in a matter of years while the state fought caste battles instead of hiring more teachers. To get the district through the next year, Pandey had won an agreement to hire a few dozen retired teachers on contract. But he felt the only long-term solution was to hire elementary and high school graduates, train them for a year and send them back to their villages as paraprofessional teachers, not unlike Dr. Zaf's approach to maternal health in Bangladesh.

We parked the Ambassador by the road and walked down a dirt

path to meet a group of Dnadua parents. None of them could deny that their situation had improved immensely since the landlords were driven out by the Naxalites. They never would have been allowed to form an organization like this under the old feudal reign, when the local lord collected rents and had first dibs on every young man's wife.

Deepan Shaw, a tall, brawny man who worked most of the year in Calcutta as a rickshaw puller, was still stunned by the change. Ten years ago, he had taken his first son to the teeming port city to apprentice as a mason and live with him in a slum. He left his second son behind in Dandua where the boy was now about to complete grade eight and go on to high school in a nearby town. "He will never have to work like I do," Deepan said.

I asked the men if any Naxalites were close by. They all shook their heads. Pandey leaned toward me and whispered that most of the men in front of us were Naxalites. In white dhotis and singlets, they looked like tired field labourers, but in their huts, Pandey said, beneath beds or sacks of grain, were guns. Dandua would never allow the landlords back.

Although the men now felt more in control of their lives, and ran the education committee, it was the women who led the social change that underpinned it all. They had to. One-quarter of the village men lived permanently in Calcutta or another city, and another quarter migrated for part of the year, in the hope of earning sixty rupees or more a day instead of the thirty or forty rupees, less than a dollar, they made in the fields at home. Once education became a common goal, it was left to the women to keep an eye on teachers and force their children to go to school. "Before, we did not think school was important," explained Saraswati, a low-caste farmer whose parents named her for the Hindu goddess of learning and then never sent her to school. "We kept our children with us in the fields. They were safer there, we thought."

With a son and daughter in the primary grades, Saraswati wanted to be on the education committee. Four years earlier, she was elected vice-president, a position reserved for women. But still, the men gathered around us kept interrupting her to clarify her points with their own opinions. Pandey suggested we find a few stools in the shade of a mud hut, where Saraswati and the other women could speak more freely.

Once we were away from the crowd, Saraswati explained that as part of the school project, the women of Dandua were encouraged to form a group to talk about problems they faced in getting their children, especially their girls, to school. Most had never belonged to any organization before, and it gave them a chance to raise ideas that never would be heard at the open meetings. One woman suggested the mothers take turns watching the school to ensure their girls' safety. Sexual harassment was a major problem in rural schools, by teachers, older boys and men working in the surrounding fields. The women also figured out ways to share their older daughter's childcare duties—a sort of village daycare system—in order to free up time for the girls to attend classes. Soon it became a social stigma to keep a child from school, especially with illiterate mothers like Saraswati showing the way. Her son was now in grade six. Her daughter—the child of two uneducated, low-caste field workers—was in grade nine.

"If my whole village is educated," Saraswati explained, "the whole village will progress."

While important, these informal women's groups were not enough to get all low-caste and adavasi girls into primary school. Many were too busy, what with all their household chores—cooking, washing, caring for younger siblings—and their mothers toiling all day in the fields. Others lived in remote hamlets or belonged to nomadic tribes, far from the reach of a little pink schoolhouse.

In the poorest and most inaccessible communities around Chatra, Pandey encouraged mothers to start their own informal entry-level schools, in a local hut or barn, with classes designed to fit around children's work schedules. All classes were taught by a villager, who had to be a woman from a scheduled caste or scheduled tribe, and usually had only a modest bit of schooling, perhaps up to grade eight. In many communities, a mothers' committee was also created to manage the school budget for chalk and books, and, more important, to encourage women to send their daughters to school. "Awake the world" was the motto of more than a hundred mothers' groups in Chatra district. "If a girl is awakening, the whole world is awakening."

The involvement of women in school management was fundamental to a broader change in society. Just as the low-caste men of Chatra did not trust the gun-toting Yadavs who controlled the state government, the women of Chatra did not trust the men who ran their villages. They did not trust male teachers with their daughters. Nor did they trust their husbands with the latrine money. For these women, running their schools more effectively was only the beginning. They wanted to change their society and its collective values, to create a culture for education in which girls' schooling would be a dominant priority, an investment and responsibility that no parent would ever again dare ignore.

To help women challenge their male-dominated society, Pandey coached them as the Maoist insurgents might coach their own cadres, with mass appeal and an elite corps of trained fighters. In the women's case, the fighters were teenaged girls plucked from the poorest and most marginal villages and sent to a training camp for one year where the most important thing they learned was how to break tradition. A girl from Dandua had gone to the camp and planned never to let her village be the same again. She would take on men. She would take on her husband. She swore she would even take on her father.

The Bihar twilight seemed to descend faster than anywhere else in India, casting darkness over the countryside before Pandey and I could find one of the training camps. It was outside the little town of Simaria, about thirty kilometres east from Dandua. There were no flickering light bulbs in the passing hamlets or the radiance of a town on the horizon, just small fires in every field as farmers burned off their remaining rice stalks to welcome a new season. At the end of the road, past a long stretch of bo trees and a gully of thorn bushes, we finally found the district education centre, lit only by our car lights. The campus of long single-storey buildings was designed around a playing field, with an entrance marked by a few banyan trees. Every district in the Bihar project had a centre like this one, used for teacher training programs, refresher courses and inspirational meetings for mothers' groups. But tucked away in one corner, at the far end of the playing field, was a small dormitory where thirty teenaged girls, many of them out of their villages for the first time, were enrolled in a gender boot camp.

When we arrived, the girls were gathered on a large blanket on the grass outside their dorm, singing and sharing folk tales. The teacher jumped to her feet and the girls quickly followed, welcoming us with folded hands and then a martial clap, 1-2-1-2-3, in the glow of a single kerosene lantern. As everyone sat down, we joined the teacher on the large carpet next to the lantern, which cast just enough light to expose a single gecko darting up and down the dormitory wall in search of mosquitoes. The ground beneath the carpet was still warm, radiating daytime heat even though the sky above was rich with stars, and the fields around us chirped loudly with the nighttime call of crickets.

When the girls arrived here three months ago, they received bedding, two sets of clothes, soap and the promise of a one-dollar monthly allowance, all financed by Pandey's larger education drive. Every day at dawn, the girls were up for prayers, calisthenics, breakfast and a morning of classes. None of them had been to school before, and now they were trying to make up for it, acquiring enough knowledge to read street signs, write a simple letter, do basic math and teach others the same. Three girls from the nomadic Birhor tribe said they were the first in their adavasi community to receive any schooling, and even their fathers were keenly awaiting their return so they could learn from them. In the afternoons, there were sports, karate and bicycling—activities the girls would never have done at home. And then there were evenings of songs and skits, not for fun but to build presentation skills and social confidence.

As the girls bunched closer around the lantern, Pandey began to ask them questions about their lives before the camp. He asked them about their time here, about their fathers and mothers, and about the lives they had left behind. Cautiously, a few of the older girls responded, and then more began to speak, interrupting each other and correcting themselves, and adding what they forgot to say earlier. They poured forth emotions and ambitions I had never heard from Indian teenagers, at least not in the countryside. The gathering had the ambience of a North American Bible camp, the sorrow and redemption, pain and joy. But when the teacher asked the girls to sing some of their village songs, their sentiments were unmistakably Indian, undeniably lower caste and unhappily female.

"God, why did you make us girls?" they sang. "When we went to school, our fathers snatched our slates."

"When we visit our father," they sang again, "he says, 'Daughter,

I have nothing for you. We have only one kilogram of wild grain and that is for our family, our dogs and cats. I have not enough to give you.'"

These girls did not deserve to be sent to school, not even grade one, they sang, because at marriage they would be out of the family, worth less than a dog or cat. That was the promise and threat with which each had been raised. And now they were here together learning to fight it.

In another nine months, they would be sent home as young women with independent minds and, Pandey hoped, a sense of community. Some would stay on here or at other centres to coach more groups. Many would become para-teachers in new community schools. But all were expected to stay with the struggle and lead a new generation. They would have to stand before older women on their own and demand to know why those women had not sent their children to school. They would be expected to stand and question older men, too, and say, for perhaps the first time in their villages, "This is my right."

One of the girls, sixteen-year-old Leela Kumari, said she came from Dandua, the village we had just visited. The pressures that the teacher spoke of—the promise and threat of emancipation—she knew all too well. The night in April when she arrived here and bedded down on the floor was the first night she had ever spent away from home. The third of five girls, Leela was put to work when she was eight years old at a local brick kiln. Her two elder sisters did the same work, were married at puberty and sent off to other villages, seldom to be seen again. The same fate awaited Leela until a year earlier when her mother gave birth to a sixth child, a boy. In celebration, Leela's mother said she could attend the training camp. She would be spared marriage for another year.

"My mother said, 'Your whole life is for working. Go and learn something. When you come back, you can work.'"

As she spoke, Leela stared at the lantern, nervously picking knots in the carpet. She was careful not to look me or Pandey in the eyes, though we sat only a short distance away. She had been raised to be shy of strangers, especially strange men.

When her father learned of her plans to go to the Simaria camp, he was angry. She was a woman of marrying age and should never leave Dandua without a male escort, he said. Then something remarkable happened. Her mother, who belonged to the Dandua women's group, told her husband that her decision was final. Leela was going. He backed down, perhaps because she had given him a son at last, or perhaps because he knew that in a changing India his daughter's marriage prospects were better if she had some education; no one wanted an illiterate daughter-in-law any more because that led to illiterate grandchildren.

The more Leela spoke, the more she glanced in our direction, across the lantern that made her white hair ribbons shine in the night. She and the others had taught each other to tie ribbons, and they liked the look.

The girls were now holding hands, laughing at their own stories. They asked Pandey to sing, which he did, and then it was my turn. I could remember only one verse of "Yesterday." The girls applauded politely, and then asked eagerly about Canada. Were girls allowed to go to school in my country? Did my sisters go to school? I'm not sure I realized how daring it was for them to ask a man a question, let alone a personal one.

I said many Canadians waited until they were in their thirties to marry. There was a stunned silence. Many of these girls expected to be grandmothers by thirty-five.

I asked them what they considered to be the ideal number of children, and there was near unanimity: two. Only a few said three. The average in Bihar, a wasteland of family planning programs, was still close to six.

"When would you prefer to get married?" I asked Leela.

"In another five years," she said. The others agreed. By then, she would be twenty-one, an old maid in rural Bihar.

"Will your father allow you to wait that long?" I asked.

"No," Leela said. Everyone laughed, and then there was another silence, this time filled with sadness.

"Our husbands will not let us study or work," another girl said. "We need these five years to teach others. Then we will marry."

Pandey was amazed at the turn of our conversation. "These girls have been away from their villages for only a few months, and here they are voicing their opinions to a strange man."

I took a few pictures of the girls and promised to send them prints. None of the girls had seen her image, except in a stained and cracked mirror. Before we left, the girls offered one more song, this one bursting with optimism. "Like flowers, we will bring a scent to the village," it went. "Like tigers, we will bring speed to our work." Leela asked me again to send photos. This time, she looked me in the eyes.

The training camps were not without their problems. Many girls had no desire to return to their villages after the year was over, not when they would be married off and shipped away to another village. Some said they would try to find work instead in a town or city, where they could enjoy some liberty. To help the young women carve new lives for themselves in their villages, the camps taught skills like embroidery and helped each village women's committee form its own savings-and-loans group to foster new enterprises. The village women who had nominated a girl were also asked to give an assurance that they would do everything they could to postpone her marriage. If they could, a new social norm might be set, and expectations raised. A new generation of mothers might demand that their elected state government hire more teachers, that teachers show up on time and that they teach something useful. Bihar, and every other Indian state, had the resources to do the rest.

This kind of demand-based development was slowly taking hold elsewhere, as some of the world's most disenfranchised people learned of their rights and lobbied for what was supposed to be theirs. A school was the most basic and obvious public good. Justice, accountability and due process were more abstract but no less important. And each of these elements in human progress required some form of democracy; nothing else could enable a society to right its social and economic imbalances.

As we drove back to Chatra in the dark, our headlights illuminated men and women walking barefoot along the road with stacks of wood on their heads. These were the Naxalites' real targets but they did not need a Maoist insurgency so much as a political movement that would give them the strength and ability to make decisions affecting their common good. This process was not just a function of consulting people or including them in a project, an approach that has become known as "participatory development." This was about people managing their own development, often from failure to failure until they found or created a better way. Few challenges were greater than this, because too many organizations believed they had the solutions and believed development was about transferring those solutions, along with money and skills, rather than about helping people find the solutions themselves. Local councils, public forums, legal measures, even Bihar's own version of the PTA: these were the weapons that millions of the poor, illiterate and hungry needed to create their own village republics.

When I returned to Gaya's train station in the middle of the night, the platform bookstall was, surprisingly, still open, lit by a kerosene lantern like the one in the Simaria girls' boot camp. It showed an assortment of titles from *You Are What You Wear* to a row of Dale Carnegie paperbacks and my favourite: *1,000 Most Obscure Words*. ("*Cicisbeo*," the jacket cover read. "A married woman's gallant.") I bought a newspaper instead, curious to read a story about a parliamentary committee "air-dashing" to Orissa to investigate a handful of tribal starvation deaths that had made front-page news a few days earlier.

When the westbound train to New Delhi arrived, late, it rolled quietly into the station, perhaps out of the conductor's concern that he might crush someone on the darkened tracks. I realized I did not know my car number and joined a small mob running from car to car, searching in the dark for the computer printouts of passenger names glued to every door and illuminated only by the moonlight. I finally found "House Stack J" just in time to throw my knapsack through the door and jump on board. No train stayed in Gaya for more than a few minutes, not with the Naxalites so close by.

Why, at any moment a revolution could break out.

RATAN DEVI AND HER GOATHERD STUDENTS, TILONIA

# 21

# The Educated Man

In New Delhi, drivers sail through red lights with impunity, killing pedestrians every day and running over traffic police several times a year. Once, in a fit of surrender, the city painted the word "Relax" on all red lights but there was no noticeable change. When one of our neighbours, home for Christmas from Philadelphia's Wharton Business School, drove the family's brand-new BMW into a police barricade, killing three policemen and two pedestrians, the family simply offered the relatives of the deceased a cash settlement, as if a criminal act could be resolved like a property dispute.

Under the weight of a large and volatile population, the judiciary was not much use anyway. So understaffed and overrun were the courts—the Allahabad High Court, the busiest in India, registered 865,455 cases in 1997—that the average wait for trial was ten years. A lawyer in central Uttar Pradesh once told me a simple doctor's note and a small payment to the right court official could win a defendant another ten years' delay.

Many Indians feared that we lived in the age of Kali, the Hindu Durga, a goddess who destroys all she sees. But in chaos, even in destruction, others saw the seeds for a new age, a time of reform. And few Indians fought more diligently for reform than Mahesh Chandra Mehta, a quiet, confident lawyer at the Supreme Court of India. In the course of one decade, Mehta had become the biggest nuisance that callous millionaires, sinister politicians and praetorian judges had seen since the imposition of income tax. Like Biharipur's angry Dalits and Orissa's Bhima Saoras, he knew that India was a society in need of profound reorganization but he didn't think the fight needed to be bloody. He believed the institutions that got India on its feet were perfectly adequate to carry it forward, and he was able to prod them along with a simple but mighty tool called public-interest litigation.

Mehta first made a name for himself in 1983 when he secured the transfer to remand homes of 190 child prisoners from an Orissa jail, where they had been living fifty to a room without any prospect of formal charges, let alone trials. A year later, he persuaded the Supreme Court to order the closure of all foundries and a thermal power plant within close range of the Taj Mahal; its marble was yellowing because of air pollution. His next major case, fought over the duration of six hundred hearings, set out to save the entire Ganges from pollution. In one victory, he persuaded a court to order five thousand industrial units along the sacred river to adopt basic pollution controls.

Mehta's one-man crusades forced the government to ban leaded gasoline, shift hazardous industries out of central New Delhi and outlaw the employment of children in hazardous industries. His greater challenge was to see those decisions enforced and supported locally. Too often, district administrators did not have the time or inclination to follow commands from on high, from either the courts or Parliament, and could not be expected to do more without local pressure. Courts, laws and administration were only as good as the society they were supposed to represent. "We call ourselves a democratic society," Mehta said of his country, when I met him outside a swarming courtroom in New Delhi. "We are not. We still have to win the confidence of the people."

He would be the first to admit that India needed a thousand more people like himself, fighting in villages and district centres for the sort of political and legal reform that secured all serious human development. I found two such people, a married couple who had gone separate ways to wage a new type of development struggle. Bunker and Aruna Roy had worked for more than a quarter century in the desert state of Rajasthan in western India. Development, they believed, was not about material benefits but about organizing people to fight for the resources and public goods that others have denied them. This very political approach to development had made them famous as iconoclasts. Yet they were more than rabble-rousers. Bunker and Aruna Roy lived among the poor, doing, every day, in those villages what Mehta was doing in the Supreme Court, and they could see the change bubbling up.

When I first came across Sanjit "Bunker" Roy's name in India's *Illustrated Monthly* magazine, I was intrigued by his comment, "Everyone hates my guts." He sounded like the kind of person I enjoy meeting. To find him, Cindy and I drove south from New Delhi for the better part of a day, beyond the posh "farm" houses and rich wheat fields of Haryana, past the Rajput forts of northern Rajasthan and into the first stretch of the Thar Desert where Bunker had been running his controversial development program since the early seventies.

The son of a prominent Calcutta family, a product of India's best schools and a favourite of Delhi society, Bunker chose at a young age to leave the capital's comforts and work in the desert with the disenfranchised. Although his father died when he was young and left little money for his children's upbringing, Bunker's mother found work and enough scholarships to see her son through the private Doon School, where Rajiv Gandhi was his classmate in the sixties, and

Delhi's prestigious St. Stephen's College. Bunker was a three-time national squash champion and should have joined the civil service or gone to Cambridge. Instead, he opted for relief work in the Bihar famine of 1966–67, where the sight of a man and a dog fighting over a scrap of food changed him forever. He decided to take up development work with the Catholic Relief Services in Rajasthan, only to realize its goal was to succour society's weakest members. He wanted to change society.

Bunker had seen how the elite of Delhi and Calcutta moulded the economy and political system to their advantage, but he was no Marxist. He wanted less to crush his own class than to help others stake their claims in the political arena, so that all of India—rich, poor, educated and ignorant—could battle it out peacefully. On a motorcycle drive across the desert state, he thought of a way to do it. He would train low-caste villagers in politics, much as he had been trained at the Doon School and St. Stephen's. And he would do it in an abandoned tuberculosis sanitarium, where Christian missionaries once worked, four hundred kilometres southwest of Delhi.

At the age of twenty-seven, Bunker started the Tilonia centre—designed not to sustain the historically meek but to help them understand how they could shape the future. Through personal contacts, he won enough financial support from Catholic Relief Services, Christian Aid, Oxfam and India's Tata Trust, funded by the country's wealthiest family, to get a modest program on its feet. His wife, Aruna, quit her coveted job in the elite Indian Administrative Services to join him. Their only mistake was the name, Social Work and Research Centre, which made Tilonia seem as boring as, well, the old tuberculosis sanitarium. Everyone else called it the Barefoot College, or simply Tilonia.

We found Tilonia (the village) set well off the highway, behind an overbearing hill of rock and thorn bush that blocked the desert winds. All around, the earth was parched and cracked. The surrounding state of Rajasthan is one of the harshest places in the subcontinent, for climate and for development. Child marriages are celebrated and child labour is rampant. Only Afghanistan and Yemen have a lower rate of female literacy.

Then we came across Tilonia (the centre), set amid a graceful clump of trees and blossoming gardens, nurtured by rain-fed water tanks and caring hands. Everything about the Barefoot College was different from the world around it. At the front gate stood a stripped-down fighter jet on a plinth, a pointed comment on India's spending priorities. Inside, there were training rooms for women to learn about politics, repairing hand pumps and installing solar panels. And beyond that was an open terrace, lit by solar panels, where more people were rehearsing the weekly Saturday evening skit, using puppets made from old World Bank reports.

We found Bunker next to the terrace, in a big mess hall where he and a few others were sitting in circles on the floor, eating dinner. He looked like a playful bear of a man, beefy and broad-shouldered, with big paws that seemed to swallow my hand—not at all like the scrawny desert people who sat around him. His grey hair was about as unruly and windblown as the thorn bushes we had passed on the road. Although Aruna had left him and the centre a few years earlier to pursue an anti-corruption crusade, Bunker remained undaunted. He invited us to grab a plate and join his group on the floor, explaining that he had thrown out the centre's chairs after discovering only upper-caste people were using them. After that episode, only Dalits were hired to prepare meals.

Once we filled our plates with the Dalit-cooked dal and rice, Bunker introduced us to a group of village women who were at the Barefoot College for a two-day refresher course in reading and writing. They did this every month, not just to refine their skills but to feel part of a bigger movement. Over the previous two decades, some three thousand women had come to the Barefoot College to learn the basics of literacy, and something about local laws, health care and the power structure of their villages. Two hundred village women had learned to install and repair solar panels, and close to a hundred more had become night-school teachers. Another twenty-seven graduates were now informal health workers, trained to buy basic medicines in town and sell them to their ailing neighbours.

The most astonishing prospect, however, were the hundreds of women—six hundred at last count—trained to repair the most important technology in rural Rajasthan, the water hand pump. The state government, with assistance from Unicef, had installed tens of thousands of hand pumps across Rajasthan, but when they broke down, which they often did, the villagers had to send someone to the nearest block centre to find the official inspector. If the man (and the inspectors were always men) was so inclined (and there was only one way to make him feel inclined), he would return to the village to inspect the damage, complete a form and file a request for assistance from the district's five-man mobile repair team. The men with the wrenches might come in a few days; usually it was a few weeks or months.

Tilonia's SWAT teams, by contrast, were all women and all uneducated, making a mockery, as Bunker liked to do, of the government's "professional" service. After graduating from the Barefoot College, the female mechanics worked in teams in their villages to fix pumps and change the leather washers twice a year. Although men jeered at them at first, attitudes changed when the men realized they no longer had to bribe a government repair team to visit the village. Soon, no one objected to the eleven-rupee-a-month user fee the women charged to cover the cost of spare parts and a small salary for themselves. Business was good enough that the Tilonia hand pump mechanics' association had banked ten thousand rupees, equivalent to about two hundred and fifty dollars.

Money was never meant to be the point of Tilonia (the centre). Women mastered technology, like a hand pump or solar panel, to gain some control over their lives. In Tilonia (the village), they would soon discover how mastering politics could do the same. What was required in each case, Bunker stressed, was "self-confidence and assurance." This they gained inside the old sanitarium, where women were able to talk freely about issues that were taboo in the village, such as family violence or condoms. Bunker gave us some examples. One woman said her husband put a condom on his fingers during intercourse, just as the health worker did during the demonstration. Another woman said she confused condoms and birth control pills and tried to swallow the condom wrapper. Another one, remembering the instructions to bury the condom after use, hid the wrapped object in her mouth during intercourse and dutifully buried it afterwards.

It was hard to believe the stories, but one of the women sitting on the floor, Ratan Devi, shook the glass bangles on her wrist and insisted they were true. But more important, she said, attitudes were changing. We needed only to visit her night school to see for ourselves.

Ratan Devi led us down the dirt road in the dark to the hut where she taught every night. It seemed like an ordinary routine, like

Rajinder's TLC classes or the low-caste schools in Bihar, until she explained her past. As a low-caste widow, she was among the lowest of society's low. By custom in Rajasthan, she should have been cast out of her husband's home to beg for alms until she died. (This was better than suttee, the ancient custom that would have required her to throw herself on her husband's funeral pyre.) But Ratan Devi was not willing to suffer the rest of her days in undignified isolation. Instead, she came to Tilonia (the centre) to make a new life, learning the basics of hand pump mechanics and enough teaching skills to instruct a small group of young goatherds every night in elementary reading and writing and to challenge their minds with new ideas.

By the time we reached the borrowed hut where the tiny woman held her classes, a dozen barefoot children had gathered around a solar-powered lantern developed at the Barefoot College. There were sixty-five night schools like this around Tilonia, with three thousand students enrolled. Each school set its own hours, managed the solar lantern and elected an MP to a district model parliament that Bunker created. The parliament met once a month to debate issues and vote confidence in its prime minister (this year a girl) and a fifteen-member cabinet. No one was allowed to mistake this for playtime. The goatherd cabinet was given an annual budget of a thousand dollars—more than double the average income in Tilonia—and made responsible for the supply of chalk, slates, light bulbs and solar lanterns to all the schools. Each minister was also assigned an adult adviser from the Barefoot College, who was named "secretary." (Bunker served as the prime minister's secretary.) If an MP felt his or her school needed more chalk, he had to make an argument before cabinet and was usually up against at least half a dozen other MPs demanding more chalk for their constituents, too. A chalk crisis could bring down the government.

Ratan Devi brought her class to order, and suggested they conduct their own mini-parliament to practise the basic skills of debating, which they had learned in a previous class. Tonight's motion, she declared after pronouncing herself speaker, was that the earth is round. The children, forgetting how tired they were from a day in the fields, dove into a free-flowing argument. Of course the earth is round, one boy said. Had no one else in the hut seen a globe? A few others said they had seen only a wall map, which they remembered as being very flat. Some of the girls admitted to not knowing what the earth was.

"Is it round like a ball?" Ratan Devi asked. "Or is it round like a plate?"

They all knew what a plate was and knew, at least intuitively, that they did not live on a plate. The children nodded to each other before the biggest boy spoke up. "Round like a ball," Ram Chandra, the night school's MP, told the house. The image of his confident face flickered in the lantern light. "Round like a ball." The motion was passed.

Ram Chandra was fourteen years old and in grade five at Tilonia's government school, which he attended every morning before tending to his family's goats in the afternoon. He came to Ratan Devi's class most evenings because, unlike the government school, he said, it was fun. It also won him the chance to go to the monthly model parliament. I asked him what he had learned from the experience.

"Before I only knew the word 'minister,'" he said. "Now I know what a minister does. I know how votes are cast."

"Is that all politics is for?" Ratan Devi asked the other children.

"No," a small boy said. "The government settles land disputes and provides drought relief."

"Is that the only difference between the school council and the village council?" she asked.

The small boy giggled. "The village council gives people alcohol to win votes," he said.

"Uh-huh," the others agreed.

Academically, the school would not win any awards or qualify many pupils for a spot in a senior school upon graduation. I also had to wonder if it would really change centuries of caste tradition in the village. There were fourteen major castes in Tilonia, but only the Jats and a few others mattered politically. Traditional landowners, the Jats controlled local agriculture. They also refused to let the lower castes touch their well, claiming it had religious value because it was attached to a Hindu temple. The upper castes had a direct line to the local administrators and politicians. How would a playful model parliament, I wondered, ever change that?

After class, Ratan Devi assured me it already had, and she began to tell us about her other life since her husband's death. In 1994, she had put her name forward in a local council election, as part of the panchayat reforms that were supposed to give Indian democracy a greater village presence. The Barefoot College graduates felt that if they could not gain access to these new levers of power, all their development work would be inconsequential. And so, forty Tilonia graduates, Ratan Devi among them, stepped forward as candidates.

The Barefoot College team became an informal party, with a common ballot symbol, the banyan tree, because that was where they often gathered, and entered their nominations in seats reserved exclusively for women. Ratan Devi found herself in the most competitive and dirtiest race of all. In her corner of Tilonia, the Congress Party had nominated the wife of a local distiller, a man who had been the elected village chief for fifteen years. He could not run again, as the seat was reserved for women only, but he could give free drinks to all those who voted for his wife. The Hindu nationalist BJP, which controlled the state government, put forward a candidate of somewhat lower profile, a woman living in purdah who had not been outside her house in more than a year. And then there was Ratan Devi, widow, Dalit and night school teacher to a group of goatherds. Her only competitive edge was a large and mobile campaign team, consisting of her students and fellow hand pump mechanics, and lots of posters financed by the Barefoot College's political action fund.

A strong man. A strong party. A stronger woman. When the voting was finished, the distiller's wife won a thousand votes. The BJP woman, the one in purdah, took five hundred. With 1,175 votes, Ratan Devi was declared the winner.

In total, the Barefoot College team won only two of nineteen seats on Tilonia's council. The BJP retained control with eleven. But Ratan Devi believed a message was sent to the higher castes. There would be more disputes on the council, no motion would be passed without her scrutiny and no water dams, schools, latrines or hand pumps would be built without her inspection. Across India, 38,791 women were elected to local councils. Although many (such as Rajinder's wife) were no more than puppets, there were enough like Ratan Devi to start something that one day might be remembered as the beginnings of a political mutiny. "There will be an increase in conflict, obviously," the widow told us as we walked back to Tilonia (the centre) for the Saturday night show. "But we will maintain our independence. We have to. It is what we have earned."

A couple of days later, Cindy and I left Tilonia, unsure whether Bunker Roy, innovator and social provocateur, had created a model for development or just an interesting experiment. Women such as Ratan Devi could no longer be treated as if they were cattle, but the higher-caste Jats still controlled the village and would continue to turn development efforts in their favour.

In its enthusiasm to revive local democracy, India had lost sight of the fact that village councils can be as corrupt and wasteful as the national government, and as much in need of checks and balances. In a thriving city or large town, this might come from independent auditors, public prosecutors or a crusading newspaper. In a village like Tilonia or Biharipur, the people in power tended to have a much tighter grip on things. Unless they ran into Aruna Roy.

Since she and Bunker decided to follow separate paths, Aruna had ventured across the Rajasthan desert to find ways to break the fossilized power structures of local society. When she did not see lives changing fast enough in Tilonia—the Jat landlords and local bureaucrats remained in cahoots—she became frustrated. What she wanted was perestroika for the peasantry.

I wanted to meet Aruna as soon as we left Tilonia, but she was as hard to track as the desert wind, a person of no fixed address, with no formal budget, office or letterhead. She was a crusader wandering from village to village, and town to town, with dozens of other activists at her side, raking muck. When she got tired, she retreated to a small town called Bhim in the middle of a district that was in the middle of nowhere in central Rajasthan. Or she drifted to Delhi to meet her friends, who ran the country. I got lucky when someone at the *Indian Express* told me she was in the city.

When we met, Aruna quickly showed why civil servants feared her so. In a land of passionate social crusaders, she was one of the most fervent, and smart enough to control the fire. Access to information rather than water pumps and solar panels was her burning ambition, which was about as esoteric as one could get in a Rajasthani village, except that Aruna knew very well what went on behind the backs of villagers. If she could help villagers see the same things as she saw, she knew what they would think.

Aruna started her campaign in 1987 in Bhim district, where she and her fellow crusaders discovered that 150 hectares of government land was under the control of a local landlord. They won an injunction from a district court, reclaimed the land and handed it over to a local forestry project. Once Aruna's corruption commandos had tasted victory, they found no opponent unassailable, no official too high to bring down. In 1990, she and the other activists formed an organization, Mazdoor Kisan Shakti Sanghathan (The Farm Workers' Movement), and launched a series of public hearings where bureaucrats and local development officers were invited to answer questions and share public documents with villagers. She called the process a "social audit." Since Aruna brought eminent jurists and journalists from major New Delhi papers to the sessions, the sheer embarrassment was often enough to bring officials into line. When it was not, she resorted to the law, taking a district official to court in New Delhi if she had to. It was as if *60 Minutes* had come to rural India.

A former civil servant, Aruna knew how the system worked, which forms to review and accounts to monitor. She had joined the IAS in 1968, at twenty-one, and was posted to a rural district in southern Tamil Nadu state. Like many fresh recruits to the "steel frame of India," as the service fancied itself, she believed her work would help the poor by ensuring justice and equity in public life. As she traversed the district with her superiors, though, she realized they had no contact with the poor. At every stop, only the village chief greeted them, and only he provided them with information. It didn't take long for Aruna to realize that in village after village the headmen and contractors were in league, cutting corners, over-invoicing and billing the state for work never done, all in the name of the poor.

Getting basic information on development projects was far from easy. Even little things such as the pay muster were guarded by the 1923 Official Secrets Act, a leftover from British colonial rule. But Aruna persisted. She challenged local council chiefs and bureaucrats to come to hearings with boxes of project documents and receipts. Hours would pass in the blistering desert heat, sometimes days, but the audiences never left—the reading of public accounts was too riveting. At one hearing, an entire village sat spellbound as their humiliated chief read the official payroll for a small construction project. People who had never been to the site shouted as their names were announced. The list included a man who had been dead for years. Another hearing exposed a state-run child care centre where, according to volunteers who signed an affidavit, the supervisor regularly demanded a fifty-rupee cut from each monthly honorarium of 350 rupees. A subsequent investigation found much of the daycare centre's edible oils, medicines and food rations had also disappeared.

The stories went on and on like a bunch of Watergate tapes. Five villagers gave sworn testimony that they had paid fifteen hundred rupees to a local official for a "free" government-built house. After the revelations, they got their money back within forty-eight hours. In another village, a company owned by relatives of local officials was reimbursed for 3.6 million rupees of work that was never done. In yet another village, the school construction budget showed the purchase of thirty bags of cement for a roof that still leaked. The contractor, speaking to the villagers, said he had been given only seventeen bags; the village chief had kept the rest.

It was hard to imagine how one woman could stop the tide by standing on the cherished rock of righteousness. Aruna was up against social swells churned by centuries of tradition and custom. She would have to create her own breakwall to survive, which was what her vigilance campaigns, she said, were all about. If we wanted to see a hearing, she suggested we meet her in a few days' time in a village called Sare Khurd, outside Alwar, a former princely fortress town on a back road several hours south of Delhi. The people there had lost their land to expropriation, and they were up in arms.

When we arrived in Sare Khurd, the farmers had gathered near a pond, under a large tent that flapped furiously in the winds blowing north from the desert. The men wore brilliant turbans of yellow, red and orange. The women were dressed in a rainbow of saris that lit up the arid landscape.

Tensions in the village first rose in 1992, when the Rajasthan Industrial Investment Corporation announced its intention to acquire sixty hectares of farmland at a predetermined price of 165,000 rupees per hectare (about six thousand dollars at the time) to make way for new industry. According to the villagers, a district official had come with police to strongly urge them to sell, or risk losing their land under the 1894 Land Acquisition Act, which allows the government to buy land for "public purposes." None of the farmers knew why their land was being purchased in bulk. Some had heard a rumour that a big poultry farm was going up. Certainly none knew that dozens of factories were relocating to the area from Delhi because of a Supreme Court order to remove hazardous industries from the national capital region. Whatever the reason for the government's sudden interest in Sare Khurd, most of the farmers sold because they felt they had no choice, even when they discovered their land was worth at least nine thousand dollars per hectare. It was time for Aruna to step in.

We followed her into the big tent as the local farmers were taking their seats on carpets laid across the floor. Most of the men and women looked confused when she took to the stage to tell them about their right to information. She might as well have been talking about quantum physics.

But then she got down to the matter at hand, the big booze factory built on the land once owned by the farmers in the crowd.

"The chief minister said two hundred people from this village came to him and asked for this factory to be built," Aruna continued, picking up the cadence of a country preacher. "If anyone here went to him, please put up your hand."

No one put up a hand, but there were murmurs of discontent.

Aruna explained the 1894 Land Acquisition Act—the one that allows expropriation in the name of "public purpose"—and asked, "Can we call the acquisition of prime agriculture land for a factory distilling alcohol to be in the 'public purpose'?"

A few men shouted, "Nay!"

"The government is ours," Aruna chanted, and the audience responded with a local saying: "It does not belong to anyone else's father."

When the slogan shouting stopped, Aruna invited Surjeet Kaur, a local woman, to the stage. Surjeet's hands trembled as she rose. She had not spoken in public before, but she was angry. She had not only lost her land to expropriation; her family had lost its honour.

"One day they came to our house and said, 'Get out. We're going to break your house,'" Surjeet said, recalling the 1995 incident when the police came to evict her and her husband and their baby. She fidgeted and pulled an end of her sari over her head in modesty. "They grabbed and pushed me, and started destroying things. They threw me to the ground. My husband came, and they beat him, too. I thought he was dead."

The police took her husband, Mongol Singh, to a local jail, where he was kept without charges for eighteen days. "Every day the police came back and said, 'I'm going to take this land, or you're going to be in more trouble.'" While Mongol was in custody, other men came and chopped down several fruit trees, and tore pieces of wood from the house.

By then, Surjeet had received advice from neighbours who said she should demand to see the notice of land acquisition, which the government is required to post publicly before it can expropriate land. "The officer came and said, 'Vacate this place.' I said, 'I will when you put it in writing.' He replied, 'Who is the officer, you or me?'"

The family accepted twenty-eight-thousand dollars for its four and a half hectares of good agricultural land. When the payment was divided among six brothers and their families, it amounted to only one year's income for each of them. People who held on to their land for another year got twice that much.

After Surjeet finished her story and returned to her seat, an older man hobbled to the stage, using a bamboo pole as a crutch. Ganga Singh said the local police broke his leg while evicting him from his land. He eventually received fifteen thousand dollars for his three hectares, but that was only enough to buy half a hectare in the next village, and the land there, he said, was not as fertile.

"I am a farmer, and for a farmer money is not important," Ganga told the crowd. "Land is important. Money will come and go, but land is always there. Where can I go without land?"

The home crowd roared and applauded.

It was time for Ram Lal Dewant, the local revenue officer who had been standing at the back of the tent, to take the stage. Mr. Dewant was responsible for all land transactions in the area. He was also new to the job and was escorted by three armed police, just in case the villagers grew hostile. "I don't know about these things," he told the crowd. "I have been in this post only two months. This does not fall under my purview anyway."

"What do you mean?" a voice shouted. It was Kanwar Singh Yadav, an elderly farmer barely able to see the stage through his thick black-rimmed glasses. His voice shook with anger, and with fear. Confronting a local bureaucrat is something a villager—even an angry one—does not undertake lightly. "I have come to your office five times, and each time someone has raised objections to my complaint," he told the hushed tent. The farmer then punched a finger in the air in the direction of the revenue officer. "The sub-registrar's office," he shouted, "is a den of corruption."

A gust of applause swept through the tent.

"Whenever I go there, there is an objection," he charged. "Yet when these big companies want land, it happens right away."

"This regime is worse than Ravana's," another man shouted, referring to the great demon of Hindu mythology.

Mr. Dewant, the revenue officer, waited patiently for the noise to die down. This was the kind of scene every administrator feared. The British used to call it "a mob." More than fifty years after colonialism ended in the subcontinent, the IAS still told would-be administrators to avoid mobs at all costs.

"It seems your grievances are real," the revenue man said, beating a retreat. He promised publicly to investigate the land transactions.

I followed Mr. Dewant to his car, an official white Ambassador guarded by more police. He seemed relieved to be out of the tent and was happy to speak to me more candidly. The villagers had been ripped off, he agreed, but that was the nature of a free market: "These people have accepted their money. The records are there. Unless a court says it is wrong, what else can be done?" As for the stories of intimidation and police abuse, he felt they were exaggerated. "People are crying now because others got more money later. It was a private deal between two parties," he said as his driver opened the back-seat door for him, "and does not concern the administration."

The people of Sare Khurd made a splash in a few Delhi magazines and newspapers, but they did not get more compensation for their land. India's bureaucracy was so vast and cumbersome that only the rarest of public complaints jolted it. And like bureaucracies everywhere, it served its own interests first. When the Rajasthan government finally responded to Aruna's movement and set up a commission on the right to information, the report was kept secret.

But Aruna and her team of corruption fighters did not feel defeated, not even in the battle of Sare Khurd. "This is a bigger struggle than independence," said Ved Kumari, a retired teacher who worked with Aruna. "That was removing a foreign power. This is our own government."

Indians took up arms and went on long Gandhian fasts to push the British out. Fifty years of democracy should allow the second independence struggle to be more peaceful. Corruption and abuse are common, to be sure, but there are checks and balances in the form of courts, autonomous media, an active Parliament, increasingly powerful state governments, elected local councils and an independent election commission that gives people like Surjeet Kaur and Mongol Singh an absolute weapon over those who try to rule them. Not long after we visited Sare Khurd, the Hindu nationalist BJP, which had held Rajasthan for eight years, was swept out of office in state elections.

This was happening more and more across the developing world. As education levels grew and voters gained access to more and better information from TV, newspapers and groups like Aruna's, they were demanding more of politicians at every level. They could no longer be duped, at least not all of the time. In India, where democracy had long been ridiculed as plodding, even as an encumbrance to economic development, I was starting to see how the political system, with free votes and free speech, was fundamental to serious social change.

Chanting in the big tent before we left, the people of Sare Khurd had at least one thing right: No government should belong to anyone else's father.

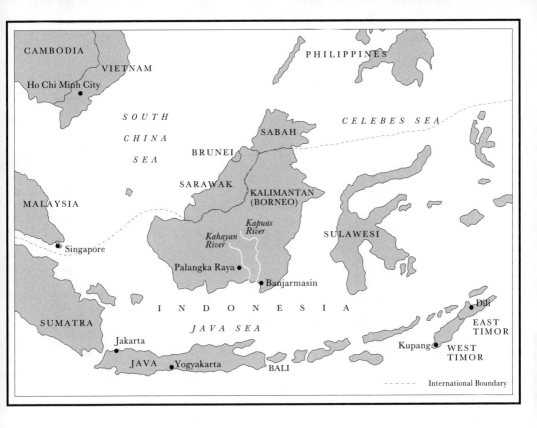

# INDONESIA

"The Turismo's American breakfast consisted of cold deep-fried eggs on a bed of grease, and boiled orange juice that was still warm. The hotel regretted that no bread was available. Anywhere."

CHRIST THE KING, DILI

# 22

## Gateway to Hell

There was no case study in development more seductive, more beguiling and, in the end, more deceptive than the incredible rise and tragic fall of Indonesia. When things were good, and for a long while they were very good, the sprawling country of two hundred million people seemed as if it had all the answers to the developing world's problems. It was a nation rich in natural resources, but so was Nigeria. Indonesia had shrewd political and economic leadership—proof to its friends that smart government, democratic or not, was essential to development. This was the country that was supposed to put all the others I had seen to shame, especially those bumbling democracies in Ghana, Bangladesh and India.

When I first visited Jakarta in 1986, the sewers were open, rats darted brazenly about the markets and just about the only places to eat were street-side noodle stalls. By 1992, *Time* magazine was writing that, "Jakarta is ablaze with lights and promise." A year later, the normally skeptical *Economist* magazine predicted that "Indonesia's long march from poverty is nearly over. By 2000 the country, once a pauper among nations, should have joined the emergent middle class."

I, too, was bitten by the enthusiasm when I returned in 1994, this time straight from Biharipur, to see growth and prosperity that excited both the mind and the senses. Jakarta was awash in air-conditioned shopping malls, expressways, posh hotels and subdivisions that sprouted up like forests, each jammed with cute little row houses, cinemas, video arcades, water parks and golf courses—a scene that looked more like Levittown of the fifties than Asia of the nineties. The average national income, a scant seventy dollars per capita when Suharto came to power in 1967, had reached 1,040 dollars, a level Bangladesh and India could only dream of.

Having crushed a Communist uprising in the 1960s, the military-backed president had created a new development regime of controlled capitalism. And he held most of the controls. The armed forces, major industries and the ruling Golkar Party were all beholden to him. He continued to fear the Communists so much that his government's foot soldiers—doctors, family planning advisers, teachers, agricultural extension agents—worked as cadres, providing services to those who respected the regime while collecting information on those who did not. If only the Communists had been so cunning.

Suharto watched as most of his opponents were killed or jailed, and his grown children became some of the richest industrialists in Asia. Rather than wave a cautionary flag or censure the regime, Western nations lined up to join the party, and few were more eager to get in than Canada.

Rich in forests, oil and gas, gold, minerals and fish, Canada and Indonesia had more in common than most Pacific nations, including old friendships with the United States and ethnically diverse populations. Prime Minister Jean Chrétien did not appear overly bothered by Suharto's bloodied past or abusive policies when in January 1996 he led a team of eight premiers and hundreds of Canadian corporate executives to Jakarta, after a swing through South Asia. During the two-day visit, not a bad word was said by Team Canada about a government that had murdered thousands of people, confiscated land from hundreds of aboriginal groups and stolen billions of dollars not only from its own people but from every major foreign aid agency on the planet. In the grand ballroom of the Jakarta Hilton, close to three hundred Canadian businessmen (and a few women) eagerly signed deals worth 2.7 billion dollars as the prime minister and premiers looked on approvingly. Chrétien, after meeting with Suharto for only fifteen minutes, went so far as to pronounce that the human rights situation in Indonesia was improving because of all this foreign money. "Isolation is the worst recipe, in my judgment, for curing human-rights problems," he told Canadian reporters gathered at the swank Hilton. "It is participation. It is being there to raise the issue, to help them to cope with their problems—that is the best way." The prime minister went on to declare, "As this country is opening up, the situation has improved. I hope the pressure all of us are putting on them is helping."

Back then, few could imagine that Suharto's forces would gun down unarmed students just metres from the Hilton's front gate, as they did in 1998. Nor did many believe such a strong nation, the very model of development, would begin to disintegrate, as it did in 1999 with the independence of a tiny territory named East Timor. Somewhere toward the end of his fifteen-minute meeting with Suharto, Chrétien had brought up the issue of East Timor, and he was apparently satisfied with the response he may or may not have received. East Timor, brutally clubbed into annexation after the withdrawal of Portuguese colonial rule in 1975, was at last, the Indonesians declared, becoming a happy member of the republic.

By historical misfortune, Timor island was divided by Portuguese and Dutch colonial regimes in the sixteenth century. Portugal seized its holding in 1515 for the rich sandalwood forests. Most of the rest of the archipelago fell to the Dutch, who retained control until 1949, with a brief interregnum during World War II. The Portuguese held on to their small outpost until 1975, when during Lisbon's colonial retreat Indonesian forces invaded the territory, ostensibly to crush a Communist attempt to seize power.

Sometime after another tray of pastries was delivered to the media room at the Jakarta Hilton, I asked my friend Dick Gordon, the New Delhi correspondent for CBC Radio, if he wanted to go to East Timor to see how happy the newest Indonesians were. Journalists were usually forbidden entry to the territory, so I suggested we pose as tourists. I figured we'd be beaten to a pulp and expelled anyway, but what choice did we have after all we had heard from our own prime minister?

Before Dick and I defected from Team Canada, a sympathetic Canadian diplomat arranged for fresh passports, free of incriminating journalist visas, to help with our tourist disguise. To add to the image, we also stopped for a night in Bali, which, as I explained with great difficulty to my editors, was the closest entry point to Timor island. I don't think they bought the story, but going to Bali gave us a chance to discard every piece of ID that suggested our profession, and to outfit ourselves with baggy orange shirts, jam shorts and rubber thongs, as well as pick up Scotch for the missionaries who we hoped would take us in. At last we could board a plane to Kupang, capital of West Timor, and from there a bus to Dili, capital of East Timor. To fly directly to Dili would be to invite the scrutiny of airport security guards who inspected all passports and identity cards to keep dissidents and journalists at bay. Besides, all direct flights to Dili were mysteriously booked weeks in advance.

The night bus from Kupang to Dili was nothing more than an oversized, overcrowded van that seemed to carry an entire village and was so short of space that we each bought an extra ticket for our legs. After climbing slowly into the central hills and jungles, the bus cut fast and sharp back to a coastal road along jagged turns and unfinished pavement, in the pitch dark of a South Seas night. How close our bus came to tumbling over a cliff, we could not see. But the sheer blackness all around meant the police at the first checkpoint could scarcely see us at the back of the bus. At the second and third checkpoints, the light was no longer an issue; the police were fast asleep, giving us a free run straight to Dili. I thought of the dozing security men as the bus flipped us like pancakes every few hundred metres, over potholes and bumps, and envied them more each time the driver played and replayed a Bobby Vinton tape at full volume, backed by a tinny synthesizer and thundering techno beat.

During the next five days in East Timor, in countless minibuses and taxis, *The Best of the '70s* on cassette was the closest thing I heard to freedom of expression, if "I Write the Songs" can be considered free expression. Surely the Timorese had suffered enough, I thought, popping my knapsack against the grille bars of the open bus window and trying again to sleep.

After dawn, a soft light raced toward us over the Flores Sea as we came around a stunning cliffside turn and saw nothing but coast ahead. The road to Dili rambled through pristine South Pacific beaches and rugged promontories, a tropical sketch touched by deserted Portuguese forts and abandoned fishing skiffs. The thinly populated coast gave way to a procession of thatched villages leading to the Iberian-styled capital, a serene outpost of palm-shaded villas, bleached-white churches and bougainvillea wedged between verdant hills and a gently lapping sea. By the time we got off the so-called bus, our jam shorts were crinkled and we had a couple of days' growth to our beards. To any self-respecting spy, we must have looked like either aging yuppies in search of some good dope or foreign journalists. Who else would come to East Timor by bus?

In the gentle warmth of a winter day, Dili exuded enough tranquility to lull itself into a slumber by noon, which was convenient because almost every shop closed then for a three-hour siesta. We took one of Dili's ancient blue taxis to the Turismo Beach Hotel, the only place foreigners were allowed to stay. Along the roads, people were just starting to open their market stalls. Children busied themselves getting ready for school. Adults waved hello—hardly the signs of a war zone. Unlike Sri Lanka, there were no bunkers on the street. Unlike Kashmir, troops did not man intersections with automatic weapons at the ready. In Dili, there did not seem to be troops anywhere at this hour.

The calm invited sleep, which was all I wanted after a bone-jarring night on the bus, but like so much else we would see in East Timor, the capital's tranquility was not what it seemed. Soon after we checked in, there came the thumping of a hundred pairs of feet on the seaside promenade across the way—a local regiment was out for its morning exercise. An hour later, a column of army trucks rumbled down the main boulevard, each with two dozen men in full combat gear, automatic weapons at the ready. Before the morning was out, military transport planes had flown overhead, and helicopters passed by so low that I feared they would lop the tops off the palm trees outside our second-storey room. There could be no mistaking this for paradise. We were in the middle of a military occupation, with all the brute force the Suharto regime said was necessary for development.

Always the pragmatist, Dick suggested we forgo sleep and plan our day over the Turismo's American breakfast, which consisted of cold deep-fried eggs on a bed of grease, and boiled orange juice that was still warm. The hotel regretted that no bread was available. Anywhere. The breakfast room looked like a bad place to talk about our plans anyway. At the next table, two Indonesian men with big arms and short hair sipped coffee.

After complimentary refills of boiled orange juice, we left the Turismo for the streets of a city that was more an emblem than a place, like Rangoon or Lhasa. And here Dili was before us, as clean and neat as Singapore. Crews of sweepers moved up and down each road, emptying garbage bins, while cars travelled in a straight line, pedestrians remained on the sidewalk, and traffic police merrily carried out their duties as if they were auditioning for *The Truman Show*.

Outside every school and government building, the Indonesian flag flapped gently in the offshore breeze. Bahasa, Indonesia's national language, was also planted firmly in young Timor minds as part of a national indoctrination program that included a daily flag-raising ceremony, singing of the national anthem and recitation of the *pancasila*, the five-point code that was meant to define an Indonesian way of life. National unity was point number three, after the belief in one God and humanitarianism. "Democracy through consensus" and "social justice" rounded out the code.

Bemused by Dili's calm, we walked down to the waterfront, where centuries-old Portuguese cannons pointed north to the Flores Sea. I had hoped to find some shade, next to a clump of trees by the cannons, but the ground was already occupied by a group of fit Indonesian men (not a pot-belly in sight) who were lounging about, apparently watching life pass by. Every now and then, a van with mirrored windows would pull up to a nearby curb for a few minutes, and then drive off—probably the *nangala*, the most dreaded of the five security forces the Indonesian military had deployed here. Every night, without fail, the secret police descended on groups of Timorese students, intellectuals and other perceived troublemakers, and broke the young men like coconuts on the pavement. Some of the nangala wore balaclavas and dark commando gear, which earned them the nickname Ninjas. Two weeks earlier, the Ninjas had exceeded their usual limits, beating two youths to death in the seaside town of Baucau. But there would be no investigation or consequence. There seldom was. The Timorese had come to accept the methods of occupation as shock therapy.

Farther along the seaside promenade, young men and women were out strolling, apparently in peace, while children played on an abandoned boat in the harbour, shrieking with delight as they dove and somersaulted into the water. That's where we saw Felix, sitting on the seawall reading an English dictionary. I sat near him on the ledge, not wanting to appear curious, and waited for him to say hello. He proudly showed me the inscription page in his dictionary, which bore an image of Jesus Christ. A crucifix dangled from his neck. He kept a Bible near his side, as much a sign of resistance in East Timor as one could dare.

As Dick walked the other way to divert at least some of the nangala's attention, Felix started to tell me, in broken English, that there were "no jobs" and "no hope" for a young Timorese university student like himself. He spoke more quietly than the water lapping against the rocks below us, but he insisted he wanted to speak. At twenty-three, he had five younger siblings to support in his home village. His only hope, he explained, was to leave his cursed homeland. His brothers and sisters would have to fend for themselves.

Felix continued, even as six young men in jeans and T-shirts, smoking Indonesian clove cigarettes, joined us on the seawall. They had much lighter skin and bigger features than the mostly small and dark Timorese, who were genetically Austronesian. The men listened attentively to our conversation. I did not know them. Felix said he did not know them. They did not seem to understand English.

"I don't mind," said Felix, whose face and neck looked badly bruised and scarred. "We don't want Indonesia here. We don't like Indonesia. I will say that."

When Felix rose and walked across the park and then the street, two of the Indonesians followed him. I wondered if I could speak to anyone else without endangering them. "There are more police here than civilians," one young man warned us on the street after dinner that night. He was keen to show us his hometown of Liqueque, where he said the Timorese way of life prevailed. When we said we had other travel plans, he pleaded with us to change them. When we said our scheduled was fixed, he begged us to extend our stay. How he wanted to speak English with his new friends. We finally had to be rude, saying we simply could not visit his village. Period. We could not tell him we were journalists without risking our necks. We could not visit his village without risking his life.

The next day, we ran into the same young man, who told us he had been followed home after our rendezvous and questioned by the nangala. "They told me not to talk about politics with foreigners," he said. "They said they knew what we talked about. They said they have special radios. They had listened to everything we said."

I remembered the Congress Party man who tried to intimidate Biharipur's Dalits with images of government spy satellites watching them vote. That was absurd and comical. A visit from the nangala was not. In East Timor, indeed anywhere in Indonesia, no one had the comfort of defying even the most ridiculous threat, because the bigger threat was everywhere. No matter what route we took, no matter how many times we changed buses, at the end of any journey there was always the same greeting: a man, a cigarette, the shade of a tree. No one knew how many Indonesian eyes were in the territory. The security forces had as many as ten thousand men and women in place and thousands more Timorese turncoats.

Unbelievably, all that we saw was considered moderate compared with what East Timor had endured, and what was left to come. In 1989, the Suharto government started to loosen its grip on the territory, allowing televisions, radios and foreigners to enter. Among them was Pope John Paul II, who came that year to give mass to three hundred thousand people, almost half the territory's population. Gradually, the Church was given greater room to work on rural development, while a massive public works program began to build roads, bridges and schools. Newspapers were also allowed to publish moderate criticisms of the Indonesian government, although not of its presence in East Timor.

Indonesia clearly hoped these gestures would win favour from the Timorese people, and some international goodwill. The gestures also pointed to the regime's most fundamental belief: that development must come before democracy. Time and again, Indonesian officials pointed to the horrendous Portuguese record of development in the territory, and they were right. The Portuguese, who were probably the most callous of colonizers, built only two roads in East Timor during 460 years of occupation. By the time they withdrew in 1975, they had educated less than 10 percent of the population. (Indonesia increased basic literacy to 60 percent.) Malaria and encephalitis ran rampant, and living conditions were so awful that the Portuguese transferred to East Timor called it *Ante-camera do Inferno*, "Gateway to Hell."

By contrast, Indonesia was spending as much as one hundred million dollars a year in East Timor, about six times more per capita than it spent in the rest of the country. The Chrétien government applauded this fact as proof that the Suharto administration somehow cared about the territory, like an abusive spouse who comes home with a lavish anniversary present. As time passed, it mattered less and less that the very same Suharto government and military had killed or starved tens of thousands of Timorese civilians during and shortly after the 1975 invasion, and had summarily executed thousands since. Forgiveness, the habitual abuser had been told, could be arranged.

Quietly, some Canadian diplomats were also trying to get out the message that, the immorality of mass murder aside, there was no reason to take the Timor issue seriously. The territory was the size of Prince Edward Island in a country as wide as Canada, and as far from Jakarta as Baffin Island is from Ottawa. "Sometimes I feel like the ambassador for Dili and Bali," a Canadian diplomat told me, implying that he had more important work than obscure lost causes or rescuing holidayers in trouble. In a country of two hundred million people, East Timor's population of eight hundred thousand (after the mass deaths) was no larger than a Jakarta suburb. In a country rich with oil and gas, timber, gold and minerals, the annexed province's small harvests of maize and coffee seemed almost laughable. About its only claim to importance was its location, five hundred kilometres north of Darwin, Australia, where there were growing fears of refugee boats sailing south. If East Timor was not such a big cause among college undergrads and left-wing intellectuals back home, its file would have been relegated to a junior political officer's desk and forgotten.

It was true that only the rarest of foreign policy analysts would recommend a Western nation stick its neck out for such an insignificant territory. Indonesia was not Zaire. It was one of the most successful development stories of the twentieth century, a well-run, diverse nation that made the most of its natural and human resources. It had a government that thought frequently about the twenty-first century, while its military joined international peacekeeping missions to keep its corner of Asia free from trouble. Indonesia also had a president who had grown up in a village, cared deeply about human development and won no fewer than six medals and awards from the UN for his development work.

The argument might have been interesting had Indonesia not wasted the bulk of its development spending in East Timor. Across the bay from the Turismo, on an empty hilltop, the Suharto government in 1995 erected a thirty-metre-high monument of Christ the King, cemented on a globe, his hands held out to the people of Dili. It was a gift from Jakarta to the people of East Timor, and in a deeply Christian land, where downtown shops specialized in Christ and Mary figurines, the Suharto regime believed the figure would be revered. Instead, the Timorese called it "Indonesia's statue."

A couple of days after we arrived in Dili, Dick and I took a taxi around the bay to the foot of Christ the King's hill, and hiked up a dirt trail to the summit, where a former army interpreter from Sulawesi seemed to be waiting for us. Perhaps he was just looking out for foreign visitors. He politely welcomed us to the site and encouraged us to photograph the magnificent Christ that towered above us. The man then started to explain that he had been here since the 1975 invasion, when Indonesia "rescued" East Timor from insurgent Communists, a nasty but important little piece of work, seeing as Saigon had just fallen to North Vietnamese forces and the Khmer

Rouge were busy depopulating Phnom Penh. "All the bad news you hear at home is propaganda from the people who fled twenty years ago," the man explained, and he asked us to thank the people of Canada for helping Indonesia.

Once he was out of earshot, a young Timorese woman who had been listening to our conversation asked us not to believe a word he had said. She was a student, paying 250 dollars a year in tuition (roughly equal to the territory's per capita income), and like Felix she had no hope of finding a job upon graduation. "I will have to move to another country," she said. "There is no hope for me here."

Almost all the skilled jobs in East Timor went to Indonesians from other islands, just as they had once gone to the Portuguese. Every week, hundreds of newcomers arrived by ship from Bali, Java and Sulawesi to start new lives with land, shops and building materials provided by the government as part of its lauded development program. If young educated Timorese wanted jobs, they would have to head for Jakarta, or abroad, which played conveniently into Indonesia's assimilation strategy. It amounted to nothing less than a second invasion, this one led by professionals and skilled workers who were transforming Dili from a quaint Portuguese town of gracious boulevards, arcades and luxuriant gardens to a prefab suburb of strip malls, split-level homes, satellite dishes and car dealerships.

Discouraged with East Timor's future, we got in our taxi and left the statue, to see if we could find some of its past. On the other side of Dili, there was something called the Museum of Timor History and Culture, a newly built cluster of dark wood huts on stilts, that was supposed to preserve the Timor identity, or at least what had survived colonial oppression and annexation. The museum was closed when we arrived at midday, but the curator, a man from Yogyakarta in central Java, agreed to open the main hut for us. When I asked how a man from Yogyakarta could preserve Timorese identity, the curator told me that all the senior staff were from Java. No Timorese, to his knowledge, had been trained in the preservation of their culture. The Javanese had not done much better, stocking display cases with a predictable collection of spears and headdresses, as if to show how backward, how undeveloped, these people were before the forces of good arrived. Sadly, even the museum's efforts were failing. Since it opened five months earlier, only eighty people had come through its doors.

On our way back downtown from the museum, we called on an economics professor at the University of East Timor, hoping he could make some sense out of this bizarre struggle to lift up and put down an entire people. In some ways, I was amazed to find Professor Armindo Maia alive. He criticized the government frequently, publicly and fearlessly. His only weapons, he explained, were logic and a poster behind his desk. "Wanted: Jesus Christ," the poster read in Portuguese, which Professor Maia translated for us: "For subversive ideas, teaching on poverty, non-violence and equality."

Maia was keen to dispel the government's myth that it was doing well in East Timor. A 7.6-million-dollar technical college built on the outskirts of Dili was rarely used, he said. Like the college, two big irrigation schemes, costing thirteen million dollars, had yet to function properly. The results were hardly surprising, considering the government refused to allow local communities and local organizations to plan, manage and account for their own development. Whether it was schools run by Javanese teachers, or roads built by Balinese contractors, little in East Timor was Timorese.

"I would say 70 to 75 percent of money for Timor is in the hands of non-Timorese," Professor Maia told us.

Rather than applauding the Suharto regime's apparent charity, the rest of the world should have seen how the folly in East Timor was a sign of much bigger troubles to come elsewhere. Across the great archipelago, which the World Bank called a "miracle" economy, anger was bubbling, and the nangala's lid would not stay on it for long. This political standoff was not the result of poverty but, ironically, would become one of its causes.

"I don't think the root of the problem is unemployment," Professor Maia continued. Development, he argued, was not about getting a job or getting rich. "There is something deeper down there. People should feel like masters of their own land. Basically, it's a type of colonization now like the old one. Before it was white colonization. Now it is black colonization. Of course there has been development, but what is development if it does not account for people's esteem and dignity? It is nothing. It is meaningless."

We returned to the Turismo, where I furiously scribbled notes disguised as letters home in case my belongings were confiscated. Dili, I noted, had become a deluded Disneyland of dictatorship, a city of facades, imported talent and make-believe happiness. If we were to find the Timorese story, it would not be in the surreal Turismo, under Christ the King or in the Museum of Timor History and Culture. East Timor's horrific past and troubled future lay well beyond us, in the hills, forests and fishing villages where terror lurked and hope continued to stir.

After another breakfast of cold deep-fried eggs the next morning, we took a taxi to the bus stand and found a crowded *bemo* headed for the coastal town of Baucau. We planned to change bemos there and continue inland to a village in the hills where a group of Salesian sisters might take us in. Or they might not. The previous night at dinner, a group of tourists, real ones, said they had heard two Canadian journalists had been detained and beaten by police. The message was out. The authorities knew we were here. Only later did I discover that a Timorese development worker we had visited was a government informer, what the locals called a "guardian angel."

The road east from Dili climbed over a denuded hill, stripped of its sandalwood trees, and lumbered across a rolling stretch of maize fields before cutting back to the coastline. The two-storey cement houses of Dili soon gave way to thatched huts, and then to a long line of fishing villages. We sat silently in the bemo, surrounded by peasants returning from the capital with bags of clothes, cooking pots and packaged foods. At Baucau, we walked slowly around the local market trying to make sure no one followed us to Venilale, the place nestled in the hills where we'd been told to ask for Sister Marlene, a Filipina nun from California.

From the coast, on a slow, twisting climb into the hills, we passed a military garrison and police checkpoints, and a cluster of caves where Japanese soldiers hid during the Australian advance in World War II. Beyond the marks of war, past and present, we climbed farther into open pastures and terraced rice paddies, through a morning mist, until we were surrounded by hills. The bemo dropped us at a fork in the road and continued south toward a place the Timorese called "The Forest," where the dregs of a Soviet-backed rebel movement hung on, almost pitiably.

On the misty roadside, there was no sign for the Catholic mission. There was no sign for anything other than a cement plaque at the fork in the road, bearing the five pancasila principles. I thought we were alone, really alone, for the first time since we had arrived in East Timor, until I saw a man and young boy walking down the road. They were our only hope for directions, and they didn't speak English. Only when we crossed ourselves in the Catholic way did the man understand what we wanted; he pointed over a ridge to the Salesian mission, where we would find vitality we had not seen in Dili. In the fields below the mission's school, volleyball and basketball games were in full swing. Beyond a church, the lineup at a small child and maternal health clinic stretched out the door and around the side. We located Sister Marlene in the school. She was as small as a lark, and as lively, and not afraid to speak to a couple of journalists. A Filipina by ancestry, a Californian by birth, she cherished free speech. She also wanted the world to see what she saw.

Up here in the hills, she told us, Indonesia's big development efforts had amounted to nothing. A nearby hut was stocked with unused government-issued fertilizer, which the farmers called "poison" because the province had not dispatched an official to explain its application in the local language, Tetum. Since the local government health clinic faced the same problem, almost all parents brought their children to the sisters instead. Measles, malaria, diarrhea and tuberculosis ran rampant. Nearly half the hillside's children died before the age of five, a rate about eight times greater than Indonesia's average.

Sister Marlene said the missionaries had learned to cope with this burden, even when the local regiment stole their supplies or came searching for the children of rebels to use as bait for surrender. The endemic fear was an emotion the Catholics could not treat so easily. The nun suggested we meet some women she knew, and sent some of her students to find them while she showed us the children's artwork. There were paintings of fighter planes and guns, and faces contorted in pain. This was the indelible sign of oppression that no quantity of roads and technical colleges could erase.

Half an hour later, the women appeared in the school hallway, brought by the children, who had found them at the health clinic. It would be safer to talk here, Sister Marlene said, explaining that one could not be too cautious in the territory, not when there were cases like the local teacher who discovered one of her ten-year-old pupils was a government informer.

The women sat down in the classroom and poured forth their traumas, while Sister Marlene translated. One woman told us of her flight by foot from rebel territory a few years earlier. She had come to surrender with her three-year-old daughter by her side and a baby in her womb. The Forest was a death trap for the young, and although her husband stayed with the rebels, she wanted to keep her children safe, even if it meant they'd be in Indonesian hands. Once out of the rebel territory, a soldier greeted her, took her daughter aside and shot the girl dead. The baby was born in prison.

Another unwed woman told us of her three children, each from a different soldier. "I had no choice," she said. "We are so poor, what can we do?"

Tragically, many of the rebels, known by their Portuguese acronym Fretelin, were not much better than Suharto's troops. They murdered anyone suspected of treason, even those unwilling to move with them through the malaria-ridden forests where they could serve as a human shield. In their wake, the guerrillas burned villages and crops, and killed hundreds, perhaps thousands, of people deemed to be traitors. One woman remembered moving with the rebels when she was a little girl. As bombs fell around her, she ran through the forest searching for water. Then she stopped for breath and sat on a log, only to realize that it was a human corpse. Then she found a pool of water, only to see that it was full of blood. Of four children in her family, she was the sole survivor.

Sister Marlene told us a special story. The school had a ten-year-old boy in its custody. His father was a leading guerrilla fighter and his mother had stayed with him in The Forest. One day, the school received a package from The Forest, and inside was an embroidered tablecloth. "To my dear son," it read. "You are the only living testimony of your father. He fought for the cause and died for the cause. Now your father is watching over both of us from heaven. I don't know when or if we will ever see each other again on earth. That is not important. It is important you know that I miss you, I pray for you, I love you." It was signed, "Mother."

I thought about the embroidery as we said goodbye to Sister

Marlene, and again as we walked by the cheering volleyball crowd. What did it mean to be a mother separated from a son? What did it mean to be a people separated from their land?

As it was late in the afternoon, we hired a bemo directly to Dili, stopping only once, in a roadside village near the sea where a few dozen women and girls had gathered in a yard to sing hymns before candles and a small altar. Their soprano harmony filled the night, and seemed stronger even than the sea crashing against the rocks below. We stood silently at the back of the service, in awe of its beauty and strength. In the face of one of Asia's greatest armies and most enduring dictators, this was all that most Timorese could offer as resistance. How hopelessly inadequate it seemed. How terribly wrong I was.

❖

The next morning, we were due to fly to Bali, where we could collect the rest of our bags and return home. We would have to show our passports at Dili airport but we hardly cared now if we were arrested or expelled. Nothing the Indonesians would do to a couple of Canadians seemed much in comparison with what they did to their own people.

Before we left, I wanted to buy some Timorese embroidery at an open-air market near the bus station. I found three pieces, which the hawker neatly folded and handed to me as I motioned with my hands to ask how much. He wrote on a slip of paper one hundred thousand rupiahs, about sixty dollars at the time. I laughed, then cursed, then dropped thirty dollars on the table and walked away. Back in India, if the hawker didn't like the price, he would run after me, shouting for more. I would shout back, and we would eventually agree on a price, laughing, cursing and playfully insulting each other until the deal was reached. But this was Indonesia. No, this was Indonesian-occupied East Timor.

We reached the bus stand before I realized the difference. I handed Dick my package and walked back. The hawker was still at his table, staring at the pavement. I handed him another thirty dollars, and apologized, uselessly, in English. Had the hawker confronted me, the nearest policeman would have slapped him. Had he chased me, the nangala would have swerved around the corner and packaged him off to God knows where. Ordinary commerce could not function in this tunnel of fear. If there was any development in East Timor, if there was any development in Indonesia, it was no longer human development; it was simply money poured into a place, like cement.

I did not return to Indonesia for another six months. In July 1996, Jakarta, the capital "ablaze in lights and promise," was at a breaking point. In a central residential neighbourhood, barely a kilometre from the presidential palace, hundreds of opposition members had blocked off traffic and were standing nose-to-nose with Indonesia's toughest riot police. Just about everyone knew this would end in an awful bloodletting, but first the government had to get rid of an embarrassing collection of the world's leading foreign ministers, Canada's Lloyd Axworthy among them, who were attending the annual meeting of the Association of Southeast Asian Nations.

On a muggy Friday afternoon, as the foreign ministers were packing their bags, I slipped by the riot police and into a bungalow that served as headquarters for the newest opposition movement to take on Suharto. The two hundred or so dissidents were hardly the Communists that haunted the mind of the aging despot. They were people like Bobbi Effendi, a Jakarta yuppie who could have been a standard-bearer for the Suharto generation. A factory manager with two children in university, Bobbi was forty-seven and prosperous by his country's standards. He had grown up in an independent nation that knew no war, owned a late-model Japanese car, lived in the suburbs, and here he was with a red bandana around his head and a rattan club in his hand, ready to do battle with riot police. How else could he make his voice heard in Suharto's Indonesia?

"This country is not a powerful country," Bobbi shouted to me. I could barely hear him over the din of a rock band playing for the protesters in the walled compound. "There is only the power of the military. If this country is to be powerful, the power must lie with the people."

Suharto's regime had never accepted this principle of power (nor did his Western allies) because it feared it would fragment the state.

It reasoned that a nation of eighteen thousand islands, five hundred or so languages and five major religions could be held together only by force—and a mock democracy. The ruling Golkar Party included the military, the civil service, the nationwide network of community development workers and anyone else who seriously wanted a government contract. To legitimize itself, Suharto's self-named New Order Government allowed two opposition parties to exist but restricted them from every notion of political freedom, although once every five years they could contest an election that Golkar was sure to win.

One of the two opposition parties represented the disaffected Muslim leadership. The other, the Indonesian Democratic Party, was left over from the former ruling party of Sukarno, the president Suharto ousted. It was a squabbling and largely irrelevant force until Sukarno's grown daughter, Megawati Sukarnoputri, emerged from the shadows to take charge in 1993. For Suharto, who believed in ghosts and spirits, the very presence of his greatest rival's daughter on the national stage was too much. The government orchestrated a putsch in the Democratic Party and virtually barred Megawati from public life. Which is when Bobbi Effendi and his yuppie friends laid siege to the party headquarters in central Jakarta.

In the nineties, the government had already put down a vocal media and an emerging labour movement, and would do the same with the disaffected demonstrators—as soon as the foreign ministers were gone. The last of them flew out of Jakarta on the Friday night. At about eight Saturday morning, the first wave of government forces attacked. Their front line was made up of young men who looked like a suburban mall gang in torn jeans and T-shirts. They threw bottles over a wall at the dissidents and started to smash street lights, street signs, phone booths, anything they could find to fill the air with fear. Then suddenly the call went out, sending the hooligans over the wall with clubs and bats. Behind them were hundreds of riot police with shields, sticks, knee pads and helmets. At the intersection of two lovely tree-lined residential streets, I stood with a group of journalists behind the riot police, shuddering to think what was happening to Bobbi Effendi. Anyone wanting to escape stood no chance.

We could see nothing but debris flying in the air. There must have been three hundred men in the small compound fighting in a pitched, almost medieval combat. The screaming, first of battle, then of pain, was shrill. And then came the bodies, dozens of them packed on stretchers and piled into ambulances and buses parked nearby.

Thinking I had seen the worst, I ran three blocks with Jonathan Head, the BBC's Jakarta correspondent, to his office, where I could scribble a few thoughts on a piece of paper, call *The Globe and Mail* in Toronto and dictate the semblance of a story. When I returned to the Democratic Party headquarters, a wave of street sweepers and cleaners had descended on the broken glass, dropped clubs and debris like maintenance staff after a rock concert. Everything seemed to have gone according to plan. The protesters were given their day and then asked to leave. When they didn't, they were beaten into submission. The New Order Government would go on.

But then I noticed something quite unusual at the next intersection. The riot police had taken up a new position, accompanied by water cannon, armoured personnel carriers and a special canine unit of German shepherds. The front row of police smacked their sticks on the pavement, preparing themselves for battle. As I got closer, I realized the force was facing a crowd that numbered in the thousands, and they looked like university students from—and this was rich with irony—the nearby Campus of the New Order Struggle.

It was too late to find a safer position. In a flash, the riot police ran forward and started clubbing a group of students who had crossed the street to taunt them. When more students ran forward, they were attacked by the dog unit. For a moment, the barking seemed louder than the screaming, but just for a moment. I turned to beat a retreat, only to see more riot police coming my way. I ducked to the side, and down a small sewerage right-of-way. Two young Indonesians had also tried to escape this way. One stood with his hands on his head and a dog snarling at his feet. The other lay on the ground as a policeman clubbed him mercilessly. With each blow, the young man rolled one way and then the other, seemingly too stunned to cry. His face streamed with blood.

Unnoticed, I walked up the other side of the right-of-way, across the street, under an elevated mass transit line and into the crowd that continued to throw rocks at the police from its position next to a McDonald's. Seething with panic and hate, waves of young people pushed forward, as if they were trying to summon the nerve to charge the police en masse. And then the water came, hard, sharp shots that knocked strong men on their backs. The crowd turned and ran through a warren of back streets and into the university campus.

I followed as fast as I could, thinking this might be the end of the clash. But when we reached the next major street, Salemba Raya, new crowds had formed, as different as the students had been from the disaffected yuppies. Many of them probably were agents provocateurs, rabble-rousers used by the obsessive military to create the kind of public disturbances needed to justify a brutal crackdown. Some Indonesians actually believed that instead of democracy, all the public needed was a good riot once in a while. Today they would get one. A few young men flagged down a city bus, ordered its driver and passengers off and set it ablaze. More youths began to tear down fences and smash windows. I followed this new crowd with frightened curiosity. One group ran inside a small army office and then raced outside, leaving the building behind them in flames. "Megawati!" the men shouted in support of the deposed opposition leader. Soon the Department of Agriculture was on fire, as was a reflecting glass branch of Bank Swansarindo International, owned by one of Suharto's children. At a Toyota dealership, one man ran inside, hot-wired a pickup truck and drove it straight through the display window, shattering glass in his wake as he continued across the parking lot and directly into a telephone pole. Another man, his friend apparently, ran through the crowd spraying a fire extinguisher in the air.

If someone in the military had hoped to create a little insecurity, the riot was now beyond their control. I walked up on an overpass to get away from the mob, and could see billows of smoke across central Jakarta, as a dozen buildings went up in flames. The crowd on the road below me had swelled into the thousands, many of them carrying cell-phones and Nikon cameras. On the other side of the overpass, a group of police faced protesters from all four directions. When a panic-stricken officer drew a pistol and fired shots in the air to disperse the crowd, I quickly got off the overpass and headed for cover, only to run into a squad of riot police about to chase a gang of youths down a side street. The pursuit was hot until the police realized they had been cut off from the rest of their unit, forcing them to turn and retreat, with scores of rock-throwing men, women and children in pursuit.

The chaos continued all afternoon and into the night. Police sealed off Selamba, the central district near the university, but could do little to calm the anger that had boiled over. Finally, in the dark, I walked down a deserted boulevard covered with rubble and glass. Every side street was barricaded with barbed wire, wooden poles and, in a few cases, furniture, erected by residents wanting to keep the mobs out. At the far end of the boulevard, hundreds of fresh soldiers stood in wait, their position given away only by the bright lights of a Dunkin' Donuts outlet. I climbed over a small neighbourhood barricade and worked my way through a series of back lanes to another major street where there was no debris, mobs or hint of dissent. Suharto's Indonesia was like that. One day, a development miracle; the next, a hotbed of trouble. I hailed a taxi to my hotel as if I were leaving a nightclub.

The next evening, over drinks, an investment banker asked me about the troubles. His wife had noticed the burning buildings during a tennis game on their rooftop club in central Jakarta. At one point, he said, black ash seemed to fall on the court. What could be so seriously wrong? he wondered. The Jakarta stock exchange was booming. Money was pouring into the country. There were jobs for anyone with an education. Wasn't this good enough?

Barely a year after the Jakarta riots, in the fall of 1997, Suharto's empire crumbled as Asia's financial crisis, the worst in decades, exposed the naked truth of Indonesia's ineffectual government. A plunging currency, hundreds of millions of dollars leaving the country, riots in the capital, ordinary citizens fighting to withdraw their savings from banks: this was not the stuff of a model country. But none of it could deter Suharto from his last great dream project. Nicknamed Megarice by the government, it involved the clearing of one million hectares of Borneo's rain forest and swamp, to make way for oil palm plantations, rice farms and housing for half a million families from the crowded island of Java. The undertaking was so fantastic, so full of hubris, so utterly arrogant that it seemed Stalinist to the core.

To make way for Megarice, the project had to torch tens of thousands of hectares of trees and peat swamp, which seemed inconsequential to the planners. They believed the equatorial rains would squelch the fires, as reliably as dawn came every day. But now, after six months without rain, the underground peat fires had raged uncontrollably from summer into autumn and soon into winter—the Suharto vision of plenty was being lost to an environmental and financial calamity. Close to twenty thousand square kilometres of land, swamp and precious rain forest were on fire, and while the Suharto regime did all in its power to downplay the disaster, the rest of the world was no longer listening.

Not only was a good part of the country on fire, the rupiah was in a free fall, banks were insolvent and the dictator of thirty years had lost all credibility at home and abroad. Indonesia, praised in development textbooks and showered with international aid and recognition, was so broke that it had stopped paying its firefighters. Yet, throughout the disaster, the government had ordered schools to stay open, ignoring a report that the haze created a health hazard equivalent to smoking four packs of cigarettes a day. The most common estimates suggested twenty million Indonesians, one-tenth of the population, could not see down their streets, and most would suffer asthma, bronchitis or skin and eye infections as a result. It was only when twenty children collapsed in a school in Sumatra's Riau province that classes were finally cancelled.

I felt I had to get to the heart of the fires, if only for a final reckoning with the post-war vision of development, and found a travelling companion in Vladimir Sakharov, a UN disaster expert based in Geneva sent to assess the damage. For Vladimir, the trip was to be less a reckoning than a quick swing through another disaster. He said he had to get back to Geneva where his wife had booked them into a spa for the weekend.

When we landed at Banjarmasin, capital of South Kalimantan, the airport was barely visible for all the haze. The outpost, once known as the Venice of the East, looked more like Sarajevo, with forces of every stripe in motion. The Indonesian army was finally heading for the fires with whatever equipment it could find or seize from other groups. Across the road from the airport, we found Canadians unloading special firefighting kits flown in from British Columbia. Malaysian teams were already deep in the forest, while American and Australian water bombers roared overhead in search of flames. What with El Niño and its rage of droughts scorching Southeast Asia, no one was going to deny the tottering Suharto regime one last airlift of international support to fight the ugly side of nature.

But as we headed into the rain forest in a rented four-wheel-drive Kijang, we began to see how the great fire of 1997 was less a product of nature than of a development dream gone mad. At the first river crossing on the road inland, a few hours away from dusk, Vladimir and I stood on a rickety ferry dock straining our eyes to see the other side as if it were the dead of night. All of Borneo and most of the Malaysian peninsula were covered by a thick, pungent haze laced with sulphuric acid, a shroud so thick it choked much of this equatorial swamp of its remaining life. There were no screeching birds. In many places, all the trees were gone, too. In their place were a few charred stumps that seemed like images from a Sebastião Salgado photograph. And in the distance, Suharto Inc. toiled on, oblivious to the fire bells ringing on satellites high above.

I bought a pint-sized bottle of Coca-Cola and rejoined Vladimir on the dock to watch the Kapuas River ferry come into view, loaded down with cars, minivans, small trucks and scores of passengers heading for fresh air. An exodus from central Kalimantan was underway, and we were headed in the wrong direction. Only a handful of cars and Kijangs rumbled onto the small boat for the return trip. The boatmen were rushing each crossing, for on the other side a lineup of vehicles stretched up a hill and down a single-track road. Hundreds of people were waiting in wood-plank beer halls and provisions shops for their turn to cross.

After the ferry docked, we headed inland across a vast peat swamp that served as a buffer between the dense jungles of central Borneo and the Java Sea. We hoped to reach Palangka Raya, a provincial outpost, by nightfall, and there seemed to be no reason to stop. On my 1996 map of Kalimantan, there was not a single road between us and the equator—only a splotch of checkered blue lines indicating a great marsh untouched by human development. This promised to be the enchanting Borneo I had read about as a child: rich with orangutans and virgin rain forest, and devoid, I hoped, of the air-conditioned boom towns we had left behind on the coast.

"Your map appears to be out of date," Vladimir said, pointing up

ahead. The jungle track we thought we could follow to the Kahayan
River and then along its banks to Palangka Raya was about to give
way to a broad dirt highway ready for paving. Along its shoulders were
Japanese-made bulldozers and construction camps that suggested
something monumental was in the works. Even in the thin light we
could see hectares of freshly cleared forests, new townships and plantations of oil palms, each spaced an identical distance from the next.

The peat lands and bog that lay before us—flat, arable and
close to rivers leading to the sea—had been the target of major
development since the twenties, when the Dutch first drew up plans
to convert these swamps to rice farms. The idea failed to win financial backing and was delayed, then scrapped when Japan took control of Borneo by force during World War II. After a brief post-war
reign, a new Dutch administration fell to nationalist forces in 1949,
and the Megarice idea did not win favour again until the nineties,
when, for the first time, Indonesia's great post-war victories in food
production and population control appeared threatened.

After all those years in power, Suharto began to worry that his
country would not be able to feed itself. The son of Javanese rice
farmers, the president had a passion for agriculture and always surprised development groups when he asked unusually detailed questions about crop yields or pest movements, or quizzed visiting
dignitaries about things like bull semen. As a former military commander, he also knew grain prices were the single most politically
explosive issue in the country. New rice production figures always
went straight to his palace in downtown Jakarta.

Initially, Megarice plowed ahead with a ten-year plan and a
three-billion-dollar budget, with much of the investment coming
from Indonesia's thriving private sector. In return for financing
roads, canals and land clearing, 176 companies were given leases to
vast tracts of land, 362,000 hectares in total, on which they were
required to build plantations for oil palms, rubber trees and other
cash crops. The government hoped to make Indonesia, in addition to
the new rice bowl, the world's biggest exporter of palm oil. Moreover,
it would achieve this through an ideal combination of industrial agriculture and small-scale farming, of billionaires and peasants, the
central characters, really, of Indonesia's greater economic miracle.
When in the mid-nineties the respected Indonesian environmental

group Walhi warned that the project would require a series of fires the likes of which modern Asia had not seen, as well as the loss of 1.4 million hectares of forest, the government barely flinched.

As we drove along the dirt road, Vladimir and I marvelled at what the tottering regime had been able to accomplish in its desperation. As part of the project's first two-hundred-million-dollar phase, work crews had started to clear an area one-third the size of Belgium, and would soon add bitumin highways and a twenty-seven-thousand-kilometre network of canals that would come together at a vast new reservoir in the forest. Even as one of the great natural disasters of the nineties burned unabated, construction workers hired by the Suharto government drained the forest of water and bulldozed trees into the ground. It mattered little that no international development agency wanted any part of Megarice, or that Indonesia's biggest environmental groups condemned it, or that the plummeting rupiah made it even more ridiculously expensive. As long as Suharto, a modern-day emperor at age seventy-six, remained in power, there seemed to be no stopping it.

We followed the development frenzy most of the way to Palangka Raya, a town that looked half abandoned when we reached it in the early evening. It had been declared a hot spot in the great fires, one of thirty-two in Borneo, and its reputation seemed justified. The town's small airport had been closed for two months, and on the main road we could see no farther than ten metres in front of us. A local official complained that the smoke had been so thick in his office one day he couldn't see the door. Another official told us one-quarter of the town's population had been evacuated, or had simply up and left. Doors and windows were taped shut. The provincial government, housed in an overbuilt Dayak longhouse that resembled a theme restaurant, seemed empty. Only the hospital was crowded, with asthma, bronchitis and pneumonia cases.

We checked into a motel on the main road, and, without thinking about the consequences, I went for an evening jog to stretch my legs after hours in the Kijang. After a few hundred metres I found myself heaving in a ditch, unable to breathe any more of the acrid air that seemed to be sprinkling ash on the streets. I walked back to the motel in the grey dark and found Vladimir in the restaurant, sensibly drinking Bintang beer and enjoying a cigarette. The only other

men in the room were managers from a plantation company active in
Palangka Raya.

We ordered more beers and a few plates of fried noodles, while
Vladimir entertained me with his long and rich career in tracking disasters. Cause, effect and solution rarely seemed to be good company.
He had just been in eastern Iran, after an earthquake, and was dis-
mayed to find medical kits from China with directions and guidebooks
written only in Chinese. Among the emergency relief supplies from
France were one hundred sets of silverware. The Iranians did not mind
the silverware so much as the fact that there was not enough to go
around, which in the egalitarian Islamic republic was very bad form
indeed. To ration the fine cutlery, it was given only to newlyweds in the
area. Although in poor taste, Vladimir said, at least the silverware was
not egregiously insensitive to the Muslim victims, not like the shipments of canned pork from Poland and the Czech Republic.

The situation in the Indonesian fires was not much better. The
U.S. and Australia offered water bombers to areas with no open water
supply. Canada sent state-of-the-art firefighting kits for the local fire
service, only to have them intercepted by a local military commander
who declared unilaterally that his men would use the equipment. He
told the Canadian training team from British Columbia and
Saskatchewan to set up camp on his base, which they did. The local
fire brigade got nothing.

But this was more than the usual aid fiasco, even for Vladimir.
Nearly forty years of dictatorship had left Indonesia without any
effective local government to sound a warning. Most towns did not
even have a fire department, and the military was so obsessed with
crushing uprisings that it had no idea how to manage a disaster.
Only a year earlier, Canada had offered to help Indonesia and its
neighbours develop a regional firefighting strategy, but Indonesia
showed no interest. At the Palangka Raya emergency centre, I found
soldiers playing chess; they referred me to a group of university students who, as part of a community service project, had resorted to
throwing plastic bags of water at the fires. Every night, the students
piled five hundred bags of water into pickup trucks and responded
to emergency calls made to their special helpline.

"The thing is to get Indonesian people involved, to get people
who feel unable to deal with the fires to make a contribution,"

explained Sulmin Gumjri, an environmental studies lecturer who started the service. "The official agencies, they do nothing."

When I suggested to Vladimir that the world had condoned Megarice by blaming the fires on El Niño, he pensively sipped his Bintang. "I'm afraid to say I already know what will be the content of my report," he admitted. It would sound something like this: A drought caused by El Niño had dried out the marshland around Palangka Raya, where greedy peasants, who would go unnamed (the poor are always unnamed), had slashed and burned thousands of hectares of land to open up more rice fields. A handful of unnamed plantation companies would take some of the blame as well. It was true that local farmers had burned fields every summer for decades, counting on September rains to stop the spread, and that, in 1997, the rains did not come until November. But the burning this autumn had also reached an epic level because of Megarice. The more the big fires spread, the more people joined in, burning scrublands allotted to them by plantation companies as if they were looting an electronics store during a blackout.

We left Palangka Raya early the next morning to drive north. Along the way, peasant farmers continued to slash away at the wilds while Suharto's last great dream smouldered under the ground in a million small fires that burst to the surface only to disappear in a flash, leaving behind nothing more than grey plumes of smoke on a dreary landscape that began to look like old London with her chimney pots. Occasionally a small bush burst into flames, igniting from its roots, but the surface was so barren that there was nothing else for the flames to catch. The surface fires died as quickly as they flamed.

Over much territory, the devastation continued in a land stripped of all natural and human life. The few trees left standing were grey with ash. The soil itself was a dull and barren black. Down side roads and country lanes, every house was boarded up and padlocked, with no sign to indicate that this land was a new frontier. Then we came across Suldani.

The young Dayak stood in a smouldering field, stripped down to his surf shorts as he dug a trench around his wood-plank house and the coop where he raised chickens for a neighbour. There was no point in leaving, he explained. His people had been in these parts for as long as the trees, and they would stay to see the forests blossom again. "This is our land," Suldani explained in a simple phrase that should have been the motto of the Asian miracle.

A Dayak from the Orang Bukit tribe, Suldani was twenty-two years old and a newcomer to the lowlands of central Kalimantan. Up in the mountainous forests, where his father and father's father lived, Suldani could earn only a subsistence from the trees and streams. Although his family grew rice in the forest and celebrated each harvest with an offering to their dead ancestors on a palm leaf altar in their longhouses, this was not the life for Suldani's generation. They watched television in their villages, and travelled by riverboat to trading posts and occasionally the provincial capital. Suldani did not wear loincloths, bird feathers or protective tattoos like his ancestors. He kept his hair short, wore Western clothes and spoke Bahasa. He preferred clove cigarettes to chewing betel nuts.

A few seasons ago, Suldani and his wife travelled downriver, first on a small longboat, then on a bigger ferry, to find a better life. He had heard about something called Megarice and the big cash economy. A plantation company gave him a one-hectare plot of land, which he was to clear and cultivate as he saw fit. Under an agreement with the national government, which owned the land, the company was then allowed to claim eight hectares for its own use.

"This was forest, thick, thick forest," Suldani said of the desolate fields around him. "People here do not appreciate the forests."

As he talked, he did not stop digging. The fire that was raging underground was moving surreptitiously through the dried peat toward his house, his wife, their eighteen-month-old son and the chickens. He planned to keep digging until he hit rock.

Although Suldani wanted to join a bigger and more comfortable world, he thought he could bring some of his Dayak traditions with him. Like the one calling for everyone to work for the common good, so that everyone will share in the benefits. The Dayak's animistic gods demanded this. But the new world of Megarice gave little respect to tradition or common beliefs. Nor did it respect the land and trees. Suharto's Indonesia was surprisingly colonial, given that the great man spent his youth in Java fighting the Dutch.

Most of the migrant farmers around Suldani's house came from other islands, Java mainly. They were given transportation by ship to Kalimantan, two hectares of forest and a wood-plank house. They could sell any wood they cleared from their new property, and for the first eighteen months, they would get a wage equal to $1.50 a day as well as subsidized food. In return, they were expected to donate a week's labour to help build roads and canals through the project area.[1]

During our visit to Palangka Raya, the military governor for the local province of 1.6 million people said he was under instructions to make way for one million more residents; they would need five hundred thousand hectares of arable land. "We have to be ready for all these people," he said with alarm. "We cannot slow down."

Once the forests around Suldani's homestead were cleared and the swamps drained, the soil became bone dry in the harsh equatorial light, perhaps for the first time in a thousand years. It would take only a cigarette to ignite some of the arid peat, but apparently more forceful means were used. Suldani said most of his neighbours lit fires so they could clear land faster and plant rice sooner. They did not want to spend a long winter cutting trees and digging up roots, as required by the plantation company.

Suldani stopped digging briefly to point to a Javanese neighbour's field, a long, charred wasteland. After one good rainfall, it would be ideal for rice planting, or better yet a new housing development. The man from Java had eight hectares of swampland to his

---

[1] This sort of coordinated population movement was not new to Indonesia, which had already shifted more than five million people, mostly from Java, to Kalimantan and other outlying islands as part of a twenty-year-old scheme called transmigration. Another five million people had moved on their own. The gigantic effort, however, had been a social and environmental disaster. It led to the clearing of twenty-thousand square kilometres of forests and violence against indigenous communities, and produced no proven economic benefit, for the migrants or the nation. The World Bank, which financed the movement of 355,000 people to Sumatra and Kalimantan, calculated the cost of moving one family to be about seven thousand dollars. Moreover, a World Bank internal review, published in 1986 shortly before the bank pulled out of transmigration, indicated that half of all people living on project sites remained in poverty, and an astonishing one in five lived at subsistence levels. Javanese rice farmers simply couldn't make ends meet in the harsh peat lands of central Kalimantan or in many other frontier lands. In the supposedly crowded region of western Java, Suharto himself lived on a thirty-thousand-hectare estate, where he built a cattle ranch, ostrich farm, private golf course and racetrack.

name, so much that he didn't even need to live here. Suldani could care for his chickens while he lived more comfortably in Palangka Raya. "Now he will be able to sell his land for more money," Suldani explained. "He will make a big profit. My neighbour will be happy."

The young man excused himself to get back to ditch digging. If he could not save his land, he said, no one else would.

Back in Palangka Raya, we stopped at the office of PT Surya, one of 136 plantation companies charged with illegally setting fires and destroying forests. Gereh Putra, the local representative, welcomed us to his small office and offered the corporate view of the growing disaster. The small fires, he explained, were set by peasants hired by his company to clear land. "My own company lost hundreds of hectares of good forest because of these small fires," he said. He rolled out a large map of the area and pinpointed where the fires were the worst, and where his company's land was. Most of the time it was the same place.

"Do you see a problem?" I asked.

"We need to develop faster," the manager insisted. He brushed the map with his hand and pointed to new forests and peatland to be cleared. The four hundred hectares of PT Surya land that had burned in 1997 was nothing. Over the next few years, the company planned to develop twelve thousand more hectares of swamp and scrubland.

Next to the map I noticed a set of official guidelines for land clearing. Mr. Putra consulted it, at our request, and told us that the official policy was this: once trees are cut, the stumps and brush should be removed by bulldozer or chemicals, not by fire. I asked if any companies did this.

"These methods are expensive." He laughed uncomfortably and dropped the hefty book of guidelines back on his desk. "Do you think we have time to read this?"

I felt as if I was back with the Barabaig, watching a big development project roll over nature and communities in the belief that countries should be built like American suburbs, with heavy emphasis on planning, investment and "vision." Like Julius Nyerere, Suharto had missed the root of Indonesia's food problems, returning to his military obsession with supply lines. Megarice was his counteroffensive. The real trouble was that his very young and rapidly urbanizing country was changing its diet, just as the Japanese, Koreans and, most recently, the Thais had done when their incomes soared. Instead of rice, Indonesians were eating noodles made from imported wheat; what these consumers really needed was a competitive, demand-based food industry. Indonesia's entire noodle business was controlled by one family, the Liems, who were among Suharto's most important corporate allies.

On our return trip to the coast, we stopped at the Megarice office, located on a river's edge. The pleasant clapboard building, neatly painted white, was set behind a military fence, out of public reach, although there was nothing worth seeing inside. The walls were decorated with pictures of Suharto touring the site and being greeted by happy farmers. The few project officers on duty, wearing military-style uniforms, explained how the surrounding fields, once the smoke had cleared, would feed their country. The area manager said he had heard the historic fires were started by a single cigarette, but there was no need to worry. Construction was proceeding apace. "*Asal Bapak senang,*" the manager told us. "As long as Bapak [the highest honorific] is happy."

I said goodbye to Vladimir in Jakarta but stayed in touch by e-mail. He told me his report was written as carefully as he had promised and filed accordingly. The UN never did criticize Bapak Suharto, not while he was in power. But others did. The World Wide Fund for Nature (WWF) called the 1997 fires "a planetary disaster," and later concluded they were less a result of El Niño than of Suharto's development policies. According to the WWF, the tycoon-president and his associates lost 493 million dollars' worth of trees in the fires. The country lost 4.4 billion dollars of wealth.

A year later, in November 1998, just five months after Suharto's fall, I was thrown out of Indonesia and barred indefinitely from returning for the crime of "doing journalist activities without proper procedure." Although several diplomats took up my case with the post-Suharto president's office, and later at cabinet level with the new democratically elected government, the reply was always the same: I was placed on the blacklist by military intelligence, and only they could remove me. The tradition of pleasing someone at the top endures— "*Asal Bapak senang*"—as it does in China, Malaysia, Kenya, and even in little Biharipur. But as Suharto discovered, and our friend Rajinder Singh Yadav would soon find out, development cannot be used to suppress the human will, at least not indefinitely. Development that does not foster liberty can only parch its roots, leaving all that it creates exposed to the kind of flames that were racing across Indonesia, and about to ignite Biharipur.

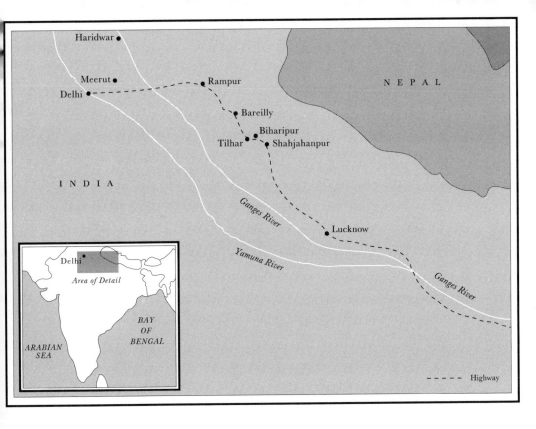

# THE VILLAGE IV

"For a moment there was silence, except for a breeze rustling the leaves of the Dalits' only tree. The two farmers, a landlord with a title and a widow with no name, had nothing more to say to each other."

# 23

## Class War

On our final trip to Biharipur, I marvelled at all that had changed in
India during our time there. Just to get out of Delhi, we had to drive
through dreary cement-block housing colonies for an hour across
what were once open fields. Out on the highway, the towering cut-
outs of Indira Gandhi had been replaced with signs offering "Beer
Ahead" and a popular whisky, "Bagpiper: 110 rupees." About halfway
to the village, a roadside dhaba had been renamed the Rock 'n' Roll
Café. It offered the same milky chai and greasy chapatis stuffed with

potatoes and peppers, but with the added draw of satellite television. Eating breakfast next to a groom's party on its way to pick up a teenaged bride, we were able to catch a glimpse of CNN.

Ahead in Bereilly, home to the pampered horse regiment, the old Kipps' Sweet Shop where we often bought presents for the villagers was now a department store, with sections for jewellery, toys, cosmetics and groceries, even Cocoa Puffs. Rama and I grabbed several chilled cans of Pepsi and continued eastward, where the number of tractors started to dwindle and more blue plastic flags appeared, bearing the Dalits' elephant symbol. Soon, every town we passed in our rented white Ambassador was draped with the militant caste flags.

But past Tilhar, beyond the railway tracks where we left our car, the changes stopped. The fields, the mud, the trees were the same. Our village emerged on the horizon as it had almost seven years ago, a cluster of mud-walled huts packed together as densely as a Bombay slum, except this time there was no haze from a hundred winter fires. It was summer, the eve of a monsoon that was already weeks late, and all the land around Biharipur was blazing hot. Only a few fields glistened in the midday sun, as Rajinder's and the Sikhs' irrigation pumps filled their neatly engineered paddies with water. The rest of the landscape, as far as the eye could see, was bone-dry—Dalit land waiting for the monsoon to decide if the coming year would be one of comfort or hunger.

Inside the village, only modest improvements had been made to the hundred or so huts. A few homes now had brick walls. Some had new cement rooftops. Rajinder had painted his house again. But nowhere in the village could we see anything that might be mistaken for public action. There were no sewers or drains, no health facilities, no signs other than a family-planning advertisement painted on a wall. Nearly seven years after we first entered this village, just about the only public investment Biharipur could lay claim to was the battered dirt path we had followed from the railway tracks.

Seeing so little progress, I felt a tinge of anger. Here, at the turn of a century when poverty was in rapid retreat in so many places, Biharipur was stagnant. Or so we thought. What lay ahead, what neither Rama nor I could fathom, was a community at war with itself, a feud so bitter and now deep that it would shake my faith in the human struggle for development.

We walked slowly through the village to Rajinder's house, where we always stayed, sensing a tension in the laneways and walled compounds that was as palpable as the monsoon air. On my last trip, some people had insulted me as a friend of Rajinder's, out to steal land. Now there was only cool silence. I no longer felt welcome, not even as an object of curiosity. Next to Rajinder's house, I was shocked to see a home in ruins, its roof, doors and windows missing and its walls knocked to bits, as if it had been shelled.

Rajinder looked no better as he welcomed us. Once a big strapping farmer and district athletics champion, he looked feebler than I had ever seen him. He told us the village was no longer safe. Not for us but for him, the landlord. He had moved his three youngest children to a new house in Tilhar, and did not go anywhere without his shotgun. He had lost twenty or so pounds, and with it most of his confidence.

"I don't know what is happening to India," the lambardar said, after greeting us. "I don't know what is happening to this village."

He began to tell us of the recent strife. A Dalit was dead, shot in his fields. Two more Dalit youths were in jail on charges of attempted murder. A young Muslim mother was also dead, found hanging by her sari in the family hut. Meanwhile, Rajinder and his oldest son, Satya Prakash, had been named in a rape case, and Amma's family, the helpless Dalits, faced charges of making small weapons in their hut. There could be no doubt: Biharipur was in the middle of a caste war. In the searing heat of July, our village was in flames. And, Rajinder said, it was all over the school.

He invited us to sit down on a charpoy, offered us cups of tea and quickly set out to explain the village war and the ugly truths it exposed about community development and local democracy.

Since my last visit, Rajinder had moved up in the world. He was now senior vice-president of the Tilhar teachers' association. With his wife on the block development council, he had access to development funds that was unrivalled in the area. His political influence was also growing. Not only was he an important player in the local Yadav political party, but his brother (whom we had never met but who lived in the district centre of Shahjahanpur) had joined the ruling Hindu nationalist BJP. This gave the family access to both government and opposition. And yet Rajinder was unable to get a school for the village. My own letters to various Shahjahanpur officials, including a personal visit to the Tilhar education office, had amounted to nothing. Rajinder met the same failure when he wrote to Satpal Singh Yadav, a distant relative who had become India's food minister in the new Hindu nationalist government. Rajinder had requested a school, electricity, brick roads, a telephone booth, tube well and health centre. Mr. Yadav apparently signed letters sanctioning a brick road and electricity for Biharipur, but the file did not move.

The lambardar carried on, writing letters and lobbying local officials to sanction a primary school. He raised the issue at his teachers' union meetings, and at sessions of the Tilhar development council. Then, finally, good news came. In 1998, Rajinder learned that a major World Bank–funded project for primary education in India would be expanded to the district of Shahjahanpur. Biharipur was on the list for a new five-room schoolhouse, worth 190,000 rupees, or about forty-five hundred dollars. All the people had to do was form an education committee to decide, among other things, on a site.

Since Rajinder controlled just about everything else in the village, he assumed an education committee would be the least of his worries. Under government guidelines, the committee was to have twenty-three members, and all the colours of India's pluralistic rainbow: teachers, women, Dalits, Muslims, youths, elders and handicapped people among them. Rajinder found names for each of the positions, but when he called a meeting, only a handful of people came. The lambardar had it all figured out anyway. He offered a parcel of land on his side of the village and told the other villagers he would not charge for it.

Then something astonishing happened. For the first time since anyone could remember, the Dalits said no. They couldn't say no to the committee because it never met. They said no to a visiting team from the education department, which had taken the extraordinary step of travelling to Biharipur to ask the uneducated, the illiterate and the ignorant what they thought. (The World Bank pressured the bureaucracy to do this sort of thing, which the experts called "inclusion.")

The process sparked arguments in every corner of the village. Some Dalits really didn't mind the school being on Rajinder's property as long as they got a school. But there was a new generation of Dalits who had been to school and had found factory jobs in nearby towns, and they refused to bend. The more militant Dalit men told the research team that they did not want the school on Rajinder's side of the village. They wanted the school as a place where their guests, especially wedding party guests, could sleep.

Rajinder agreed to the Dalits' request and proposed a piece of government land for the school on the other side of the village, near the mango grove. Initially, no one voiced any disagreement, and soon bricks and cement sacks arrived from Tilhar. That was when a small group of Dalits came forward to announce that the new site was not feasible because the land was where they stored mounds of rice and wheat. Where would they put their harvest if a school were built there? In protest, the Dalit farmers smashed some of the bricks piled up for the school, until an infuriated Rajinder sold all the building supplies and put the money aside for a time when agreement might prevail.

As the summer of 1998 turned to winter, and another bumper harvest was taken to market, the arguments grew so intractable that the district education team announced Biharipur was no longer going to get a school. The allotment was awarded to another village, on the other side of Tilhar, where at least the community had agreed on a site. Rajinder resumed his role as a political lobbyist, pleading with the Tilhar development council to keep his village on the list. The next time an education team returned to Biharipur, it asked the villagers to sit together to make a collective, community decision. No meeting was ever held. No decision was made.

That was about the time that Rameshwar was found dead.

One of the new militant Dalits, Rameshwar was part of the resistance to Biharipur's middle-caste dominance. He was also believed to be carrying on with several village women outside his caste. Indian villages are rife with rumour, usually malicious and untrue, but just the circulation of a rumour, no matter how ludicrous, can cost a man his honour and require stern reprisals. A few years earlier, the suggestion that one man's wife had a liaison with Rameshwar drove her husband to commit suicide by consuming fertilizer. More recently, as rumours swirled again in the village, another jealous husband, Radhey Shyam, said he would not tolerate such innuendo. After all, Radhey Shyam was a Yadav, and the Yadavs thought they controlled Biharipur.

When Rameshwar was found a few days later, shot dead outside the village, Tilhar police said the young Dalit had been summoned to the fields by a group of Yadavs. They had no other information about the death and no evidence with which to press charges.

Aside from the killing, there was caste tension over a small temple built by Bola, one of Rajinder's middle-caste neighbours. A Dalit family said the temple was on their land, and knocked it down. Then, one night, an educated Dalit youth named Sri Pal attacked the temple builder's house with a group of friends. They smashed the door, ripped off the roof and demolished walls and window frames, forcing Bola and his family to flee the village.

Rajinder surely would have stopped the fight had he been at home, but he was away that night. Maintaining the village peace fell to the bullying Satya Prakash. Unlike the angry young Sri Pal, who had finished elementary school and moved to Bereilly to work in a factory, Satya Prakash, a high school dropout, could not leave Biharipur. Ever. As the eldest son, he would have to spend his life here, protecting the family's land, honour and the traditions on which their power rested. Someone like Sri Pal could venture forth and provoke the established. For Satya Prakash, change was something to be fiercely resisted.

On that angry night, during the vandalism, Rajinder's son emerged on the family's roof and shouted at the Dalits to return to their homes. "Who are you to speak to us like this?" Sri Pal shouted back. A few of the Dalits who had gathered in the ruins of Bola's house drew pistols and pointed them at Rajinder's son. Satya Prakash ducked inside and returned with his father's rifle in his hands. He fired a shot in the air. The Dalits scattered.

The next day, Sri Pal came to Rajinder's house with the Tilhar police, who announced that the previous night's shot in the air had grazed the young Dalit. They also announced assault charges against Rajinder and Satya Prakash for the gun incident and for allegedly raping Sri Pal's wife. There was no evidence, and never would be. Under India's remarkable Dalit protection law, a female Dalit's accusation was all police needed to lay rape charges, and Sri Pal's wife had come forward to give a statement. Even a verbal insult, such as calling a Dalit "untouchable," was considered rape.

But if Indian law is firm, its application is flexible. Rajinder quickly got the charges against himself dropped, a favour that he said cost him five thousand rupees. "I want you to write this down. The police here take money," the lambardar said to me, his voice stern. "The police here are corrupt." The police said they couldn't drop the charges against Satya Prakash so quickly, since he had acted violently, but they agreed to "go slow" in their investigation. Everyone knew that meant "go nowhere."

I had never seen Biharipur in this state. Families weren't talking to their neighbours. Guns proliferated. Rajinder figured there were as many as two hundred weapons in the village. Only a year earlier, Amma's family had been charged with manufacturing small guns from metal pipes in their hut. Several Dalits were taken to the county jail, and returned only after they gave police a wristwatch, fifteen hundred rupees and a pledge to pay another three thousand rupees later.

That night, Rajinder told us not to sleep in his guest courtyard where we had stayed on every visit since 1993; it was too easily accessible from the public alleyway. He told his sons to carry our charpoys into the main yard and place them next to his tractor, where we would be better protected. He would sleep on the roof above us, with his gun and a round of bullets.

"I used to be proud of my village," Rajinder said. "I used to want to do things for my village. Now I'm feeling very bitter. Even officials are telling me, 'Why do you bother here? We'll find you another posting.'

"Instead of gratitude there is abuse. My wife and I are sick of this place."

He had already sent three of his seven children to a private school in Tilhar, where he had bought a small house for them to stay with his parents. He was building another house outside Shahjahanpur and hoped to move there with his wife and the younger children. Satya Prakash would stay behind to protect the remaining landholdings, though Rajinder was scaling that back, too. This year, he had rented seven of twelve hectares to the Sikhs.

"I don't like violence," Rajinder said, slinging his rifle over his shoulder before climbing up to the roof. "I would rather walk away but people would see that as a sign of weakness. They will push you if you walk away."

I was amazed at two things. First, how rich Rajinder had become—three houses and a tractor—since he got his secluded wife elected to the Tilhar development council. And second, how much he now had to fight to keep what he had acquired.

The only disturbance that night, other than the usual summer swarms of mosquitoes, was a midnight drizzle that forced us to move our charpoys under the tractor shed. I slept the rest of the night facing a big rear wheel covered with mud.

The next morning, we visited our other friends in the village, and in each home a little more of my hope evaporated. Down the laneway and around the corner from Bola's razed house, a liquor shop had opened in the spring, run by Prem Pal, the youngest son of the witch doctor, Natu Lal, who had died the previous year from a fever. In the end, Natu Lal's prescription—mud on the forehead—did him no good. He passed away at midday, when the gods were at rest. A few months later, his wife took ill. Their three farmer sons spent twenty-five thousand rupees for her to stay in a private cancer hospital in western Uttar Pradesh, but that too was futile. Within a month, she was gone.

Once his parents were dead, Prem Pal bid for a liquor licence, the most lucrative new business in the countryside. Still in his first year of operation, he was selling seventy-five small plastic bags of whisky a day—clear 36-proof and dark 25-proof—to field workers who for the first time in modern India had some disposable income. His only marketing was a sign outside the family hut: "The price of alcohol is very low these days."

On the other side of the village, we called on Dalchand, who was decidedly thinner and greyer than I remembered. He sat glumly inside his dark hut; his eyesight was failing, and he had trouble digesting his food. But he was most upset about his daughter Kanya, whose wedding we had attended six years earlier. The previous week, Dalchand had been to Kanya's village, about forty kilometres away, where she lived with her in-laws and her five-year-old son. Producing a son so quickly after marriage should have raised young Kanya's status in her new community, but it had not. Her husband had moved to Delhi, to work in a soap factory, leaving her to fend for herself. Her in-laws refused to give her food, even for their grandson.

Her husband never sent money from Delhi, either, and rarely returned. Since he had no land to his name, she had to find fieldwork just to earn enough to feed herself and her boy, not unlike Amma's circumstance forty years earlier.

"She is very weak. She can hardly move," Dalchand told us. "I fear she will starve to death."

I asked him why he had not brought her and his grandson back to Biharipur—custom allows a father to bring his daughter home—at the very least to give them a good meal. "Believe me," he said, "she was too weak to move. For three or four days, she had not had food." He sighed. His other grandson, the three-year-old who had cried through most of Kanya's wedding, had died. Diarrhea again. And now his two granddaughters were of marrying age. He and his son Bishram would have to find cash for that, as well as money to fix the roof that collapsed during the previous monsoon. "Can you look for a son-in-law who has a job?" Dalchand asked us earnestly.

At least Dalchand's eldest daughter, the one who had been thrown out of her husband's village for losing her first baby in childbirth, had been taken back by her in-laws. That was a load off Dalchand's mind, not having an abandoned daughter in his home. His wife, Kamla, entered the room with a couple of fans she had made with toffee wrappers. She handed one to me and one to Rama. "What can we do?" Dalchand asked. "If you are poor, you have no way out."

Across the pathway from Dalchand's, I noticed the clump of eucalyptus trees was gone. It had belonged to Biharipur's only Muslim woman, Manna, who was out front trying to sell a small basket of potatoes to passersby. She looked despondent, too. Six of her ten children were dead from a variety of causes, the most common being diarrhea. We sat down on a charpoy to find out more about the children's deaths, but Manna pulled her sari over her head and refused to look at us as she spoke. Her rambunctious teenaged daughter, Shakila, the one who looked after her younger siblings while Manna worked in the fields, had been married a few years earlier, leaving the mother with the extra burden.

What about her son's wife, Rahisa? I asked. She had three small children of her own, but surely she could help out. "Rahisa is dead," Manna muttered. A few months earlier, the young woman was found hanging from her sari in the family hut.

"It just happened like that," Manna said, not looking up from the potato basket. "Everyone was in the fields at the time. No one knows why she did this thing."

Apparently, Rahisa's parents had been as incredulous as we were. Young women were murdered every day in north India for not pleasing their in-laws. Sometimes it was a failure to produce a son. Sometimes it was bad cooking.

Rahisa was buried in the fields outside Biharipur by her parents, who came from their village when they heard the news. They also announced plans to notify local police—unless Manna gave them forty thousand rupees. That was when she cut and sold her twelve eucalyptus trees and rented a corner of her already crowded house to relatives from Tilhar who wanted to try their luck as field labourers. The in-laws accepted the money and had not been seen since.

We left Manna sitting in the blazing July sun, on the hard ground that her trees once shaded. She held two hundred rupees in her hand, tuition for her crippled boy, Ishaq, the one who used to crawl through the mud, to attend private classes in Rajinder's court-yard. During the height of the school fight, Manna and several other women had asked Rajinder to pursue his plans. Which is what he did. On July 5, when north India's schools opened for a new academic year, he used his authority as headteacher of the non-existent Biharipur primary school to hold his first classes in the cement courtyard where we usually slept. He had saved a few dozen small slates and chalk from the ridiculous adult literacy drive, and put one thousand rupees of his own money into other supplies. The rest of the money, for notebooks and texts, came from mothers like Manna.

On the first day of class, fifty-two of Biharipur's one hundred school-aged children showed up in the yard. More than half, thirty in all, were girls. Seventeen were Dalits. It seemed the mothers were right. Rajinder even managed to get a second teacher sanctioned for his school, although the first candidate, a Muslim woman from Tilhar, did not meet his standards. "Her family approached me and asked if it would be okay if she came only once a week," Rajinder said, shaking his head. The corruption and negligence of his fellow teachers never ceased to amaze him. "I said no, it would not, so the family arranged for her transfer to another village." The next junior teacher sent to Biharipur was a Yadav, like himself.

❖

On our last day in Biharipur, we rose early and visited the Sikhs in their oasis beyond the village. They had invited us for breakfast, a feast of fresh, steaming rotis, curried vegetables and hot sweet chai. As usual, no one except Jeet, the grandmother, sat with us for more than a few minutes. There were too many chores to complete in the morning. At the very mention of the school feud, the older Sikhs huffed in disgust. They wanted nothing more to do with Biharipur. The village, Kartar Singh said, was sick. "It has a bad name," Jeet added. "We do not go there any more."

I gave Jeet a box of sweets to celebrate our second child, not yet born. She remembered the last sweets I had given her. "Why are you working so much for us?" she asked. How strange, I thought, for her to equate a gift with work, but in this family, everything was equated with work.

I had also wanted to see Amma one more time, if she was still alive. We found her beyond the mosquito-infested pond, in her mud-walled home where the weapons were allegedly made. She had lived in this place for more than fifty years, ever since she came to Biharipur as a child bride, had five children and saw her husband die. With half a hectare of land, she now watched over twenty-four great-grandchildren whose lives were not noticeably better than hers.

Amma welcomed us with a gruff namaste and asked immediately where Cindy was. I said she was pregnant and had gone home to her mother's. She said that was wise, and then asked where the sweets were before I had the chance to hand her a box. Amma took one for herself and then carefully gave one sweet to each of the children clustered around her charpoy, never letting the box move beyond her elbow range. For a moment, the weak old lady looked as tough as the matron of a school kitchen. She had to be. Dhan Devi, the young Dalit mother, was of little aid. She had recently given birth to her fifth child, a boy, whom she breast-fed while sitting on the dirt at Amma's feet. The baby was red with scabies. The rest of the brood, most of then naked, crawled all over the old woman to get more sweets.

I asked the Dalits about Rajinder's new informal school, only to discover that none of this clan's children attended. They didn't know about the classes, the parents said. How they could not know about a school twenty metres away was beyond me, but that's what they said. The eldest girl, Pinky, was too busy anyway, learning how to make chapatis and preparing for marriage. She was twelve. Archana, another of Amma's great-grandchildren, was already married and had given birth the previous year to a son, the widow with no name's first great-great-grandchild.

The children continued to pull at Amma's sari, pleading for sweets. A few sat on the dirt, looking dazed as they sucked on the chunks of milky sugar. "I haven't had one," one of the bigger girls told the old woman. The girl looked as if she had not eaten in days but Amma, the survivor, was unconvinced. "The only thing you haven't had is three smacks on the head," she said scoldingly and continued to hold the box tightly in her lap.

Before long, Rajinder found us at Amma's house and told us his tractor was ready to drive us to the railway tracks. It was the first time I had seen him on this side of the mosquito pond.

"Lambardar," the old lady greeted him with folded hands. He responded with folded hands and no words.

"Lambardar, it is so hot, and all the children are sick," Amma continued.

"It is hot," he replied, looking only at the sky.

And for a moment there was silence, except for a breeze rustling the leaves of the Dalits' only tree. The two farmers, a landlord with a title and a widow with no name, had nothing more to say to each other.

I folded my hands and wished Amma well. Rajinder turned away to survey the fields.

"Go, brother," the old woman said. And we left.

Rajinder took us as far as the railway tracks on his tractor, and then asked if he could hitch a ride in our car to Tilhar. We could be of some help, he said, by coming with him to see the local police chief. I could not offend my friend and host of seven years by saying no. Besides, it would be interesting to see the inside of Tilhar county jail. We piled into the Ambassador, Rajinder choosing to sit in the front passenger seat with his rifle at his side. His second son, the DM, drove the tractor back to the village. The ambitious, courteous, efficient young DM was nineteen, with big shoulders and a struggling beard. He had failed grade ten three times and was to be married the following year. "There will be no DM," he said to us sadly before we got into the car. Rajinder's best hope for the boy was for him to join the army. India and Pakistan were fighting again, in remote and mountainous Kashmir, and having a son on the battlefield would bring honour to any farmer, even a lambardar.

Tilhar's main bazaar that Sunday morning was teeming with farmers from scores of local villages, landlords and peasants bustling like shoppers in a North American mall. After Rajinder pointed out the small house he had built there, he took us to a sweet shop. The best in central Uttar Pradesh, he said. He insisted we try its delights, which were covered in flies, and then popped into a clothing shop to buy a pair of shorts and a T-shirt as a gift for my son.

We piled back into the Ambassador and drove to the county jail at the edge of town, set amid a small clump of old banyan trees that kept it shaded in the summer. On the front porch, a few officers in pants and undershirts sat at small student desks, taking depositions from farmers who had come to lodge complaints. One was the son of the only woman other than Rajinder's wife on the Tilhar development council. Although she was chairperson, the son attended every meeting on her behalf.

"What's new in your village?" the young man asked Rajinder.

"There is a liquor stand," the lambardar said.

"Ohhhhhh. That's good." The young man beamed.

"It brings in a lot of criminal elements," Rajinder said.

"Oh, that's bad," the son replied obligingly.

"What caste is the owner?" asked one of the officers, who had stopped a deposition to listen to our conversation. He leaned back in his small wooden chair so that we could see his full stomach as it stretched the thin white fibres of his undershirt.

"Kashyap," Rajinder said. It was a backward caste, lower than the Yadavs but still higher than the Dalits.

"That means trouble," the officer, an upper-caste Thakur, said, shaking his head.

The police, all men from middle and the so-called forward castes, used this bit of information as a pretext to talk about the rise of the Dalits and all the trouble it meant. They warned Rajinder to watch his back.

We said goodbye to Rajinder's friend and the officers, and walked past the jail to a small bungalow where the police chief lived. A peon emerged from the house and asked what we wanted. Rajinder, so tough in his village, seemed flustered, so Rama and I gave our business cards to the peon, who took them inside. A few minutes later, the police chief emerged and ordered the peon to make sweet lassis and tea for us, and bring an electric fan to the porch where we sat.

The chief had started his career as a journalist in Uttar Pradesh's crime capital, Meerut, and seemed eager to talk with two reporters from New Delhi. Unfortunately, he had spent too much time in rural jails where his conversation skills had deteriorated. Whenever we asked about the Biharipur crime wave, he changed the topic to a word game. "India is made up of North, East, West and South," he said at one point, tapping the four edges of his table with a teaspoon. "That means N-E-W-S. India is news. You know how to make news, don't you?" he asked with an impish smile. "N.E.W.S. North. East. West. South."

Rajinder fiddled nervously with his drink and tried to steer the conversation to the rape charge against Satya Prakash. Unsure of the facts, I quickly told the chief that I had no intention of interfering in the good works of the Indian Police Service other than to speak of Rajinder's good character.

The chief, a Thakur, leaned back in his chair and laughed.

"Your friend is not so helpless," he said, smiling mischievously again. "He is a zamindar [landlord]. A zamin-*dar*! You know what *dar* [lord] means, don't you?"

We knew very well what he meant: the Yadavs were losing to the Dalits what the Thakurs had lost to the Yadavs thirty years earlier.

Before we left, Rajinder asked the police chief to post a guard at his house in Biharipur. I had never seen the lambardar look worried, and now he was fearing for his life. The chief leaned across the desk and softly said that Rajinder should lie low. He had no intention of pursuing the charges, but at the same time, a Thakur police chief who was seen as going soft on a Dalit rape case would be courting trouble. He might just as well sign his own transfer papers to Naxalite country. "You could create problems for yourself and for me," the chief said.

He told Rajinder that a personal guard would only attract more attention to his dispute. The two men agreed to leave things as they were.

We thanked the police chief for the lassis and drove back to the highway with Rajinder, who asked if we could drop him at the bazaar. He needed to buy a few things for the village and then check on his Tilhar house. I wondered when we would see him again. Seven years earlier, when we asked people along this road for directions to the village, he was known as a lambardar, a prince. We came to know him as the pillar of Biharipur: schoolteacher, healer, mystic, athlete, election fixer, farmer. For much of those seven years, I had thought of him as the best hope for India, the type of can-do man who could turn his village around. But now I watched in sympathy and bewilderment as Rajinder took his rifle from the Ambassador, waved goodbye and slipped into the crowd of Sunday shoppers.

We left Tilhar in silence, in the scorching heat of an early July afternoon. Our village was in shambles. Our lambardar was disgraced. I felt a bit stunned and ashamed, but mostly confused about all that had gone wrong. As the Tilhar crowds thinned and the car lurched into fourth gear, I realized that the seemingly senseless struggle in Biharipur was no different from the Barabaig's demise or the flames of Borneo. In its striving for a school, the village was going through a painful transition, one that might become much more violent, or might not, but one that was necessary. Development, if it is to mean anything, is not about a school or any other product. It is about the process of a community coming together and deciding to change. Only when the people of Biharipur sit down together, when men face women and Yadavs face Dalits, when the lambardar and the widow with no name argue until they agree on a site for their school, when they finally refer to it as *their* school, will their work become lasting.

Beyond that, I had no idea how the village would move forward. Rajinder could be chased away. There could be more clashes. There could be more deaths. But change didn't have to be violent. With the right kind of guidance from the communities around them— from district officials, caste leaders and local social organizations— the people of Biharipur could find ways to plan their shared future and then create it.

There is enough evidence of this happening in other places, from

Tilonia to Timbuktu, in Bangladesh, Bihar, the shea-nut forests of Ghana and Segou, to assure Rajinder, Amma, the Sikhs and their neighbours that they are not alone. This quiet struggle to take charge of their lives is the greatest struggle that the world carries into the twenty-first century. It isn't about past grudges, encumbering traditions or debilitating histories. It's about their future as a community.

When Biharipur finally sees itself as a community, only then will its people begin to find that elusive process called development.

# CONCLUSION

The fields of Biharipur seemed a world away from where this journey began, at Bangkok's World Bank–IMF meetings. In many ways they were, but in many more ways they were not.

I began my travels with the poor in 1991 in that gorgeous Thai palace of prosperity, with a very affluent crowd—the bankers and pinstriped finance ministers who preside over Third World development. At the time, I was convinced that if people were given control over the basic decisions of their lives, in markets and government, they would do whatever was needed to better those lives. I thought that was simply human nature.

Along the way, I met remarkable individuals who bore witness to this notion that human development is more the result of personal effort than of the workings of larger forces in a society. In Uganda, a country that endured more suffering than most nations in the twentieth century, George Mpango, the humble chemistry professor, had managed to take what his father had left him and make it better. Of course, he had to contend with his derelict brothers. But in a place more commonly associated with despair, George had expanded his father's farm, brought new farming techniques to the area, built a private school specializing in science and developed a protein biscuit, all the while maintaining a full professorship and raising his three children on a pittance of a salary.

For all his gumption, however, George would not have succeeded without a reformist government, or international aid donors who had taken a liking to Uganda. Directly or indirectly, they made each of his tasks easier, just as the same forces often made life harder for others.

In West Africa, in the long shadows of kleptocratic dictators, cruel soldiers, fickle climates and colonial horrors, Nené Coulibaly, a Mama Benz, was able to run her own little factory in the backwaters of Mali. A credit union helped her finance her business and profit from her savings. Canadian assistance helped that credit union expand.

Even in Biharipur, in a village where progress seemed so elusive, Kartar Singh and the Sikhs brought profound change to their own lives through hard work, thrift and risk. For the village's Sikhs, as for Nené Coulibaly, geography, history, climate and global economics were less significant than individual resourcefulness. Too often this personal resourcefulness is overlooked in the passionate, and often irrational, public debate about poverty. The poor, at least the ones I met on this journey, do not need a radical new economic system or a utopian society to change their lives. They usually can do that on their own, once some basic obstacles—often raised in the name of poverty reduction—are removed from the path.

Human liberty is important to development, but that does not mean there is a diminished role for public action. I hope this book has shown how public voices—Aruna Roy's anti-corruption campaign, the PTAs of Bihar, the village councils of Bangladesh—are as important as individual choices. In northern Ghana, the shea-nut gatherers could not have struck an equitable deal with the Body Shop without some sort of organizational support from the regional government, international aid agencies and the British retailer itself, so that they could buy processing equipment, finance their inventories and ride through the rough storms of fluctuating prices. This is collective action at its best.

But too many development programs confuse this sort of action with one of the aid industry's favourite buzzwords—"participation." Development is not about people participating in a program, as if they were going to the county fair. Development is about people managing the process—running their own fair. Some aid agencies call this "ownership," but very few I've encountered are willing to cede control to the people most affected by decisions. This is why local democratic government—the most basic form of "ownership" known to public action— is fundamental to eradicating poverty.

Although most of the developing world now favours democracy, at least as a method of selecting national governments, the emergence of local democracy is still slow. India has been at it longer than most, running the world's biggest elections for more than half a century, yet in Biharipur the Dalits are only now, at the start of the twenty-first century, gaining a say in something as simple as the functioning of a school. A PTA would help, but democracy is about more than elected councils and such counterweights as courts, an independent media and accountability commissions. For democracy, and therefore development, to flourish in the village, its residents must feel they have equal opportunities in life. No challenge could be more difficult in a village rooted in traditions that are as old as the landscape.

India's new market economy is at least halfway democratic. For decades, the village's farmers could buy and sell only what the government allowed, and only at prices it determined fair. Since the introduction of agricultural reforms in India, the area around Biharipur has enjoyed a remarkable transformation. Over the course of the 1990s, rice production in the administrative block of Tilhar grew by fifty percent. The area's wheat output almost doubled, while new cash crops like mustard and peanuts took root.

This was one of the quiet miracles of the late twentieth century, and it raised with it the standard of living of thousands of poor families in Tilhar. The farmers with access to land, seeds and credit were suddenly tasting a prosperity previously known only to Tilhar's princely families. The great remaining challenge lies in the distribution of opportunity so that it reaches families that lie on the other side of the democratic divide, without land or credit.

Since Rama and I first stopped in Tilhar to ask directions to the lambardar's house in 1992, the infant mortality rate has been cut nearly in half, enough to save about ninety lives a year in this one county. During the same period, the number of boys enrolled in primary school has doubled to 8,535. The number of girls in school has more than tripled, to 6,284. Most of these changes, of course, happened in Tilhar town and in some of the more prosperous farming villages where landholdings were large. According to the government's own statistics, fully forty-six percent of Tilhar county continues to live in poverty. Villages like Biharipur still lack a school and basic immunization program. The benefits from the developing world's great decade of economic reform, so boldly presented in Bangkok, are simply not trickling down.

It was only when we left Tilhar town in 1999, with Rajinder fading from our view, that I noticed a small shop with a fax machine, the first to reach this area, and realized how much more prosperous this crowded, dirty farming centre was compared with the crowded, dirty village of Biharipur just five kilometres away. The global wealth gap could be seen right here, in one county, between people who faxed letters to

New Delhi and others who could not yet write letters. Later, when we moved back to Canada, people often asked if I had experienced culture shock. Not like I did, I said, returning to New Delhi from Biharipur.

Ensuring development reaches places like Biharipur has to be one of the great challenges facing the world. What is needed to meet it are more democratic and stronger local governments. These are the bodies that can help communities decide on the location of a school, challenge the corruption of a local sugar mill and allocate development funds more wisely than any charity. These are matters of efficiency, but what local governments do best is to give citizens a feeling that they *are* citizens with a role and a responsibility in everything their community does.

This is as true for big cities, stalked by anonymity, as for small, remote villages. In New Delhi, for instance, there was a crime spree in the summer of 1999, when I returned from Biharipur for the last time. The city's newspapers, normally given to endless political analysis, were filled with stories of domestic murders, gangland assassinations and shootouts in some of the chic bars that had flourished with economic liberalization. New Delhi's murder rate was now higher than New York's. Its traffic was even worse. Congestion was so bad that I took to driving through red lights and along sidewalks because that's what everyone did. The diesel-belching trucks and buses clogging the regular lanes had made the city's air almost unbreathable. And there seemed almost no hope for public transport. Worse than the delays was the harassment. Sexual abuse of women on Delhi's buses became so rampant the police had to dispatch a special force of undercover women cops to ride the transit lines.

In this sort of chaotic urban environment, many of my neighbours wanted a firm dictatorship, not more democracy. Yet democracy was what would make their city more liveable. With so many civic issues at everyone's doorsteps, Delhi's local elections were no longer fought along caste or ethnic lines; they were battles over mass transit, drinking water, even a proposal to ban taxis built before 1975. Between elections, civic action groups—newspapers, courts, neighbourhood associations, business groups—kept the municipal government on its toes.

Rather than addressing these parochial challenges, most development groups in the West seem consumed by global issues—global warming, global trade, global government. But as I prepared to leave India I came to believe that the world's future lay more at the local level, as mundane as that often seems. Rajinder's struggle with the Dalits to build a school. Aruna Roy's barefoot campaign against rural corruption. The simple expansion of credit unions down the Niger River valley. These hardly seem like events that can change the world, but they are. And they can change it for the better.

In each of these cases, if people can be given the support they need to make important decisions in their own communities, to build their own democracies in their own ways, they can do the rest themselves. In doing so, they will not only move their own communities out of poverty, they will take the world with them.

A month after my last visit to Biharipur, I packed my remaining books, notes, files and clothes in three hockey bags and called the Punjab Taxi Stand for the last time. Cindy, who was pregnant, and our two-year-old son Matthew had already left for Canada, and so an hour before midnight I crossed New Delhi alone in an old Ambassador taxi, this one with its doors firmly on their hinges. Out of nostalgia, I rolled down the window once more to breathe the Delhi air. Chaos on the airport road no longer bothered me. Cars lined up three abreast in a single turning lane no longer seemed irrational. Grinding as it could be, apocalyptic as it seems to so many visitors, this was a society sorting itself out. Ultimately that is what development must be about.

The British Airways flight to London left on time, crowded with summertime trekkers heading home to Europe. As we took off, I watched the lights of Delhi sprawl in every direction, sparkling like the remaining drops of a wave that had crashed ashore. Soon, the city lights dwindled and all I could see through the small window were dimly lit clusters, the villages of northern India. The settlements looked like they could reach to eternity, but they, too, began to fade as we rose above the mountains, jostled through a bank of monsoon clouds and finally broke into the still night above.

Out the window there was darkness everywhere except on the very edge of one horizon. There a faint brush of light could only mean the coming of a new dawn.

# ACKNOWLEDGEMENTS

I finished this book with more debts than I can ever repay, owed mostly to people who would never think of collecting them. I have relied on hundreds of people to lead me to new places and introduce me to new ideas. Some of their stories are told here; most go without mention. I am grateful to them all.

In India, I owe my greatest debt to Rama Lakshmi of *The Washington Post*, who helped me find Biharipur and who offered immeasurable wit, laughter, insight and criticism on our many trips to the village. Early on in my time in India, Ashok Khosla, Anil Agarwal and Sunita Narain helped me understand the country's development challenges. Professor C.J. Daswani, architect of India's most innovative curriculum reforms, walked me through the troubling state of the country's schools. Delhi's most colourful historian and bon vivant, Patwant Singh, used the excuse of wonderful dinners and long walks in Lodhi Gardens to explain more than I could understand about modern Indian society and politics. Dimandeep Singh, an outstanding environmental journalist, helped me perceive the bridge between politics and poverty. At the World Bank mission in New Delhi, I relied on dozens of staff members for information over the years, but found none more giving of their time than Gitanjali Chopra and Bimla Bissell. Similarly, Anjali Nayyar at the Population Council and Gillian Wilcox of Unicef provided a constant stream of documents and ideas. In the southern city of Chennai, the great development economist M.S. Swaminathan always provided a voice of reason on complex issues, and a welcome retreat to his research centre. In Orissa, Narayan Gopalakrishnan of Gram Vikas took Cindy and me on one of our most remarkable journeys. In Bihar, Tejinder Sandhu of Unicef helped me understand the uglier side of school reform, while his colleague Baikunth Pandey found two full days in his overloaded schedule to lead me through an insurgency and all its hopes.

Bangladesh often felt like my home away from India, not just because I spent so much time there but because the people were always so welcoming. In 1996, Cindy and I travelled the length of the country to see its awesome inland fisheries. Doris Capistrano of the Ford Foundation helped us find our way, intellectually as well as geographically. Development researcher Atiur Rahman, Caritas workers Albert Mankin and Marcel d'Costa, and, most important, Mokammel Hossain, a tireless bureaucrat in the fisheries ministry, guided us along the way. In the southwestern shrimp belt, Manik Saha of the *Daily Sangbad* travelled up and down the backwaters and back roads with us to witness an awful devastation. In Dhaka, environmentalist Saleem Samad was instrumental in sending us to the wash-away islands called chars. Qazi Faruque Ahmed, founder of the NGO, Proshika, graciously spent several hours with me in December 1998, explaining the modern history of Bangladesh's poverty. During the same trip, two Canadians, Faruque Sarkar and Russell Pepe, also went to great lengths to show me how development was changing across the countryside. At the Grameen Bank, Muhammad Yunus and Muzammel Huq met with me again and again to explain rural banking and poverty. At the World Bank mission, the former resident representative Pierre Landell-Mills prodded me to clearer thinking on poverty, while Subrata Dhar provided me with so many documents I needed a separate bookcase for Bangladesh back in New Delhi.

Roger Young, a Canadian development consultant, gave me helpful information about development thinking in both Bangladesh and Tanzania. His insights into Canadian aid to Tanzania in the eighties led to an important rethinking of this country's aid policy. In Katesh, home of the infamous Canadian wheat farms, John Mnuve, formerly of CUSO, introduced me to other local activists who took me to the Barabaig people. Several employees of the National Agriculture and Food Corporation, who must remain unnamed, also assisted me with useful criticisms of their own work and that of the Canadian government. In West Africa, the Canadian diplomatic missions in Accra, Abidjan and Bamako provided an invaluable service in arranging interviews and field trips while never apparently trying to steer my thinking. Similarly, in Indonesia, Canadian political officers offered valuable insights into the bizarre workings of the Suharto regime. I am especially grateful to a former diplomat, Colin Stewart, now with the UN in Dili, for his remarkably accurate views of the Indonesian government and the situation in East Timor.

❖

While writing this book, I relied excessively on many friends in New Delhi. One of them, Roger Finan of the International Development Research Centre, gave me a desk and computer so that I could escape from my own office for a few hours every day to focus on the book. Despite my imposition, the IRDC staff—especially Roger's assistant, Prabha Sethuraman—were exceptionally kind; they should not be held responsible for any of this book's contents.

After Cindy left India, our friends Ruth and Arthur Max allowed me to stay with them for a month, never minding my late-night work habits. In Toronto, where I finished writing the book, I stayed much longer with my father-in-law Donald Andrew and Margaret Anderson than any of us had anticipated, and thank them for their kindness and understanding. During this time, Kevin Omura provided me with a temporary computer and considerable advice on the new electronic world.

Before all this started, my literary agent Bruce Westwood persuaded me to write the book for Random House Canada and, more specifically, for Anne Collins, and I am grateful for his wisdom. Anne pushed me to rewrite and rethink several chapters, to add important stories and ideas, and to delete much of my ramblings. Not once did she express impatience or lack of confidence, though both were often warranted. Her assistant, Pamela Robertson, was equally tolerant, shepherding four drafts of the manuscript on more computer disks than I could keep track of. Fortunately, she could. This book's designer, Jenny Armour, performed miracles, including rescuing a cover photo that had lost its negative.

At the *Globe and Mail,* I am greatly indebted to William Thorsell, who as editor in 1991 assigned me to the development beat and moved me to India. His passion for reporting on issues beyond the news, on the small events that continuously shape our world, deserves much credit. For most of my time overseas, Patrick Martin was my foreign editor and Linda Hossie his deputy, and they always provided sage advice, good humour and great tolerance of a correspondent's unusual mood swings. Sue Andrew was a wellspring of sanity. Lastly, I am extremely grateful to Richard Addis, the *Globe and Mail*'s new editor, and Drew Fagan, the new foreign editor, who offered nothing but support in the home stretch of this journey.

I am especially grateful to my children, Matthew and Lauren, for tolerating my long absences and for sharing with me the beauty of human development, as I am to my parents, Margaret and Reginald, who provided much inspiration for this work. This journey, of course, would not have even begun had it not been for my wife and closest friend, Cindy. After our first trip to India, she said it was "a nice place but I wouldn't want to live there." She moved there anyway, and stayed seven and a half years. Her photographs lavish this book. Her spirit inspires its words. My thanks to her will never be adequately expressed.

# INDEX